Democracy in Ghana

Rapid urbanization and political liberalization is changing the nature of African politics and societies. This book develops a framework for the study of democracy and development that emphasizes informal institutions and the politics of belonging in the context of daily life, in contrast to the formal and electoral paradigms that dominate the social sciences.

Based on fifteen months of field research including ethnographic observation, focus group interviews, and original quantitative survey analysis in Ghana, the book intervenes in major debates about public goods provision, civic participation, ethnic politics and democratization, and the future of urban sustainability in a rapidly changing world. By developing new understandings of democracy, as well as providing novel explanations for good governance and development in poor urban neighborhoods, the book transcends the narrative of a failing and corrupt Africa and charts a new way forward for the study of democracy and development.

JEFFREY W. PALLER is an assistant professor of politics at the University of San Francisco. He has conducted fieldwork in Ghana, Kenya, Uganda, and South Africa and his work is published in *Polity, African Studies Review, Africa Today, Journal of Modern African Studies, Africa Spectrum,* and *Current History.* His dissertation won the African Politics Conference Group-Lynne Rienner Best Dissertation in African Politics Award. He is secretary for the African Politics Conference Group and chair of the Comparative Urban Politics Related Group for the American Political Science Association. He curates the weekly news bulletin, *This Week in Africa.*

D1127891

Democracy in Ghana

Everyday Politics in Urban Africa

JEFFREY W. PALLER
University of San Francisco

CAMBRIDGE
UNIVERSITY PRESS

CAMBRIDGE
UNIVERSITY PRESS

University Printing House, Cambridge CB2 8BS, United Kingdom

One Liberty Plaza, 20th Floor, New York, NY 10006, USA

477 Williamstown Road, Port Melbourne, VIC 3207, Australia

314-321, 3rd Floor, Plot 3, Splendor Forum, Jasola District Centre, New Delhi - 110025, India

79 Anson Road, #06-04/06, Singapore 079906

Cambridge University Press is part of the University of Cambridge.

It furthers the University's mission by disseminating knowledge in the pursuit of education, learning and research at the highest international levels of excellence.

www.cambridge.org
Information on this title: www.cambridge.org/9781108466431
DOI: 10.1017/9781108578721

© Jeffrey W. Paller 2019

First published 2019
First paperback edition 2020

A catalogue record for this publication is available from the British Library

Library of Congress Cataloging in Publication data
Names: Paller, Jeffrey, author.
Title: Democracy in Ghana : everyday politics in urban Africa / Jeffrey W. Paller.
Description: New York : Cambridge University Press, 2018.
Identifiers: LCCN 2018041842 | ISBN 9781316513309 (hardback)
Subjects: LCSH: Democracy–Ghana. | Politics, Practical–Ghana. | Political corruption–
   Ghana. | Urbanization–Political aspects–Ghana.
Classification: LCC JQ3036 .P35 2018 | DDC 320.4667–dc23
   LC record available at https://lccn.loc.gov/2018041842

ISBN 978-1-316-51330-9 Hardback
ISBN 978-1-108-46643-1 Paperback

For Kathleen

Contents

Figures

Tables

Preface

Ghana is one of Africa's most successful democracies. It holds free and fair elections, has experienced multiple turnovers of power, and hosts an unrestricted press and independent judiciary. These institutional developments emerge in a broader context of political liberalization and urbanization, placing the country on what should be a healthy path toward democratic deepening and consolidation. Yet this formal institutional progress coincides with nondemocratic developments, including the persistence of political clientelism, the capture of public goods for private gain, and the sustenance of ethnic politics. This prompts a puzzling question: Why do these nondemocratic elements endure despite the strengthening of liberal democratic institutions? Moreover, how do societies overcome these challenges to their political systems? Conventional accounts of democratization blame governance failures on formal institutions or entrenched societal structures, failing to account for the ways in which these formal institutions interact with informal social organizations in the context of everyday life.

These nondemocratic characteristics are even more surprising in cities, where economic modernization and rapid population growth are transforming Ghanaian society. Yet the reality is that the impact of urbanization is uneven, contributing to different political developments in distinct neighborhoods within the same city. This book provides a view from below, giving a glimpse into how local urban communities make democracy work – or fail to overcome existing nondemocratic elements. The book's main argument is that informal norms of settlement and belonging continue to structure everyday politics in Ghana's cities, helping to explain logics of political clientelism, elite capture of public goods, and ethnic politics. But they can also contribute to the development of legitimate and responsive representatives, public spheres of collective decision-making, and a multiethnic civic life in Ghana's poorest neighborhoods. A democratic politics in Ghana's cities depends on how informal norms of settlement and belonging shape the everyday politics of its neighborhoods.

Acknowledgments

My mind often wanders to my first full day of ethnographic research in 2011 when I surprised Philip Kumah at his tailor shop in Old Fadama. I was excited to work with Mr. Kumah on issues of governance and urban development, and he walked me through the neighborhood and introduced me to the big shots: I Don't Mind, Abdullah, Ayatu, Chief Inspector Paul, Inspector Saibu, Chief Zachi, M. Suala, Laryee, Bujati, Mosi Chief, Mallam, Nii Ayi, and Billy. I would later meet Chairman, Frederick Opoku, Latif Osman, Bright Dzila, Ato, Kobe, Jima and many others. It took me a full year to understand their importance to the community, but I could not have done my research without their support and willingness to have me wander through the paths of their neighborhood. The same can be said for Honorable Latif, Mr. Ashalley, Nii Lantey Vanderpuye, Nii Tackey, Lena, Victor Okaikoi, and Hussein Addy in Ga Mashie, and Mr. Zonyira, Jonathan Avisah, Selormey, Charles, Fawaz, and Bronx in Ashaiman.

Mama Angela in Ashaiman and Mama Rose Thompson in Ga Mashie made sure that I never went hungry, and taught me what real Ghanaian food tastes like. Faidal-Rahman Haruna spent one of my favorite days of research with me watching the Champions League final. Governor explained to me the intricate details of Ga culture, as well as local politics. His friends carried me through the streets of Ga Mashie on their shoulders during the Homowo Festival. Isaac was a master at campaign strategy and I had some of the most interesting conversations about Odododiodioo politics with him. Sarah and Mabel were always around Ga Mashie for a laugh, and became close friends. Belinda, Samira, and Joyce made sure I was fed and comfortable at the tailor shop. Hamid introduced me to many great people in Nima. Raymond provided great insights and friendship during my visits to Ashaiman. Former mayor of Accra Nat Nunoo Amarteifio provided rich details about governance in Accra, and the development of informal settlements in the city.

Five people were essential to my research, and helped shape the contours of the project. They offered novel insights, introduced me to diverse networks of leaders and residents, and discussed their personal challenges and neighborhood struggles with me. We became partners in the research process. In many ways, we were co-ethnographers. Philip Kumah opened his tailor shop, his family, and his decision-making process to me. He translated interviews, led focus groups, and enumerated the survey. I constantly asked myself "What would Mr. Kumah do? What would Mr. Kumah think?"

Innocent Adamadu Onyx served a similar role in Ashaiman. He took his role as social worker seriously, and was deeply interested in the project for his own intellectual development. Nii Addo Quaynor's passion for Odododiodioo politics is unprecedented, and he made sure to pass that excitement onto me. Addo knows everyone in Ga Mashie, and walking through the neighborhood with him introduced me to the who's who of indigenous Ga politics. Alhassan Ibn Abdallah's intuition about politics is unparalleled. On many occasions he explained to me the politics of Northern Ghana, the settlement of Old Fadama, and the intricacies of the NDC party. Every time I spoke with Abdallah I learned critical facts about Ghanaian politics, and when we discussed his culture and family, I felt like I somehow knew Ghana better. Abubakar Addy is a true scholar, and always knew exactly the type of information I was looking for. He was more than a research assistant; he became an economist. I grew up with these five men, and my project evolved with them.

Eric Tei Kumadoe helped me negotiate the University of Ghana at Legon. Farouk Braimah of People's Dialogue is the preeminent expert on slum issues in Ghana, and was very generous with his time. Bernice Naah of Amnesty International and Yaw Asante of Self Help Initiatives Support Services offered interesting perspectives about slum rights as human rights. I enjoyed my conversations with Martin Davies, Nicky Morrison, Dagna Rams, Afia Afenah, Naaborko Sackeyfio-Lenoch, Victoria Okoye, Dennis Chirawurah, Greg Ofosu, Sarah Brierley, and Jamie Hitchen while in Ghana. Noah Nathan's expertise on electoral demography in urban Ghana has been invaluable, and I always look forward to our discussions at conferences and in the field.

The Center for Democratic Development served as an excellent research host. Professor Emmanuel Gyimah-Boadi introduced me to an impressive network of scholars, and graciously offered his time while providing insights about Ghanaian politics. Victor Brobbey, Kojo Asante, Kakra Duayeden, Franklin Oduro, Daniel Armah-Attoh, Joe Asunka, and Edem Solermey were great research collaborators. Mohammed Awal became a coauthor and a close friend, as did George Bob-Milliar and Abdul Gafaru-Abdulai. A major highlight of my research was learning from these great scholars and conceptualizing new projects with them.

A few professors are particularly notable in my development as a scholar. Will Reno advised my undergraduate thesis and sparked my interest in African politics when I was an undergrad at Northwestern. Lauren MacLean helped me find my scholarly voice, and has been a great mentor throughout the years. Howard Schweber constantly urged me to incorporate political theory into my work, and has pushed me to develop my research focus beyond Africa. Michael Schatzberg, my dissertation adviser, pushed me to expand the boundaries of the political and consider historical and cultural sources of legitimacy in my study sites. His influence is evident across all of my research, and I would not be the scholar I am today without his mentorship.

I was lucky to learn from numerous scholars at the University of Wisconsin where I completed my doctorate, including Rikhil Bhavnani, Edward Friedman, Benjamin Marquez, Leigh Payne, Erica Simmons, Scott Straus, and Aili Tripp. I enjoyed going through coursework and dissertation writing with Mehreen Zahra-Malik, Brian Ekdale, Melissa Tully, Matthew Scharf, Jennifer Petersen, Barry Driscoll, Charlie Taylor, Taylor Price, Alice Kang, Brandon Kendhammer, Joschka Philipps, Michael Pisapia, and Matthew Mitchell. They were there when the highs were high and the lows were low.

I benefited from great comments at the APSA Africa Workshop "Local Communities and the State" in Gabarone, Botswana in 2012. At this workshop, I met fantastic scholars from all over the continent, and began new work friendships with Danielle Carter Kushner, Martha Wilfahrt and Parakh Hoon. Eric Kramon provided great comments as a discussant at the "Methodological Innovation in Urban Research in the Developing World" conference hosted by American University in 2015. I received great feedback from Erika Weinthal, Erik Wibbels, Anirudh Krishna, Alison Post, and Adam Auerbach at the "Workshop on Urban Poverty in Developing Countries Workshop" at Duke University in 2016.

My discussions with Sarah Charlton, Kate Owens, Maureen Donaghy, Alisha Holland, Lauren Honig, Josef Woldense, Dennis Galvan, Shelby Grossman, Cat Kelly, Dominika Koter, and Chris Gore at various APSA and ASA meetings have been extremely fruitful. I also received great discussant comments from Chris Day, Kristin McKie, Andy Harris, Peter Lewis, Shana Warren, and Tariq Thachil at these conferences. Jeremy Menchik, Tim Longman, and Noora Lori helped me with conceptualization and framing of the project at my talk at Boston University. Ellen Lust hosted a very productive Program on Governance and Local Development conference at Gothenburg University called "Seeking Solutions" in 2017. I enjoyed conversations with and feedback from Ruth Carlitz, Adam Harris, Ato Kwamena Onoma, Zoe Marks, Lise Rakner, John McCauley, Daniel Masterson, Diana Greenwald, Stephen Commins, Kristin Kao, Stephen Marr, and Diane Singerman. Happy Kayuni, Joachim De Weerdt, Pierre Landry, and Anja Franck provided great discussant comments. I have really enjoyed putting together panels with Anne Pitcher, who also helped me strengthen my introductory chapter at a crucial stage of the writing process. I've presented portions of the research at Stanford University, UC Berkeley, University of Florida, University of Gothenburg, Duke University, Columbia University, Northwestern University, Elmhurst College, University of Sheffield, American University, Free University, City College of New York, Bates College, Boston University, and University of Wisconsin.

I am very fortunate to have had great colleagues and friends in my various academic positions. Clarisa Perez-Armendariz, William Corlett, Jim Richter, Áslaug Ásgeirsdóttir, Stephen Engel, Michael Rocque, Michael Sargent, and Senem Aslam helped make my first teaching job a very enjoyable and productive experience. Colleen Laird, Alero Akporiaye, and Joshua Rubin became great friends. Jackie Klopp was a fantastic mentor at the Earth Institute, as she pushed me to consider the forces of urban development outside the context of the neighborhood. I learned so much from Katya Vasilaky, Kimberly Oremus, Eyal Frank, Martina Kirchberger, Eugenie Dugoua, Aaron Blum, Francis Annan, and Anthony D'Agostino during my year in New York. Monthly meetups with Nick Smith forced me to think about my work in new ways, and pushed me to address aspects of my research that I had not thought about before.

My colleagues at the University of San Francisco have provided a strong support network and vibrant intellectual environment in which to share ideas. I especially want to thank Annick Wibben, Elisabeth Friedman, Kathy Coll, Brian Dowd-Uribe, Christopher Loperena, Lucia Cantero, Jesse Anttila-Hughes, Sadia Saeed, Noopur Agarwal, Jessica Blum, Dana Zartner, Omar Miranda, and Karen Bouwer for their support and friendship. Keally McBride has been an excellent faculty mentor, and provided helpful comments on the introductory chapter. In the Bay Area, Leo Arriola has been extremely generous, and has had made me feel very welcome at UC Berkeley's Africa Research Seminar, which has become a second intellectual home. I have greatly benefited from comments by Danny Choi, Justine Davis, Lindsay Bayham, Fiona Shen-Bayh, Paul Thissen, Martha Saavedra, Ann Swidler, and many others.

Macartan Humphreys, Adrienne LeBas, Brenda Chalfin, Nicolas van de Walle, Jackie Klopp, and Nick Smith participated in my book manuscript workshop hosted by the Earth Institute at Columbia University, and provided invaluable suggestions. Martina Kirchberger, Anouch Missirian, Anthony D'Agostino, Jonathan Westin, Elizabeth Sperber, Jonathan Blake, Alex Daugherty, and Kimuli Kasara also attended the workshop and added very helpful comments. This day-long intensive discussion greatly helped me improve the manuscript. My editor Maria Marsh provided great guidance during all stages of the book publication process.

The Social Science Research Council generously funded my year of ethnographic fieldwork, and the National Science Foundation funded the household survey. I also benefited from grants at the University of Wisconsin, and from faculty development funds from Bates College and the University of San Francisco. I was able to make significant progress on the book while I was an Earth Institute Postdoctoral Fellow at Columbia University. Portions of the research have been published in "Informal Institutions and Personal Rule in Urban Ghana" in *African Studies Review*; "Informal Networks and Access to Power to Obtain Housing in Urban Slums in Ghana" in *Africa Today*; "From Urban Crisis to Political Opportunity: African Slums" in *Africa under Neoliberalism*; and "Defending the City, Defending Votes: Campaign Strategies in Urban Ghana" in *Journal of Modern African Studies*.

My parents nurtured my curiosity from day one, and are always there for me. Most importantly, I owe the greatest amount of thanks to my partner, Kathleen. She has been at every step of the journey with me, from conceptualizing the project in graduate school to submitting the final manuscript in San Francisco. In between, we conducted our research in Ghana and Kenya, completed our PhDs at the University of Wisconsin, and traversed the country as we took various fellowships and academic jobs. We are collaborators, coauthors, and best friends. In many ways, this book is the product of our dinner table conversations over the last ten years.

1 | Democracy, Development, and Daily Life

On a hot morning, a traditional fetish priest sat beside a major street drinking a beer in Ga Mashie, the oldest neighborhood in Accra, Ghana. This was not any street, but *his* street – the street for which his family was custodian of the land and he was the family elder. On this particular day, he basked in his latest accomplishment: securing the government contract to rebuild the local food market. He has no contracting skills and has never been to technical school. Instead, his close personal connections to the Member of Parliament (MP) helped secure him the contract. But this was not merely petty corruption or vote buying. The MP needed the support of a traditional elder to build on the property. He needed to offer state concessions to a traditional leader in order to develop a market on the land. The contract was the prize outcome of a long political struggle for the rights to rebuild the market, one that spanned political parties, market women's associations, and various MPs and local leaders.

The fetish priest is just one of dozens of traditional leaders in the neighborhood to engage in multiparty politics as a way to build local support and legitimacy, as well as make money. Though ethnically diverse, community decision-making is restricted to a narrow club in indigenous neighborhoods like Ga Mashie: members of the ethnic group who claim ancestral rights to the land, called indigenes. Community governance follows customary norms and procedures, and spills over into the practice of multiparty politics.

Despite its long history as the political center of the country and the spiritual core of the indigenous ethnic group, these underlying political dynamics contribute to a situation where houses are substandard, sewers overflow, and poverty and unemployment rates are high. The situation is even more surprising because elections are extremely competitive, civil society organizations are active, and the community is directly next to Ghana's central business district. Yet the neighborhood descends into squalor as clientelism is rampant, its leaders empower their own families at the expense of the common good, and ethnic politics persist.

The situation is very different in a stranger community in Ashaiman, a settlement on the outskirts of Accra. On a rainy day in a notorious poor neighborhood, a drunk driver drove his truck into an electricity pole. A blackout ensued, and the entire neighborhood went without power. As water flooded the muddy roads, a respected landlord rushed to the scene to calm tempers. A group of residents followed, arguing and deliberating about what should be done. Some of them threatened to beat up the driver. They debated whether to send the driver to the police station, knowing that if he were charged he would not be able to pay for a new pole. He worked for a known "big man" in town, causing concern that he had influence over the police.[1]

Filing a complaint with the electricity company would take too long. The Municipal Assembly and police officers were ineffective. Community members had to resolve the issue themselves. Twenty residents, including the local assemblyman, landlords, and the owner of the vehicle – respected and legitimate authorities called "opinion leaders" in Ghana – piled into a local store and came up with a plan.[2] The owner of the vehicle was pressured to pay for most of the new pole, while residents contributed a small amount. The assemblyman drove straight to the utility company to demand they fix the pole immediately. Residents were able to hold their leaders to account and get them to do their jobs, contributing to collective decision-making and community governance. By the early evening, electricity was restored to the entire neighborhood. This outcome was even more surprising because the neighborhood is ethnically diverse, highly impoverished, and has weak and often ineffective formal institutions. In contrast to Ga Mashie, this Ashaiman neighborhood has responsive and effective leaders, a robust public sphere that facilitates community decision-making, and a multiethnic civic life.

Despite similar demographic patterns to Ashaiman, the practice of politics contributed to a very different development outcome in Old

---

[1] A "big man" in Ghanaian society is a leader perceived for his high degree of wealth and virtue and privileges the public demonstration of power, generosity, and consumption of expensive goods (Price 1974).

[2] Assembly persons are elected representatives of Ghana's 254 decentralized assemblies whose role is to "spearhead development projects such as [the] drainage system, [and] rural, urban electrification among others."

Fadama, Accra's largest squatter settlement. A few months earlier, families sat alongside trash heaps with as many of their possessions as they could salvage. Their own community leaders had just collaborated with municipal authorities to demolish their structures and they had nowhere to go. But they were far from surprised: Their neighborhood has been under the threat of eviction since 2002, and their leaders had since become untrustworthy and concerned only with their self-interest.

During Accra's annual floods, squatter settlements become scapegoats for the city's larger problems. Municipal authorities cannot keep up with Ghana's rapid urbanization, build enough infrastructure, prevent squatters from settling on flood plains, and clean sewers and drains. Instead, they blame residents in the poorest of neighborhoods for causing the urban crisis. During this particular flooding season, the government used the crisis as an excuse to demolish hundreds of structures illegally built along a central lagoon. But community leaders saw the exercise as an opportunity to lead the demolition themselves, to provide an employment contract, and a way to show strength and bolster their power in the community. Within weeks, residents had rebuilt their houses and the neighborhood continued to grow larger.

The view from within the neighborhood is largely an untold story. Residents work long hours as scrap dealers and market sellers. Opinion leaders hold weekly meetings to discuss issues in their hometown, as well as ways to support new migrants to the city. Entrepreneurs start private shower and toilet businesses, as well as microloan institutions to service a growing population. Political parties extend sophisticated organizing machinery into the deepest corners of the settlement, providing a mechanism to ensure votes and distribute patronage. Representatives of the state form coalitions with community leaders, political party activists, and NGOs to maintain a low level of control in these areas. Yet as the example of the demolition demonstrates, the political process serves private interests, empowering leaders and brokers who are not accountable to the entire population, but rather to a small slice of people from the same ethnic group. While residents engage in collective decision-making, the community is governed along private lines – often ethnic, personal, and partisan. Despite vibrant struggles for power, political clientelism persists, the political arena is reduced to private decision-making, and an associational life is organized along ethnic lines.

These introductory vignettes illustrate an intriguing puzzle in African urban development. Poor neighborhoods with similar demographic and institutional characteristics demonstrate very different patterns of collective decision-making and community governance. Despite having many of the variables that scholars have put forth to explain how communities can improve their livelihoods and demand development, including vibrant civil societies, high political competition, and robust political participation, the Ga Mashie and Old Fadama neighborhoods continue to suffer from political clientelism, the elite capture of public goods for private gain, and ethnic politics. Yet with a seemingly similar demographic profile, the Ashaiman neighborhood – the community in the second vignette – has overcome these nondemocratic politics to construct a public sphere that serves the interests of a majority of residents. This variation in governance and development across city neighborhoods in Ghana serves as the empirical puzzle in this book.

Conventional political science theories are limited in their ability to explain these divergent development outcomes. One approach narrowly focuses on the role that elections play in fostering accountability and distributing public goods and services. The second approach zooms in on societal characteristics, and emphasizes factors like ethnic diversity and poverty to explain why certain areas struggle to develop. Yet as these introductory vignettes suggest – and as I will demonstrate in this book – these theories overlook the everyday politics in urban neighborhoods that bring representatives and their constituents together or keep them apart in daily affairs. Everyday politics refers to the institutional context of daily decision-making in a neighborhood – how people act, think, and feel about power on a daily basis. The everyday politics of urban neighborhoods helps explain why clientelism persists, the capture of state resources for private gain, and entrenched ethnic politics.

The context of daily life is important to African politics because this is where leaders legitimate their authority, as well as make decisions about how to distribute resources. Politicians and political parties are motivated by appealing to constituents' daily struggles, and gain their support by engaging them in face-to-face deliberation. Citizens, on the other hand, expect their leaders to be available and concerned with personal issues and affairs. This is also where governance of goods and resources occurs. People make decisions about keeping the neighborhood clean, educating students, providing healthcare, and contracting infrastructure projects on the streets of neighborhoods and in quotidian interactions. Yet in most political science scholarship, everyday politics is treated as merely a reflection of formal political forces like elections, or as representative of broader societal processes. The motivations, behaviors, and decision-making are overlooked. This book treats daily life as an arena of politics in its own right, providing a lens into an aspect of democratization that has been mostly overlooked.

The second major argument of the book is that informal norms of settlement and belonging continue to structure everyday politics in Ghana's cities, despite significant changes in the formal and societal realms. In particular, norms of indigeneity – that groups native to a territory hold special rights and entitlements – remain sticky, setting cities on a path of urban development where host–migrant relationships dictate the politics of its neighborhoods. These cleavages are apparent in everyday politics, but extend to the formal realm during elections and in courts over claims to property rights. By combining survey methods, historical analysis, and ethnographic research, I provide a comprehensive look at leadership and civic life in Ghana. In doing so, I provide a more complete picture of the political process of urbanization.

Since African governments inherited structures of authority in the late 1950s and 1960s that were significantly impacted by colonial rule, African cities have grown rapidly and unequally. And they keep growing: By 2050, 70 percent of all Africans are projected to live in urban areas, signaling a huge transformation away from rural life. But the majority of these people will live in conditions where infrastructure is poor, services are under-provided, and property rights are insecure. The increasing number of poor neighborhoods, many of which are not recognized by formal authorities, raises important questions about claims to land and incorporation of migrants into political society, as new communities form, identities change, and relationships between representatives and constituents are altered. As African countries adopt more politically and economically liberal policies, and their societies become more urban, this book demonstrates that everyday politics requires a central place in the study of urban development.

An Urban Future

Africa is undergoing an urban revolution that is remaking polities and societies (Parnell and Pieterse 2014). Its 3.5 percent urbanization rate per year during the past two decades is the highest regional urbanization rate in the world (African Development Bank 2012). Currently, 40 percent of the population lives in urban areas, making up more than 414 million people (United Nations 2014). A result of this rapid urbanization is the growth of under-resourced neighborhoods across the continent. As of 2010, an estimated 200 million people (Vidal 2010), or 62 percent of the urban population in sub-Saharan Africa resides in neighborhoods often called slums (UN-Habitat 2012; Arimah 2010).[3]

This urban transformation poses an enormous societal challenge. Cities are at the forefront of political struggles as previously marginalized communities demand citizenship rights and seek inclusion into democratic polities (Holston 2008; Resnick 2013). It also poses a policy challenge. The recently launched sustainable development goals specifically call to "make cities and human settlements inclusive, safe, resilient and sustainable." This reflects growing recognition that human development depends on how well urbanization is managed. According to Dr. Joan Clos, Executive Director of UN-Habitat and former mayor of Barcelona, the global view of "cities as containers of problems" must change. Cities are, in fact, "accelerators of development."

The rise of megacities, especially in the Global South, has left large populations to suffer congestion and pollution in poor neighborhoods (Van der Ploeg and Poehlhekke 2008). Urbanization has often occurred without economic growth and industrialization, contributing to a process of urban informalization and the growth of the urban poor (Fay and Opal 2000; Ravallion et al. 2007). Mike Davis popularized this alarmist sentiment in his book *Planet of Slums*, where he argues that the 1970s debt crisis and IMF-led restructuring of Third World economies in the 1980s decreased wages, increased unemployment, and led to an informal proletariat and urban crisis (Davis 2006). Scholars and pundits suggest that rising land prices,

---

[3] UN-Habitat (2003) defines slums by their physical conditions. Slum neighborhoods lack durable housing of a permanent nature; sufficient living space; easy access to safe water at an affordable price; access to adequate sanitation in the form of a private or public toilet; and security of tenure that prevents forced evictions. Slums are neighborhoods that have these observable conditions (though they might not have all five characteristics).

privatization of subsistence agriculture, and declining state and social safety nets has forced rural dwellers to the city to sustain basic livelihoods (Mahmud 2010; Almeida 2012).

The restructuring of economies in the 1980s and 1990s hit African cities particularly hard (O'Connor 1993). Its state and civil service was hampered by policies that contributed to capital flight, the collapse of manufacturing, marginal or negative increase in export incomes, drastic cutbacks in urban public services, soaring prices, and a steep decline in real wages (Rakodi 1997; Myers 2005). These challenges occurred in the context of poor economic policies and political instability that had already constrained development across the continent (Bates 1981). By the 2000s, many in the development and policy-making industry expressed how these policies backfired, and were never fully implemented (van de Walle 2001). The most important report on the failures of urban policy was published by the United Nations in 2003, and concluded: "Instead of being a focus for growth and prosperity, the cities have become a dumping ground for a surplus population working in unskilled, unprotected and low-wage informal service industries and trade ... The rise of [this] informal sector is ... a direct result of liberalization" (United Nations 2003: 76).

But these significant changes also signaled a political opportunity. The increasing liberalization of the 1990s resulted in a strange paradox: It exacerbated socioeconomic inequalities, but also created political space independent from the state (Tripp 1997; Chalfin 2008). In countries like South Africa, Kenya, and Ghana, cities were the main setting for political change, becoming sources for homegrown political opposition that would usher in a new era of democratization (Chazan and Rothschild 1988; Bratton and van de Walle 1994). The first protests broke out in highly urbanized countries, mostly in cities (Bratton and van de Walle 1997). But the rise of democracy in the third wave opened new mechanisms for political dissent (LeBas 2011). The wave of democratization in the 1990s coincided with the development of an urban middle class and a burgeoning civil society in many African countries.

Political liberalization in the 1990s coincided with a shift in international development policy: Democracy, good governance, and human rights became priorities (Young 2012). For urban planners and development specialists, governance included setting out to fix what went wrong with African cities (Myers 2005). But this also meant limiting the role of the state in this process, while strengthening decentralization through the empowerment of local administrative units (Eyoh and Stren 2003).

These shifts in priorities forced urban residents to confront livelihood and welfare challenges without the assistance of the state (Azarya and Chazan 1987; Chalfin 2014). Residents were resilient, and devised various strategies to cope with insecure living conditions.[4] They formed grassroots associations that were involved in a range of activities including community management, provision of social services and infrastructure, finance and credit, and religious and social affairs (Tostensen et al. 2001). They relied on informal networks because the formal structures of the city or the state did not protect them.[5] These responses were not always democratic or egalitarian. In some cases, populations politicize conceptions of belonging and notions of citizenship, making new claims over territory and land (Geschiere and Gugler 1998; Geschiere and Jackson 2006). Nonetheless, communities depend on the strength of their social networks and underlying networks of reciprocity and social capital.[6]

Political scientists have been slow to respond to the changing urban landscape in Africa. While political liberalization, good governance, and urbanization have all received significant attention, their impact on African politics and how the urban poor are integrated into modern political systems remains understudied. Moreover, scholars of political clientelism, distributive politics, and ethnicity focus their attention primarily on rural settings, overlooking crucial sites of democratizing societies. This book shows how the dual process of political liberalization alongside rapid urbanization in Ghana interacts, supports, and even shapes each other. Africa's urban future rests on poor neighborhoods as emerging spaces of intense political importance.

---

[4] Some of the most influential studies in urban Africa focus on the different ways that individuals and groups confront governance and economic challenges in the context of state failure. See: Maylam and Edwards (1996); Ferguson (1999); Simone (2004).

[5] See the following studies for this perspective: Attahi (1997); Hart (2000); Appadurai (2001).

[6] Putnam (1993, 2001) has documented the importance of social capital in Italy and the United States, respectively. In Ghanaian politics, community associations and pressure groups have a long history, as I show in the next section.

Democracy in Ghana

Ghana is an ideal site to study the parallel processes of urbanization and democratization. While much of the continent is in the early stages of urbanization, Ghana's experience with these processes dates back to the colonial era, where rural residents began flocking to its cities in large numbers to take advantage of budding industries and economic opportunities (Acquah 1958). In addition, its vibrant and well-established two-party political system emerged in the struggle for Independence in the 1940s, and these distinct political traditions now shape party politics (Fridy 2007).[7] Today, the National Democratic Congress (NDC) and the New Patriotic Party (NPP) dominate the political arena. Examining these dual processes of urbanization and liberalization in Ghana provide a lens into the role that they might play in other countries across the continent.

The political importance of Ghanaian cities dates back to the colonial era when the city acted as both a system of control and a space to engage in political struggle against colonial authorities (Austin 1970). In 1957, Ghana became the first country in Africa to gain independence.[8] The impetus for this early transition came from pressure from its political parties, particularly the Convention People's Party (CPP) led by founding president Kwame Nkrumah, which drew support from the grassroots. Nkrumah rallied support based on his slogan "Independence Now," as opposed to the United Gold Coast Convention's (UGCC) call for "Independence at the shortest possible time." Most of this resistance emerged in Accra, where "disgruntled commoners" like returned ex-servicemen, unemployed youth, and "elementary-school-leavers" who had little chance of social mobility protested rising prices of goods, as well as colonial rule more generally (Apter 1955; Austin 1970).

Local *asafo* companies – groups of military bands organized in towns, villages, and traditional states – provided an organizational framework for popular mobilization during the colonial period (Datta and Porter 1971; Shaloff 1974; Simensen 1974, 1975; Fortescue 1990; Akyeampong 2002). By the 1940s, the CPP and the UGCC existed side

[7] See: Sebastian Elischer (2013) and Rachel Riedl (2014) for a discussion of the origins of Ghana's political parties.
[8] Ethiopia was never colonized by a European power, but was occupied by Italy.

by side with these youth associations, fighting to gain their support and hoping to subsume them into party organizations. We see legacies of these earlier struggles in Ghana's neighborhoods today, with the contemporary manifestation of the CPP and UGCC – the NDC and NPP, respectively – rallying support in these urban areas (Klaus and Paller 2017).

Throughout Ghana's postcolonial history, including periods of authoritarian rule, political parties have been very active in mobilizing local communities. Prior to the current multiparty era, which began in 1992 and is called the Fourth Republic, the country experienced numerous coup d'états and threats to freedom of association and expression. Nonetheless, nonstate actors like traditional authorities, religious figures, and other local leaders have long contributed to an active and vibrant associational life. For example, during the authoritarian regime of Jerry John Rawlings (1981–1992), a group of market women at Accra's Makola Market served as a de facto representative group for the opposition. The government made concerted efforts to decentralize administrative control and devolve budgets to district assemblies. Politicians used these assemblies to fund their party machinery, while trying to co-opt grassroots organizations like keep-fit clubs, cleanup committees, and "fisher folk" in order to strengthen political control (Gocking 2005).[9] Local leaders and associations have long been a crucial part of Ghana's process of democratization.

While Ghana has avoided the large-scale electoral violence that has broken out in other African democracies like Kenya and Cote d'Ivoire (Klaus and Mitchell 2015), elections have contributed to communal conflicts in Northern Ghana (Jockers et al. 2010) that have played out in cities, as well as low-intensity electoral violence in urban Ghana (Bob-Milliar 2014). This is often because local leaders use political parties and elections to advance their own personal agendas (Onoma 2009). But political parties also exploit these local divisions, many of which draw on long-standing grievances over claims to land and territory (Lentz 2013; Klaus 2015).

All this is to say that Ghana is a vibrant multiparty democracy, and is considered to have some of the most robust liberal-democratic institutions on the continent. The country has had six free and fair elections, and has experienced three peaceful transfers of power between

---

[9] Keep-fit clubs are local youth athletic clubs made up of mostly young men.

political parties – in 2000 when the NPP took power; in 2008 when the NDC reestablished authority; and in 2016 when the NPP acquired the reins of the state.[10] Most elections have been decided by a narrow vote margin, demonstrating the high intensity of party competition. In addition, political participation is high, which is bolstered by a vibrant civil society and free media (Gyimah-Boadi 2009; Arthur 2010; Ninsin 2016). The population is maturing as a democratic citizenry, and Ghanaians now vote based on issues rather than narrow parochial interests (Lindberg and Morrison 2008; Harding 2015).

Despite these improvements in Ghana's institutional development, the country is beset by political clientelism, elite capture of state resources, and ethnic politics.[11] This history has contributed to a large body of literature evaluating its democratic performance. Most of these studies focus either on formal institutional development, or the social structure underlying decision-making. Largely missing in the study of Ghana's democracy is the way these formal institutions interact with informal social organization in everyday life.[12]

A notable exception is the research by anthropologist Maxwell Owusu. He shows how traditional beliefs interacted with colonialism to privilege a politics where Ghanaians consider government to exist for instrumental purposes (Owusu 1970).[13] Owusu writes, "Material interests have been related to and controlled by shared values that stress the primary end of political action not civic responsibility and duty, but material and economic benefits directly related to matters of status and prestige" (Owusu 1970: 68). Importantly, Owusu pays close attention to how tradition and historical forms of authority interact with modern day democracy and political systems. For example, he considers how the "ideas and beliefs people have about

---

[10] The NPP boycotted the 1992 elections, which was beset by procedural irregularities.

[11] For new research on clientelism, distributive politics, and ethnicity in Ghana, see: Abdulai and Hickey (2016); Asunka (2016, 2017); Asunka et al. (2017); Gadjanova (2017).

[12] George Bob-Milliar is one of the few scholars that focuses on how political parties gain support in the context of daily life; why ordinary Ghanaians join parties; and the different norms and strategies that shape political competition. See: Bob-Milliar (2011, 2012, 2014).

[13] Peter Ekeh (1975) provides a similar explanation for this in Nigeria, explaining that there is both a civic and primordial public in postcolonial sub-Saharan African countries.

social stratification and about systems of authority in society" contribute to the way that Ghanaians understand and practice democracy (71). The importance of face-to-face relations, social and familial networks, and reciprocity are embedded in Ghana's rich political culture. As I've demonstrated elsewhere, they shape the process of democratization today (Paller 2014).

Maxwell Owusu's insights into Ghana's democracy suggest that traditional views of authority and political culture continue to influence contemporary politics. As Ann Swidler (1986) emphasizes, culture provides the repertoire or "tool kit" of habits, skills, and styles through which individuals construct "strategies of action." While political culture provides what is thinkable (Schatzberg 2001), individuals then navigate the political arena strategically and rationally depending on the cultural tool kit that is available to them.

In other words, while Owusu's insights describe a lot of the practices that are evident in contemporary politics, they risk essentializing Ghana's democracy. Empirically, there is a lot of variation across the country with respect to the interests, incentives, and behaviors of Ghana's politicians, as well as the motivations and actions of the citizenry. As the introductory vignettes describe, there is even significant variation across Ghana's cities. An approach to democracy that relies solely on a unified political culture cannot explain this important variation.[14] Instead, it is important to treat urban neighborhoods as sites of politics in their own right, where a new politics emerges and extends far beyond a clash between traditional systems of authority, colonial ruptures in government, and modern democracy. Uncovering the informal institutions of a neighborhood sheds light on the available strategies of action.

Leadership and Civic Life in Africa

To better understand how democracy works in practice, this book pays close attention to leadership and civic life. One of the most convincing accounts of how social structure and state power interact at the local level is Lauren M. MacLean's *Informal Institutions and Citizenship in Rural Africa*. In the book, MacLean offers an account of how distinct

---

[14] For the best account of the role of political culture in African democracies, see: Schatzberg (2001).

experiences of state formation shaped different informal institutions of reciprocity, or long-term ties of exchange between members in a group (MacLean 2010). MacLean's argument is notable because it uncovers how associational life is an outcome of the historical process of state formation, as well as how these ties are reproduced in social engagements in everyday life. This approach demonstrates how micro-level norms of reciprocity contribute to different political outcomes and exercises of citizenship. In particular, it shows how "local patterns of social and political exclusion and the ways that rural people were linked (or not) to the broader national political system" help explain matters of ethnic conflict and democratization.[15] In this way, MacLean focuses attention on an arena of politics that most political science studies of public goods and service provision leave out: how local communities experience the state in everyday life, and how residents interpret democratic citizenship. I draw from this critical insight and apply it to the historical evolution of leadership and civic life in Ghana's cities.

A comprehensive understanding of leadership and civic life requires paying close attention to the interaction between formal and informal institutions, and suggests that this relationship is crucial to the study of democracy (Helmke and Levitsky 2006). Informal institutions are "the socially shared rules that are created, communicated, and enforced outside of officially sanctioned channels" (Helmke and Levitsky 2004). Institutions are distinct from culture because they include a sanctioning mechanism that constrains and enables human behavior (North 1990). Informal institutions shape the modes of behavior and attitudes at a stage prior to formal political participation by defining the risks and opportunities of action and options available to political actors (Lauth 2000).

In the context of weak formal institutions, they can provide a powerful social logic by way of an "economy of affection," through a network of communication, support, and interactions at the local level (Hyden 1983). In a new democracy, these rules and norms are important because they are often the real rules and norms being followed because the political process is informally institutionalized

---

[15] For example, ethnic grievances in Ghana are mediated at the local level, due to the reciprocity networks that emerge after a long process of state formation (MacLean 2004).

(O'Donnell 1996). The "informal rules shape how democratic institutions work" by reinforcing, subverting, and superseding formal rules, procedures, and organizations (Helmke and Levitsky 2006: 2). Therefore, a true representation of leadership and civic life requires an investigation into the underlying informal institutions.

Dennis Galvan's (2004) *The State Must Be Our Master of Fire* applies these insights to African democracy and development. In his book, Galvan combines insights from the political culture literature with institutional analysis. Drawing from the case study of sustainable development in rural Senegal, he emphasizes the importance of considering local knowledge in a particular society. Local populations actively make political institutions their own by giving meaning to "foreign" concepts.[16] Conceptualizing culture as fluid and changing provides the theoretical basis for understanding how nonindigenous institutions and practices become "thinkable" in rapidly changing societies. In later work with Gerald Berk, he suggests that people "live through" their institutions by viewing them as bundles of resources available for creative reinterpretation and recombination (Berk and Galvan 2009). The authors label the construction and disfiguring of institutions through this process "creative syncretism." This process guides my conceptualization of everyday politics, which I discuss in the next section.

Most of the studies that provide this type of close analysis between institutions, social life, and political culture focus on rural Africa. Very few studies look at African cities. Those that do either emphasize formal institutions like elections, or social organization independent from formal power structures. Importantly, they do not consider the interaction between the two – how leaders and residents navigate their local context and subscribe to informal norms. The few studies that do this are anthropological studies that examine leadership patterns and public life. Most notably, Enid Schildkrout (1978), Deborah Pellow (2002), and Brenda Chalfin (2010, 2014) provide the most detailed accounts of leadership and civic life in urban Ghana. In *Landlords and Lodgers,* Pellow traces the origins of leadership in Sabon Zongo, a poor migrant neighborhood in Accra. She discusses the social practices that bring leaders and their followers together in daily life, and suggests

---

[16] Frederic Schaffer (1998) provides a similar analysis for the concept of democracy, analyzing how Senegalese understand elections.

that the control of urban space dictates these terms of interaction. The book situates the neighborhood in the broader development of the city, but also discusses how internal social organization – based on temporal settlement patterns and religion – shape the everyday politics of the neighborhood.

Schildkrout's book *People of the Zongo* provides a similar exercise for the growth of Kumasi. Schildkrout's analysis is central to the approach I take in this book, that migration in West Africa is not only a temporal process, but also a structural situation where "the dichotomy between hosts and strangers is not a temporary phase of interaction" but "more or less a permanent identity" (Schildkrout 1978: 6).[17] Enid Schildkrout's claim is particularly strong: Immigrant or stranger status is permanent, and the relationship between hosts and strangers is structural and deterministic. I maintain this focus on host-settler relationships being a defining feature of group relations, but I suggest that they are not deterministic, but rather are negotiated and navigated in everyday situations. Interestingly, Schildkrout notes how migrant populations in Kumasi in the 1960s relied on patronage relationships with political parties in order to secure their tenure and avoid eviction, and even deportation. The close attention paid to the relationship between formal and informal institutions provides a lens into the way norms of indigeneity overlapped with party politics in the early years of Independence. The category of host, stranger, and squatter, which I introduce later, are sticky and persistent categories of Ghanaian politics.

Brenda Chalfin's (2014) recent research in Tema and Ashaiman explains patterns of leadership and public life in the context of the current global political economy and state retrenchment. In doing so, it opens up new ways to think about civic life. In particular, she explains how the governance of public services, like toilets, extends beyond distribution and management, to claims to a right to the city. In other words, she demonstrates how urban populations co-opt public services and transform them into "sites of political possibility." In this process, public infrastructure takes on new meaning to local populations. The governance of public services provides the possibility for new leaders

---

[17] Also see: Fortes (1975). I define migrant as any individual who was born in another city and claims another city, town, or village as his or her hometown. They include both international and internal migrants.

to emerge, daily interactions to coalesce into strong social ties, and deliberation to strengthen an emerging public sphere.[18] Thinking about the governance and management of resources in the broader context of the right to the city and the emergence of civic life opens new possibilities for the study of leadership, political authority, and distributive politics.

These scholars provide important reflections on the study of leadership and civic life in urban Ghana. In particular, they shed light on the way political clientelism, distributive politics, and ethnicity interacts. Importantly, they emphasize the centrality of everyday politics to the study of these important concepts. Moreover, they emphasize how these patterns of politics emerge in an urban context given specific historical developments. In particular, the informal norms of indigeneity continue to structure the arena of political competition, broadening our understanding of multiparty politics.

Yet despite these crucial insights, the arena of everyday life has not been adequately incorporated into political science theories of clientelism, distributive politics, and ethnic politics. Instead, these bodies of literature overemphasize elections, without placing voting and campaigns in their broader political context. Studies that focus on social organization tend to discuss identity and class without reference to historical patterns of urban development, overlooking the centrality of host-stranger relations in contemporary affairs. Alternatively, the anthropological accounts of urban Ghana just discussed do not contribute to generalizable theories of democracy. While part of the reason for this is disciplinary, the other reason is that the empirical material that they draw from focuses on a single neighborhood in a much larger city.[19] As I explain in Chapter 3, they do not account for the broader process of urbanization in distinct neighborhoods across the same city. For this, a comparative analysis of urban neighborhoods is required.

This book provides a necessary addition by using the anthropological tools of everyday politics to uncover the patterns of leadership and civic life in Ghana's cities, and then incorporating them into a generalizable theory of democracy. In doing so, it provides a rich

---

[18] *Neoliberal Frontiers* explores these concepts in the broader framework of everyday state building (Chalfin 2010).

[19] All three studies focus on stranger communities called *zongos*, which I explain in more depth in the next chapter.

account of how local populations make democracy work – or fail to overcome politico-institutional challenges.

Everyday Urban Politics

The first argument of this book is that everyday politics provides a lens into understanding the variation in governance and development across Ghana's cities. Specifically, the everyday politics of urban neighborhoods helps explain why clientelism persists, the capture of state resources for private gain, and entrenched ethnic politics. Everyday urban politics is the institutional context of daily decision-making in a neighborhood – how people act, think, and feel about power on a daily basis. Four characteristics distinguish this approach from other theoretical frameworks.

First, it is embedded in the social practices of individuals. These social practices include formal political actors like presidents, politicians, technocrats, and business elites, as well as ordinary people. An emphasis on social practices blurs these crude lines between formal political behavior and informal activity, or action that occurs outside of officially sanctioned rules and regulations. The observable implications of these social practices are the actions, events, customs, and behaviors of people involved in a study.

Second, power shapes what happens in daily life. The concept is most concerned with the first dimension of power (Lukes 1974), or the ability of individuals, organizations, or institutions to influence decision-making. Power is also about relationships, and uncovering the ties between people helps explain how power is structured. The observable implications of these political relationships are the networks that form from social interactions that occur over time, as well as the social ties between people.

Third, everyday politics includes the structures of authority that might not be measurable or observable, but are nonetheless shaping peoples' behavior. I suggest that political scientists' focus on institutions, or the rules and norms that govern societies, is an important addition to understanding everyday life. Everyday politics examines how political institutions work each day because this is where elites and ordinary people interact, as well as where prospects for stability and change occur. This is because people contribute to the constructing and disfiguring of institutions through the process of creative syncretism (Berk and Galvan 2009). Important institutions that require analysis include elections, legislatures, administrative bodies, property rights regimes, and customary authority. The observable implications of these political institutions are the rules and norms themselves, as well as the strength, functionality, and utility of them from day to day – what they make people do.

Fourth, the concept requires uncovering the emotions that people feel on a daily basis. Specifically, the emotions of theoretical interest are those linked to the social practices, power dynamics, and institutions that govern behavior. This is because emotions motivate people to act, think, and feel in a certain way. These emotions have political consequences. They might include "public opinion" and "political attitudes," but they might not be clearly specified as such. For example, the way a politician makes a citizen feel might tell us more about his or her likelihood to participate in multiparty politics than whether he or she "supports democracy." Alternatively, how a resident feels on a particular day might motivate him or her to engage in collective action. While there are other ways to study emotions like using surveys, experiments, and lab techniques, everyday politics requires a focus on how individuals make sense of their daily environment through a process of meaning-making (Wedeen 2002). This approach also underlies a theory of political change because it can uncover when, where, and how emotions shift and behaviors change. The observable implications of these emotions are the feelings that research subjects have that propel them to act or acquiesce.

Informal Norms of Settlement and Belonging

The second argument of this book builds off a large body of scholarship that points to the informal norms of settlement and belonging as a defining feature of African urban politics.[20] This approach follows the volume *African Cities: Competing Claims on Urban Spaces*, suggesting that "the identification of old and new competing claims on urban spaces and the understanding of how city dwellers forge their own way of dealing with expansion—by creating notions of the 'stranger'" is an important heuristic for broader political struggles (Locatelli and

---

[20] Other scholars who take this approach include Schildkrout (1978); Cooper (1983); Locatelli and Nugent (2009).

Nugent 2009: 4).[21] A focus on informal norms of settlement and belonging privilege a focus on the everyday politics that uncovers interests and motivations in the neighborhoods themselves. Following the insights of Patrick Chabal, belonging is not just a material claim, but is central to selfhood and comes with certain obligations, "To have no obligations is not to belong; it is not to be fully and socially human" (Chabal 2008: 48).

This approach suggests that the way people understand ownership and view their relationship to territory and urban space shapes the urbanization process (Van Leeuwen and Van der Haar 2016). In empirical terms, I suggest that relationships between host, stranger, and squatter populations form the dominant cleavages across urban neighborhoods. Therefore, urban neighborhoods are best categorized with respect to these cleavages, contributing to three distinct types of settlements that I label indigenous, stranger, and squatter settlements.

Indigenous settlements are the oldest neighborhoods in a city, where populations make indigenous or autochthonous claims to land and territory. In Ghana, customary law dictates property ownership, privileging this form of land tenure. Politically, these claims contribute to a conception of citizenship that provides these groups the entitlement "to enter the struggle for resources" based on ethnic origin (Mamdani 2002: 505). Leadership and community governance are dominated by customary norms and practices, contributing to political clientelism that is shaped by traditional and familial institutions. It also shapes distributive politics because populations feel entitled to state resources because they are the original inhabitants of the land. Members of the indigenous ethnic group claim customary entitlements as a club good, in exchange for support and votes. Not surprisingly, ethnic politics persists, as the indigenous group restricts decision-making to members from its own group.

---

[21] In the volume, competition for urban land in Lagos takes the form of struggles over legitimate ownership of land and territory, rooted in understandings of indigeneity and belonging (Akinyele 2009: 109–133). In Kumasi, outsiders are scapegoated for water scarcity, demonstrating how host-stranger relations explain political cleavages in the city. In related work, host-stranger relations contribute to urban land conflict in Ethiopia, Johannesburg, and Juba. See: Keller (2014); Marx (2016); McMichael (2016) for more scholarship that takes this approach.

Ghanaian cities have a long history of migration, and when migrants were not assimilated into indigenous neighborhoods, they formed *stranger settlements* on the outskirts of the city. Early settlers – usually migrant leaders – purchased plots of land directly from indigenous landowners. The informal settlement pattern contributes to a situation of peaceful existence between host indigenous populations and migrant residents. Because these settlements subscribe to informal norms of settlement and belonging, these neighborhoods are publicly legitimate in the eyes of the broader population, even though they are poor and under-resourced. Although most of these residents are poor, and many are recent migrants, they do not feel threatened about their tenure security in the city. This contributes to patterns of authority where leaders are expected to respond to the needs of all residents. In addition, a public sphere emerges where residents from different groups engage in collective decision-making. Therefore, civic life develops along multiethnic lines.

In the 1980s and 1990s, *squatter settlements* emerged as new neighborhoods for poor migrants to settle, as rapid urban growth and liberalization outpaced formal urban planning and government-sanctioned housing. These settlements are analytically distinct from stranger settlements because they violate the informal norms of settlement and belonging. The population squats on the land, without purchasing land directly from the owners or custodians of the land. Therefore, they are illegitimate in the eyes of the local population and government agencies often do not officially recognize them. Although they have strong and active leaders, they are motivated by a personal agenda to accumulate power and support a constituency elsewhere, usually in the home region from which they migrated. Therefore, distributive politics follows a private logic, where leaders capture state resources for personal gain. Ethnicity remains highly salient, as there is very little trust and reciprocity across ethnic groups.

In Chapter 2, I explain these settlement patterns in more depth. Throughout the book, I demonstrate how the informal norms of settlement and belonging go a long way toward explaining the persistence of political clientelism, the type of distributive politics, and the resolve or decline of ethnic politics. In Chapter 3 I explain the origins of these neighborhoods in the context of Ghana's urban development.

The Role of Urban Space

This book rests on the simple premise that politics in African cities are conceptually different from politics in rural areas. This is for all of the demographic reasons we might expect, including that most cities are more ethnically diverse, have higher densities, and provide better access to education and health services. There are also institutional reasons, including that most cities are closer to formal political and economic power.

But urban politics in Africa is different from rural or national politics for less obvious reasons too, and this rests on the importance of urban space. Urban space refers to two dimensions: the physical territory in a city, and the social and institutional arrangements that establish order. Because of higher densities, urban space is often more restricted and less plentiful. As urbanization occurs, land prices typically increase, raising the material value of property. In addition, urban land has often been sold to different individuals or companies, often making it harder than in many rural areas to trace ownership to a particular plot or territory. The social and institutional arrangements are also more varied, with diverse forms of authority. These parallel authority structures include nonstate actors like NGOs, customary authorities, religious figures, and politicians and political parties. In these ways, competition for power over urban space is often more complex and varied than in rural areas.

Therefore, control of urban space has great economic value, as prices for properties rise. But it also has great political value because the struggle for followers and support takes new forms in cities. These forms can manifest in securing tenure of residents, provisioning water and electricity, and providing safety. This control of urban space can translate directly into formal political power. But it is not as simple as existing scholarship suggests. This is because most studies of democracy in Ghana focus on clientelism, distributive politics, and ethnic politics at the national level, which restrict analysis to understanding political competition mostly in rural areas. In rural Africa, populations are less diverse and constituencies often form durable voting blocs. In addition, local authority structures compete less with other political actors, leading to stable relationships between traditional authorities and political parties. Ethnicity tends to overlap with territorial boundaries, restricting the scope of political competition so that elect-oral constituencies overlap with societal organizations. Therefore, the avenue toward political and economic empowerment moves in one direction – and elections can be a rewarding way of attaining these material assets.

But in urban spaces, individuals and groups have multiple options toward political and economic empowerment that extend far beyond elections. This can include forming new jurisdictions of traditional authority, profiting off property, and making new alliances with NGOs, both local and foreign. What this means is that elections – and the clientelism and distributive politics that come with them – are embedded in broader struggles over control of the city. The control of urban space is the most important political struggle, beyond just winning elections. This has significant repercussions for the way democracy works in urban Africa.

Research Design and Methods

I first traveled to Ghana to conduct exploratory research in the summer of 2009. I began my research in the three neighborhoods of Old Fadama, Tulako (Ashaiman), and Ga Mashie, all located in the Greater Accra Region.[22] I selected these cases based on a most-similar systems research design. They exhibit comparable demographic characteristics in terms of household income, education, and health indices (Table 1.1). In addition, they have high levels of political competition and party institutionalization, state capacity, legacies of state-building, and ethnic diversity. Yet the outcomes in governance and development are stark. Old Fadama residents lack tenure security, sanitation, and access to public services. Ashaiman residents, on the other hand, have cleaner streets, better services, and safer neighborhoods. Finally, while Ga Mashie has the best roads, secure structures, and quality public services, they struggle to maintain and manage them effectively. At the very early stages of the project, it was obvious that these neighborhoods were governed very differently and practiced a distinct type of politics.

[22] Old Fadama is colloquially called "Sodom and Gomorrah" by locals. Ashaiman is a growing municipality outside the port city of Tema. I focused most of my work in Ashaiman in two neighborhoods, Tulako and Ashaiman Zongo. Ga Mashie includes James Town and Ussher Town.

Table 1.1 *Most-similar systems case selection for ethnographic research*

	Ga Mashie	Ashaiman Zongo	Old Fadama
Settlement Type	Indigenous	Stranger	Squatter
Party Affiliation	NDC	NDC	NDC
Pol. Competition	High	High	High
Ethnic Diversity[23]	2.0263	1.7875	2.1625
Indigenous Group	Ga	Dangbe	Ga
Lived Poverty[24]	1.169	1.175	0.9

I devised a survey that borrowed many questions from the *Afrobarometer*, a reputable public opinion survey that asks ordinary citizens about their attitudes toward the state and democracy. I included questions drawn from the existing literature that measure explanatory variables for governance and development outcomes. These included a battery of questions about voting and political participation, as well as others about civil society and social structure. Surprisingly, there was very little variation in responses between the three neighborhoods. None of the conventional explanations for governance and development could explain the divergent outcomes I noticed in these three urban neighborhoods.

Most of these questions are devised to explain national-level political patterns. Those that focus on local factors attempt to uncover social structure, demographic characteristics, and individual attitudes toward generic political actors and institutions. However, they are unable to account for the political behavior and community decision-making that actually takes place in respondents' neighborhoods. Additionally, they do not incorporate the informal norms and multiple authorities that are so important to governance in local communities. They do not pay enough attention to local political context, and how leaders control urban space.

---

[23] Measured as the mean of the answers for the following question: "Does a person from a different group live next to you?" 0 = No; 1 = 2–5; 2 = 3–5; 3 = More than 5. Distribution is 1.61–2.44.

[24] Measured as the mean of the answers for the following question: "In the past year, how often, if ever, have you or anyone in this household gone without medicines or medical treatment?" 0 = Never; 1 = Just once or twice; 2 = Several times or many times or always.

To understand the process of political decision-making in these neighborhoods, I needed to immerse myself in the daily lives of the residents and leaders. Over the course of one year, August 2011–2012, I conducted ethnographic research in these three neighborhoods (Figure 1.1).[25] Ethnography is the "immersion in the lives of the people under study" (Wedeen 2010).[26] This research method helps uncover the process of politics, the informal networks that underlie political arrangements, and the spontaneity in decision-making that shapes institutional pathways. I visited at least one of the case study communities on a daily basis. I ate meals with residents and leaders, observed community meetings, visited the private offices of politicians and chiefs, participated in party rallies, and attended ritual events. By interacting with community residents and leaders on a daily basis, I gained crucial insights into their motivations and incentives – as well as their emotions and habits. Often, we would make decisions together, giving me in-depth understandings of urban Ghanaians' decision-making process. I documented empirical observations in field notes (Emerson et al. 2011).

I supplement the ethnography with archival research and historical process tracing that uncovers the timing and sequence of the democratic consolidation process. Specifically, I analyze the history of each community from the early migration period to the present, placing special emphasis on the original settlement pattern.[27] In this way, variation in political development extends beyond space to include the important temporal dimension.

I also draw from focus groups with local leaders and residents. Focus groups are "a research technique that collects data through group interaction on a topic determined by the researcher" (Morgan 1997: 6). The focus groups helped me uncover the practices of accountability that residents use to make sure that their leaders do their jobs. The method sheds light on how residents understand the meaning of

[25] See: Marcus (1995); Chalfin (2010) for examples of multi-sited ethnography.
[26] See: Schatz (2009) for a broader discussion of political ethnography, especially to understand the different approaches to the method.
[27] For discussions of process tracing in political science research, see: Brady and Collier (2004); Pierson (2004); George and Bennett (2005).

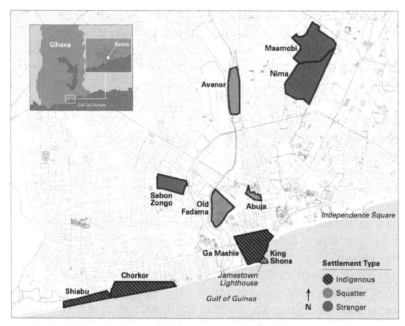

Figure 1.1 Map of poor neighborhoods included in research in Accra (designed by Niki Wolfe)

accountability and democracy (Kendhammer 2013). Questions were conducted in their native languages.[28]

To broaden the scope of the study, I developed a household survey to test the qualitatively induced hypotheses across a larger sample of urban residents in poor neighborhoods across Ghana.[29] This is the first comprehensive survey to my knowledge that examines different types of poor neighborhoods in Accra in a comparative framework, particularly the squatter settlements. While NGOs and academic institutions

---

[28] I used various techniques to get at the challenges and successes of local decision-making in Africa, using philosophical, hypothetical, and real scenarios that might occur in daily political affairs. The focus groups helped me design context-relevant questions for the household survey.

[29] I conducted the survey in April 2013 in tandem with the Center for Democratic Development – Ghana (CDD). CDD has extensive experience conducting surveys in Africa; they also administer the *Afrobarometer* surveys for the continent.

have conducted human development surveys in various settlements, none have systematically examined all of them together.[30]

The survey categorizes poor neighborhoods based on local knowledge, rather than official, formal designations. Boundaries of neighborhoods are determined by a rich assessment of how residents and officials designate certain neighborhoods based on insights acquired after qualitative research. The survey asks questions about political conditions in the neighborhoods, and specifically the nature of local-level decision-making.[31] The survey includes approximately eighty respondents in sixteen distinct neighborhoods in Accra, Ashaiman and Kumasi, totaling 1,183 total respondents; neighborhoods were selected to vary by settlement type. Due to lack of adequate baseline data in these communities, I utilize a spatial sampling technique.[32]

Most studies of urban Africa, and urban Ghana in particular, either rely on qualitative case studies of one neighborhood, or quantitative surveys of human development. Most of the surveys include questions that are more relevant for a rural African context, failing to uncover the important factors that are distinct to cities. My mixed-method approach based on a comparative research design overcomes these shortcomings by using qualitative research to induct the context-relevant characteristics of urban politics in Ghana, and then testing them deductively across a larger sample of neighborhoods and residents.

Ghana's Urban Poor

This book focuses primarily on Ghana's urban poor. Of course, the country's urban population extends far beyond this group, and includes a growing middle class and entrenched elite.[33] Nonetheless,

---

[30] The Ghana Census does not consider many informal settlements that are not recognized in their enumeration.

[31] The questions are tailored to fit local context and consider dynamics that are specific to urban life. The questions include attitudinal, behavioral, and experimental tests of the level of trust and feelings of reciprocity that residents have with their leaders, associations and pressure groups, and other community members.

[32] The technique is similar to that used by Landry and Shen (2005). See: Appendix for details into the questionnaire and sampling procedure.

[33] Noah Nathan provides some of the most exciting research to date on the role of the middle class in Ghanaian politics (see: Nathan 2016a, 2016b). Richard

the majority of Ghana's urban residents remain poor and play a very important, yet understudied role, in the country's political system. While Africa's poor now includes millions of people living in cities, there are surprisingly few studies that examine how they participate in politics. Danielle Resnick's (2013) *Urban Poverty and Party Populism in African Democracies* is one of the few studies that examines how political parties interact with poor voters, explaining how opposition dynamics in Zambia and Senegal contribute to certain groups having formal political power.[34] While a large literature in Latin America investigates the political behavior of the urban poor and the inter-actions they have with political machines, this scholarship does not yet exist in the study of African politics.

I focus most of my attention on poor urban neighborhoods because these areas are often neglected by scholars and misunderstood by the popular press. An investigation into these neighborhoods provides a glimpse into the characteristics of the urban poor, and what their needs and motivations might be. While Ghana's census provides a relatively accurate portrait of its overall population, an accurate representation of urban residents remains difficult to configure because of logistical and demographic challenges. In the poorest city neighborhoods, it is incredibly difficult to compile representative samples of populations, due to the mobility of people and their ability to "hide" from surveyors (Vigneswaran and Quirk 2012).

In urban Ghana, reliable baseline data on urban populations is nonexistent. Previous studies rely on the 2000 census, for which population figures have drastically changed in the last decade.[35] For example, the population of Accra has risen from 2.26 million to 4.3 million. Further, many residents of poor neighborhoods, particularly squatter settlements like Old Fadama, anecdotally reported that enu-merators did not survey all parts of the settlement. This leads to under-reporting of a crucial population who live in informal settlements. The Ghana Statistical Service even acknowledges this in their report: They

---

Grant (2009) documents the spatial differences between poor neighborhoods like slums, and middle- and upper-class neighborhoods on the outskirts of Accra.

[34] The classic political science account of the urban poor and its role in politics is Nelson (1979).

[35] Noah Nathan (2016a, 2016b) is an exception. He geocoded the 2010 census data and combined it with electoral returns.

estimate a population of one million migrants living in Accra who do not fit neatly into the household sampling procedure and enumeration area methodology to which they subscribed (Ghana Statistical Service 2012).

A true representative sample of urban residents, therefore, is not available in Ghana, due to the lack of baseline data and fluidity of migratory populations. Therefore, I adopted spatial sampling techniques and applied them to urban Ghanaian neighborhoods. The results are telling. The urban poor are not a homogenous group of people. They vary by age, socioeconomic characteristics, occupation status, education levels, and ethnic affiliation. In my survey, the majority of residents, or 68 percent, are less than forty years of age.[36] Similarly, levels of education vary significantly, with 21 percent indicating no formal schooling, 16 percent having attended primary school, 29 percent junior high school, and 34 percent indicating some secondary schooling. Twenty-nine percent of respondents are illiterate, 39 percent can "read a little," and 30 percent are literate. The literacy rate in Accra is 66 percent, Kumasi is 69 percent, and Ashaiman is 77 percent.

Most residents are employed in the informal economy (Hart 1973).[37] Fifty-three percent respond that they work full time in the informal sector, while 14 percent are employed part time in this sector. A small 10 percent are employed in the formal sector. Only 19 percent of respondents are unemployed, calling into question the claim that poor neighborhoods are filled with large numbers of unemployed. By and large, these numbers represent the national average: The African Development Bank reports that an estimated 54 percent of the labor force is engaged in informal economic activities while only 11.5 percent work in the formal sector (African Development Bank 2012). They further report that the age group of fifteen to twenty-four has an unemployment rate of 25.6 percent, twice that of the twenty-five to forty-four age group and three times the forty-five to sixty-four age group. In terms of occupation status, the urban poor resident looks very much like the ordinary Ghanaian.

---

[36] This means that 31 percent of respondents are over forty years of age, demonstrating that poor neighborhoods are not merely depositories of urban youth as the conventional wisdom suggests.

[37] The informal economy includes all businesses that are not regulated by the state. See: Meagher (2010).

The mean household daily income is twenty-one *cedis*, approximately seventeen dollars at the time of the survey. The majority of residential households, or 61 percent, makes less than thirty *cedis* per day. While some of these respondents have several dependents, respondents still seem to be comfortably above the $1.25/day national poverty line, and even above the two dollars per day designation of the middle class. In my sample, only 12.1 percent of households indicated making less than five *cedis* (three dollars) per day. While this figure does not take into account the number of dependents, it does suggest that urban poor fare better than the national average, which reports a 24.2 percent poverty rate (Cooke et al. 2016). This suggests that the urban poor might fare better economically than the rural poor.

It appears that these trends in household income translate into quality of life indicators as well. For example, only 10 percent of respondents indicate that they "many times" or "always" go long periods of time without medicines or medical treatment. Thirty-seven percent of residents have not experienced this problem in the past year, while 29 percent have only experienced this problem once or twice in the past year. One potential explanation for this is that most residents, or 65 percent, are enrolled in the National Health Insurance Scheme. These data suggest that the lived experience of poverty is quite low for the urban poor. The problem facing poor Ghanaian city residents appears to be different from residents in other cities across the continent, where the UN has reported, "two out of five African slum-dwellers live in a poverty that is literally 'life-threatening'" (UN-Habitat 2003). More likely, however, is that more data is needed to validate these alarming policy reports to provide a clearer assessment of the livelihoods, challenges, and opportunities of the urban poor across Africa. This book provides one in-depth account of the lives, and especially the politics, of Ghana's urban poor.[38]

Outline of the Book

Chapter 1 introduces the major contributions of the book. Chapter 2 outlines a theory of leadership and civic life in urban Ghana. The

---

[38] See Table A.1 in the Appendix for summary statistics about how these variables compare across settlement types.

chapter starts with inductive logic, and traces the evolution of leadership, the origins of settlement, the history of migration, and the growth of squatter settlements. From this information, I create a typology of urban settlements that fits these empirical patterns of African urban development. I introduce the analytical differences between indigenous, stranger, and squatter settlements. The second half of the chapter explains how these settlement patterns shape governance and development outcomes today. In particular, it suggests how they shape the construction of legitimate authority, the type of distributive politics, and the organization of civic life. In doing so, I explain how the theory contributes to existing theories of political clientelism, distributive politics, and ethnic politics, respectively.

Chapter 3 provides an addition to conventional accounts of Ghanaian urbanization by reconstructing the political history of urban growth from precolonial times to the modern day. I emphasize how informal norms of settlement and belonging help explain the political development of Ghanaian cities at different stages of urbanization, despite changes in social structure and formal institutions. While much has changed in Ghana, the leaders' and residents' desire to control territory and urban space has maintained its importance throughout history.

Chapter 4 asks why political clientelism persists in many neighborhoods despite advancements in liberal-democratic institutions. I show how the evolution of political clientelism in urban Ghana has its roots in precolonial and colonial structures of power, as well as how cities developed over time. My approach calls into question the conventional wisdom in political science scholarship that patrons rely on clients to win elections in exchange for goods and services needed for poor people to survive. This simplistic view of political clientelism overlooks how leaders control space and territory, the historical evolution of leadership, and how leaders bolster their reputation by gaining admiration and respect among followers. I suggest that scholars need to pay close attention to the construction of legitimate authority. Drawing from ethnographic data, I show how stranger settlements have developed responsive and legitimate leaders to serve the interests of the public, while indigenous and squatter settlements have not.

Chapter 5 provides ethnographic and survey evidence to substantiate a theory of distributive politics for an urbanizing continent. I pay close attention to the historical evolution of urban neighborhoods, as well as how certain residents and groups make meaning of specific goods and resources. This is particularly important in cities where land is scarce while property values rise, enabling politicians and leaders to politicize the commons. The chapter provides an alternative to conventional accounts of distributive politics by considering how informal norms of settlement and belonging shape certain types of distributive politics across neighborhoods. I show how Ashaiman residents and leaders constructed a public sphere in their city, while Ga Mashie and Old Fadama restrict decision-making along club and private lines, respectively.

Chapter 6 demonstrates how a focus on everyday politics provides a lens into the organization of civic life in urban neighborhoods. This approach magnifies the persistence and social resilience of underlying institutions, especially traditional authorities and the chieftaincy. I explain why in neighborhoods like Ga Mashie and Old Fadama, ethnicity continues to be the defining feature of the organization of civic life, while in Ashaiman it dissipates into the background. The informal norms of settlement and belonging help explain these divergent outcomes. I demonstrate how the study of ethnicity must extend beyond elections and social organization, to the ways in which it contributes to control over urban space.

Chapter 7 concludes with the empirical and theoretical implications of the study. I demonstrate how the theory is best generalizable to other West African countries – particularly countries like Nigeria and Cote d'Ivoire – where customary law structures land access and the historical experience of indigeneity and settler dynamics are similar. Nonetheless, the theory of everyday urban politics and the importance of informal norms of settlement and belonging go a long way to explaining developmental outcomes in urban Africa. I briefly discuss the urban experience in Kenya to show how my theory applies to Eastern Africa, as well as discuss the policy implications of the study. I conclude that everyday politics is a central and crucial aspect of the democratization process in urban Africa, and goes a long way toward explaining political clientelism, distributive politics, and ethnic politics.

The Roots of Urban Politics in Africa

What are the roots of urban politics in Africa? What shapes the practice of politics across urban neighborhoods? How does urbanization affect the political practices of African governments and politicians? Part I provides preliminary answers to these important questions. The chapters outline the important theories that have been advanced to explain urban politics across Africa, as well as the concepts that are useful for empirical analysis of African cities. The first chapter brings together empirical and theoretical scholarship from across the continent and theorizes a new way of understanding urban development. The chapter understands African urbanization to be a contentious political process that dates back centuries. I trace how precolonial patterns of authority, colonial investments, and structural adjustment policies contribute to the historical and political roots of African cities today. An African city grows from an indigenous core, to a multiethnic city, to a sprawling cosmopolitan metropolis.

The next chapter applies this theory of urban political development to urban Ghana. While the chapter focuses mostly on the development of Accra, it provides suggestive evidence of similar urban processes in Kumasi and Sekondi-Takoradi. The chapter retells the political history of urbanization in Ghana by focusing on the diverse types of neighborhoods that make up Ghanaian cities today. Part I sets the stage for the everyday political practices that will be documented in Part II. In this way, it uncovers the roots of urban politics in Ghana.

2 | Leadership and Civic Life in Urban Africa

In an influential article in *The Atlantic*, journalist Howard French suggests that Africa's new urban centers are shifting its old colonial boundaries. He describes a process in Lagos, Nigeria where the development of tax infrastructure and local economic growth has "dramatically reduc[ed] dependence on redistributed oil income" (French 2013). But even more important than the economic activity, is the emergence of a middle class and cosmopolitan identity that transcends ethnic and tribal divisions, in which citizens form a social contract with the local government. Urbanization could signal the end of the tribalism that has affected the continent since Independence, by creating a public sphere that extends across distinct groups.

French's article touches on one of the most important questions facing African societies today: How does urbanization affect Africa and its political systems? Will rapid urbanization transform the continent? Scholars have been grappling with these questions for many years, largely focusing on how urbanization affects formal political change, as well as how the movement of people to cities transforms societal divisions and identities. Yet understudied are the interactions between formal institutional change and informal societal organization. Paying close attention to leadership and civic life in urban neighborhoods can help fill this gap.

This chapter suggests that urbanization, on its own, is limited in its transformative potential. This is because the underlying informal norms of settlement continue to structure the practice of politics at the neighborhood level. But not all neighborhoods share the same politics of belonging. Instead, there is considerable variation in the construction of legitimate authorities, type of distributive politics, and organization of civic life across different urban neighborhoods. These elements of neighborhood politics deepen our understanding of political clientelism, distributive politics, and ethnicity on the continent. By embedding conventional social science concepts in the context of everyday politics, we are better able to understand why sustainable urban development is so difficult to achieve but also how, given the right institutional context, a new and more democratic practice of politics can emerge.

In this chapter, I review existing accounts of African urbanization. I then explain why it is important to consider informal norms of settlement and belonging in studies of African urbanization. I provide a theoretical framework for understanding how informal norms continue to influence the practice of politics. In particular, I discuss how the construction of legitimate authorities, the type of distributive politics, and the organization of civic life varies across urban neighborhoods, setting the stage for the variation in political practices that I will discuss in the rest of the book.

Accounts of African Urbanization

The field of African urban politics emerged in the 1950s and 1960s as scholars examined the large influx of workers moving to towns to work in mines (Mayer 1962). Most of these studies examined the Rhodesian copper belt, investigating the shifting identities of the migrants and documenting their new lives in the urban areas. Anthropologist Max Gluckman argued that the town opened up new arenas of social relations, suggesting that "An African townsman is a townsman, an African miner is a miner: he is only secondarily a tribesman" (Gluckman 1960: 57–58). He continues, "When a man returns from the towns into the political area of his tribe he is tribalised—de-urbanised—though not outside the influence of the town."

Ethnicity emerged as a category that distinguished new migrants from those already living in the town, as well as a way to identify the many different groups of people who were now sharing the same urban space (Gluckman 1960: 55).[1] Most of these early studies relied on a structural or functionalist approach, emphasizing the role of modernization and urbanization and their ability to transform social identity (Epstein 1958). The theories suggest that individuals seek new identities to replace their rural, kinship affiliations.

More recent scholarship offers a slight corrective. Scholars like Mahmood Mamdani maintain a structural focus, but conceptualize

---

[1] For an insightful review of the literature, see: Lentz (1995).

the city as a modern form that emerged during colonial rule. For Mamdani, the urban–rural dichotomy was institutionalized and became the basis of the new African class structure (Mamdani 1996). He calls this process "decentralized despotism," and explains how the colonial practice of indirect rule created a modern, urban elite that sought domination over the traditional, rural masses.[2] The urban–rural distinction was a societal cleavage that had significant social, cultural, and political implications that grew out of the colonial experience.

Urbanization also had direct impacts on the organization of civic life in urban neighborhoods. At the grassroots, some migrants formed strong ethnic affiliations for instrumental reasons. Migrants organized with others who shared a common descent, language, and history, forming hometown associations, mutual aid societies, and social networks (Mitchell 1969). This led to an interesting paradox: Groups were losing their cultural distinctiveness while at the same time retaining and emphasizing their ethnic diversity (Cohen 1969).[3] Ethnic groups functioned as interest groups: Indigenous populations labeled outsiders to assert control, while strangers and settlers established their own identifying characteristics to claim rights and housing, occupation, and connections to local headmen and politicians (Cohen 1969: 33). Robert Bates (1981) formalizes these ideas and argues that ethnic groups functioned as political coalitions to aggregate interests and overcome collective action problems for strategic gains.[4]

These changes were especially pronounced in urban centers, where people from diverse ethnic groups were now living in close contact with one another, and engagement with the state was easier and possible. Formal political competition became more intense, and evident to outside observers. Most studies of urban African politics today

---

[2] Similarly, Achille Mbembe (2001a) explains how postcolonial leaders inherited a form of domination that was institutionalized in a *commandement*, where the new African bourgeoisie internalized these differences and used their leadership status as a way to further bolster ethnic divisions. Alternatively, Ferguson (1992) documents how Zambian urban elite manufactured the concept of an "authentic" Zambian-ness to "open up some space between their own cosmopolitan style and the specifically Western cosmopolitanism of the white settlers" (83).

[3] Claire Adida (2011) observes a similar dynamic among Hausa and Yoruba communities in Ghana today.

[4] Colonialism's impact on the African state was severe, and reordered social hierarchies and ethnic cleavages in the process (Young 1994).

emerge from this tradition, emphasizing the importance of formal institutional rules, dynamics of political competition, and demographic characteristics.[5]

Most of these accounts of African urbanization and transformation place significant emphasis on the state and national-level political factors. By doing so, they often overlook the relationships between leaders and their followers at the local level. In reality, many of these relationships withstood large-scale formal institutional change, and the struggles for governance and power extended far beyond official institutions. Alternatively, a focus on social organization treats ethnic groups as fixed and unchanging, without uncovering the political dynamics that might spark ethnic conflict at the local level, like control of housing, territory, and urban space. Missing in these studies are the unofficial norms and duties – the informal institutions – that have shaped governance and development throughout precolonial, colonial, and postcolonial Africa.

Settlement and Belonging in African Urbanization

There is very little attempt to connect the historical context with contemporary forms of authority and practices of political power in urban Africa today.[6] But as Michael Schatzberg (2014) has argued, leaders and their followers throughout African history search for political space to experiment with new modes of governance, or the rules that shape daily life and everyday affairs.[7] The successful experiments form the basis of community governance, and in turn the practice of politics.

Urban neighborhoods provide leaders the opportunity to exploit new opportunities to expand territorial authority and political

---

[5] For example, Danielle Resnick studies populism and opposition dynamics in Zambia and Senegal, focusing on how political parties mobilize the urban poor (Resnick 2013). Other studies focus on the impact of changing demographics, including the growth of the middle class (Green 2014; Resnick 2015; Nathan 2016a). Ethnic segregation is also an emerging topic of study (Ejdemyr et al. 2017).

[6] Even the studies that focus on precolonial Africa emphasize geographic constraints (Herbst 2000), and centralization of power (Englebert 2002). Martha Wilfahrt's research links historical patterns of leadership with contemporary public goods provision. But like most studies, it focuses on rural Africa (Wilfahrt 2018a, 2018b).

[7] Schatzberg cites Barrington Moore's claim that leaders need "room to experiment with making the future" (Moore 1978: 482).

power.[8] Local leaders seek alliances with decentralized authorities but also interact with state actors with the intention of expanding their power and economic base. These political opportunities extend beyond instrumental and material concerns: They offer leaders new chances to gain admiration and respect from followers. In cities, an important way that leaders can gain legitimacy and respect is by controlling access to housing and providing security of tenure in a fair and just manner. For example, indigenous leaders rent houses, sell land to developers, and create important links to politicians. They take advantage of their historical ties to territory and property. Alternatively, migrant leaders can establish territorial authority by founding new neighborhoods, taking in other guests and strangers, selling land as de facto landlords, and serving as representatives and spokesmen for social networks and interest groups (Paller 2015).

The ability of leaders to control access and security of land and territory rests on the land tenure regime of African societies. Most West African land tenure regimes are what Catherine Boone calls neo-customary: Host populations claim ancestral rights to the land based on their indigenous or first-comer status (Boone 2014). Historically, the state never acquired ownership of land (Casely-Hayford 1903). But this land tenure system can also reproduce ethnicity, creating distinctions between ethnic insiders and outsiders (Boone 2014: 93). These land tenure regimes are typically fluid, negotiated, and ambiguous, contributing to land conflicts when there are pressures to clarify or formalize land rights, register property, or distribute title (Berry 1993, 2009). These land tenure regimes give considerable power to indigenous groups who are custodians of land, but also places the control of territory and housing outside the purview of state and formal jurisdiction. In theory, this means that all land has an owner.[9] The land tenure

---

[8] This is especially crucial in Africa given its experience with colonialism. In many countries, including Ghana, the capital city became the social, political, and economic center of the country. These are called primate cities. Populations in far-off rural areas were further marginalized. In Ghana, the Northern Region has experienced underdevelopment and underrepresentation since 1957 (Abdulai 2017). Urbanization opens up opportunities for Northerners, and other groups from marginalized areas, to seek political and economic power in cities like Accra.

[9] In the Ghana context, see: Ollenu (1962); Ollenu and Woodman (1985); Konadu-Agyemang (1991).

regime therefore privileges legitimacy, or the popular acceptance of authority and ownership, over formal or state rights. It also creates distinctions based on settlement and ownership, as "a person of a different tribal origin is regarded as a stranger" (Pogucki 1954: 31). The struggle for legitimacy, often played out between groups, is therefore a deeply political struggle.

Due to this underlying land tenure regime, the relationship between strangers, host societies or indigenes, and the state shapes narratives of belonging and exclusion. These narratives have developed throughout history, and have been further intensified by interventions like the slave trade, colonial rule, and refugee flows. Today, these narratives are exacerbated by foreign investment and international NGOs.

Narratives of belonging and exclusion become institutionalized in the daily practices of individuals and leaders, and are central to everyday politics. They shape the ways individuals and groups make meaning of their daily environments. These narratives become cultural resources that leaders and residents use to guide the politics and governance in daily affairs, and earn the admiration and respect of their constituents. These narratives include claims to legal and political recognition, rights of ownership, declarations of citizenship, and challenges of incorporation.

I focus particular attention on the informal norms of settlement and belonging. In urban neighborhoods, these norms and procedures are most often attached to the question "who settled first, and how." These rules and regulations are unofficial, but coincide with the settlement patterns by which different populations migrated and settled in the city. These narratives become politicized as urban populations fight over temporal concerns, claiming to have arrived in the city first. Populations might also disagree about the legitimacy of the original inhabitation, leading to civil conflict between host and migrant communities.

Original Claimants of the City

Informal norms of settlement and belonging start with the observation that claims to indigeneity and autochthony form the basis of legitimate ownership and control of land and territory. Autochthon means "of the soil itself," privileging a rightful claim to a particular territory

(Loraux 1996; Geschiere and Jackson 2006).[10] "Indigenous" means literally "born inside" with the connotation in classical Greek of being born "inside the house" (Ceuppens and Geschiere 2005). Some populations claim authoritatively their first comer status and prioritize the time of arrival, leaving no doubt to the question "who settled first, and how" (Daes 1996). This is especially important in neo-customary property rights regimes, where access to land is determined by traditional norms. In these contexts, indigenous populations claim to be the rightful owners of the land, providing them an important source of profits. For example, Ga traditional authorities in Ghana took advantage of this privileged position throughout its history, particularly during the colonial period when Ga chiefs benefited from selling land to the colonial government (Sackeyfio 2012), as did Ashanti leaders in the cocoa regions (Austin 2005).

In most of these historical contexts, migrants settled in new lands as "allochthons," or strangers, and established patron-client relationships with traditional "landowners" (Chauveau 2001). This settlement status sets the stage for a powerful way to limit the citizenship rights of foreigners or outsiders, providing indigenes the claim they are rightful "heirs to the property" while settlers will always be considered strangers (Nzongola-Ntalaja 2011). Strangers are therefore defined in opposition to the indigenous group, creating a political cleavage based on origin. This leads to the "synthesis of nearness and distance which constitutes the formal position of the stranger" (Simmel 1908: 404). But it is important to emphasize that the labeling and ongoing political salience of the category of stranger is socially constructed and politically manipulated, and is an "actively generated condition" (Whitehouse 2012: 13). The indigene-stranger dichotomy is always relative (Geschiere and Jackson 2006), with individuals and groups, even those of the same ethnic group, negotiating and making claims to first comer status (Hodgson 2002; Kuper 2003, 2005).

These dynamics are particularly salient in neighborhoods with large populations claiming indigenous status. In urban Ghana, these

---

[10] Jeremy Waldron explains that "'Indigeneity' is derived from 'indigenous' which means '[b]orn or produced naturally in a land or region; native or belonging naturally to (the soil, region, etc.),' from *indu*, an old Latin root meaning 'within' (like the Greek *endon*) and *gignere* meaning 'to beget'" (2003: 1).

neighborhoods include Ga Mashie, Chorkor, and Shiabu in Accra; Ashanti New Town in Kumasi; and Taabo in Ashaiman.[11] Norms of indigeneity play an important factor in everyday governance. Throughout Ghana's history, the indigenous ethnic group has restricted the scope of the political community, limiting the number of individuals able to participate in community decision-making to members of their own group. This leaves a large number of residents, particularly migrants and strangers, on the outside of the decision-making process.[12] In the most severe cases, strangers are "unassimilable aliens" who never gain full citizenship status (Fortes 1975: 245). In many settings, these "tales of origin" become the most important political cleavage there is (Boas 2009).

The politicization of indigeneity was further institutionalized under colonial rule, and was an important legacy of the colonial state. Colonists in the late nineteenth century first conceived of indigeneity as a system and strategy of rule and used it as a classification and organization strategy to establish social control.[13] Postcolonial leaders then used claims of authenticity, belonging, and exclusion as political strategies in authoritarian and multiparty contexts (Bayart 2005). Yet local struggles over "who settled first, and how" date back to precolonial times, and leaders used this rhetoric to extend their territorial power and fight for political space (Lentz 2003). In this way, claims to indigeneity have a political and material aim (Mamdani 2002; Pelican 2009).

In many respects, the development of the postcolonial state remains bifurcated through the institutionalization of ethnic entitlements and alternative conceptions of citizenship.[14] In the context of state failure and limited resources, struggles over citizenship rights can become important sources of ethnic conflict (Bates 2008; Keller 2014).

---

[11] In related work, we define these neighborhoods as having "indigene advantage," where at least 40 percent of the residents are of the indigenous ethnic group (Klaus and Paller 2017).

[12] This is true in many settings across the continent. For example, Habyarimana et al. (2009) find this trend in Kampala, Uganda with respect to the Buganda ethnic group.

[13] Ceuppens and Geschiere (2005) discuss this in the context of French Sudan.

[14] Several political scientists have investigated the impact of alternative conceptions of citizenship at the national level in postcolonial Africa. See: Ekeh (1975); Laitin (1986); Mamdani (1996); Ndegwa (1997); Adejumobi (2001).

Tribalism and playing the ethnic card become political strategies to claim resources and citizenship rights from the state. Tribalism and ethnic chauvinism, therefore, are outcomes of an interaction between informal institutional politics that privilege autochthony and indigenous claims due to original settlement patterns and multiparty politics. I examine this interaction throughout the book.

The dual transition of political liberalization and rapid urbanization has actually contributed to the heightening of claims to indigeneity and autochthony (Geschiere and Nyamjoh 2000). These struggles play a prominent role in the national politics across many African countries (Geschiere and Gugler 1998), but also are played out locally through efforts of boundary making and closure, central aspects of politics of belonging (Appadurai 1996).[15] Politicians in Africa have a long history of manipulating citizenship laws to benefit their groups and constituents, and this worrisome trend is heightened in the context of political liberalization (Manby 2009). In these contexts of liberalization and decentralization, local elections, land management, and citizenship are often linked, leading to electoral strategies that attempt to displace and disenfranchise strangers (M. Hilgers 2011). Not surprisingly, then, the political salience of indigeneity and autochthony is much more intense in competitive electoral districts, in the same way that the salience of ethnicity might depend on the need to form a minimum winning coalition (Posner 2005). Yet formal electoral arrangements and informal norms of settlement often work in concert, especially in neighborhoods in capital cities where the national government impacts daily governance. Throughout the book, I show how early settlers in indigenous settlements like Ga Mashie use norms of indigeneity to mobilize voters and select their political candidates, demonstrating the overlap between informal and formal institutions.

---

[15] In the rapidly globalizing environment, some scholars argue that discourses of belonging evoke local claims to access global goods and resources (Simone 2001; Mbembe 2001b, 2002). These discourses lead to a "global conjecture of belonging" (Li 2000) and what one scholar has termed "glocalization" (Robertson 1992). In countries that experienced significant decentralization, many of these claims for belonging became an important source of friction in local communities (Adejumobi 2001). This is evident in countries like Nigeria where a preoccupation with indigeneity shapes local government administrative bodies (Ejobowah 2012).

A Long History of Migration

Norms of settlement and belonging are complicated as migrant communities move to cities and seek citizenship rights and public goods in their new neighborhoods. Historically, early settlers purchase plots of land directly from legitimate landowners, usually traditional authorities or family elders (Peil 1976; Konadu-Agyemang 1991). The consequence of this is that the relationship between host and migrant communities is relatively stable. The host community does not question the legitimacy of the neighborhood, even though there might be numerous property disputes that exist between families in these settlements.

This settlement pattern and societal arrangement exists outside of formal rules of ownership and legality. Historically, the coalition between indigenous and migrant populations creates *de facto* land security. These relationships become institutionalized in patron-client networks, as migrants rely on indigenous authorities for protection of their property rights. In Accra, this meant establishing clientelist networks with the indigenous Ga (Pellow 2002: 47). The same was true for stranger communities in other cities, as migrants formed coalitions with indigenous Ashantis in Kumasi (Schildkrout 1970, 1978; Arhin 1971).[16] Over time, these neighborhoods become multiethnic, integrating Hausas, Yorubas, and other groups. While ethnic networks dominate daily life, leaders and groups form alliances with other leaders and groups to form more powerful coalitions in the face of state power.[17]

This settlement pattern is consistent with customary law, as the new settlers in the city legitimately acquired land from original inhabitants. During times of urban expansion, the close ties that ethnic headmen have with indigenous traditional authorities provide the needed legitimacy to gain formal incorporation and political recognition. Once the neighborhood gains legal status, political entrepreneurs jockey for formal recognition to become official representatives to their followers.

---

[16] Sandra Barnes (1986) documents these patterns in urban Nigeria.

[17] Ousmane Kobo (2010) has demonstrated how religion can play a powerful organizing force in migrant communities. Muslims inhabit many migrant settlements, which can take on a more powerful organizing logic than ethnicity. In addition, the Hausa language is often the lingua franca, also undermining the power of ethnicity.

Therefore, they establish close political ties with the host city and need to reward loyal followers because they intend to stay in the city. Ethnic leaders become opinion leaders through this political and contentious process, as well as through their ability to care for newer migrants. Throughout the book I demonstrate this historical process in the formation of Ashaiman, and I explain how this creates an optimal institutional environment for effective community governance and democratic politics.

The Proliferation of Squatter Settlements

More recently, rapid urbanization has contributed to the proliferation of squatter settlements. These neighborhoods are distinct because they violate customary law: New settlers do not purchase plots directly from the indigenous family elders who claim ownership of the land. Nonetheless, squatter settlements have emerged as a space for previously marginalized communities to extend their territorial authority and place demands on governments for democratic dividends. Migrant leaders arrive in the city, settle on an unauthorized piece of land, and establish a political stronghold, backed by dense social networks. These neighborhoods develop and grow as new residents tap into networks of trusted friends, migrants, and coethnics for assistance in finding housing (Agyei-Mensah and Owusu 2012). Residents join social networks that make up a distinct cluster in a particular neighborhood. For new migrants to the city, these clusters often link to one's hometown. Residents from the rural countryside migrate in coordinated efforts to cities, and often settle in clusters within the same neighborhood of a low-income community.

The emergence of squatter settlements has contributed to the rise of urban land conflicts across the continent.[18] Rakodi attributes these conflicts – which often result in evictions and demolitions – to conflicts between the "occupiers" and government agencies over the political recognition of urban space (Rakodi 2016). The lack of clarity between different land regimes, as well as overlapping authority structures and ambiguous tenure jurisdictions, contribute to these problems (Payne 2001; McAuslan 2003). At the grassroots, claims to urban space, as

---

[18] Lombard and Rakodi (2016) provide an overview of this phenomenon across the world.

well as demands for rights to the city, are interpreted differently by various actors, and framed by politicians and powerful actors to empower themselves and serve private interests (Van Leeuwen and Van der Haar 2016). In addition, informality is often used as a way to maintain power, reinforce patron-client relationships, and maintain the political status quo (Roy 2009). In Ghana, scholars have emphasized the relationship between state power and community resistance, showing how these unauthorized settlements resist forced evictions and demolitions (Grant 2006, 2009; Afenah 2012). Yet less attention has been paid to the informal norms that play a crucial role in the persistence of squatter settlements across the continent.

Squatters do not have formal legal rights to claim housing and tenure security from the state. But perhaps more importantly is that they cannot make legitimate claims to land ownership from traditional authorities or indigenous family elders. Therefore, they are forced to make demands on their political parties and other nonstate actors. While squatter settlements have recently gained attention due to the growth of poor neighborhoods in the developing world and the international community's focus on forced evictions as a human rights concern, state policy toward these neighborhoods – and squatter settlements in particular – have their roots in colonial health policy. For example, indigenous and migrant African communities were kept out of city planning and largely left unregulated (Njoh 2006). Africans lived in communities that were not regulated formally, and they developed in an unplanned nature. Public services were not provisioned. Colonial authorities used zoning laws and building codes in an attempt to control urban development and strengthen social control over native populations (Njoh 2009). Urban development that deviated from colonial codes and laws was considered illegal and was not condoned (Ocheje 2007).

Colonial urban policy left an important legacy: "The norm of city planning consisted of slum clearance, relocation and redevelopment. For this reason, planners in Africa refuse to accept the notion that unauthorized settlements, no matter how they came about, should be 'regularized', as that would be to condone illegality" (Ocheje 2007: 183). Governments use the threat of forced eviction and forceful demolitions to counter the fear that authorities have of poor urban populations. They also do so to counter short-term urban problems like flooding without tackling larger structural problems that contribute to large-scale urban growth (Obeng-Odoom 2010). These strategies are forcefully used against squatter settlements, and little has been done to change these tactics. This is one reason why squatter settlements are unable to gain legal recognition from the state.

While state policy toward squatter settlements might have originated out of colonial health policy, perhaps just as important is that residents are viewed as illegitimate inhabitants because of the way they settled in the neighborhood, which violated indigenous norms of property ownership. In other words, insecure land rights and crumbling infrastructure persists – while the population continues to grow – because squatting violates informal norms of indigeneity and belonging. Throughout the book I document how informal norms of indigeneity underlie state policies toward eviction and demolition, enabling a small cadre of leaders to take advantage of the insecurity for their own private gain. This is most apparent in neighborhoods like Old Fadama, which have grown rapidly in the current era of multiparty democracy.

This retelling of African urbanization with a focus on informal norms of settlement and belonging offers a new way to look at the history of cities. It suggests that the conventional focus of African urbanization obscures important local-level variation between neighborhoods and the host-migrant relationships that form the basis of property relations and control of territory today. These spatial differences have their roots in the political history of urbanization that I will document in Chapter 3, where a Ghanaian city like Accra evolved from an indigenous town, to a multiethnic city, to a sprawling metropolitan area with illegitimate squatter settlements.

Typology of Urban Neighborhoods

In line with the process of urbanization I have just described, this book considers neighborhoods based on the underlying informal norms of settlement and belonging. This typology reflects the way that urban Ghanaians understand their own claims to urban space, and how these understandings of illegitimacy and legality become institutionalized over time. While urban neighborhoods form at different times throughout history, the differences in how host populations understand outsider claims to the city persist. Yet original settlement patterns are not necessarily deterministic: Norms and understandings of urban space

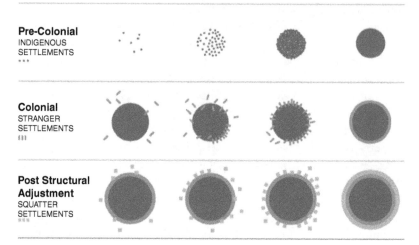

Pre-Colonial
INDIGENOUS
SETTLEMENTS
• • •

Colonial
STRANGER
SETTLEMENTS
ⅰⅰⅰ

**Post Structural
Adjustment**
SQUATTER
SETTLEMENTS

Figure 2.1 Stages of urban political development (Graphic by Noopur Agarwal)

can change due to political struggles, bargaining between leaders, and collective action by residents themselves.

I discuss three different types of neighborhoods in this book: indigenous, stranger, and squatter settlements (Figure 2.1).[19] To represent the urban growth patterns just described, the type of settlement corresponds with a core-periphery matrix – illustrated by a concentric circle – in which the expansion of the city gains a new layer of neighborhoods, either stranger communities or squatter settlements, over time.

Indigenous settlements are defined as neighborhoods inhabited by a majority of indigenous residents, whereby these populations make autochthonous ownership claims to land and territory. Therefore, informal norms of indigeneity govern these neighborhoods. *Stranger settlements* are defined as neighborhoods inhabited by a majority of migrant settlers, whereby early residents purchased land and territory directly from indigenous landlords or custodians of the land. Therefore, informal norms of cooperation and public legitimacy govern

[19] There are other types of neighborhoods in urban Ghana as well, most notably gated communities (Grant 2009) and middle-class neighborhoods where formal plans and private property rights shape the allocation and development process. These neighborhoods are certainly important, but are left out of the analysis in this book.

these neighborhoods. *Squatter settlements* are defined as neighborhoods that are also inhabited by a majority of migrants, but they are considered temporary residents or squatters because they did not purchase land and territory directly from indigenous landlords or custodians of the land. Therefore, informal norms of personal empowerment and privatization of the commons govern these neighborhoods.

These neighborhood types are mutually exclusive. But this does not mean that variation in specific sections of a given neighborhood does not exist. Instead, I treat neighborhoods as urban space with unified and distinct boundaries. In the rest of this chapter, I discuss how these types of neighborhoods exhibit different forms of everyday politics. In particular, I show how they shape the construction of legitimate authority, condition the type of distributive politics, and structure the civic life of communities. In doing so, I provide a new way of thinking about distributive politics, political clientelism, and ethnic politics, respectively.

The Construction of Legitimate Authority

One of the puzzling realities in urban Ghana today is the persistence of clientelism despite the strengthening of liberal democratic institutions (Lindberg 2010; Paller 2014). This has led several scholars to deem Ghana a "patronage democracy" embedded in a political economy of "competitive clientelism" (Abdulai and Hickey 2016; Gadjanova 2017). Political scientists offer explanations for the persistence of clientelism that range from colonial legacies, illegitimate state institutions, "perverse" machine politics, inability of politicians to make credible commitments, role of party brokers, high levels of poverty, and electoral competition, to weak indigenous industries and easy state financing from foreign aid.[20]

In contrast to this growing body of scholarship, this book argues that the evolution of political clientelism in urban Ghana has its roots in precolonial and colonial structures of power, as well as how cities developed over time. As I will demonstrate in Chapter 3, patron-client

---

[20] See: Ekeh (1975); Englebert (2000); Stokes (2005); Keefer (2007); Kitschelt and Wilkinson (2007); Lindberg and Morrison (2008); Whitfield (2011); Stokes et al. (2013).

relationships emerged at different stages of the urbanization process, and were reshaped by significant changes in governance during colonial rule and multiparty democracy. In other words, patron-client relationships predate the rise of Ghana's two major political parties in the early 1950s, and far precede Ghana's return to multiparty democracy in 1992. This simple observation suggests that the drivers of political clientelism exist outside formal institutions of power and is largely epiphenomenal to the multiparty process. But multiparty democracy complicates these relationships, and can further entrench them.

This approach complicates the conventional wisdom in political science scholarship that patrons rely on clients solely to win elections in exchange for goods and services needed for poor people to survive. This simplistic view of political clientelism overlooks how leaders control space and territory; the historical evolution of leadership, and; how leaders bolster their reputation by gaining admiration and respect among followers.

I advocate a strong analytical shift from conventional studies. Instead of using the terms patrons and brokers, I label these people what they are considered in the neighborhood: opinion leaders. "Opinion leader" is a term that Ghanaians use to describe local leaders in their community. They gain admiration and respect from their constituents by accumulating wisdom and providing advice, and they achieve a social status and reputation based on these characteristics. In addition, they are expected to control territory and urban space. This shift in thinking about clientelism provides a more accurate account of local leadership in urban Ghana.

Rethinking Clientelism in Urban Africa

A growing research agenda examines political clientelism as a central element in the politics of distribution. This literature, which emerged in the early 2000s, focuses on the instrumental and particularistic elements of the electoral process (Stokes et al. 2013). Clientelism and patronage are "strategies for the acquisition, maintenance, and aggrandizement of political power, on the part of the patrons, and strategies for the protection and promotion of their interests, on the part of the clients" (Piattoni 2001: 2). For ordinary people, this offers new avenues of political accountability, whereby a citizen's vote can be exchanged for "direct payments or continuing access to employment, goods, and services" (Kitschelt and Wilkinson 2007: 2). Institutional features including levels of political competition, economic development, ethnic heterogeneity, and public sector involvement in the economy can shape these incentives.

These studies provide instrumental explanations to various electoral outcomes. In other words, they emphasize how parties win elections, and why citizens vote in the ways that they do. These studies follow the important contributions made in the 1980s and 1990s that suggest clientelism will not fade away with the rise of market capitalism, political and economic modernization, and the rise of civil societies across the world.[21] Nonetheless, these scholars focus exclusively on elections and organizational capacity of political parties. The assumed outcome for all patrons and brokers is the desire to win elections.

These studies stand in direct contrast to scholarship that emerged in the 1960s and 1970s that embed patron-client relationships in a cultural and historical context. The 1977 volume *Friends, Followers, and Factions* edited by Schmidt et al. includes a series of influential articles that demonstrate how cultural ties and low levels of economic and political modernization maintain clientelism. With no mention of elections, political clientelism is defined as: "A vertical dyadic alliance, i.e., an alliance between two persons of unequal status, power or resources each of whom finds it useful to have as an ally someone superior or inferior to himself" (Schmidt 1977: xx). In these models, the core attributes of clientelism are longevity, diffuseness, face-to-face contact, and inequality (T. Hilgers 2011).[22] The concern for others' social welfare is at the center of these relationships, providing an important mode of representation. The recent scholarship discussed overlooks many of these important daily features of political activity, focusing exclusively on instrumental and electoral logics.[23] In doing so, they miss a powerful representative – the patron – who shows concern for his client's social welfare.

Javier Auyero attempts to bridge these two approaches by developing a theory of electoral clientelism that relies on the underlying reciprocity and concern for others' social welfare. In effect, Auyero

---

[21] Roniger (2004) and Hicken (2011) argue this convincingly.

[22] Most of these models build off a norm of reciprocity, namely that: "1) people should help those who have helped them, and 2) people should not injure those who have helped them" (Gouldner 1960).

[23] Exceptions include Finan and Schecter (2012) and Lawson and Greene (2014).

argues that formal party politics are outcomes of "ongoing informal problem-solving networks meant to ensure material survival and of shared cultural representations" in the context of daily life (Auyero 2001: 14). Most importantly, he draws from Pierre Bourdieu to describe a system that is institutionalized in demands for recognition in the practices of daily life. He explains, "The emphasis that inner-circle members place on their 'friendship' with their brokers and on the affective ties so contracted hints at the meanings that emerge and sustain these ties: clients' desires to be cared for and recognized should be considered the central cause of their behavior" (Auyero 2001: 180–181).

Contemporary scholars of clientelism are now drawing from Auyero's critical insight and incorporating it into their models. For example, Stokes et al. (2013) integrate the important role of the broker, describing them as "local intermediaries who provide targeted benefits and solve problems for their followers; in exchange, they request followers' participation in political activities such as rallies—and often demand their votes" (Stokes et al. 2013: 75). In the context of the secret ballot, politicians require brokers to monitor the activity of voters. The authors explain: "Brokers are neighbors who have acquired reputations for their abilities to solve voters' problems." Brokers are embedded in the social context of ordinary people and have the information the parties need. This might serve as an important element of representation if brokers are adequately incorporated into the party apparatus and have the power to demand public goods and resources from the state through mechanisms of clientelist accountability. Nonetheless, the authors do not actually examine the representative element of the broker, and instead focus exclusively on their instrumental utility for the political party machine.[24]

While the Stokes et al. volume accurately examines the conditions under which brokers help the machine win elections (and empower themselves), they stop short of analyzing the broker as a possible democratic representative in his or her own right. Further, they do not consider how "the least privileged elements of the population demand or claim as right" (Gay 1998: 15) through clientelism, providing a potential solution to the "problem of democratic representation"

---

[24] Stokes et al. (2013) make it clear that party leaders have different incentives than brokers.

(Piattoni 2001). In this way, the dichotomy between "client" and "citizen" is reinforced, even while scholars like Roniger have convincingly demonstrated that the distinction between private and public gets blurred in many developing societies (Roniger 2004).[25]

By contrast, I treat the broker as a representative in his or her own right. By treating the broker as an "opinion leader," I am able to disentangle when and why he or she serves the public interest versus a private or club interest. In other words, I bring opinion leaders to the forefront of the democratic process – something that is largely missing in studies of democracy in Ghana, where politicians and voters dominate scholarship. In doing so, I uncover the importance of neighborhood-level motivations, namely how the struggle to control territory and urban space shapes the interests and incentives of local leaders.

While formal institutions of accountability and representation clearly matter, they have limitations. The structure of the political economy, informal rules and norms, political culture, and the policy-making environments all shape incentives and constraints for political leaders. This critique of the instrumental and electoral logic is forcefully argued by Auyero in the context of clientelism: "This point of view assumes—wrongly—that, because favors, goods, and services circulate one way and support attendance at rallies, and—ultimately —votes circulate the other way, the former are causing the latter, that is, that votes and support come *because of* goods, services and particular favors. Confusing the circulation with the generative principles of action, this scholastic point of view makes a serious epistemological mistake" (Auyero 2001: 23).

Most contemporary studies of clientelism suffer from this same mistake. While they do a fine job of demonstrating the electoral incentives of brokers, they fail to recognize that brokers face a menu of options and incentives to extend their political power and territorial authority. Electoral mobilization is one of many strategies in a broader political game that lies outside of formal institutional channels, and incorporate broader struggles over control of urban space. In effect, the answers to these questions demand a return to earlier studies of

---

[25] For example, Ayşe Güneş-Ayata argues that clientelist strategies are attempts to "search for flexible solutions oriented toward individual needs, taking private concerns into consideration and integrating everyday concerns as public issues" (Güneş-Ayata 1994 in Roniger 1994: 26).

clientelism (e.g., Scott 1972) that examine formal institutions embedded in the context of everyday life. It requires a focus on the norms and "cements" that tie ordinary people to their representative. It is these "generative principles of action," as Auyero calls them, that require more attention in studies of clientelism, and in which the current focus on electoral and instrumental approaches to clientelism overlook.

The Limits of Neopatrimonialism

An additional shortcoming of the political clientelism literature is that most of the empirical case studies are drawn from Latin America and Europe. The related literature on neopatrimonialism in Africa provides similar insights, but pays very close attention to the historical, social, and cultural context of Africa. Neopatrimonialism is a political system that relies on social hierarchies where patrons use state resources to secure loyalty from clients. Nicolas van de Walle's *African Economies and the Politics of Permanent Crisis, 1979–1999* effectively shows how informal patron-client relationships stall economic reform and development (van de Walle 2001). The claim has important implications: neopatrimonial rule is inherently antidemocratic, and is a grave threat to African democracy.

But what the neopatrimonialism literature overlooks is that clientelism is one of the most effective strategies for citizens to get representatives to do their jobs. For the urban poor, it can be the only effective accountability mechanism available to citizens (Nelson 1979). In some cases, citizens have significant power by controlling politicians through the demands of rents (Kitschelt and Wilkinson 2007), building on the reciprocal and social exchanges between leaders and their constituents that are a central feature of politics in many societies. At the local level, residents often rely on their patrons – or more appropriately their personal problem-solving networks – for daily survival needs (Auyero 2001). Representatives and citizens have complex social relationships that extend far beyond electoral arrangements.

In their influential article, Pitcher et al. (2009) argue that a close reading of Max Weber – on which the neopatrimonialism theories are based – highlights the diverse ways that the legitimate exercise of power is culturally framed (Pitcher et al. 2009: 127). In many patrimonial societies, legitimacy is derived from reciprocities based on personal, unequal, and status loyalties – extending far beyond material exchange that dominates the focus of political clientelism literature. When these relationships are maintained by voluntary compliance, they constitute a system of legitimate governance. Critically, this legitimacy is maintained only insofar as both parties recognize the responsibilities of the other, deeming it a collective endeavor (Pitcher et al. 2009). Building off this insight, I suggest that these relationships of voluntary compliance help construct legitimate authority in urban Ghana.

Therefore, the concept of the "opinion leader" captures legitimate political authority. "Opinion leader" is a term that Ghanaians use to describe local leaders in their community. They gain admiration and respect from their constituents by accumulating wisdom and providing advice, and they achieve a social status and reputation based on these characteristics. They can then use this legitimacy to settle disputes, link constituents up to jobs, and organize collective action. But the causal arrow goes both ways: People also gain legitimacy by settling disputes, providing jobs, and organizing activities. All leaders, including chiefs, ethnic headman, pastors, imams, political party brokers, assemblypersons, members of Parliament, and many others, strive to gain the status of opinion leader, giving them important legitimacy that is independent of their formal positions of power. These informal expectations are expected of formal representatives as well, blurring the boundaries between formal and informal institutions (Lindberg 2010; Paller 2014).

Opinion leaders engage in daily social practices to gain the respect of their followers. They help enroll the children of new migrants into schools, and get deals on school uniforms from neighborhood tailors. They introduce women to the leaders of the market associations in order to secure a stall, or link young men to potential employers. If a neighbor is sick, they might help organize money to send the resident to the hospital. In the meantime, they care for the sick person, and pray for them. They open the compounds of their houses to the youth to discuss politics and community affairs, and they might also provide food. Most importantly, they listen to the needs of their constituents, providing necessary guidance and attempting to do what they can to help with the situation. In return, they are publicly honored as good leaders.

Opinion leaders are especially important in Ghanaian cities where residents rely on leaders to access and secure housing, yet cannot rely only on ethnic or religious authority for these needs. Residents, many of whom are new migrants, are particularly vulnerable in cities, where they don't have deep social ties and embedded histories with other residents. In the informal and cash economies that are prevalent in urban Ghana, residents might struggle to make enough money in a day to put food on the table (Hart 1973). They often seek help from established patrons for daily survival, and opinion leaders step in to fill this need. They rely on opinion leaders as nodes in their personal problem-solving networks (Auyero 2001).

But these relationships extend beyond instrumental concerns of material exchange, to bonds of mutual respect. Constituents seek admiration from their opinion leaders, and they demand respect in return. Attaining the status of an opinion leader takes time and effort, and it extends beyond elections and campaigns. Leaders respond to reputational incentives of public shame and honor, and these mechanisms motivate their behavior in the context of daily life. While reciprocity and trust are created through these repeated interactions, they are endogenous to the relationships of dignity that are created through the process of seeking and providing opinions. Stated another way, leaders must establish respectful modes of interactive communication with their followers. They do this by literally giving their opinion – they advise and care for their followers. Mutual respect develops and admiration is achieved.

In political science literature, opinion leaders are often reduced to political brokers, or local actors who "operate in an informal space between citizens and the state in which they facilitate the exchange of electoral support for access to goods, services, and protection" (Auerbach and Thachil 2016). But the act of brokerage is one of many duties that local leaders must fulfill. This book makes a conceptual break from the mainstream scholarship by situating the role of brokers in their broader social and institutional context. This is necessary because political brokers in urban Ghana establish authority and legitimacy ex ante to electoral competition, and they do so by subscribing to social and cultural norms (Paller 2014). Political brokerage is just one of many avenues toward personal empowerment for local leaders.

Missing in conventional understandings of political clientelism are the motivations and incentives that shape peoples' daily political behavior. Most approaches limit their analysis to elections, legislatures, and the rule of law. Similarly, institutional variables like political competition and regime type are assumed to drive patron-client relationships, contributing to theories of politics that emphasize incentives and interests without actually talking to and understanding the motivations of the actors involved. In doing so, they overlook the meanings that leaders and followers attach to the political process that provide a crucial aspect of the evolution of local leaders.

Toward a Theory of Legitimate Authority

To devise a theory of legitimate authority, it is important to consider how leaders control space and territory; the historical evolution of leadership, and; how leaders bolster their reputation by gaining admiration and respect among followers. But as I argue earlier in this chapter, these patterns vary depending on neighborhood, and the informal norms of settlement and belonging that govern urban space. In particular, leaders have different relationships to their constituents and attachments to territory depending on whether the neighborhood is an indigenous, stranger, or squatter settlement.

Opinion leaders in indigenous settlements can gain their authority through traditional ties, ownership over land, and control of territory. It creates opportunities for traditional authorities to amass wealth, at the expense of ordinary residents. For example, traditional leaders might have the incentive to perpetuate ambiguous property rights so that they can exploit double allocation of land (Onoma 2009). Original owners of the land are not incentivized to go through state channels to secure resources because their leaders benefit from informality. This makes it very difficult for private developers and the government to purchase land for public development. Instead, opinion leaders can make demands on local authorities by way of customary entitlements – they can offer land access in exchange for goods, services, and resources.

Another avenue of power in indigenous neighborhoods is the chieftaincy. The institution of the chieftaincy has a long history of being politicized for personal gain. Indigenous norms can contribute to chieftaincy disputes that severely undermine local development because they create serious divisions within the community that harbors deep mistrust and resentment. But these neighborhoods also often have distinct political advantages when compared to other settlements: The government officially recognizes these neighborhoods; they form the historical center of cities; and residents maintain close links to national politicians (Razzu 2005).

These settings offer a powerful example of transplanted institutions being creatively syncretized in local environments (Galvan 2004). In many contexts, indigeneity continues to structure selection in formal political positions.[26] For example, politicians will only be considered if they are from important indigenous families and are from the underlying territory (Paller 2014). They must demonstrate themselves as family heads with the ability to feed and care for their family members. Family is often privileged over merit, and leaders are expected to share goods with their kin fostering a certain type of patronage relationship.

While this focus on family can have positive implications for members of a leader's club, it can lead to exclusion of those who do not belong. In many cases, these leaders become "autochthony entrepreneurs," or those who "share a similar goal—the exclusion of 'illegitimate' residents from both political and economic arenas, often by violent means" (Mitchell 2012: 268). In other words, residents who are not ethnically aligned with the indigenous group nor related to the family from which the leader comes are left without fair and equal representation.

Leaders in stranger communities face different constraints in their endeavor to control urban space and establish a political following. Opinion leaders gain respect and authority through their service to the community. Leadership is not restricted to ethnicity or political affiliation. Opinion leaders provide service to the neighborhood because of their long time horizon: They plan on living there indefinitely. In this way, community well-being underlies governance in the neighborhood: If leaders do not serve the community interest, they will be shamed into action. Opinion leaders will then hold each other to account and come together to push for effective change. Leaders are expected to live in the neighborhood. This is necessary because residents have the opportunity to voice their grievances and make life difficult for leaders who do not do their jobs – they do not have an exit option (Ermakoff 2011).

---

[26] Evidence of the importance of indigeneity in African politics is found in Cameroon (Jackson 2006), Cote d'Ivoire (Chauveau 2001; Mbembe 2001b; Banégas and Marshall-Fratani 2003; Boas 2009; Mitchell 2012), the Congo (Autesserre 2010), Ghana (Lentz 2003), Burkina Faso (Lentz 2003), Nigeria (Nzongola-Ntalaja 2011; Ejobowah 2012), and Kenya (Klaus and Mitchell 2015).

This opens up the space for constituents to meet their leaders and engage in collective decision-making.

Finally, leaders in squatter settlements face the most constraints because their neighborhoods are seen as illegitimate in the eyes of the host population. The temporary status and ambiguous relationship with the host population has important implications for how opinion leaders gain admiration and respect. Leaders maintain active political ties to their hometown with the hope of running for political office or gaining chieftaincy status there in the near future. They use the new urban settlement as a space to accumulate power and goods to reward followers back home. This urban–rural connection is bolstered by the historical precedent that young migrants who move to the city but have family in their rural hometown are expected to remit money and accumulated resources back home, fundamentally shaping the nature of urban–rural political and economic cleavages (Bates 1983).

In a context of insecurity and illegality and without access to public services, opinion leaders provide services and de facto security of tenure to their residents. Leaders are not selected based on government performance or responsiveness – their ability to secure public services or citizens' concerns on these matters. But they can still control large vote banks that political parties rely on for support. Opinion leaders can capitalize on patron-client relationships to bolster their own personal power. They make connections with politicians and offer their mobilization skills and "political muscle" in exchange for private goods and security.

In line with precolonial patterns of authority and legitimacy, the time of arrival to the city as well as the accumulation of wealth greatly enhances admiration and respect, as opinion leaders establish personal power by extending territorial authority. Without formal security apparatuses in place, they often use coercive means to strengthen power. Leaders take advantage of the insecure and informal property rights institutions to enhance their wealth and power through private operations of "public services" like shower and toilet businesses, scrap recycling, and exploiting the informal land market. Additionally, leaders take advantage of increasing international funding from NGOs to build political followings, make money, and travel outside of their home country and even continent. But this also leads to intense internal rivalries over the sharing of goods and opportunities, which are often distributed unequally and along ethnic lines.

Table 2.1 *Types of legitimate authorities*

Settlement type	Opinion leaders
Indigenous	Chiefs, family elders, religious leaders, landowners
Stranger	Teachers, religious leaders, landlords, early settlers, civic leaders
Squatter	Slumlords, scrap dealers, political party brokers, NGO leaders, youth leaders

The different forms of legitimate authority are summarized in Table 2.1.

The Type of Distributive Politics

Ghana is often called a "winner takes all" political system. This raises the stakes of elections, enabling the capture of state resources by governing elites and the subsequent distribution of goods to their own political constituencies. Ever since Harold D. Lasswell's claim that politics is "who gets what, when, how," distributive politics has been at the forefront of the study of democracy and authoritarianism. In Ghana, this has led to a burgeoning literature on the calculations that elites make when distributing resources, as well as the role that voters play in demanding state goods and services. Most of these studies take elections as the point of departure, focusing exclusively on how election campaigns shape the distribution of resources, and how the final vote tallies represent this process.

Yet the view from within urban neighborhoods provides a puzzling finding: Some communities construct a public sphere in which goods are distributed equally, while others restrict the governance of resources along private or group lines. This suggests that the winner-take-all politics is not possible everywhere, and that leaders face different constraints and sanctioning mechanisms depending on local context.

My approach calls into question the conventional wisdom in political science scholarship that distributive politics is solely an outcome of electoral politics, where politicians provide goods and services needed for poor people to survive, in exchange for their votes. This simplistic view of distributive politics overlooks three important facets of distributive politics in urban Ghana, namely how claims to space and territory create different entitlements to resources; the historical evolution of cities and its neighborhoods, and; how leaders control the urban space and politicize the concept of the commons. I suggest rethinking how local populations understand goods and rights, as well as how leaders politicize these concepts for their own personal empowerment. This forces us to rethink governance in urban Africa so that is more in line with the historical development of its cities.

Rethinking Distributive Politics for an Urbanizing Africa

A growing research agenda examines resource distribution as a central feature of African politics. These studies focus on the decisions that politicians make to win elections, treating distribution as the key mechanism through which they garner votes and govern their constituencies. As Miriam Golden and Brian Min summarize, "Underlying each set of studies is the assumption that the goal of politicians in allocating resources is exquisitely electoral, highly partisan, and ultimately a function of attempts at political survival" (Golden and Min 2013: 74). In addition, these studies suggest that elections serve as accountability mechanisms, enabling citizens to sanction leaders out of office if they do not perform.[27]

A similar approach suggests that elections contribute to policy responsiveness, whereby leaders respond to the desires of voters, and the median voter in particular (Przeworski et al. 1999; Golden and Min 2013). These studies focus on how policies are responsive to the needs and interests of constituents, and whether they maximize the welfare of the broader population. All of these studies rest on the very simple premise that elections deliver accountability because they legitimate authority and allow citizens to select good leaders and remove bad leaders from office (Fearon 1999). Elections provide the channel for citizens to get their representatives to do their jobs, and ensure that their ideas and interests are incorporated into policies.[28]

Various scholars have found support for these claims in Ghana. Most notably, Robin Harding finds that voters do in fact attribute

[27] For a critique of the electoral logic of accountability, see: Paller (2018a).
[28] Schaffer (1998) and Schatzberg (2001) critique the notion that elections legitimate authority in the African context. Instead, they emphasize the importance of embedding elections in their cultural context.

their vote to government performance, reporting that vote shares in constituencies are positively affected by the condition of local roads (Harding 2015). Similarly, voters are likely to support the politician that is associated with the dominant ethnic group of a given place (Ichino and Nathan 2013). They do this because local community and geographic contexts convey information about the nonexcludable goods that they are likely to receive. By taking local geography and neighborhood-level motivations seriously, Ichino and Nathan highlight the importance of local-level motivations to patterns of distribution.

The electoral approach requires voters to have significant control over their representatives (Manin et al. 1999). Citizens must be able to access information about their representatives. They must know what they did with their budgets and where their money has been spent. They must understand how the political process works, and what is expected of their representatives. Information must be accessible, transparent, and unbiased. A burgeoning research agenda examines the role that information plays in electoral accountability, drawing on the logic that citizens will control their representatives if they have complete information about these issues: If the politician is still underperforming, they will vote him or her out of office.[29]

The limitations of electoral sanctioning theories have opened a new focus in African politics that focuses on the spread of information. This scholarship emphasizes the role of constituency service. Politicians, and MPs in particular, are expected to visit their constituencies on a regular basis, engage in face-to-face communication with their constituents, and pay for personal needs like funerals and birthdays. Moreover, they are expected to distribute contracts, provide government jobs, and secure development projects for supporters. Distributive politics thus becomes closer to the expectation of clientelism: the distribution of electoral handouts in exchange for votes, which is usually defined as vote buying (Nichter 2008).

This type of behavior is well documented in studies of Ghana (Lindberg 2003, 2010; Nugent 2007; Lindberg and Morrison 2008;

---

[29] There is an abundance of empirical scholarship that finds support for this theory by assessing the role of newspaper circulation (Besley and Burgess 2002; Adsera et al. 2003), public disclosure laws (Djankov et al. 2010), and public audits (Ferraz and Finan 2008). Grossman and Michelitch (2018) emphasize the role that information plays in competitive districts in Uganda.

Paller 2018a). Eric Kramon advances a novel theory drawing on evidence from Kenya, suggesting "the distribution of electoral handouts is a strategy by which politicians make their promises more credible with respect to the provision of resources to the poor" (2016: 461). The distribution of electoral handouts establishes credibility with voters, signaling that the candidate is likely to deliver on his or her promises in the future. Credibility thus takes on three dimensions: knowledge, expertise, and competence; perceptions of shared interests and trustworthiness, and; electoral viability (Kramon 2016: 463). These "electoral handouts" are meant to spark a pattern of loyalty between the representative and constituent, establishing "credibility with respect to the future provision of resources" (Kramon 2016: 464).

Kramon's theory goes a long way toward explaining why electoral handouts can be a viable campaign strategy in Africa. But by conceptualizing constituency service solely within a context of elections, he treats activities like providing for the health of constituents and paying schools fees as simply "delivering the goods." This approach narrows in on the behavior of the politician, without considering the broader meaning of constituency service. These "electoral handouts" are more than strategies that politicians use to signal credibility for formal political office, but also important features of the way those opinion leaders legitimate their authority outside of the electoral context.[30] Leaders have been engaging in this type of behavior for many years, even when not running for elections. In addition, opinion leaders who are not actively campaigning also engage in similar behavior to maintain followers and establish authority.

The exclusive focus on elections, without considering the context in which the distribution of electoral handouts is embedded, overlooks the process through which respect and admiration between constituents and representatives is achieved. Theories like Kramon's privilege the importance of elections above all, prioritizing the distribution of resources as a purely instrumental exchange. But they lack historical and cultural context, instead treating elections and the voting process as the only mode of representation there is. Distributive

---

[30] Auyero (2001) describes these tactics as everyday survival tactics. Holland (2016) provides a similar (though alternative) logic in her theory of forbearance, suggesting that politicians choose not to enforce the law as an informal welfare mechanism. Resnick (2013) discusses similar strategies as populist.

politics through elections is reduced to the only game in town, separate from broader struggles of power, including those over land, territory, water, and traditional authority. In cities, these include conflicts to control urban space. Instead, I draw from Schaffer's (2007) insight that vote buying – and distributive politics more generally – takes on different meanings in distinct cultural and historical contexts.

I argue that a focus on legitimacy, rather than credibility, can better explain how opinion leaders maintain control and authority even when the resources dry up and goods are not able to be delivered: Admiration and respect are much harder to lose than credibility.[31] In other words, opinion leaders can persist despite losing the credibility of their constituents.

Instead of a solely electoral approach, I borrow from the insights of Erica Simmons who suggests that we also need to consider "what is perceived to be at stake" in distributive politics (Simmons 2016). This forces us to think about the types of claims made, as well as what particular resources are being provided (Kramon and Posner 2013). Simmons emphasizes the importance of the meaning-making process – how communities make sense of their resources, and the symbolic (as well as material value) they hold. She distinguishes between quotidian communities and national communities to interrogate the importance of resources to groups of people. Quotidian communities are "built on face-to-face, routine interactions where members know each other personally," and the daily governance of resources can help bring residents and citizens together (Simmons 2014). Alternatively, "goods can serve as a symbol of national belonging, a vehicle through which particular regional identifications are reproduced, or as a way of indexing membership in an ethnic category of identification," helping solidify national communities (Simmons 2016: 41).

It is in this distinction where the type of resource matters. For example, Simmons explains how water and corn in Bolivia and Mexico, respectively, galvanized a broad-based coalition of protesters in the face of market privatization. Neighborhood-level relationships take on new importance – with governance of specific resources

---

[31] I thank Michael Bernhard for drawing my attention to this point.

playing a central role in the formation of grievances – in the context of economic and political liberalization. Distribution is not merely an instrumental exchange between politicians and voters, but rather a larger struggle over identity, claims making, and community.

This is especially important in the context of postcolonial Africa, where infrastructure – which is often reduced to public goods in studies of distributive politics – cannot be separated from modes of social control. Brian Larkin goes so far as to suggest that in the early years of independence, infrastructure operated as "a mode of address whereby the ... state offered development and technological progress in return for political subjection" (Larkin 2008: 245 quoted in Chalfin 2014: 97). In other words, investments in infrastructure signaled modernization, but often through displacement of local populations in the process. Infrastructure, therefore, took on specific meanings in the context of urban planning and the control of urban territory after colonialism, and the debates around these infrastructural improvements extended far beyond the narrow electoral scope of "delivering the goods" as "electoral handouts."

Debates over urban infrastructure open up public conversations about governance, democracy, and nationhood. Yet the recent period of structural adjustment and neoliberal restructuring has coincided with a privatization of the state and public goods (Mbembe 2001a). This has had severe implications for public services, as Brenda Chalfin explains, with respect to services like public toilets: "The built environments of sewerage and sanitation offer people an opportunity to wrest a space for urban existence outside the grasp of political institutions and elites" (Chalfin 2014: 93). Moreover, governance of public goods and services has its own politics, offering the potential to "enable the 'public' as social formation, realm of interaction, and collective consciousness" (Chalfin 2014: 106). This approach to public services suggests that the distribution of goods and services is part of a larger political struggle over governance and authority, which takes on very specific meanings in African cities.

Resources, goods, and infrastructure mean different things to different groups of people. It is insufficient to reduce the struggles over distribution and governance to logics of electoral handouts in exchange for votes, without considering the historical and cultural context in which electoral politics is embedded. In urban Africa, land, territory, water, and housing take on specific meanings depending on whether you are a native or stranger to the city, as noted earlier in this chapter.[32] For squatters, distributive politics is better understood in a broader context of urban and national citizenship. I now turn to a discussion of governance that considers treating urban space – and neighborhoods in particular – as a commons.

The Politicization of the Commons

The electoral approach to distribution is not the only way to study distributive politics. Alternatively, a long tradition of scholarship builds from theories of collective action and governing the commons (Olson 1965; Hardin 1968). This framework treats decision-making as a collective action problem that requires governing space and territory as a commons (Olson 1965; Ostrom 1990). This approach is particularly attractive in contexts where formal institutions are weak, and populations are forced to come together to make decisions for themselves and engage in collective decision-making. However, this form of governance is susceptible to the free-rider problem, also called the zero-contribution thesis: "Rational, self-interested individuals will not act to achieve their common or group interests" (Olson 1965: 2) because they can benefit from shirking, contributing to the underproduction of public goods. Over time, cooperation and public goods provision declines. The challenge for scholars is to uncover the institutions that local communities devise to govern their goods so that all individuals participate in collective action.

Elinor Ostrom's influential work suggests that groups can invest in self-monitoring and sanctioning institutions, so as to reduce the probability of free riding (Ostrom 1990). Ostrom notes that this is an evolutionary process, where social norms and learning develop over time (Ostrom 2000). Social norms are "shared understandings about actions that are obligatory, permitted, or forbidden" (Crawford and Ostrom 1995). The goal for collective action scholars is to uncover the "set of norms and values that can support cooperation" (Ostrom 2000: 146). It is in this domain where context matters, because fair rules of distribution depend on trusting relationships, where people

---

[32] For new work on the distribution of housing, see: Paller (2015); Croese and Pitcher (2017).

decide to abide by the rules and engage in collective action because they share the same concept of fairness (Bowles 1998).

When context is taken into account, collective governance and decision-making is complicated. This is particularly true in cities, where neighborhoods are not static – new groups form often, and rules are misunderstood or simply not followed by newcomers. Ostrom argues, "in-migration may bring new participants who do not trust others and do not rapidly learn social norms that have been established over a long period of time" (Ostrom 2000: 153). Of course, populations must also coordinate with government authorities, which are often tasked with providing public goods and services to local populations. Termed coproduction, it involves the process through which individuals who are not in the same organization are transformed into goods and services (Ostrom 1996).[33] This form of governance requires synergy and hybridity between local communities and formal governments.[34]

Coproduction is not a given, largely due to competing norms of reciprocity and fairness, but also because of contentious struggles over control and authority of the commons. Political entrepreneurs might not represent the interests of all residents, and instead restrict decision-making to a select few individuals. In reality, the commons are often politicized – subject to power dynamics that are not easily categorized or distributed along lines of economic rationality and efficiency. The social norms framework, therefore, suffers from some of the same shortcomings as the electoral distribution approach: the assumption that all groups and individuals make equal claims to the same goods and resources.

---

[33] Sheely (2013) finds evidence for this in Kenya, suggesting that community institutions and government agencies must work in tandem to promote the maintenance of public goods over time.

[34] Scholars are starting to take this seriously (Cammett and MacLean 2013; Brass 2016; Post et al. 2017). But most of these studies emphasize the relationship between state and nonstate actors. This treats them as analytically distinct, which might not be the case. These studies are state-centric, suggesting that variation is an outcome of the strength and penetration of the state. My framework explains the *type* of hybrid service provision we will see, providing an explanation as to where we might see different outcomes. In a recent article, Post et al. (2017) outline a framework that captures variation in hybrid provision. While Post et al. suggest that variation exists, they attribute it solely to subnational state capacity, while I attribute it to informal norms of settlement and belonging.

As I suggest earlier in this chapter, groups make distinct claims to urban space depending on the informal norms of settlement and belonging. These claims to urban space shape the entire distribution process, from the development of a public sphere to the privatization of the commons. In other words, the commons is not a theoretical model, but rather a real space and territory embedded in a broader political imaginary. Who has a right to this space – and the goods distributed to it – is a political question, not one that merely evolves socially.

A second limitation of this framework is that the social norms that evolve to generate collective action take time to develop, and the early stages are critical. Ostrom (2000) suggests "the presence of a leader or entrepreneur, who articulates different ways of organizing to improve joint outcomes, is frequently an important initial stimulus" (149).[35] Strong opinion leaders can play this role, helping forge trust and reciprocity across diverse groups. But leaders and political entrepreneurs can also be divisive, instigating tension when cooperation might be likely to develop organically. What this means is that the formation of a commons is political, and that a commons can also be politicized along certain social cleavages.

The dynamic nature of the commons suggests a rethinking of the term so that it is more in line with concepts of politics, rather than merely economic and social phenomena. Treating the commons as a public space or sphere introduces the importance of justice, claims making, and rights into the study of public goods distribution and collective decision-making.[36] Public spheres are actively generated conditions, where individuals engage with one another through deliberation and social engagement (Habermas 1991). In other words, it is worth thinking about the commons as a potential space, where "the common world . . . gathers us together and yet prevents our falling over each other . . . providing a sense of common object while permitting the expression of multiple perspectives" (Arendt 1958: 52 quoted in Chalfin 2014: 101).

---

[35] Ostrom cites Frohlich et al. (1971); Varughese (1999). Grossman (2014) provides evidence of how leadership selection rules shape collective action in Uganda.

[36] I use the definition of claim-making advanced by Gabrielle Kruks-Wisner: "Action—direct or mediated—through which citizens pursue access to social welfare goods and services, understood as publicly provided resources intended to protect and improve well-being and social security" (2018: 124).

By bringing the focus of everyday life into conversation with theories of the commons, we can better understand residents' and groups' connection to the commons, and how they generate a public life that represents their interests and ideals. In the context of urban space, this forces us to think about who has a right to the city – who can claim, govern, and shape urban space.[37] In other words, the distribution of resources is embedded in this broader struggle for control and authority in the city. This shift toward focusing on urban citizenship – the allocation and negotiation of rights and resources in a city – embeds the distribution of goods and resources to a specific political community in the city. My analysis takes this concept of the urban commons one step further, and suggests that the political sphere varies across urban neighborhoods. My theory of distributive politics outlines this variation in the next section, demonstrating the importance of informal norms of settlement and belonging to the construction of a public sphere, as well as to the politicization of the commons.

Toward a Theory of Distributive Politics

My framework considers how populations politicize the commons and incorporates how groups think their resources should be distributed and governed. As I have suggested, opinion leaders and local residents condition their attitudes about distribution based on the informal norms of settlement and belonging. Indigeneity remains a salient political identity in urban Ghana today (Nathan 2016a; Klaus and Paller 2017). Historically, indigenous neighborhoods have had distinct political advantages when compared to other poor neighborhoods because they form the historical center of cities, allowing them to develop with close ties to the political and economic centers of the country. Yet one of the more surprising developments in African cities with neo-customary land tenure regimes is the "downgrading" of these

[37] The dominant approach to claims-making and citizenship take a state-centric approach, attempting to understand why certain individuals or groups claim access to resources or membership in a national political community (see: Hanagan and Tilly 1999; MacLean 2010; Kruks-Wisner 2018). My approach shifts claims to the territory of urban space – the city. In addition, citizenship entails both rights and privileges that citizens gain by being a member of a political community, as well as the duties and obligations to which he or she has to perform.

neighborhoods, where some traditional and central urban neighborhoods have descended into slums (Melara Arguello et al. 2013).

In these neighborhoods, claims to indigeneity and autochthony provide alternative conceptions of citizenship among the first comers to the land, providing these groups the entitlement "to enter the struggle for resources" (Mamdani 2002: 505). These claims are evident in the indigenous residents' attitudes toward distribution: They feel entitled to state resources because they are the original inhabitants of the land. The informal norm suggests that because other communities include squatters, they do not deserve state resources when indigenous populations arrived first and also require resources for development.

This strong sense of entitlement and first-comer claims to the land strikes fear among residents in indigenous settlements that they are losing the control and authority of the city to outsiders. This sparks what in the literature is often deemed a psychological mechanism stemming from fear of outsiders and the stimulation of stereotypes (Allport 1954; Blumer 1958; Bobo and Hutchings 1996; Putnam 2007; Enos 2015). In particular, it triggers an emotional response, similar to what Christopher Claassen calls a "violation of group entitlement" – the feeling that an "out-group" is getting what the "in-group" deserves (2014: 134).

Therefore, neighborhoods governed by indigenous norms and practices privilege club goods that are excludable and non-rivalrous: Members of families of the indigenous ethnic group secure customary entitlements in the form of government contracts to build education and health facilities, jobs, or welfare projects. Resources also extend to public toilets and water outlets. The benefits are distributed to members of the club, typically along family lines. Those who are not members of the "indigenous club," are not entitled to the public services of the state.[38]

The host population does not view migrants in stranger settlements as a threat to taking over the city, and therefore support the equitable distribution of resources to these neighborhoods. Again, the public legitimacy of settlement goes a long way toward explaining this

---

[38] It is important to note that in my research I find that most Ghanaians believe that all residents should have access to education and health care. But they believe there should be a distinction between governing brick-and-mortar goods tied to a particular territory versus health care and educational facilities, which are allocated as national citizenship rights.

outcome. Many people live in neighborhoods that are considered publicly legitimate today because of the way the territory was settled: Early settlers purchased plots of land directly from indigenous landowners. While state agencies and private individuals might have the official land title, I refer to purchases directly from customary authorities or indigenous families. The state, as well as residents of the host city, does not question the legitimacy of the neighborhood, even though there are numerous property disputes that might exist within these settlements and often have a history of resisting eviction and demolition.

Although most of these residents are poor, and many are recent migrants, they do not feel threatened about their security of tenure in the city. Nor do they worry that their control of urban space will be threatened with the influx of new people or the distribution of limited resources to other neighborhoods.[39] Therefore, a public sphere emerges that relies on collective decision-making among members of diverse ethnic groups.

Distribution of goods, therefore, takes the form of common goods that are rivalrous and non-excludable, or public goods that are non-rivalrous and non-excludable. In both of these scenarios, the public interest is served by public goods projects like water stations, public toilets, and education and health facilities. Both of these scenarios are positive outcomes, but the major difference between common goods and public goods in these neighborhoods is that common goods are governed by customary norms to manage common pool resources (Ostrom 1990).

Of course, not all stranger settlements that develop this way are legally recognized by the state. The informal norm of settlement and belonging fosters legitimacy, but it does not necessarily mean that the state legally recognizes the neighborhood, or the homes within it. In neighborhoods that have not been legally recognized by the state, residents often come together to fight for legal recognition. They make claims based on their history of purchasing the plot, and these struggles are contentious and political.

Neighborhoods that have legal recognition, therefore, are well demarcated and incorporated into administrative assemblies' development

---

[39] See Table A.1 in the Appendix for measures of these indicators across settlements.

plans. The provision of public services is mandated, and the local struggle for power revolves around who will manage the public services, like toilets. This does not mean that service provision is a given or that politicians will be accountable to the citizenry, but it does mean that public service provision is the jurisdiction of the formal political domain. That said, informal political activity continues to structure provision of services through the form of "toilet wars" and struggles for government contracts, where the fight for power occurs within the governing political party (Ayee and Crook 2003). Opinion leaders try to consolidate their control through their involvement in the governing party.

As mentioned earlier in this chapter, squatter settlements where populations illegitimately inhabit land have grown rapidly across urban Africa since 1990. Because they are illegitimate in the eyes of the local population, government agencies often do not officially recognize them. This public perception is directly translated into attitudes about distribution: People think that squatter settlements do not deserve public services because they were settled illegitimately.[40]

Squatter settlements that lack formal land tenure and legitimate ownership privilege private goods that are rivalrous and excludable: Opinion leaders and their followers secure their democratic dividend in the form of a private reward like a government contract, cash gift in exchange for votes, and protection for serving as a de facto landlord. In this way, the commons is privatized by powerful actors, being used as a space for political entrepreneurs to empower themselves personally at the expense of the common good.

The different types of goods distribution are summarized in Table 2.2. I then turn to explaining how these different norms of settlement and belonging shape diverse organizations of civic life.

The Organization of Civic Life

Ethnicity – shared cultural attributes, consciousness, and boundaries (Young 2014) – continues to influence politics in Ghana. Distinct groups are affiliated with specific political parties, contributing to the persistence of patronage along ethnic lines. This has led to a

---

[40] They are universally perceived as illegitimate and hence unworthy of public recognition and investment.

Table 2.2 *The type of distributive politics*

Squatter	Stranger
Private Goods (rivalrous and excludable)	Common Goods (rivalrous and non-excludable)
Indigenous	**Stranger/Other**
Club Goods (non-rivalrous and excludable)	Public Goods (non-rivalrous and non-excludable)

burgeoning literature on the role of ethnicity in African politics.[41] The importance of traditional authorities in everyday affairs – specifically over the control of land – amplifies the importance of ethnicity. Most of these studies take elections as the point of departure, focusing exclusively on how ethnicity serves as a cognitive shortcut in matters of voting. In addition, ethnicity has been shown to explain collective action at the societal level. Ethnicity can be a barrier to a democratic and progressive politics by preventing the formation of nationalism that could unify and modernize African countries.[42] Yet the view from urban neighborhoods provides a puzzling finding: Some communities are governed across ethnic lines, privileging a civic life that extends to all of its residents. This suggests that ethnic politics can be overcome in certain contexts. Why does ethnicity shape the decision-making process in some neighborhoods but not others?

In contrast to the conventional scholarship, this book argues that the organization of civic life is an outcome of how cities developed over time. It is also an outcome of a long historical and political process. By the organization of civic life, I refer to the patterns of authority and structure of associational life – how daily affairs are constructed and institutionalized in a neighborhood. As I will demonstrate in Chapter 3, different types of associational structures emerged at different stages of the urbanization process, and were reshaped by significant changes in governance during colonial rule and multiparty democracy. This calls into question the conventional wisdom in political science scholarship that ethnic politics is an outcome of formal institutions or entrenched social organizations. This simplistic view of ethnic politics overlooks

---

[41] For a very good review, see: Young (2014).
[42] For example, see: Miguel (2004).

three important facets of ethnicity in urban Ghana, namely how claims to space and territory magnify the salience of ethnic identity; the historical evolution of cities and its neighborhoods, and; how leaders control urban space and politicize the concept of ethnicity. Therefore, I suggest rethinking how local populations understand ethnicity, as well as how leaders politicize these concepts for their own personal empowerment.

Ethnic Politics and Elections

The general expectation in African politics is that citizens prefer politicians from their own ethnic group. Robert Bates is one of the most influential scholars to explain why ethnicity plays a central role in politics. He suggests that ethnic groups are "coalitions which have been formed as a part of rational efforts to secure benefits created by the forces of modernization" (1983: 152). But people have many different identities, and this rationale does not explain why certain identities become salient versus others. To fill this gap, Daniel Posner (2005) shows how formal political competition structures which identities become salient. He provides a very strategic rationale: "They will consider each of the principles of group division that divide the political community (religion, language, race, clan, etc.), compare the size of their own group with that of the other groups that each of these cleavages defines, and then select the identity that puts them in a minimum winning coalition" (2005: 4). African voters choose their ethnic identities for strategic reasons – to gain material rewards during elections. Citizens also use ethnicity as a group heuristic for evaluating public policies (Lieberman and McClendon 2013).

There is significant support for these arguments in Ghana. Regional identification representing distinct ethnic homelands is crucial to the electoral process (Nugent 2001; Fridy 2007). Voters in the Upper East, Upper West, Northern, and Volta regions typically identify with the NDC, while the NPP enjoys substantial support from the Ashanti and Eastern regions. In this way, voter preferences have long been linked to ethnic considerations, especially the instrumentalization of ethnicity in party platforms (Nugent 2001; Fridy 2007).

Expanding beyond Ghana, Dominika Koter (2013) shifts the attention to the social structure of society, explaining why ethnic electoral blocs emerge in countries like Benin, but not in countries like Senegal.

Importantly, she finds that "politicians respond to preexisting networks and channels of authority" (Koter 2013: 189). Baldwin and Huber (2010) also focus attention on the structure of society, suggesting that "between-group inequality" better explains governance outcomes, in contrast to ethnic or cultural fractionalization. These studies go a long way toward explaining the relationship between social structure, elections, and public goods provision.

Yet these studies suffer from two major shortcomings. First, because they are largely concerned with national-level political factors, they treat elections as the primary institution that shapes political competition and power. They do not account for the importance of informal institutions of settlement and belonging that are critical in African cities, providing an alternative rationale for why the salience of certain ethnicities are operated over others. Second, they treat ethnicity as fixed and unchanging. Similarly, because they focus on mostly rural areas, ethnicity and territory are understood to be contiguous. This is not always the case in urban areas, where migration and mobility contributes to a social structure that is always changing and in flux. A focus on the everyday life of urban neighborhoods can help overcome these limitations.

Ethnicity and Civic Life

Related theories emerge from the social capital literature emphasizing the structure of associational life, placing attention on the norms of trust and reciprocity in a community (Putnam 1993). Civic life, therefore, refers to "the part of our life that exists between the state on one hand and families on the other, that allows people to come together for a whole variety of public activities, and that is relatively independent of the state" (Varshney 2002: 4). These are the preexisting networks of engagement that underlie social life – who is connected, how they engage with one another, and why these social ties emerge. Civic life encompasses behaviors, including routine interactions, quotidian activities, and political practices. In Africa, civic life is often organized along ethnic lines, privileging the dominant majority ethnic group over minorities.[43]

---

[43] For good discussions of how ethnicity structures political life, see: Ekeh (1975); Ndegwa (1997); Bayart (2005).

One of the most robust findings in studies of collective action is that ethnic diversity erodes cooperation (Banerjee et al. 2005: 639; Miguel and Gugerty 2005). The volume *Coethnicity* attempts to explain why, and finds that "individuals cooperate with coethnics at a higher rate than with non-coethnics, not because of biases toward in-group members, but because they expect coethnics to cooperate with them and because they believe that, should they fail to cooperate, they might be punished" (Habyarimana et al. 2009: 23).[44] This is not because coethnics value the welfare of their own over that of non-coethnics.[45] Instead, a strategy selection mechanism is at play, whereby ethnicity signals to players that they should cooperate with one another, over other possible alternatives. The authors suggest that there are ways for cooperation to emerge in ethnically diverse settings: "When and where collective action succeeds, it is generally among homogenous subsets of the community or within narrow associations that have developed mechanisms for policing contributions" (Habyarimana et al. 2009: 133).[46]

Coethnicity does not leave much room for cooperation and effective governance in ethnically diverse settings, especially in the absence of a third-party sanctioning mechanism. There is now a growing literature that attempts to explain cooperation in this context. For example, Dionne (2015) shows how dense social connections can overcome ethnic diversity and facilitate cooperation in Malawi. Internal central-ized authorities selected by democratic elections have also been shown to promote cooperation in Uganda (Grossman and Baldassarri 2012). A strong national identity (Charnysh et al. 2015; Robinson 2016;), crosscutting social cleavages (Dunning and Harrison 2010), and a sense of belonging to a common polity (Singh 2011) have all been shown to help overcome ethnic divisions as well.

Yet these studies overlook the fact that ethnicity might be endogen-ous to other important institutional features, like the informal norms

---

[44] This is due to several mechanisms, including what the authors call readability, frequency, reachability, and strategy selection mechanisms. The authors conclude that a norm of reciprocity exists among coethnics, which can substitute as a sanctioning mechanism (106). The results are driven mostly by the fact that coethnicity enables egoists to act more like altruists (112).

[45] The authors call this a preference mechanism (Habyarimana et al. 2009).

[46] A relatively small subset of homogenous groups contributes to successful collective action, rather than broad-based, multiethnic activity (146).

of settlement and belonging. In cities this is especially important because ties to urban space are arguably more important than ethnic identity itself. This is because urban space refers to territory, and the social and institutional arrangements that establish order. Civic life emerges out of this historical context, thereby conditioning when and where multiethnic coalitions form, and the conditions under which ethnic groups work together to enact change. This is where institutions can play an important role, beyond solely societal characteristics and organization.

Finally, social interaction and the development of strong and weak ties might impact the political salience of ethnicity (Granovetter 1973). In places where there are quotidian and organizational interactions between and across ethnic groups, we are likely to see more cooperation.[47] One mechanism advanced by the social contact hypothesis suggests that interpersonal contact between individuals from differing groups will alleviate prejudice and promote friendships across a social divide, as long as there are underlying networks of solidarity and equality (Allport 1954).[48] I draw from these theories, but provide an explanation as to why cooperative behavior emerges in urban neighborhoods.

Toward a Theory of Multiethnic Governance

As urbanization confronts African societies, multiethnic civic life has emerged in spaces that historically were dominated by a single group. But not all neighborhoods experience this kind of social transformation. While the structure of civic life varies across urban Ghana, no explanation exists for why these differences persist. What accounts for the difference in civic life between urban neighborhoods?

In line with the broader argument of this book, I argue that informal norms of settlement and belonging shape the civic life of urban Ghanaian neighborhoods. In the indigenous core of a city, norms of indigeneity contribute to social engagement along ethnic lines. Indigenous residents often have the incentive to organize themselves ethnically in order to maintain their indigenous status, a label that they view as an

---

[47] Drawing from this insight, Varshney (2001) finds that there are fewer riots in Indian neighborhoods with strong associational ties between groups.

[48] A new social contact experimental study does not find evidence that social contact decreases prejudice, but does alter and contribute to more cooperative behavior (Scacco and Warren 2018).

important economic and political resource.[49] This insight is consistent with a growing literature that suggests norms of reciprocity and social capital can serve exclusionary purposes.[50] In the capital city where migrants come in large numbers and land values continue to increase – while outsiders buy large swaths of land – indigenes often worry that they are "losing their city." A narrative of indigeneity offers a strong incentive to organize ethnically and not incorporate outsiders; indigenes can then maintain their entrenched patronage network with politicians and the city authorities. It can serve as a way for community leaders to organize members, especially when the economy is struggling. Additionally, claims to indigeneity might privilege the hoarding of resources by family, undermining public goods.

Norms of indigeneity can also create severe disputes among members of the indigenous group, creating longstanding conflict that divides the community and seeds distrust. It contributes to placing legal residents of the settlement versus "illegal" residents in surrounding neighborhoods, thereby undercutting a powerful class identity or alliance that ends up undermining a collective cause. In other words, claims to indigeneity contribute to the division of the poor to the benefit of a small "traditional" elite. It creates opportunities for residents and community leaders to place patronage demands on political parties through claims of land ownership, to solicit international organizations and nonstate actors to secure resources, and fill municipal positions with coethnic members at the expense of technical expertise.

The informal norm of indigeneity serves a competing function: It coexists with formal institutions but structures incentives that are incompatible with formal rules, and undermines the formal rules of the game (Helmke and Levitsky 2006: 15). While corruption and patrimonialism are often associated with competing informal institutions (e.g., O'Donnell 1996; Borocz 2000; Lauth 2000), the interaction between norms of indigeneity and multiparty politics helps explain why corruption and patrimonialism persists: It shapes incentives and behaviors to serve ethnic interests, creating a logic of politics that might be considered patrimonial and corrupt.

---

[49] Hilgers (2011) goes so far as to argue that autochthony is a product derived from social capital, and confers status, prestige, and access to networks. It works as capital, and this "allows it to play the role of an actual form of capital that can be invested, valued and protected from" (M. Hilgers 2011: 35).

[50] See: Berman (1997); Acemoglu et al. (2014); Satyanath et al. (2017).

Alternatively, migration to a city shapes distinct patterns of leadership and civic life. The legitimacy of a group's settlement in the city can have significant implications for social engagement. This is the çase in stranger settlements. In these neighborhoods, social engagement develops cross-ethnically because residents and leaders have incentives to build multi-ethnic coalitions in the face of state power. Settler groups need positive relationships with the indigenous ethnic group to protect their security of tenure, secure citizenship rights, and access public services. Therefore, they are encouraged to strengthen coalitions with other ethnic groups to place more pressure on the state. The more pressure they put on the state, the more public services they can secure. Opinion leaders have incentives to work with other headmen for similar reasons: The cooperation between leaders from different groups has the effect of trickling down to group members (Acemoglu and Jackson 2015). Therefore, patron-client relationships develop cross-ethnically, with rewards being distributed across diverse groups in the neighborhood.

Community organization also has the potential to develop along programmatic lines, not solely ethnic, class, or religious lines. Residents join friends clubs, self-help groups, football fan clubs, and political associations that extend beyond ethnic affiliation. This fosters cross-ethnic social engagement, where the sharing of goods and services extends across ethnic groups. Residents organize formal local associations because opportunities are distributed to formally organized groups. This includes private goods through political parties and NGOs, but also public services from municipal assemblies. Local youth must respect leaders and authority because they provide jobs. These factors facilitate the growth of cross-ethnic social engagement, where the social expectation of sharing goods and resources with members from different ethnic groups is institutionalized in daily life.

The informal norm of indigeneity serves a complementary function: It coexists with formal institutions and structures incentives that are compatible with formal rules (Helmke and Levitsky 2006: 15). The interaction between informal norms of settlement and belonging and formal party politics opens up the political arena to include multiple ethnic groups, contributing to a multiethnic associational life.

Squatter settlements, on the other hand, privilege the organization of civic life along ethnic lines. Without a long-term time horizon to stay in the neighborhood, residents and leaders maintain strong connections to their rural homeland, and their coethnics from these places. Therefore,

Table 2.3 *Organization of civic life*

	Civic life
Indigenous	Ethnic (indigenous) – Competing
Stranger	Multiethnic – Complementary
Squatter	Ethnic (ties to hometown) – Substitutive

there are pockets of ethnic strongholds across the neighborhood. In addition, in the absence of external sanctioning mechanisms (as Habyarimana et al. 2009 suggest), cooperation is undermined by distrust between ethnic groups. Social interactions are largely restricted along ethnic lines as well. While these behaviors are certainly not deterministic, the organization of civic life maintains a very ethnic calculus. Therefore, informal norms of settlement play a substitutive role, replacing the formal rules and providing alternative rules of the game, restricting the sphere of urban governance along ethnic lines (Helmke and Levitsky 2006).

Ethnicity and the organization of civic life are summarized in Table 2.3.

Conclusion

This chapter presents a stylized theory of local politics in poor African city neighborhoods. I outline ideal types, noting that there is incredible variation within each type of neighborhood. Yet by rethinking African urbanization with respect to informal norms of settlement and belonging, we gain a better understanding about how leaders emerge, political communities form, and neighborhoods evolve. In particular, I show how indigenous settlements maintain restrictive governance along the lines of the indigenous ethnic group; public spheres emerge in stranger settlements that open up the arena of urban governance to a diverse set of residents that span beyond clientelistic and ethnic linkages, and; squatter settlements privilege a practice of politics that substitute for formal institutions, thereby privatizing the commons. The next chapter explains the growth of Ghana's cities over time, paying close attention to how the informal institutions of settlement and belonging shape the political development of its neighborhoods.

3 | The Political History of Urbanization in Ghana

Ghana's history of urbanization has been well documented by historians, anthropologists, and geographers. Ethnographers like Margaret Field (1937, 1940) and J. M. Bruce-Myers (1927) provide intricate accounts of the origins of Ga society, and the process of change in precolonial Accra. Historians like John Parker (2000a, 2000b) provide insightful accounts of colonialism's impact on Ga politics and society, while Naaborko Sackeyfio-Lenoch (2012, 2014) extends this analysis to include the ways in which colonial rule provided new opportunities for financial gain among indigenous landowners. Ivor Wilks (1989) provides a similar service for Kumasi. Another set of scholars document the early migration process, describing the different ways that stranger communities are integrated into indigenous societies and the complex local politics that shape the growth of stranger communities (Schildkrout 1978; Kobo 2010; Ntewusu 2012). These sets of studies demonstrate the early challenges that Ghanaian cities had in shifting from ethnically homogenous towns to multiethnic cities. Finally, contemporary geographers like Richard Grant (2006, 2009), Franklin Obeng-Odoom (2010), and Ian Yeboah (2000) emphasize the current growth patterns of Ghanaian cities, demonstrating how factors in the global political economy have contributed to the growth of squatter settlements today.

Yet most of these studies focus on one particular element in the process of urbanization – a specific time period, sub-population of residents, or area of the city – without providing a holistic view of the growth of Ghanaian cities across time and space. This chapter provides an addition to conventional accounts of Ghanaian urbanization by reconstructing the political history of urban growth from precolonial times to the modern day. I emphasize how informal norms of settlement and belonging help explain the political development of Ghanaian cities at different stages of urbanization, despite changes in social structure and formal institutions.

As a scholar of politics, I focus on the local political economy of urban growth. I suggest that community leaders seek to control territory and urban space through tactics like seeking alliances with colonial authorities and joining political party machines. Yet they must develop admiration and respect among their followers to be seen as legitimate leaders. It is through this political history of urbanization that Ghanaian cities develop from indigenous towns, to multiethnic cities, to sprawling metropolises inclusive of illegitimate squatter settlements. These underlying patterns of authority set the stage for the everyday politics in Chapters 4, 5, and 6.

The chapter combines a variety of sources. I summarize some of the most important research from ethnographers and historians that document processes of political change in the precolonial and colonial era. I supplement this with my own archival research that provides a view of decision-making within the Accra Town Council, focusing particularly on poor neighborhoods and revenue collection. I then incorporate original oral histories from early settlers of Ashaiman and Old Fadama to demonstrate what urban growth looked like from below at the neighborhood level. These insights provide an important, yet untold perspective to the process of urbanization. By utilizing these various sources, I demonstrate that while much has changed in Ghana's cities, the leaders' and residents' desire to control territory and urban space has maintained its importance throughout history.

The chapter continues as follows. I explain the origins of Accra and demonstrate the impact that colonialism had on the development of Ghanaian cities. I then recount the challenge that cities had in integrating migrants, and explain how municipal authorities attempted to govern poor neighborhoods under colonial rule in Accra and Sekondi-Takoradi. I document the patterns of leadership that emerge in urban neighborhoods in Accra and Kumasi. I discuss the early stages of Kwame Nkrumah's rule by emphasizing his complicated relationship with local chiefs, as well as his modernization campaign's impact on new neighborhoods like Ashaiman. I end by summarizing how Ghana's failed housing policies have contributed to the growth of squatter settlements in its larger cities, and the contentious process of urban growth in neighborhoods like Ashaiman and Old Fadama. I conclude with a short discussion of how multiparty democracy contributes to the uneven growth of cities today.

The Birth of Accra

Accra became an economic center of the region in the 1600s, as settlers profited from trading slaves, gold dust, and palm oil in exchange for European goods like guns and gunpowder.[1] As early settlers, the family emerged as the most important group identity in controlling the town. The settlers – migrants of the Ga ethnic group – established "quarters" based on family lineage, and these quarters became modern-day neighborhoods. Men arrived as "a harried gang of refugees ... The gangs appeared at different times and each consisted of 'a few men and their sons and brothers and many wives and children.' Each gang seems to have fortified one of several hills ... to have removed later to the coast and settled there permanently, deciding that coastal sites were safer as they needed protecting on one side only" (Field 1937: 2). As first-comers to the land, the Ga claimed indigeneity to the city of Accra.

Ga families rooted themselves in the authority structure of the neighborhoods, labeling the combination of these early settlements Ga Mashie. The basic social unit of the Ga is the *we,* or the ancestral house through which all inhabitants trace their descent through a common male ancestor (Odotei 1991). The ancestral house has physical implications because it marks the political space of the neighborhood, providing ways to mark differences in the community (Osei-Tutu 2000). Territory is particularly important because the important markers in the community are where ancestors are buried.[2] The control of space and territory emerged as the defining feature of power and leadership.[3]

From this emphasis on space and settlement, where early settlers are marked physically by where they live and their dividing boundaries they set, an insider-outsider narrative emerged: Families established political structures and *asafo* companies, or military bands, to protect themselves from potential raids from "inland raiders."[4] This

---

[1] The first Europeans arrived in the 1400s, constructing a fort in Elmina in 1471. At first, they were mostly interested in gold.

[2] For example, the founders of the Gbese quarter are buried under the Ussher Fort, marking an important location in the community.

[3] Pellow 2002 explains how this focus on space and territory maintains its importance in the local dynamics of urban neighborhoods today.

[4] The *asafo* company also represented the voice and interests of the commoner: The "*asafoi* were seen as the institutional expression of 'commoner' interests, ready

first-settler status developed into a sense of entitlement to land and territory (Quartey-Papafio 1914). As a contemporary politician maintains: "The Gas have never been conquered and made slaves. The soil of the land has always been, and is, the property of the Ga people" (Josiah-Aryeh 1997).

At the center of the narratives that developed was origin: Ga people trace their histories to central Africa, where they came into contact with Ancient civilizations and even adopted parts of the Hebrew language.[5] But more importantly in the origin narratives is the importance of first arrival, or who came to Accra first.[6] This represents who is a "true Ga." For example, descendants of the Otubluhom quarter of Ga Mashie are originally Akwamus, and do not hold the highest prestige (Bruce-Myers 1927: 72). The descendants of Kinka, on the other hand, claim to be the oldest quarter and point to this first-settler status for garnering respect (Daniell 1856: 2).

The Ga were under constant attack from the Akwapim people of the north, and depended on their links with Europeans for guns, economic power, and other wealth. The killing of King Okaikoi by the Akwamus in 1677 threatened the centralization of power in the Ga state, leading to the development of seven quarters in Ga Mashie around the 1730s (Arn 1996). Ga people remember this point as a critical juncture when the Ga lost unity and cohesion. After the defeat, powerful Ga leaders claimed autonomy from the centralized authority in Accra. The indigenous core of the Ga split into five different quarters, and two immigrant groups also established quarters due to the "wealth of their founders, their association with Ga war efforts, and, lastly, their alliance with powerful African as well as European allies" (Osei-Tutu 2000: 64). Otubluhom, Abola, Asere, and Gbese made up Dutch Accra (Ussher Town), while Sempe, Akumadjzei, and Alata were part of British Accra (Jamestown). These quarters developed their own paramount chieftaincies and were hardly unified, developing *asafo* companies and political networks based on these new family alliances.

---

to defend the rights of the ordinary *manbii* [townspeople] and keep in check the prerogatives of the chiefs" (Parker 2000a: 19).

[5] Bruce-Myers (1927: 72). Others trace their origin to Benin City in Eastern Nigeria.

[6] Parker (2000a: 8). Parker writes: "Despite their lack of historicity, such claims [of origin] are striking characters for cultural tensions in early colonial Accra, when traditions of origin were mobilized and further elaborated in Ga political action" (Parker 2000a: 8).

There were constant military battles and struggles for power between the different quarters in the 1700s and 1800s. The divisional rulers of these quarters controlled land, and were not ruled directly by a centralized Ga Mantse, or king. Many of the important divisions that remain in Ga Mashie today are outcomes of political struggles that can be traced back to the seventeenth century (Osei-Tutu 2000: 63).

The control of land provided family elders with the source of political authority (Shipton 1994). In this way, the origins of authority and leadership derive from control of land, military power, and ability to strengthen the stool, a central part of Ga society. Political incorporation and leadership developed through those who would help perpetuate the power of the Ga state. The policy of incorporation adopted by the Ga was aimed at giving the immigrants a sense of belonging to the state: "With the defeat of the Ga by Akwamu in 1680, the power of the Ga rulers was shattered. Immigrants who displayed certain qualities and had the ability to help in protecting and defending the Ga were elevated ... By giving them a position in the government, they identified themselves with the stability of the government and the survival of the state" (Odotei 1991: 67).

The conflict over authority and power was further complicated by the role of Europeans. The Ga people established a lucrative business in trading slaves and gold, particularly in the late 1600s and early 1700s, and later in palm oil after gold decreased after 1850. To bolster their strength in trade, Europeans erected forts: The Dutch built the Ussher Fort (then called Crevecoeur) in 1650; the Swedes built Christiansborg Castle in 1657; and the British built James Fort in 1673. It was during this time that the Ga political entrepreneur established himself as a middleman between the Europeans and his own people by exchanging land for the construction of forts in exchange for economic power (Acquah 1958: 16). The Ga people benefited from the role as middlemen in the larger long-distance trading routes.

The control of land was central to the role of Ga middlemen: They controlled the land and therefore required a certain level of goodwill, or respect, but also a direct exchange of profits. The desire to control the coast, and its vast trading routes, was at the forefront of local politics (Arn 1996). This also contributed to the development of a stratified class system, where new "merchant princes" served apprenticeships under the Europeans and gained wealth, prestige, and territory (Daaku 1970 cited in Arn 1996). Political entrepreneurs gained power and extended territorial authority based on their control of followers and access to firearms.[7] The role of Ga leaders as middlemen between Europeans and inland tribes underlie the logic of social exchange and marks an early point in the evolution of patron-client relationships in Ga Mashie.

In the 1830s a group of Nigerians and freed slaves from Brazil arrived in Ussher Town, and one of the local chiefs gave land to the settlers. But what is most notable is that they absorbed into Ga society by marrying Ga people, speaking their language, and trading and participating in daily life (Field 1940; Gocking 1999). By 1840 the Abola Mantse became the Ga Mantse – the king of the Ga state – due to his leadership in the Ashanti-Fanti War (Sanjek 1972: 35). Throughout the 1800s, "strangers" incorporated themselves into one of these seven quarters, learned the Ga language, intermarried with indigenous Ga, and assimilated into the Ga ethnic group. Power was not based on kinship, but rather the number of followers, and the addition of immigrants was part of this accumulation of political power.

In Ga Mashie, this involved the process of "becoming Ga," as the Ga maxim *"Ablekuma aba kuma wo"* suggests: "May strangers be added onto us" (Parker 2000a: 16).[8] It also included joining *asafo* companies and "defending the town" (Parker 2000a: 48). This was also at the forefront of male honor: To become an honorable Ga man, you had to fight and defend the town (Field 1940). Social engagement and bonds of respect, therefore, emerged along ethnic lines – allegiance to the Ga state. But it was a particular type of ethnic solidarity, one that involved an indigenous esprit de corps.

The Impact of Colonialism

From the earliest years of Accra's population growth, the Ga attempted to protect territory from ethnic outsiders, using its custodianship over land as an important political resource in establishing middlemen status with European traders. These relationships became further

---

[7] For example, this was the case with the rise of Wetse Kojo and the Alata stool (Parker 2000a: 14).

[8] Parker notes that the final custom that distinguished Gas from inland tribes was their circumcision: "Three centuries later the lament could still be heard in Accra: *Nye ha folio eha Nkranpon fee*—'You let uncircumcised people snatch Great Accra'" (Parker 2000a: 16).

entrenched under colonial rule, as the British formally institutionalized these roles in their system of indirect rule. Ga traditional authorities used these privileged positions to gain power, status, and prestige in their own city (Parker 2000a; Sackeyfio-Lenoch 2014).[9] Accra became the administrative capital of the Gold Coast in 1877, contributing to its growth, as it became the headquarters for business dealings and political decision-making. Ga leaders became important figures in the real estate market when the British passed the Public Lands Ordinance in 1876, shifting the land tenure regime from a traditional system to a modern one that witnessed the rise of land alienation in the subsequent colonial period (Quarcoopome 1992). Modern urban development contributed to rising land prices, as well as the shift to a rights-based land tenure regime (Pogucki 1954: 21).

The early economic and political origins set Accra on the path to the primate city it is today. The colonial government was relatively autonomous from indigenous leaders, allowing local authority structures to exit the formal system and rule their populations informally. Indigenous populations lived in neighborhoods outside the formal town planning structures, designated slums or urban villages in the official documents. Colonial rulers made early attempts at incorporation of local chiefs to maintain stability and expropriate land, but these measures were never formally institutionalized.

The administration of the town was never easy, as the British attempted to win over indigenous chiefs and integrate them into municipal governance, relying on them to collect taxes and manage sanitation measures. But the chiefs did not carry out their mandate quietly. For example, in 1859 chiefs incited residents to protest paying the municipal tax rate (Acquah 1958: 22). Resistance to colonial tax policy was ongoing throughout colonial rule, and the main impediment to establishing the Municipal Council; an ordinance to set up the council was finally passed in 1898 (Akyeampong 2002). But colonial administrators never fully depended on indigenous neighborhoods for facilitating development, and the neighborhoods did not pose a significant threat to urban security or livelihoods.

---

[9] Intermixing also contributed to a new class of people. These mulattoes, called "merchant princes," gained a privileged status in society and became part of the intellectual and political class over time (Daniell 1856).

Public health concerns changed the dynamics of urban politics, forging a new alliance between the colonial government and indigenous neighborhoods to prevent mass insecurity. The bubonic plague outbreak in 1907 intensified the need for formal institutionalization and stronger state capacity, demonstrating to commoners the value of the Municipal Council. A key part of the sanitation measures involved the organization of a demolition committee after the outbreak. But it failed in its efforts because it did not consult with traditional authorities at the grassroots (Quarcoopome 1993: 23). An additional shift in leadership patterns occurred in 1910 when the Colonial Administration began recognizing stranger headman outside the authority structure of the Ga traditional chieftaincy system, serving as a strategy of divide and rule that contributed to more power for the Accra Municipal Council (Arn 1996: 436).

The implementation of multiple levels of authority and governance of Accra led to struggles between diverse factions of the Ga community. For example, the 1884 "Civil War" between residents of Ussher Town and James Town erupted when groups of residents in James Town insulted King Tacki Tawia I (Osei-Tutu 2000: 66). Testimony at the 1907 Commission of Enquiry into Ga indigenous institutions highlights the "importance of military organization and of warfare in determining the form of Ga institutions and the dynamics of political competition" (Parker 2000a: 46). These "fights" over the process of incorporation began to change in the early years of colonial rule. The introduction of indirect rule and rising land values in the 1920s and 1930s led to intense stool disputes (Sackeyfio-Lenoch 2014). In fact, stool succession disputes became "the curse of Ga politics" (Field 1940: 51). This contributed to local rivalries and competitive struggles for followers, but in new arenas of politics (Parker 2000b).

Chieftaincy Disputes and Everyday Politics

Stool succession disputes dominated Ga politics in the late colonial period. I summarize the following case because it illustrates how stool succession disputes undermine formal institutions and city governance. In 1924, the British administration in the Gold Coast published a new law that conceded a majority of Town Council seats to African merchants and elites (Osei-Tutu 2000). The law also implemented new revenue raising measures including property rate increases and license fees. The incumbent Ga Mantse Nii Tackie Yaoboi (1919–1929) supported the ordinance, along with African educated elite. The Ga Mantse was also the local representative for the Aborigines Protection Rights Society, an organization that represented the rights of customary law and ownership (Nworah 1971).

The *asafobii*, or group of youth who view themselves as military figures and protectors of the Ga state, organized against the ordinance claiming that it disrupted their Ga indigenous culture. They claimed that the Ga Mantse did not have the authority to rule over the entire Ga Mashie community without their popular support. The details of the account are more striking. The mass of *asafobii* marched to the bedroom of the King at dawn – "traditionally, a time for sober reflections and level-headed discussions" (Osei-Tutu 2000: 71) – and offered their disapproval. The Ga Mantse strongly disagreed and stated his plan to continue supporting the ordinance. The Ga Mantse refused to succumb to popular pressure and was later deposed by his people in 1925 and officially destooled in 1929.

One of the crucial mistakes the Ga Mantse made was that he did not make his decision by subscribing to informal norms and duties of Ga political culture. He did not discuss the decision in a public meeting where he could come face-to-face with those he ruled (Osei-Tutu 2000: 73). When the Ga Mantse did finally call the populace together, he gathered them at a local place that signified belligerence or war, not compromise (Osei-Tutu 2000: 75). In these ways, he could not legitimate his decision, but rather was accused of forcing the ordinance on his people, and doing so on behalf of the colonial authorities. But this was not simply a struggle between the colonial state and Ga society. Instead, local political entrepreneurs used the institutional and cultural resources available to them to consolidate their own power.

Upon closer investigation, the situation represented a political struggle between Western educated elite Ga and the traditional "stable" poor, both of which sought the necessary political space to govern their daily affairs (Quarcoopome 1987). In fact, initially local Ga residents were not as forcefully resistant to the state or colonial rule: After the bubonic plague outbreak in 1908 residents understood the value of paying rates and cooperated with the Town Council. Instead, Quarcoopome explains: "This action, by a section of the people of Accra led by some divisional chiefs, was to make the

Ordinance unpopular and then to associate its enactments with the Ga Mantse with whom they were engaged in a dispute" (Quarcoopome 1987: 30).

The underlying political struggle involved the sitting Ga Mantse and the Asere Paramount Chief. In other words, the struggle over the Municipal Corporations Ordinance "was used as a tool in a chieftaincy dispute" (Quarcoopome 1987: 45). This approach to urban development shows how local political entrepreneurs build followings from the ground up, with the desire to dominate and control political space. The politicization of the chieftaincy is an enduring feature of Ga Mashie political life, as chiefs were deposed in the 1950s depending on which side of the political divide they lay and continues today (Austin 1970).

Incorporating Migrants into a Growing City

The growth of Accra involved the influx of Northerners, who were instrumental in transport and trade (Ntewusu 2012).[10] Increased migration to Accra was also the result of conflicts in other parts of the country, like the 1894 disagreements between Northerners and the indigenous leaders of Kete-Krachi, which initially controlled the kola nut trade (Maier 1980).[11] Northerners were influential members of the Gold Coast Constabulary, a police force that was used in the wars against the Ashanti, and in quelling riots in Accra (Parker 2000a: 105).

The formation of new neighborhoods made up of mostly Northerners was part of the urbanization process, as migrant leaders jockeyed for political position and mobilized their followers for privileged positions among indigenous landowners, as well as colonial authorities (Pellow 2002).[12] With declining cooperation of indigenous Ga leaders

---

[10] These include people from Northern, Upper East, and Upper West Regions, as well as people originating from Burkina Faso, Niger, Togo, and Nigeria. The most common ethnic groups are the Yoruba, Hausa, Fulani, Kotokoli, Mossi, Dagomba, Mamprusi, Grushi, and Gonja.

[11] There was also an influx of Northern migrants in 1874 as a result of the British-Ashanti War (Ntewusu 2012). There was another influx in the early 1900s as a result of the burgeoning cocoa trade (Brand 1972).

[12] Even the naming of neighborhoods is contentious, because "the power to control how the community is referred to by others" becomes a powerful "historical text" (Dakubu 1997: 10).

in municipal governance, especially with respect to collecting taxes, colonial administrators allied with migrant leaders and integrated them into the decision-making process (Ntewusu 2012: 37). Importantly, the formation of new neighborhoods was not a linear story of natural population growth, but a political process and response to disease outbreaks, where migrant leaders jockeyed for space to extend their political power. For example, Chief Braimah founded the neighborhood of Tudu in 1911, and Sabon Zongo was founded around 1912.[13]

Fulani herdsmen moved from Tudu and Adabraka to the new neighborhood called Nima in the early 1920s, preferring more space and control (Dakubu 1997). The origin of Nima traces back to cattle dealer and prominent Muslim teacher Alhaji Futa, who secured cattle grazing land from the Odukpong family of Osu and the Gbese people of Old Accra (Chambas 1979). Migrants moved in large numbers to Nima in the 1930s because they could not find accommodation in the growing city center, but also to avoid taxation as it sat outside the Accra Municipal boundary (Chambas 1979: 37). In this way, community leadership chose to exit the formal political system, allowing them to control their populations and provide informal services outside the control of colonial administrators.

Though Accra does not have natural resource endowments, it benefitted from the Gold Coast's growing cocoa trade as the commercial capital and port city. The 1919 and 1920 cocoa booms "brought an air of prosperity" to Accra, contributing to population growth, including the arrival of Asian, Lebanese, and Syrian merchants (Acquah 1958: 20). This coincided with the governorship of Sir Frederick Gordon Guggisberg (1919–1926) who is credited with the modernization of the capital city. The insertion of Accra into a global trading network "revolutionized" the city, contributing to the rise of land values, influx of capital and currency, and increasing dependency on the British (McPhee 1926: 2). The emerging kola nut and palm oil industries contributed to the increase in Northern migrants living in Accra (Ntewusu 2012).

The indigenous chiefs used this atmosphere of prosperity as an opportunity to demand public services; they collectively mobilized and secured the construction of gutters and wells (McPhee 1926).

---

[13] Sabon Zongo saw 12 percent growth between World War I and II (Brand 1972).

Benefitting from an enabling economy, the colonial government relied on close ties to indigenous leaders for access to land. The government built Achimota School, Korle Bu Teaching Hospital, and many other structures that signaled modern development. The colonial government sought to centralize planning, and the incorporation of indigenous populations into the decision-making apparatus was part of this strategy. The 1939 earthquake further intensified the need to build more housing and centralize planning, leading to the incorporation of Labadi in 1943, and government-built housing estates in many surrounding suburbs (Acquah 1958: 28).

Additional relocation of populations occurred after the earthquake, including resettled populations in Korle Gonno. During World War II, Nima residents served military officials in the nearby service barracks, working as cooks, stewards, laborers, porters, and prostitutes (Chambas 1979: 37). The demobilization of African troops in 1947 led to the move of ex-servicemen – many of northern descent, as well as people from the Gambia, Sierra Leone, and Nigeria – to Nima. Though the Gold Coast Housing Authority prepared a plan for the systematic growth of the neighborhood in 1945, no real infrastructural improvements were made. Residents relied on ethnic headmen for support, establishing patron-client relationships with them. Chiefs offered accommodation, job opportunities, and protection in exchange for honor and esteem. By the end of colonial rule, a stable equilibrium existed between indigenous leaders, migrant headmen, and formal government representatives. Yet it also signaled new opportunities for indigenous leaders and migrants to stake a new claim to decision-making power (Hart 2016).

The Challenge of Governing Poor Neighborhoods

The colonial administrators introduced the term "slum" for poor and underdeveloped indigenous and migrant neighborhoods outside of formal town plans and grids. Slums presented a serious governance challenge and were at the forefront of policymaking during colonial rule. They were considered a massive public health concern, with outbreaks of tuberculosis and the bubonic plague catching the attention of colonial authorities. Quality of housing was also central to debates in the Accra Town Council, the administrative body tasked with urban governance. The debates, politicking, and eventual inaction under colonialism demonstrate a consistent pathway in the growth of poor neighborhoods from the colonial period to the present.[14]

In the following pages I document examples of the process of decision-making in the Accra Town Council.[15] In the 1930s the Accra Town Council debated whether the municipal authorities should allow temporary "swish buildings" in Sabon Zongo, a poor neighborhood near the center of Accra.[16] The official building code did not allow these types of structures, but some members of the assembly appealed to the "prevailing depression" and "sympathy" for the poor residents. Those who supported the ordinance to demolish all structures made with swish materials made "slippery slope" arguments, suggesting that "if they were relaxed in this instance, other divisions in Accra as well as other communities throughout the Colony and Ashanti would ask for the same amendments for their building regulations."

The medical authorities framed the situation as a public health concern, claiming that "swish buildings harboured rats, termites, and other pests, and that after these houses had been built, dangerous borrow pits were left." Most notable in this account is that the authorities deemed the population of residents as squatters, and thereby temporary dwellers in Accra. The Medical Officer of Health further declared "that when houses are put up for sale for default of rates the Accra Town Council should buy them with a view to their demolition, if necessary, and the clearance of slum areas."[17] Bureaucrats attempted to politicize norms of belonging by emphasizing its temporary status. Yet on the ground, the neighborhoods were considered legitimate settlements because of the agreement made between the host population and the leaders of the migrant population.

For this reason, the communities were not defenseless. Three council members came to the defense of the Sabon Zongo residents, most likely as a way to score political points. Councillor Michael Thompson was perhaps the most vocal. He argued: "masons generally make

[14] I focus specifically on migrant communities in this section. But the persistence of government inaction was consistent across indigenous communities as well. For example, a 1908 ordinance in response to the need for disease control recommended demolishing houses of ethnic Ga on land near the new Harbour Works and Customs Office. However, the local Ga population resisted and would not relocate (PRO CO 96/470, Rodger to Crewe, No. 326, July 1, 1908, enclosed).

[15] All archival documents are from the National Archives Ghana Search Room.

[16] CSO/20/5. October 8, 1934.   [17] October 8, 1934.

mistakes in laying the foundations of buildings ... he asked that the owner of the building should not be penalized."[18] More importantly, he appealed to their plight: "He stated that Council should take into consideration the condition of the poor people, and if they could live in properly built swish houses, they should be encouraged to do so to avoid congestion."

Councillor Kitson Mills made a similar point that "he had brought up the question at the request of the people living at Sabon Zongo, who were poor and could not afford to put up cement block buildings." Another argument suggested that "Sabon Zongo was outside Accra proper and he failed to see why the poor people there should be bound by the Regulations." And perhaps most forcefully, one councillor added, "It would be bad policy to force our people to build beyond their means. He expressed the hope that Councillors would be sympathetic and consider the question seriously."

In the end, the ordinance to demolish these structures passed by a vote of four to three in favor of the demolition of the structures. But this did not mean that they actually were demolished. In fact, the situation persisted with government inaction.[19] The discussion of Sabon Zongo came up again on September 12, 1938 when the Municipal Executive's office issued the following: "I appeal to the President to stop the collection of hawker's licenses in this area until the Council has been able to discharge its own obligations."[20] The government did not demolish the structures but were still collecting rents, creating a confusing situation for residents and their political representatives. The inaction of the Assembly came up again with regard to the construction of the Municipal Sports Stadium in 1938.[21] Councillor Jones Nelson motioned that the demolition "will only be made possible by

---

[18] CSO/20/5. October 8, 1934.

[19] Government inaction was a consistent trait of colonial rule. Gale describes how in 1878 the Town Council passed the Towns, Police and Public Health Ordinance. The ordinance was meant to keep the town clean and provide proper sanitary conditions. The provision included: "No building could be erected without the Governor's permission, and decayed buildings must be repaired or demolished; the Colonial Surveyor was given the task of clearing and draining the streets, and the government could impose fines on those who committed public nuisances." Nonetheless, the ordinance was rarely enforced, and even inspired the Gold Coast proverb "Laws are passed to throw dust in the eyes of the Colonial office" (Gale 1995: 191).

[20] September 12, 1938.   [21] December 12, 1938.

being carried out by installments, a reasonable sum being provided each year in the Estimates of the colony for that purpose."

The Council politicized the issue of slum clearance to attract potential relocation packages for either themselves or those whose structures were to be removed. But in reality, the situation persisted: "Councillor Jones Nelson noted that since the outbreak of the plague in 1907 nothing had been done in the matter of slum clearance in Accra."

While there was a clear policy in place to remove unauthorized structures and demolition notices were handed out, government inaction continued:

The President had a list of 600 unauthorised structures. It seemed to him that the responsible employees of the Council were not doing their work properly but that failure on their part to report the presence of unauthorised structures might be due to a mental attitude induced by seeing unauthorised buildings springing up on all sides and their inability to take any action to remove these structures before the lapse of six or seven weeks ... The President remarked that he himself was shocked when he saw the list. If any one took the trouble to go round Accra he would find there were many buildings which should not be allowed to stand.[22]

Yet the reply to this statement by Councillor Mark Addy demonstrates that the Council's response was not due to a "mental attitude" but rather to rational political calculations: "Much suffering of privation is being felt and a general outcry against their removal exists." In other words, councilors adapted and responded to popular pressure.

Slum Clearance in Sekondi-Takoradi

The politicization of slum clearance was not just a problem facing Accra, but confronted other cities across the country as well, including Sekondi-Takoradi. In June 1938, the Sekondi Town Council deliberated slum clearance in their city.[23] They discussed the "congestion" in the city as well as a challenge to figure out what to do with the large "floating population" in the Gold Coast. At the heart of the matter was what to do with the people who would lose their structures, many of whom were fishermen.

[22] February 13, 1939.   [23] CSO 11/14/352. June 20, 1938.

One councillor argued: "It was undesirable to embark upon any scheme of slum clearance until the Council was assured that there was available land which could be placed at the disposal of the dispossessed."[24] Meanwhile, the Medical Health Officer urged for action: "It has to be borne in mind also that, quite apart from being overcrowded, many of these houses are crudely constructed, inadequately ventilated and lack almost all the minor comforts and conveniences appropriate to reasonably good habitations." But nonetheless, nothing was done and the situation persisted because "it will be possible to do more than complete the preliminary work connected with the formulation of a scheme of slum clearance until after the war."

Like Sabon Zongo, the situation in Sekondi presents a situation of congestion, over-crowdedness, substandard housing, and underdevelopment. While the government was attune to this situation and sought to fix it, it could not due to practical constraints. In this case, the political will was not there during the time period of World War II. Yet what these deliberations in the Accra and Sekondi Town Councils demonstrate is the overarching politicization of slum clearance schemes. State administrators used demolition notices and building regulations as a way to enforce social control. Politicians and councillors used the ensuing insecurity as a way to gain political support of local communities. With insecure property rights, local communities relied on politicians to support their cause.

The Construction of Legitimate Authority

In the context of slum clearance and insecurity, residents in poor neighborhoods found creative ways to secure protection and security of tenure. Local groups and populations formed patron-client relationships with members of the Town Council, colonial administration, and later political parties: They offered votes and support for protection and security of tenure. But the formation of these political constituencies occurred from the ground up outside of officially sanctioned activity. Groups jockeyed for local power, political entrepreneurs navigated the insecure institutional context in ways to personally enrich themselves, state administrators extracted rents and issued eviction and

[24] CSO 11/14/352. 1941.

demolition threats to establish social control, and bonds of social engagement developed between leaders and their constituents.

These patron-client relationships had an informal, but rational, logic. At the root of the situation was the settlement pattern by which populations settled the land, as strangers and squatters, respectively. Without formal housing rights, these populations were pawns in a larger political game, one in which the politicization of the situation simply led to the persistence of the status quo. State administrators established social control without having to provide services, or expend financial obligations. They could continue to extract rents from the populations.[25] Politicians acted as representatives of the local communities, and established themselves as powerbrokers. With the threat of demolition, communities relied on these politicians for security of tenure and protection from eviction. This pattern continued into the Independence period.[26]

Land and housing were at the center of these early political struggles. Early settlers to the city established authority on the ground and struggled to establish control of the housing market. The family heads became "headmen," or a sort of chief (*odikro*), in the new neighborhood, extending custodianship over land held by family members and new settlers not related to him (Apter 1955: 90). He distributed land to newcomers, providing economic power. These original settlers quickly became political figures, and strong opinion leaders in their neighborhood.

In the absence of state social welfare, they played a role as caretakers of the community. Deborah Pellow argues, "A man could establish himself by providing others with lodging. This primarily meant enacting the traditional role of the *mai gida* or patron. Such a man not only

---

[25] Colonial officials were really only interested in their own well-being.
F. Fitzgerald, a London editor of the *African Times*, wrote condemningly of the colonial officials as people who could "enjoy their mistresses and drink their brandy and champagne upon a dungheap, provided they may occupy the highest positions on the stinking mess" (Gale 1995: 187).

[26] The situation was further propagated by specific policies that encouraged extraction of resources over investments in urban sustainability and planning. Gale writes: "It was clear that African towns were being permitted to grow in much the same unplanned, unhealthy manner in which early British industrial towns had developed ... The problem was not simply a lack of funds ... [but] the lack of commitment to spend money on major sanitary projects" (Gale 1995: 197–198).

needed to have money, but also had to be generous with others ... In this foreign situation, if a man died on the street and had no kin nearby, the *mai gida* would buy the necessary cloth and coffin and see to his burial" (Pellow 1985: 431). While these figures certainly resonate with African cultural patterns, they were also notable for their economic and political importance.

The most important resource that they controlled was housing because they could provide accommodation for clients, which included brokers, assistant-brokers, clerks, servants, and errand boys.[27] Most of the important local political disputes were the result of underlying struggles for control over housing. Securing land and housing brought great political power to local leaders. These so-called business land-lords had important political power, and served as authority figures in these new settlements.

For migrant noncitizens, the establishment of patron-client relation-ships was particularly acute (Peil 1971). This is because residents relied on these connections for protection of their livelihoods: They feared being deported. In the context of Kumasi – the second largest city in Ghana – Schildkrout writes, "Their settlement was encouraged, for as strangers they had no traditional authority and were dependent on the government for permission to remain in the town and, even more, for any rights and privileges they required" (Schildkrout 1978: 67). There were also significant differences between first- and second-generation migrants (Skinner 1963). Early stranger populations had closer con-nections to traditional African authorities while second-generation migrants established closer links with Europeans and had more auton-omy in relation to customary authorities like local chiefs. Yet, trad-itional chiefs still had power via their control of land, and distributed it in exchange for presents and indebtedness (Skinner 1972: 1211).

Local communities forged alliances with those who provided access to housing and land, and while these relationships changed with formal institutional change, the groups in these communities still self-organized in ways to protect their economic livelihoods. The most effective patron is usually felt to be the one with whom a group of strangers has a close relationship at a particular time, and this depends

---

[27] Cohen describes this function in his discussion of a migrant neighborhood in Ibadan, Nigeria (Cohen 1969: 72). This pattern is documented elsewhere: Skinner (1963, 1972); Arhin (1971); Schildkrout (1970, 1978); Peil (1971); Pellow (1985, 2002); Barnes (1986); Allman (1991); Kobo (2010).

upon the exchange of favors, including political support. Since many strangers are vulnerable because they are not citizens, "they are in need of protection from officials; strained relations with those in power can mean a real risk of deportation" (Schildkrout 1970: 258).

Yet, locally, ethnic groups jockeyed for political alliances and protection; poor communities were not homogenous entities (Allman 1991). Ethnic groups acted as interest or pressure groups: They self-organized to put pressure on state authorities for distribution of services (Cohen 1969). For example, in the aftermath of the 1939 earthquake, organizations from stranger settlements entered the political fray to demand humanitarian assistance (Allman 1991). Therefore, groups formed locally in order to extend their political power.[28]

Leaders also needed the recognition from state authorities to legitimate their rule within their own communities – they sought being "gazetted" in local newspapers to recognize their role as headmen in particular ethnic communities (Pellow 1985: 434). This allowed them to serve as judges in local disputes, which brought gifts, status, and prestige. This anthropological approach to the study of urban political development shows the role that ordinary residents, political entrepreneurs, and social networks play in the construction of political communities.

Settling in Kumasi

These political dynamics were not restricted to Accra or Sekondi-Takoradi. Enid Schildkrout carefully documents how politics of settlement and belonging characterized the urbanization process in Kumasi. For example, in the thick of Britain's colonial project in the Gold Coast in 1927, a chief of a Kumasi migrant settlement was officially incorporated into the Native Administration, the bureaucratic section of the colonial government in charge of indigenous African affairs.[29] Until this point, leaders of these *zongo* communities held local authority but

---

[28] Similar patterns were observed in urban Nigeria: Leaders used their patron and middleman roles in their quest for authority, and used patron-client relationships to generate attention and "move upward in the political hierarchy" (Barnes 1986: 11).

[29] The following history of political development in Kumasi's *zongos* derives from Schildkrout (1970).

were not officially recognized by the government.[30] In this capacity, the newly installed chief was nominated to serve on the Kumasi Public Health Board, ran his own court tribunal, and successfully mobilized unpaid laborers for community labor exercises. The power of the position was emboldened by his link to colonial authorities.

Kumasi's urbanization was well on its way, but the integration of migrants into the state apparatus was neither linear, nor passive. Rather, it was a contentious and political process that included extensive jockeying between groups and political factions for formal recognition. These political battles extended well into the 1950s, when most *zongo* leaders in Kumasi aligned with the Asantehene, the king of the indigenous Ashanti ethnic group. The leaders directly involved themselves in multiparty politics, forming a political bloc that opposed the governing CPP. But underlying these alliances were new deportation laws in 1957 that expelled many leaders, accusing them of being non-Ghanaian citizens.

But these leaders had a rival. In 1958, the CPP constituency chairman gained formal recognition as chief of the *zongo* even though he did not have majority support in the neighborhood. The CPP consolidated its power in the *zongo* communities and established voluntary organizations that were closely aligned with the party. Residents were interested in party politics only insofar as they related to the appointment of ethnic headmen. Ethnic leaders received their authority directly from the government, through their alliances made with the CPP. Yet without cross-ethnic alliances and popular legitimacy on the ground, these leaders could not effectively govern or mobilize support in their own neighborhoods.

Urbanization after Independence

Ghana's path to Independence is typically described in linear terms: The urbanization of society coupled with a growing and ever-powerful political class contributed to a vibrant Independence movement. The

---

[30] In Nigeria, *zongo* is used to refer to a cattle market (Cohen 1969). In Ghana, early inhabitants of these neighborhoods were Muslims from the Northern Territories. Today, they are generally understood to contain a strong Muslim identity and speak the Hausa language, although not all are of the Hausa ethnic group (Kobo 2010).

dominant narrative suggests that a cross-ethnic and cross-class move-ment emerged in Accra, leading to collective mobilization, but never guerilla warfare in the countryside or mass violence. In addition, the lack of a settler colony in British West Africa was seen as a boon to indirect rule and eventual independent rule, allowing a shift of author-ity that was already working in concert. But this linear approach obscures the rise of contention between a growing urban intelligentsia and traditional authorities that date back to early years of colonial rule. The introduction of multiparty politics intensified these rivalries (Yakah 2016).

Early signs of unrest occurred in the 1930s over the price of cocoa, as Ashanti chiefs aligned with colonial authorities to raise the price of cacao (Austin 1970: 10). These growing divisions played out in pro-tests in the Accra riots of 1948, where an estimated twenty-nine people were killed and 200 injured in demonstrations over food prices. These protests signaled more than an elite fracture, but also the rise of ordinary commoners in the political process, especially "elementary-school-leavers" who were looking for a political voice (Austin 1970: 15). The CPP took advantage of these disgruntled commoners, and mobilized them into their organizational machinery – especially in urban areas like Accra: "The youth societies became branches, and the malcontents party secretaries" (ibid: 27).

This had important implications for urban governance: The CPP co-opted metropolitan affairs, and there was little separation between the party's organization and city hall. The urban poor remained loyal to the CPP, receiving private and club goods in return, even though no large-scale development occurred. The CPP could win the necessary votes by catering to the private needs of the urban masses, while overlooking urban development projects. During this period, the CPP was particularly concerned with winning enough votes, as political competition was incredibly high, as well as quashing opposition.

The CPP saw important resistance to their leadership in the early years of its rule in Accra, when the *Ga Shifimo Kpee* – "Ga Standfast Association" – split off from the CPP in Nkrumah's own Odododio-dioo constituency – which encompassed the heart of Old Accra called Ga Mashie. The Ga nationalist organization demanded better servi-ces, employment opportunities, and housing accommodation (Hodge 1964). They couched these demands in tribal and ethnic language, relying on demands of indigeneity and entitlement drawn from their roots to the capital city. But these fears extended to issues of land alienation, where Ga feared the influx of outsiders into their city, particularly those of the Akan (Fridy and Brobbey 2009). The political economy of land contributed to these fears: Due to a demand for government and private firms, the price of land increased significantly in the early 1950s, and Ga landlords alienated thousands of acres of land to turn a profit (Pogucki 1955). Land speculation became a lucrative business, and Ga leaders and politicians benefited from the rising land values (Onoma 2009).

By the early 1950s, the land question was the most contentious issue in Accra, with prominent Ga leaders accusing Nkrumah of selling off their land to outsiders (Quarcoopome 1992: 47). While the *Ga Shifimo Kpee* did not gain widespread support due to its close connections to the political opposition, it did force the CPP to confront the land question, and organize its own counter Ga nationalist organization, the *Ga ekomefeemo kpee*. Battles between these two groups in the streets of Old Accra became rowdy and violent (Hodge 1964). But more importantly, it encouraged the state to get more involved in land deals and restrict the sales of land to foreign businesses, contributing to the politicization of land rights in the city. Just as importantly, the CPP used the state apparatus to weaken its opposition. Nkrumah went as far as to arrest forty-three members of the *Ga Shifimo Kpee,* accusing them of trying to overthrow the government (Quarcoopome 1992: 49).

Nkrumah's centralization of power was a political strategy to counteract growing opposition from various parts of the country, including Ashanti and northern regions (Rathbone 2000; Yakah 2016). The tightening of power spilled over to urban governance, contributing to coercive management including demolitions and displacements. State-led development projects were central to Nkrumah's plan to modernize the country, and cities were at the forefront of his industrialization policies. For example, the government of Ghana acquired the land surrounding the Korle Lagoon (which includes modern-day Old Fadama) in 1961 for purposes of urban development, paying relevant compensation to the Gbese and Korle stools, and relocating residents to New Fadama (Grant 2006). Additionally, Nkrumah developed the city of Tema on the outskirts of Accra, and moved the major port there (Chalfin 2014). These strategies had consequences: They established social control over certain populations, and institutionalized patterns of loyalty and patronage with selected neighborhoods and community leaders. Nkrumah cracked down on opposition, making political opposition a costly strategy. Nkrumah's industrial strategy also undermined the price of agricultural goods, contributing to the rapid migration of rural dwellers to cities looking for work (Bates 1981). Once in cities, migrants competed with indigenous traders for jobs and economic influence, contributing to local tensions during the ensuing decades (Peil 1974; Kobo 2010; Honig 2016).

The government also had to deal with growing dissatisfaction in Accra stranger communities, like Nima and Sabon Zongo. These neighborhoods symbolized Accra's growing population, as well as the rise of a heterogeneous population and the formation of a cosmopolitan city.[31] For example, in 1949 the Nima Development Committee formed to demand development and represent the interests of residents (Chambas 1979: 85). The committee was set up to lobby the government to provide services to the neighborhood.[32] In 1951 Nima was officially incorporated into the city limits of Accra. In 1952, Kwame Nkrumah led a large rally in the neighborhood and promised to transform Nima into a "city in a city," a slogan that has not been forgotten by the residents of the neighborhood (Chambas 1979: 88). The struggle for authority deepened when the CPP extended its organizational machinery into the neighborhood in 1953, co-opting already existing groups like the Young Pioneers and the Worker's Brigade (ibid).[33]

The Ghanaian government specifically highlighted settlements with large migrant communities like Nima and Maamobi as neighborhoods that were under resourced and in need of upgrading in its urban plans. In 1954, local ward members aligned with the governing political party were successful in getting four public latrines built for residents. The struggle to upgrade Nima, as well as distribute resources to the neighborhood, was highly contentious. Arn (1996) tells the history of

---

[31] By 1960, the African stranger population had risen to 98,780 people, making up approximately 30 percent of the population (Quarcoopome 1993: 29). By this time, the Ga population made up only 51.6 percent of the population (Acquah 1958).

[32] Kobo (2010) suggests that a *zongo* Muslim identity arose after the 1948 earthquake. Muslim leaders organized to demand help to rebuild their homes, presenting a new challenge to Nkrumah's rule (Kobo 2010: 72).

[33] Nkrumah personally elicited the support of *zongo* leaders in the lead up to the 1956 elections, giving them the title "chief of propaganda" (Rouch 1956: 58–59).

attempted intervention in Nima, documenting the proposed campaigns of slum clearance that started with the "Accra Slum Clearance Committee" formed in 1961. The committee identified Labadi, Nima, and James Town as potential spaces for upgrading, but Nima leaders never organized effectively to make the plan a reality. Over the course of the 1950s and 1960s, the government shifted from a strategy of recognition and service provision, to ignoring them altogether. While it threatened to evict and displace them, the CPP's dependence on their political support contributed to an equilibrium where the communities exited formal governance, and the government continued to ignore the needs of the population.

Meanwhile, Nkrumah used citizenship laws to weaken his opposition. In 1957 he deported several opposition leaders and Lebanese and Syrian merchants because they were "threats of the social order" (Kobo 2010: 75). Subsequently, the Aliens Act of 1963 required all noncitizens to have residence permits. In 1968, the Legislative Instrument 553 ordered all migrants to have a work permit (Peil 1971).

After the overthrow of the CPP in 1966, there was a small political opening at the grassroots for collective action. For example, the residents' committee in Nima was reformed and renamed the Nima Development and Welfare Committee. Though chiefs showed up at early meetings, recruiting members was needed because the chiefs and tribal elders stopped showing up to community meetings, signaling their political apathy (Chambas 1979: 87). Independent political voice was difficult to achieve, as political parties quickly got involved. Politicians in the Progress Party like I. C. Quaye, attempted to disband the welfare committee due to its expected allegiance to the CPP. Residents were also afraid to get involved in community affairs because of widespread condemnation by the new government; citizens feared that their previous connections to the CPP could get them in trouble, even jailed.

In 1970, a more serious plan came from the Accra-Tema Metropolitan Planning Office, calling for the relocation of more than 50 percent of residents for redevelopment (ibid: 438). The headline of a *Daily Graphic* article on March 4, 1970 was "Nima to Go." A "commercial speculative scheme" was introduced in 1972, with plans to relocate residents to Madina, Ashaiman, or Dansoman. In 1973, Ghana's head of state Col. Acheampong led a sod cutting ceremony for this project. As the population of Accra spread out from downtown, Nima now sat on valuable land in the center of the city. Redeveloping the neighborhood could help modernize the city, and provide investment and kickbacks to the political and business class.

Vibrant collective action among community members was crucial to the community's resistance to eviction and demolition. Chiefs and landlords were most vocal against the redevelopment plans, realizing that it was an attack on their authority. In 1968, Christian students from the University of Ghana formed Operation Help Nima (OHN) to resist the redevelopment plans.[34] Their strategy shifted from demanding help from the outside to "help the people of Nima help themselves" (Chambas 1979: 99). OHN centralized leadership in the community, even bringing leaders of Nima and Maamobi into a unified structure. But the group was also instrumental in getting the Odorkwei family, the traditional landowners of Nima, into the political decision-making in Nima by incorporating them into the welfare committee (Chambas 1979: 69). This bargain had an important consequence: It signaled a political alliance with the indigenous Ga, lessening the fear that indigenes had of the new migrants.

The organization was also instrumental in getting compensation and relocation options for residents when construction for the Nima Highway began in 1975. But there was internal contention: Some residents accused them of serving the interests of the landlords, and not the majority of poor dwellers in the neighborhood. Over time, OHN became the de facto speaker for the community, contributing to friction between them and community leaders and chiefs.[35] But the neighborhood's collective capacity placed important pressure on government authorities to provide services and development, and to prevent forceful evictions from their property.

The incorporation of "aliens" remained a contentious issue. In 1969 the Busiá government decreed the Aliens Compliance Order, demanding all "aliens" without residency permits to leave the country within

---

[34] OHN was funded by Christian organizations in Britain, the Netherlands, the United States, and other Western countries through the Christian Council of Ghana.

[35] As one leader said, "Every year the OHN people get money from abroad on our behalf but they never let us know how much. And always they tell us they have discussed so and so with the government – sometimes we don't really understand the proposals they put forward to the government on our behalf but we hope they are actually going to be in our interests in the future" (quoted in Chambas 1979: 108).

two weeks. The Order severely impacted the Yoruba and Igbo immigrants, who were seen as a local economic threat to indigenous urban traders (Honig 2016). During a severe economic downturn, migrants threatened the governing regime, and expelling them was a tactic used to undermine the political power of the opposition (Kobo 2010). But alliances with host populations allowed these populations to overcome these expulsions and return to these neighborhoods when relations were regularized. The Order solidified *zongo* neighborhoods as reliable vote banks for parties of the Nkrumahist tradition, as *zongo* residents could no longer trust parties in the Danquah-Busia tradition. Clearly, government policies significantly shaped residential and political patterns in postcolonial urban development.

The Search for Greener Pastures

The housing shortages in cities, as well as the dilapidation of poor neighborhoods, intensified during the Independence period. In response, at the early years of Independence President Nkrumah launched a modernization campaign that placed access to affordable housing at the center of the agenda (Elleh 2002). The government formed the State Housing Corporation and the Tema Development Corporation (TDC) to deal with housing issues. TDC, for example, purchased sixty-four miles of land seventeen miles outside of Accra and formed the city of Tema.

While Tema and Ghana's modernization campaign served as important pull factors from the countryside to the city, not all migrants could afford formal housing. Instead, neighborhoods like Ashaiman developed as squatter settlements in the early 1960s. Located just across the Tema motorway, the settlement provided low-cost housing to workers who could not afford accommodation in the planned city. Residents constructed houses made of cardboard cartons from shipping containers, corrugated iron sheets, and simple sheets of plywood. Non-natives of Tema who were displaced when the government constructed the port were also designated plots in Ashaiman, but the area was meant to be a temporary settlement (Owunsu 1991).

Ashaiman quickly grew due to lack of affordable housing in Tema, unregulated official land and housing control, and nearby opportunities for employment. During the 1960s and 1970s, it developed a burgeoning informal business sector, where an estimated 79 percent of residents were employed (Kirchherr 1968 cited in Owusu 1999; Mazeau, Scott, and Tuffuor 2012). At the early stages of settlement, many of the settlers were skilled or semiskilled workers (Sandbrook and Arn 1977). The population rapidly grew from 185 in 1948, 2,624 in 1960, 22,000 in 1970, to 50,000 in 1984, and today is estimated at over 230,000 people. The settlement is now part of the "Accra-Tema city-region" (Yeboah et al. 2013).

At first, the entire community was a squatter settlement. But parts of the settlement developed on customary land while others developed on government land, leading to distinct developmental trajectories of particular neighborhoods (Peil 1976). Residents who purchased customary ownership have legitimacy, while those squatting on government land fear that a politician, soldier, or other government worker might take the land away for "the good of the nation" (Peil 1976: 165). This contributes to variation between Ashaiman neighborhoods today, and is the reason why the neighborhood variation displays different authority structures.

For example, the neighborhood called Tulako developed as a squatter settlement. The word Tulako means "logs" in Hausa and the settlement was labeled this because the early settlers tied their cattle to logs, and from there a large cattle market developed. In the early 1960s, there were very few structures and people in the area. Rather than formal land title, customary ownership, or other markers that might designate control of property, early arrival and subsequent local control mark the roots of political development.

Today, Tulako rests along the major thoroughfare, alongside the only traffic light in the city. In the 1960s and 1970s, there were few houses around the traffic light, but there was a church with a mud house made with thatch and "some one or two scattered houses here and there."[36] The early settlers were Nigerian migrants who were involved in cattle rearing. As is typical in most Ghanaian informal settlements, local spots within Tulako were named after the local big men who established territorial control. But they were given indigenous Dangbe names, because as an indigenous resident explains: "We will not sit down [and allow] aliens to come and name the places."[37] The neighborhood remains a first stop for new migrant arrivals, especially those coming for economic opportunities. "It is a place where

[36] May 5, 2012.   [37] May 5, 2012.

they can lay their heads while looking for what they came for," one leader explains, "until they get where they can finally work and get their daily bread."

The settlement of Ashaiman was not without its problems. "When settlers came," one resident recounts, "some were able to acquire land by dubious means. Sometimes the people would sell land to 2 or 3 people. When the authorities came to demarcate the land, 2 or 3 would come. People have to be fast enough to 'create documents.' People will fake documents. The strongest people will win. If people know people, it will happen." For these reasons, political alliances matter a great deal in the control of urban space.

But the early settlers worked together to solve these disputes, and had the authority to determine cases. In the early years, even the police and the state stayed out of these affairs. Other settlers remember the lack of order and security during the early years of settlement. "Ashaiman started as a 'haven'—just like Australia did—with convicts. As a kind of slum. There is a place called Site 1 where laborers were housed. They moved toward this place as settlers. It started to develop in a haphazard manner. Lots more people started coming in," one early settler, who came in 1974, recounts. "All this area was actually a forest. Around '68 and '74 you dare not be around the Station at 3PM. You'd be attacked."[38] Little by little, the early settlers attempted to clean up their community: "You'd see pigs destroying all the gardens. We had to help control the pigs. People would steal fuel. We'd have clean up campaigns."

Yet Ashaiman was well organized from the early days of settlement. Each ethnic group had their respective hometown associations; friends' clubs met on Sundays; religious groups met during the week; youth clubs met throughout the week.[39] When Rawlings implemented the People's Defense Committees – the mobilization structures of his revolutionary government – Ashaiman residents were easily regimented to participate. Leaders quickly gained the legitimacy of their land by

---

[38] February 27, 2012.

[39] Sandbrook and Arn documented this local associational activity in the 1970s, "The local chieftaincy and Northern Ghanaian headmen dominate the existing Ashaiman Development Committee, with the established churches, market women and the Youth Council also having representation ... As well, there is an Ashaiman Landlords Welfare Association which provides a specific service to landlords in Ashaiman" (Sandbrook and Arn 1977: 63–64).

aligning with customary authorities and securing the legal recognition of their neighborhoods.

These community leaders play an instrumental role in local politics. Landlords tried to secure title in various ways, through giving gifts to customary authorities or by formal sales (Barnes 1974 quoted in Peil 1976: 162). Landlord associations became active in local politics, helping bring together neighbors from different ethnic groups. As demand outpaced housing supply in the 1960s, Tema realized that there was a growing problem and allowed the building to continue (Owusu 2004). Moreover, they tried to control some neighborhoods in town by aligning with local leaders to demarcate formal plot sizes, allowing them to regulate the development and extract taxes from residents.

Ashaiman is distinct from other neighborhoods because the migrants' claim to most of the land is considered a legitimate purchase in the eyes of customary authorities: They are not squatters who are staying temporarily. For early settlers, moving to Ashaiman provided not only an opportunity to purchase land and property, but also the chance to found a political community and expand authority. This is consistent with the settlement of *zongos* across the Greater Accra region. For example, Alhaji Seidu Kardi exchanged gifts with customary authorities for Madina in order to "play a more important role as local leader" (Peil 1976: 163); Malam Nelu purchased a plot of land at Zongo Malam; Malam Bako founded Sabon Zongo (Pellow 1985); and Braimah founded Tudu in in the early 1900s (Ntewusu 2012). Establishing roots in Ashaiman provided these same political opportunities. The legitimacy of settlement and inhabitancy provides the basis for urban development that serves the public interest in stranger settlements today.

Failed Government Housing Policies

Despite Ghanaians search for greener pastures in the outskirts of Accra in neighborhoods like Ashaiman, the housing shortage in urban Ghana continued into the 1970s.[40] Ghana faced a housing deficit of 736,657 in 1970; 1,184,636 in 1984; 1,526,275 in 2000; and 1,600,000 in 2010 (Awuvafoge 2013: 13). In 1986, the Ministry of Works and Housing formed a National Housing Policy Committee to examine

---

[40] This section is adapted from Paller (2015).

the housing situation in Ghana (Bank of Ghana 2007). The report detailed a comprehensive strategy to improve service delivery across the country, mainly focusing on institutional mechanisms that could coordinate the process. This new plan was part of a broader strategy, instigated by structural adjustment programs, to shift the focus of affordable housing from the government to the private sector.

The state withdrew from direct housing production and financing and attempted to stimulate the growth of the real estate sector and the indigenous market. The 1980s also marked the emergence of the new interest group Ghana Real Estate Developers Association, who represented the private interests. In effect, quasi-government agencies like Social Security and National Insurance Trust, entrusted with the responsibility of public housing development, have decreased their investment in public housing by 50 percent over time (Arku 2009).

The government's strategy in 1991 shifted from an emphasis on direct provision to coordination. Further, "the shortage of housing has given rise to very high occupancy levels, unaffordable rents, unstable tenancies and poor living conditions. These factors, combined with issues of land litigation, high cost of building materials, shortage of skilled manpower and infrastructure services, underline the seriousness of the problems facing housing delivery in the metropolitan area" (Republic of Ghana 1991). Until 1990, the strategic plan estimates that 15 percent of the housing stock was government provisioned housing; it rapidly declined with structural adjustment and the inability of the State to finance and provision more housing. In 1990, the plan estimates that the housing shortage was 19,135 units of accommodation.

The government's shift toward a liberal approach to development included the attempt to regularize land tenure security. According to this perspective, affordable housing in neighborhoods where housing rights are not secured and owners are unable to produce capital are problematic. This informal housing market produces "dead capital," and residents are unable to invest in their homes and leverage their ownership assets into other progressive development (De Soto 2003). To deal with this challenge, the World Bank-supported Land Administration Project was implemented to "harmonize statutory laws and customary interests bearing on Land" (World Bank 2013).

The ambiguous and insecure land tenure regime has long been recognized as an impediment to economic growth in Ghana, and an impediment to accessible affordable housing (Besley 1995; Goldstein and Udry 2008). The Bank of Ghana recently found that, along with the rising cost of inputs, land acquisition is the driving force behind the rising price of housing in Ghana (Bank of Ghana 2007). The high costs complement the fact that land transactions are not recorded, titles are not provisioned, and multiple individuals and families claim the same plot of land (Onoma 2009). The government recognized that customary law needed to be better incorporated into the formal state property rights regime (Blocher 2006), and the Land Administration Project attempted to do this. But the project has been for the most part unsatisfactory due to its inability to register the majority of land, and effectively manage the land allocation process (World Bank 2013).

By the end of the twentieth century, the state and formal private enterprises had failed in their attempts to provide sufficient housing to urban residents, including upgrading poor neighborhoods. The international community has attempted to play a role in facilitating the process of increasing access to housing for poor urban Africans (Arimah 2010). For example, the Ghana Poverty Reduction Strategy (GPRS) I, implemented in 2001, focused on attracting foreign capital to fund housing development. The GPRS II (2006–2009) specifically focused on poor and marginalized populations, detailing a special program for slum upgrading. The Cities without Slums action plan, under the auspices of the Cities Alliance and the Slum Upgrading Facility are the cornerstones of the agenda. These programs seek to mobilize foreign capital and to link this financial assistance with local actors. The projects seek to package the financial, technical, and political elements of development projects (Durand-Lasserve 2006).

While the outcomes of these policies are still incomplete, several scholars blame them for contributing to a housing market privileging the rich over the poor, increasing income inequality, and undermining an indigenous housing market that favors the poor (Gruffyd Jones 2009; Obeng-Odoom 2012). Despite the formal housing shortage, Ghanaians continue to migrate to cities in large numbers. With the government, international community, and private businesses unable to keep up with the growing demand of housing, residents seek alternative means to access and secure housing. The outcome of these failed public policies is the growth of squatter settlements and the rising number of urban residents living in these neighborhoods.

The Growth of Squatter Settlements in the Era of Democracy

Today, Accra is an ethnically diverse city in a multiparty democracy.[41] The rapid population growth of the city coupled with insecure and ambiguous property rights has transformed Accra's cityscape (Grant 2009). While squatter settlements were rare in West Africa before 1990 (Peil 1976; Konadu-Agyemang 1991), they have proliferated across the continent in the last twenty-five years (Fox 2014). Increasing land values mixed with rapid urbanization has forced poor migrants to squat on government land and private property. Government policies have been unable to solve these challenges. They have not produced improvements in neighborhood infrastructure and youth unemployment, instead focusing on land tenure formalization and public-private partnerships that advantage the elite (Obeng-Odoom 2010).

Ghana's government frames squatters as a nuisance, dangerous, and unsanitary (Afenah 2012). Today, this stage of urbanization exists alongside rising globalization, contributing to new political geographies that connect the local and the global scales (Grant 2009). The growing importance of international organizations like the World Bank, Slum Dwellers International, and Amnesty International in urban planning and slum-upgrading projects shifts incentives on the ground, and provide new sources of funding for urban priorities (Gulyani and Talukdar 2007; Huchzermeyer 2011). They also contribute to neighborhood political rivalries and new types of community decision-making (Paller 2015; Stacey and Lund 2016).

Globalization and multiparty democracy has greatly impacted the struggle for incorporation among urban neighborhoods like Old Fadama, and it has been well documented (Grant 2006; Braimah 2010; Afenah 2012). But the role that neighborhood leaders play, as well as the incentives of NGOs and their intermediaries is less understood. The rapid growth of Old Fadama is illustrative of the rise in the population of squatters across the country.[42] In 2002, the community received an eviction notice, ordered to quit the neighborhood to give

---

[41] According to the 2010 census, 40 percent of the city is Akan; 27 percent is Ga; 20 percent is Ewe; and 13 percent is Northern ethnic groups.

[42] In 2004, the Ghana Homeless People's Federation estimated the population of Old Fadama at 24,165. By 2006, community leaders estimated the number to be closer to 35,000 (Grant 2006). A community-led enumeration in 2009 counted 79,684 residents (Braimah and Owusu 2012).

way to the Korle Lagoon Ecological Restoration Project. The Centre for Public Interest Law fought on behalf of the evicted in court, but lost. Though the government did not follow through with the eviction, it continued to use early morning sweeps – locally called "join the line" – to spark fear in the population and impose social control. While the government wanted to develop the land as part of its campaign to modernize the capital city, the residents made up an important vote bank in the very important and competitive Odododiodioo Constituency. The campaign in the lead up to the 2004 election quelled the immediate eviction, and the defeat of the NPP parliamentary candidate provided a short-term safety net for Old Fadama residents, who helped win the election for the NDC candidate.

Leaders in the neighborhood organized with help from the NGO People's Dialogue for Human Settlements (PD), an affiliate of the international Shack/Slum Dwellers International (SDI). The NGO immediately became the speaker for the community, forming the Ghana Federation for the Urban Poor (GHAFUP) as a subsidiary that it could control and collectively organize when need be, as well as OFADA as a leadership body. Farouk Braimah, the executive director of the organization and expert on urban development, established close ties with the Ministry of Water Resources, Works & Housing, Ministry of Local Government and Rural Development, and the Ministry of Tourism and Diaspora Relations, as well as the mayor of Accra (Braimah 2010). A plan was put in place to resettle the residents, making PD the de facto organization that would control the process on the ground, giving it control over funding and selecting recipients. PD urged residents not to build permanent houses, nor invest in public services, wanting to signal to the metropolitan authorities that it was ready to relocate.[43]

But the 2008 elections changed these tactics. The incoming NDC government appointed a new mayor, and internally disputed what to do about the neighborhood. The mayor had alliances with the Ga chiefs, and promoted eviction and demolition without supporting compensation. The chiefs viewed the squatters as trespassers on their land and city, and an impediment to potential kickbacks on development deals. The President, on the other hand, urged the protection of

---

[43] There are also rumors that the Vice President was in charge of negotiations, but could not broker a solution in a timely manner.

human rights and "eviction with a human face." When John Mahama became President in 2012, rumors spread that his brother had plans to redevelop the Korle Lagoon environs, sparking new fears of potential eviction.

Meanwhile, the neighborhood had grown to 80,000 residents, and NDC politicians relied on these people for votes. From 2008–2016, the NDC extended its organizational machinery even more, expanding from eleven local branches to twenty-seven. Without the capacity to demolish all the structures at once, the mayor targeted sections of the neighborhood, focusing on the outer edges of the neighborhood. Demolitions occurred in 2012 and 2015, signaling the coercive capacity of the metropolitan government.

With new eviction threats, PD now had something to fight for again, and reentered the decision-making sphere.[44] Evictions offer opportunities for NGOs to enter political decision-making. PD revived OFADA after the demolition, and began organizing community leaders. With a recent victory by the NPP in the 2016 elections, new calculations will likely form.[45] One of the major changes is that the city authorities now recognize the Yam Market, which sits on the edge of the neighborhood. Leaders of the market have direct interaction with city authorities without passing through OFADA. Accra Metropolitan Assembly now provides sanitation in the market.[46] They also pay market tolls to AMA. Therefore, the immediate surroundings of the market are considered safe from demolition. Because this neighborhood is made up of people from the Konkomba ethnic group, their chief has become very powerful. The assemblyman also plays a political role as more parts of the neighborhood become legally recognized due to the vibrant commercial activity.

All of these developments have led to what Stacey and Lund (2016) label a "state of slum," where there is "a sharp contrast between

---

[44] Stacey and Lund (2016) assert "OFADA interprets interactions with government as a validation of their claims as a legitimate local authority and facilitator of local development" (610).

[45] One of the major contributions to the NPP's electoral victory was its ability to make inroads to *zongo* communities, increasing its support in urban areas (Bob-Milliar and Paller 2018).

[46] During my fieldwork there were 216 administrative units – called MMDAs – that are in charge of local government affairs. There are now 254. The President appoints the chief executive, or mayor. The goal of the assemblies is to promote local economic development.

locally produced institutions that enjoy the power to govern but do not have the legal backing to exercise authority, and statutory institutions that are assigned the formal authority to rule but do not have the power to do so" (Stacey and Lund 2016: 611). The constant, daily interactions between informal authorities and municipal workers, party agents and opinion leaders, blur the neat line between state and society. One thing is clear: The battle for legitimacy and recognition in the city is a political one, and extends far beyond NGOs like PD and municipal authorities like AMA, to the opinion leaders and political parties that govern these urban spaces.

Conclusion

As the historical development of Accra suggests, urbanization is not a linear process. Rather, it is the outcome of a politically contentious struggle over claims to territory and control over space in the city. This struggle traces back to precolonial times, and persists today.[47] Failing to account for the diverse ways that leaders and residents gain power and control urban space ignores how Ghanaian cities actually grew over time. By reconstructing the political history of urbanization in Ghana, I set the stage for understanding how the everyday politics in Ghana's neighborhoods is the outcome of a long and contentious political struggle over authority and control of the city.

---

[47] See Figure 2.1.

Everyday Politics in Urban Ghana

Part II provides a glimpse into the everyday politics of Ghana's urban neighborhoods. The bulk of the empirical evidence is qualitative, drawn from my multi-sighted ethnography. I document the day in which I recorded the observation – either through an interview, informal conversation, or observation at an event in the neighborhood – in the footnotes to be very transparent about the process through which knowledge is created. Each chapter starts with a discussion of everyday politics of Ga Mashie, the indigenous core of Accra. I then explain how stranger neighborhoods in Ashaiman overcame political clientelism, created public spheres for a diverse set of residents, and overcame ethnic politics – despite occasional setbacks. The third section of each chapter explains the politics of Old Fadama, pointing to the challenges of sustainable urban development in the squatter settlements of these sprawling Ghanaian cities. The empirical evidence of these three neighborhoods is meant to illustrate the politics of indigenous, stranger, and squatter settlements, respectively.

Chapters 5 and 6 also include evidence from my household survey to show that the mechanisms, processes, and practices evident in the three case studies generalize to a broader sample of sixteen neighborhoods across the country (also see Table A.1 in Appendix). The quantitative evidence is not meant to prove the theory. Rather, the survey data provide additional evidence that the everyday practices evident in the case study neighborhoods represent broader patterns of politics across the country. Both sources of data present a view from below – how leaders and residents construct institutions and participate in decision-making processes in their neighborhoods.

4 | The Construction of Legitimate Authority

Ghana's Fourth Republic – the period of multiparty politics since 1992 – is one of the most successful periods of democratization on the African continent. During this period, there have been three turnovers of power between political parties. The Ghanaian voter has become more educated and knowledgeable about the democratic process, and demanding of his or her political representatives. Despite the process of democratic learning, experts are quick to declare Ghana a "patronage democracy" with a political settlement based on "competitive clientelism" (Abdulai and Hickey 2016; Gadjanova 2017). On the ground, Ghanaians call this a "winner-takes-all" political system – the governing party captures state resources and distributes them to their followers. A burgeoning literature in African politics attempts to explain this phenomenon by relying on an instrumental understanding of political clientelism, namely that patrons rely on clients to win elections in exchange for goods and services needed for poor people to survive.

Yet the conventional political science approach overlooks how leaders control space and territory, as well as how leaders evolve in Ghanaian cities. Moreover, it fails to consider how leaders bolster their reputation by gaining admiration and respect among followers. In urban areas, there are multiple avenues of personal advancement for leaders, and elections are only one means to achieve these aims. By focusing solely on the electoral process, these theories miss how legitimate authority is constituted in neighborhoods in the context of daily life. Politicians, party brokers, and assembly persons must legitimate their authority at the grassroots first, achieving the status of opinion leader before they enter formal positions of power. They gain admiration and respect from their constituents by accumulating wisdom and providing advice, and they achieve a social status and reputation based on these characteristics. This, in turn, helps them control territory and urban space, a prerequisite for formal political power.

119

These patterns of legitimate authority vary across settlements. The informal norms of settlement and belonging shape distinct authority structures, providing an explanation as to why neighborhoods have different kinds of opinion leaders. This chapter draws from ethnographic observations to demonstrate these differences. First, I explain how Ga leaders in indigenous neighborhoods must subscribe to customary norms, as well as be from traditional families that control land. They are typically chiefs, family elders, religious leaders, and landowners.[1] I then discuss how leaders in stranger communities like Ashaiman must help people from different groups and ages, demonstrating a commitment to the neighborhood that expands beyond their family or clan. These opinion leaders include teachers, religious leaders, landlords, and other civic leaders.

Finally, in squatter settlements like Old Fadama, leaders can rely on fear and coercion to maintain authority, especially because residents rely on "big men" to secure their tenure. In addition, leaders seek alliances with political parties, but capture goods and services to distribute to a narrow following from their hometown, using their newfound power to potentially enter formal positions of power back home. Opinion leaders are slumlords, scrap dealers, political party branch representatives, NGO workers, and youth club executives. The chapter provides an institutional explanation based on informal norms of settlement and belonging to demonstrate why political clientelism in urban Ghana persists.

History and the Control of Space in the Indigenous Core of a City

In the indigenous core of a city, including the neighborhood Ga Mashie, the evolution of leadership dates back to the earliest settlers. The historical evolution of these neighborhoods shapes the type of leaders that emerge. These leaders must come from powerful traditional families, suggesting that lineage and chieftaincy institutions still shape the selection of community leadership today. These dynamics are apparent in the everyday politics of indigenous neighborhoods, where the following event illustrates how the control of space and territory is tied to the construction of legitimate authority.

[1] See Table 2.1.

In June 2012, the Ga State lifted the ban on noise making and drumming in the lead up to its annual Homowo Festival.[2] The Ga community held a large ceremony at a royal family palace entitled "Peace, Progress and Development."[3] The official statement was posted on the website of the Government of Ghana with the following statement: "It is the prayer of the elders that the entire political leadership in the country, will live up to their word, to give mother Ghana peace, progress and development." The ceremony included royal family members like those of the Tackie Komme We, luminaries and politicians including the Regional Minister, Minister of Works and Housing, area MPs, and local youth hired to serve as security guards. Tourists and the media also attended the event.

The Ga community wanted to project a unified, glamorous celebration to the outside world. Hundreds of residents and visitors attended the event, royal family members paraded through the streets in their traditional garb, and the party lasted late into the night. While the ceremony was indicative of traditional ceremonies that take place across the country, it was most notable for the underlying informal politics that structured the event: Only a portion of the Ga community attended the festival because since 2007 there has been a divisive chieftaincy dispute that has pitted family members against one another and divided the community.[4]

At this particular event, most of the political leaders were affiliated with the NDC and were of Ga-Dangbe origin.[5] But everyone in

---

[2] June 7, 2012. The Homowo Festival is the annual harvest festival of the Ga people. There is an annual festival and parade through the streets of Ga Mashie. See: Quartey-Papafio (1920).

[3] The event was held at the Gbese Blohum. Ghana's government commissioned the sign as a token of respect. It provided recognition of the Ga people, while also securing legitimacy in the process.

[4] Those in attendance supported the controversial Nii Ayi-Bonte II as the Gbese Mantse, and the accredited Wulomei of the Ga State led by Nuumo Ogbarmey III (Sakumo Wulomo).

[5] Politicians included (at the time) E. T. Mensah, the Minister for Works and Housing, Nii Laryea Afotey Agbo, the Greater Accra Regional Minister, and Odododiodioo Constituency MP Jonathan Nii Tackie Komme. Numo Blafo, the Public Relations Officer for Accra Metropolitan Assembly participated in the ceremony. The Tackie Komme We strongly endorses Ayi-Bonte II, as the Odododiodioo Constituency MP and his brother marched in the ceremony. Nii Okai and Brunos, two local "thugs" who are known to support Tommy Okine and other NDC politicians, led the security guards; they also work as land guards for various Ga big men.

attendance supported Ayi Bonte II, aka Tommy Okine, as the chief of the disputed Gbese stool.[6] Contrary to the fears of many community members, the celebration was peaceful. In 2010, fights broke out at the event and gunshots were shot near the royal palace. In 2011, only a very small crowd gathered for the celebration. The chieftaincy dispute continues in court, with both sides winning important judgments in various levels of the court system.[7] The fact that it is an election year only seemed to heighten the tension. This is because the NPP is perceived to support Okine's opponent, Nii Okaidja III. The belief is that if the NPP wins the 2012 election, Nii Okaidja will gain the upper hand and take over the royal palace.[8] While none of the leaders who support Nii Okaidja attended the celebration, the ability of the opposing claimants to carry out peaceful events on behalf of the Ga community bolsters Ayi-Bonte's power and legitimacy in the community.

The close alliance with the Accra Metropolitan Assembly (AMA) among this Gbese faction also bolsters their popular legitimacy and demonstrates how Ga indigenous politics underlies formal politics and development. Ayi-Bonte II's backing by AMA, as evidenced by the appearance of its spokesperson and the government's official announcement of the event, gives him important political backing and ability to influence decision-making. This is further evidenced by the ability of Okine and the Ga Mantse to align with city authorities like AMA to carry out issues of development.[9] For example, earlier in the year the mayor of Accra and a caravan that included several cars of Ga traditional authorities arrived in Old Fadama and along the railways with the goal to evict squatters: They painted the words "Gbese land" on structures that they wanted demolished.[10] The mayor used

---

[6] Tommy Okine is former CEO of Hearts of Oak, the football team that is perceived to align with the NDC and draws support from Accra, particularly its indigenous areas like Ga Mashie (Fridy and Brobbey 2009).

[7] For example, in 2014 the Supreme Court ruled in favor of Nii Okaidja III, which ruled the 2003 ruling null and void (which enstooled Tommy Okine). Nii Okaidja III was again enstooled in 2007. A group of kingmakers enstooled Okine again in 2016.

[8] Okaidja has the support of NPP big men like former Regional Minister Sheik I. C. Quaye, former Accra mayor Stanley Adjeri Blankson, and current MP aspirant Victor Okaikoi. These fears have been reignited after the NPP won the 2016 presidential election.

[9] There are allegations that Adama Lantse Ayi Bonte II, a recently enstooled chief, also receives support from AMA.

[10] November 18, 2011.

his close alliance with this faction of the Gbese people to bolster his popular support to carry out his plan for redeveloping and moderniz- ing the city. This would allow him to reward his loyal followers and bolster his support among his club.

The popular perception among Accra residents is that the mayor was appointed as AMA Chief Executive because of the support he had from the Ga chiefs. The Ga chiefs are important brokers because they are the custodians of the land, a very important condition in a country under the jurisdiction of customary land ownership.[11] But perhaps just as importantly, the Ga authorities use formal political institutions to broaden their own support at the local level. As one Old Fadama resident explained, "Sometimes Ga chiefs do this to extract and make money—and to put fear into people."[12] According to a Ga Mashie resident, they are simply trying to build their case as the legitim- ate traditional authorities of the Ga people: "By coming through the community it looks like they are doing something for their people. This is especially true when the Adama Lantse is trying to build support for his case to the throne."[13] In this way, multiparty politics is embedded in the context of indigenous institutions that frame daily political life in Ga Mashie. In other words, Ga community leaders use multiparty democ- racy to bolster their own support in underlying chieftaincy struggles.[14]

In recent years, there has been a resurgence of African politics schol- arship on traditional chiefs.[15] Perhaps the most important book to date is Kate Baldwin's (2016) *The Paradox of Traditional Chiefs in Demo- cratic Africa*, which suggests that the return to multiparty elections has empowered chiefs to become more important to the political process. Baldwin argues that chiefs can help improve the democratic process by improving the responsiveness of governments. She argues, "Elected politicians can respond most effectively to rural constituents through

---

[11] For example, the Acting Chairman of the Ga Traditional Council, Nii Dodoo Nsakie, claims that the Ga authorities will not support the mayor unless he demolishes structures and evicts squatters on Ga land: "Until Dr. Vanderpuije demolishes Sodom and Gomorrah, all his effort will be null and void. If he does that, we (Ga Traditional Council) will give him the needed support to stay in office."

[12] November 22, 2011.   [13] November 22, 2011.

[14] There is a long history of this across the country. See: Jockers et al. (2010); Stacey (2015).

[15] Studies include Williams (2004); Ntsebeza (2005); Logan (2009); Onoma (2009); Englebert (2010); Acemoglu et al. (2014); Boone (2014); Wilfahrt (2018a, 2018b).

institutions constructed and maintained by unelected leaders who are unconcerned about losing power" (5). In later chapters, she calls chiefs "development brokers," perpetuating the idea that chiefs "serve" the formal government representatives.

While Baldwin's book addresses the role of rural chiefs in weak states – not urban areas like Ghana – it suffers from another limitation: a formal institutional bias that treats them as subsidiaries in a larger political game. Even the way she sets out her premise demonstrates this bias: "The logic behind and the effects of *allowing* traditional leaders increased authority in developing democracies" (italics my emphasis, page 5). By stating the issue in this way, she takes agency away from the chiefs, and suggests that the democratic system "allows" traditional authorities increased authority. This negates the historical evolution of chiefs as opinion leaders in their communities, struggling for control and authority over territory since the precolonial era.[16] It undermines the agency that chiefs have in building their own case as legitimate authorities.[17]

In this way, cities provide multiple avenues toward political and economic empowerment, which rests on the ability to profit from rising property values, as well as compete for positions in social institutions like chieftaincies and family stools. A focus on the everyday politics of neighborhoods calls into question the formal bias, and treats traditional and customary institutions as actors in their own right, with motivations and incentives that extend beyond the instrumental role of winning elections. In indigenous neighborhoods, chiefs are important opinion leaders that control urban space and territory.

Everyday Politics of Chieftaincy Disputes

There is a vibrant anthropological literature that critically examines the role of chiefs in Ghanaian society, and treats them as independent

---

[16] In fact, there is a long history of traditional authorities and elites fighting against state power in Ghana. Most notably, the Aborigines' Rights Protection Society (ARPS) was formed in 1897 to contest the Crown Lands Bill of 1896 and the Lands Bill of 1897. These bills threatened customary land tenure. The defeat of these bills institutionalized the power of traditional authorities, especially with respect to control of land.

[17] For a more empirically accurate description of the politics of the chieftaincy in Accra, see: Naaborko Sackeyfio-Lenoch (2014). To understand the role that colonialism plays in the development of the chieftaincy, see: Mamdani (1996).

actors. For example, Carola Lentz and Christian Lund have described the ways chiefs compete for authority, especially in Northern Ghana (Lentz 1998; Lund 2006; also Stacey 2015). As I traced in Chapter 3, the tensions between traditional authorities, politicians, and government representatives date back to colonial times, and emerged as an important arena of competition during Kwame Nkrumah's presidency (Rathbone 2000; Parker 2000a; Sackeyfio-Lenoch 2014). While this approach captures the importance of traditional authorities to local communities, it underemphasizes the way that they engage with political parties.[18] Both approaches miss how these different actors form coalitions – but also divide residents – in the context of daily life. The following example explains how chieftaincy disputes manifest in the daily politics of indigenous neighborhoods.

In Ga Mashie, politicians publicly acknowledge their support to certain sides of a chieftaincy dispute, contributing to divisions in the community. Residents and leaders on the ground attach political party affiliation to certain sides of the dispute. In the recent Ga Mantse dispute, one side claims that King Tackie Tawiah, aka Joe Blankson, was enstooled by the NPP government. While traditional authorities rarely publicly pronounce their support for a political party, residents verify alliances by indicating which events the leaders attend, as noted in the vignette just described. But the opponents use this against them. "We have people who are Chief Contractors," the Asere Kingmaker explains, for example "Blankson is not from the Royal House. He is a politician from the NPP government. He was put in by force."[19]

Disputes over the Gbese Chieftaincy and Ga Mantse continue to divide the community, thus affecting the developmental prospects of the settlement more generally. Because of the Ga Mantse dispute, all money that is allocated for development to the Ga Traditional Council is frozen until disputes are settled. Nii Okaidja III, one of the claimants to the Gbese throne explains how chieftaincy disputes undermine development, "When governments come to power, they work hand-in-hand with the traditional Councils to fast-track development in the various communities. But when there are chieftaincy disputes, it retards development and that is the problem we are facing. Chieftaincy

---

[18] This is the strength of Baldwin's (2016) book.
[19] July 5, 2012. A Kingmaker is a position in the royal family that plays a central role in the selection of chiefs and kings.

disputes have, actually, retarded the progress of Ga State and this must stop now" (Odoi-Larbi 2012). Yet these disputes are deeply rooted.

In a focus group, Ga Mashie youth explain their frustration with the chieftaincy disputes. "When you look at Sempe, they have two chiefs, two queen mothers," a respondent explains. "At Gbese, someone knows he is not fit to be a Chief but he is forcing himself to be one. When you see people fighting for position it means there is some wealth to be looted that explains that behavior."[20] More damaging, is that the chieftaincy disputes divide the community and impede development. Residents recount the time after a chief was dethroned that biscuits, shoes, and dresses for children were left inside the palace and were never distributed to those in need. While unemployment often draws the attention of politicians, policymakers, and the media, a major problem lies in the lack of accountability of Ga Mashie's community leaders.

There are no accountability mechanisms to hold the traditional authorities and chiefs to account. Most residents do not think the Chiefs do anything for the community. One man said, "They get slush funds from the government and use it to enrich themselves. They don't even live in the community."[21] For these reasons, residents do not respect their chiefs. "We do not fear [respect] them," one resident said.[22] But the traditional authorities matter for more than symbolic reasons: They control the family land, and developers and politicians must rely on them if they want to pursue development projects. In his excellent book *The Politics of Property Rights Institutions in Africa,* Ato Kwamena Onoma explains how Ga chiefs have used this to their advantage, empowering themselves through allocating land multiple times (Onoma 2009). In the indigenous core of a city, government administrators must work with chiefs to pursue their policy agenda. As I will explain in the next chapter, politicians offer customary entitlements in exchange for land and property needed for development.

This is apparent in the opening vignette of this book where Member of Parliament Nii Lantey Vanderpuye cozies up with a fetish priest to pursue his development agenda. The relationship between the two figures is performed in quotidian practices and habits, similar to what Javier Auyero (2001) describes in his study of clientelism in Buenos

[20] June 20, 2012.   [21] December 7, 2011.   [22] December 15, 2011.

Aires. For example, in May 2012, the fetish priest celebrated his fiftieth birthday party. To honor Nana Odupon Okomfo Abeka Sikafo II, and to thank him for his valuable support, Vanderpuye donated 500 Ghana cedis for his birthday party. The priest has been an NDC insider since former President Rawlings staged his first coup d'état in 1979. He is also the father of sixteen children with ten different women. At his birthday party he relished his role as father figure. While various women cooked large bowls of rice, stew, and chicken, he was in charge of dishing out the food on people's plates. He made sure that all visitors would eat. This activity held symbolic power: As a leader, he fed his followers. His various children brought the plates out to the important visitors from the community, thereby strengthening social support for the priest and indirectly solidifying political support for Vanderpuye.

An ethnographic approach to the everyday politics of Ga Mashie highlights the importance of these otherwise unobserved details. As Clifford Geertz (1973) carefully observed the power dynamics of a Balinese cockfight many years ago, and Lisa Wedeen (2007) makes meaning of the $qa\bar{t}$ chews in Yemen, the priest's actions demonstrate the important ways that he legitimates his authority as an opinion leader. The fetish priest, and by extension Vanderpuye, was fulfilling what Michael Schatzberg (2001) calls the moral matrix of legitimate governance. Leaders are expected to fulfill their role as fathers and caretakers, and they do so quite literally throughout the practices of daily life.

During the Homowo Festival, Vanderpuye sponsored another event at the fetish priest's house. He made a banner with both of their pictures on it and displayed it on the main street. The banner symbolized Vanderpuye's support of Ga indigenous culture, as well as the fetish priest's political support for Vanderpuye. The metaphor of legitimate governance took on a very instrumental role during campaign season: Politicians rely on family heads to secure votes and improve their electoral chances, as Staffan Lindberg suggested in his discussion of how informal institutions contribute to the persistence of clientelism (Lindberg 2010). In this way, Vanderpuye tapped into his "cultural tool kit," as Swidler (1986) called it, and used the underlying norms of indigeneity to advance his own political power. The reality in daily life complicates Baldwin's (2016) optimistic picture of the relationship between chiefs and political parties. While family heads serve as intermediaries between the party and the residents on the ground, many locals also see them as an impediment to progress and development.

How Indigenous Norms Structure Leadership Selection

Family lineage continues to shape politics in indigenous neighborhoods. While political campaigns might try to withdraw publicly from engaging in chieftaincy struggles, family lineage continues to influence voters and legitimate candidates. In other words, politicians must prove themselves to be opinion leaders in their community before they can win elections. Because family lineage shapes legitimate authority, it structures the leadership selection of its politicians. While these underlying norms have the potential to complement formal governance, they play a competing function in Ga Mashie because the informal norms of indigeneity "structure incentives that are incompatible with the formal rules: to follow one rule, actors must violate another" (Helmke and Levitsky 2006: 15). In order to win "democratic" elections, candidates must subscribe to the informal norms of indigeneity that structure leadership selection.

For example, Vanderpuye's campaign highlighted that he comes from a very powerful clan, Lante Djan-We.[23] This clan is "steeped in tradition" as they are the first clan to celebrate the Homowo Festival, the most important annual ceremony of the Ga. But Vanderpuye's family connections are not without dispute. Some members of the opposition claimed that he is not really from the Lante Djan-We family, but rather from Otubluhom, a different quarter of Ga Mashie.[24] These family alliances are particularly important in indigenous settlements because they signal "who came first, and how," marking an important political resource to extend authority. The politics of indigeneity translates directly into leadership selection for formal political positions.

The importance of family requires a brief history in Ga Mashie and Odododiodioo formal politics.[25] Since multiparty democracy emerged in 1992, family lineage continued to influence the choice of candidates.

---

[23] December 17, 2011.

[24] As one member of this family said, "We have the Blanksons, Lawsons, Mays, etc. But we do not have the Vanderpuyes" (July 3, 2012).

[25] This section was first published in Paller (2014).

For example, in 1996, New Patriotic Party (NPP) candidate Samuel Odoi Sykes struggled to overcome the fact that he is perceived to be from La, outside of Ga Mashie with different family histories. His opponent, Nii Okaidja Adamafio is from Gbese, in Ga Mashie, greatly bolstering his electoral chances. Adamafio narrowly won the election. "The message caught up with people," one politician said.[26] In 2000, Nii Ayi Bonte won the election for the NPP. He was selected as NPP's candidate largely because he is from Gbese, his father was Chief of Gbese from 1959–1978, his great-grandfather was Chief of Gbese from 1911–1940, and the acting Chief is his father's first cousin. As Ayi Bonte said frankly, "You are an indigene, you are the Chief's son, so they voted for me."[27]

In the by-election of 2005, the NDC considered similar family dynamics when choosing its parliamentary candidate. The NPP selected a candidate who happened to be a "Captain of War." Anis Mankattah was an "Asafoatse" – traditional Ga leaders who are marshals of war. In response, the NDC then decided they needed someone to counter this captain of war, so they selected Jonathan Nii Tackie Komme who is a royal king. The NDC believed that because the king trumps the captain of war, they could get more supporters. As one man said, "It worked—you follow the king." In 2008, the NPP selected a man named Adjei Sowa to contest against Tackie Komme. He lost to Tackie Komme. As one politician explained, "He [Adjei Sowa] did not have support because of his name. He comes from Teshie. They look at names. Tackie Komme used this against him."[28] In contrast to government performance, ideology, or programmatic ideas, the institution of family continues to influence leadership selection in the local politics of indigenous neighborhoods, contributing to a specific type of political clientelism.

Conventional theories of political accountability posit that elections serve as a way for voters to sanction leaders for poor performance, or select candidates that are thought likely to respond to the needs of constituents (Przeworksi et al. 1999; Golden and Min 2013). But as this evidence demonstrates, elections serve as an arena for underlying informal norms of indigeneity to become actualized. Formal institutions do not have independent effects; informal

[26] June 8, 2012.   [27] June 8, 2012.   [28] June 8, 2012.

institutions compete with formal rules and procedures in indigenous settlements like Ga Mashie.

Legitimate Authorities, Shameless Opinion Leaders

In the literature on political clientelism, brokers are typically viewed as the people who bridge political parties with constituents, who might include traditional authorities.[29] But in urban indigenous neighborhoods, local opinion leaders often represent the parties and the traditional authorities, complicating the relationship between politicians and voters. While opinion leaders might hold important legitimacy stemming from their ties to important families in the community, they do not necessarily represent the interests of the broader public, or even a large voting bloc. They often serve the needs of a narrow "club."

The example of Nii Kwatelei Owoo suggests how opinion leaders can be legitimate, but act without shame. This runs counter to studies of informal institutions whereby leaders subscribe to social norms of shame and honor (Tsai 2007). Nii Owoo is a family elder and his family is engulfed in a court case over land. The Owoo clan is trying to reclaim land that Owoo's ancestors sold to the colonial government in 1921. The family is suing the Achimota School, arguing that the school has not used the land for the educational purposes that they expressed when they bought the land in 1921. The school is now using it for an ecotourism park. The family is embroiled in a court case demanding the land back.

Owoo constantly said that it is a burden on him as a family elder to lead his people without land. "It will be difficult to take care of my people," he said.[30] Here, Owoo notes that leaders are expected to control land and urban space in order to constitute legitimacy. His court documents state that the family has lost more than 90 percent of its lands through government acquisitions, "rendering the family virtually landless." Nii Owoo emphasized the injustice and how his family is suffering. The document continued, "The Nii Owoo family is desperate and concerned about the plight of the indigent and landless Gamashie people." He then emphasized the injustices of colonialism.

---

[29] Most recent studies of political clientelism take this approach, including Hicken (2011); Stokes et al. (2013); Larreguy et al. (2016).
[30] July 5, 2012.

"The land was compulsorily acquired," he explained. "We did not buy it according to proper value. We were forced to sell it."[31]

But Nii Owoo is a controversial and polarizing figure. He is the head pastor of the Rejected Cornerstone International Ministry, a charismatic church in Ga Mashie. While the church boasts more than 200 followers, some residents in the surrounding area express their distrust of the church. One resident says the church steals the money of the followers and the pastor uses it for his personal empowerment. He is accused of being a false prophet. Nii Owoo is also a political figure. He explains, "If a pastor says he is not a politician, he may not know what he is doing. All pastors are politicians. And pretending does not bring us anywhere." He is an NDC activist and works on Vanderpuye's campaign and publicly supports him. "As regards for Nii Lantey, I see what he can do. How he relates to the indigenous people. I choose him," he says. He uses his political connections to assist him with his court case. He explains, "He is helpful with relations to the President." Nii Owoo is also the Executive Director for a land investment firm, and he attempts to use his political connections and influential Ga networks to profit from the growing Accra land market. Many other family heads have also stepped into this position of power (Paller 2014).

The claims of historical injustices through the rhetoric of indigeneity are common in Accra today. The Asere Kingmaker makes a similar claim: "We are not lucky. All the Natives of the city, in every country, the government has taken lots of land without paying any compensation. It deprives you of taking care of your people. If our grandfathers did not give our land out, we could take care of our people."[32]

But skeptics blame the chiefs for "filling their own pockets" and not investing back in the community. This is consistent with Onoma's (2009) argument that in urban settings, chiefs do not have the incentive to secure private property rights, but instead allocate plots to multiple

---

[31] Sara Berry's (1993) excellent book documents how indirect colonial rule in Ghana started commercializing property, while the government attempted to subscribe to customary norms and rules of land tenure. However, many land transactions occurred where there were still disputes over property, as well as the meaning of "native" and "custom." These legacies have not been adequately dealt with in postcolonial Ghana, and ambiguous land tenure rights and property disputes persist.

[32] July 5, 2012.

individuals to enrich themselves. Many youth complain that "Our leaders don't help us, they care about themselves alone."[33] Because the traditional authorities control access to land, they can make a heavy profit when land is sold. The Asere Kingmaker explains the process: "The lands belong to the family. The family has to sell the land. Then the family brings the paper to me and I sign it. So my name is on the paper. I don't sell land. I just get the signing fee."[34] But even the Asere Kingmaker's position is in dispute – his brother is now claiming the position. The problem is that his brother is a known supporter of the NPP and is a well-educated lawyer who is affiliated with the Ga Traditional Council. The Asere Kingmaker, on the other hand, is aligned with the NDC (although he claims that he "does not do politics") and has enstooled a disputed Gbese Mantse and Ga Mantse. The belief on the ground is that customary law privileges big men and politicians to take advantage of the land market. Land access and control is then politicized, contributing to insecurity and deep divisions in the neighborhood.

Catherine Boone (2014) traces these chieftaincy conflicts to the colonial patterns of land settlement, whereby British authorities never confiscated land from indigenous populations. In systems of customary ownership, conflict then takes the form of communal struggles whereby lines of struggle emerge within groups and neighborhoods. These kinds of internal rivalries are apparent in Accra, where many of the forms of political violence can be traced to chieftaincy disputes and intra-Ga struggles over power and authority.

While the true motivations of leaders like Nii Owoo and the Asere Kingmaker are conjecture, the role of Ga leaders in the Accra land market is undisputed. What is less known is the way that local leaders benefit from the customary land institutions. Customary law and norms shape the incentives for community leaders to keep land and property rights ambiguous in order to benefit from rising land values (Onoma 2009).

A fetish priest explains how the land market works: "One of our brothers will sell a piece of land. They will collect the money and immediately tell their cousin. The cousin will then go to the plot with macho men and demand payment, saying it is their plot. They do this constantly."[35] The land market has established an illicit business where

---

[33] June 20, 2012.   [34] July 5, 2012.   [35] April 5, 2012.

community members serve as land guards and "macho men" for area big men. These deals can be extremely lucrative. For example, one known land guard now drives around Ga Mashie with a Mercedes convertible.[36] But it is also important to emphasize that these behaviors signal a high status and prestige, providing a moral basis of legitimacy that should not be overlooked (Owusu 1970). Many residents perceive this behavior as subscribing to the competing informal institution of indigeneity.

In a neighborhood like Ga Mashie, unemployed and uneducated young men find lucrative employment opportunities by working as land guards and macho men. Indigenous status incentivizes this behavior through the logic that the Ga people are the owners and custodians of the land. Therefore, they have the right to control it, access it, and profit from it. These young men often also work for political parties as "political muscle" and foot soldiers (Bob-Milliar 2012; Klaus and Paller 2017). While it is difficult to get accurate data on how widespread this behavior is, the ethnographic evidence suggests that land ownership and entitlement to Accra shapes the power dynamics of Ga Mashie in daily life. Residents also perceive it to be a big problem, and many family struggles and rivalries are fought because of land disputes.

These dynamics are intensified in the current era of democratization. The Ghanaian government has a mandate to develop neighborhoods. With the political and economic center of the country in Accra, the government relies on their close connections with Ga family heads to purchase land for development. Therefore, the exchange of customary entitlements for land becomes a self-enforcing mechanism of particularistic politics. Chiefs and traditional authorities act in these ways across the entire country, including in squatter and stranger settlements. The difference is that in indigenous settlements this behavior is considered legitimate, and residents expect their leaders to make strong claims to land, as well as state resources. Even without access to elections or state resources, these patterns of legitimate authority emerge, calling into question theories of political clientelism that privilege the desire to win elections above all else.

---

[36] April 9, 2012.

Expansion and the Struggle for Space in a Growing City

The growth of cities like Accra has changed the dynamics of African societies by bringing together people from different ethnic groups into a limited physical space. These previously unsettled neighborhoods become arenas of politics where early settlers establish themselves as leaders, creating new authority structures distinct from indigenous chiefs and elders. These patterns have been well documented by anthropologists and historians like Sandra Barnes and Deborah Pellow. For example, in *Patrons and Power*, Barnes (1986) intricately details the different ways that a migrant community forms in Lagos, Nigeria, documenting how chiefs, traditional authorities, and landlords settle disputes, serve as intermediaries between political parties and residents, and solve collective action problems. Similarly, Pellow's (2002) *Landlords and Lodgers* documents the internal organization of a Ghanaian *zongo* community, demonstrating how daily practices, physical space, and struggles for power overlap in a rapidly changing city.

These books are essential for understanding how opinion leaders emerge in migrant communities, and how they engage with indigenous leaders and populations. Additionally, these neighborhoods have rich histories, emerging in the early 1900s when colonialism changed the economic vitality of cities, as well as in the early years of the Independence era when state-led modernization campaigns infused new investment into urban centers. The following sections build on Pellow's and Barnes' important arguments, but address how these authority structures continue to shape multiparty politics today.

The "Old Pioneers"

Explaining the origins of Ashaiman, Mr. Selassie said "If you want[ed] a place to sleep … you just clear[ed] the place, and put your head [down]." In the early 1960s, he was one of the early settlers in the community, looking for a cheaper alternative to Tema, a planned and expensive housing estate nearby.[37] "Then Ewes come in … then there was one Dagomba man who shifted the refuse dump here to the next

---

[37] For a good discussion of the historical development of Tema, see: Chalfin (2010, 2014).

house," he said, referring to the large garbage dump that was cleared and moved to make way for more settlers.

"Then one old man, Mr. Narter, from Ningo, came to clear the place, he is also a cattle farmer and a cattle trader. Then came a Dagomba man called One-one, he is still alive." Selassie's voice trailed off, until he remembered the others. "That is when my brother came in. My brother put up three wooden structures for the first time then it was rented by these Ewes ... so in short we have Hausas, we have Ewes, we have Dagombas, as well as Dangbes." Selassie was especially proud of the multiethnic settlement that developed. His recollection of the settlement reflects the nature of how property rights are understood informally, in relation to the early settlers who originally laid claim to the land. In this way, leaders became "stationary," laying claim to a piece of land and establishing authority in that place.[38]

A teacher at Christian International School, Selassie was one of the founding elders of Ashaiman. These elders maintain authority and are prideful of the city they helped settle. They refer to themselves as the "Old Pioneers." Selassie recounts one of the pioneers: "Doctor Afenyo used to call people and tell them to clean up. He was strict." He started a private school in the center of town, and his son is now a leading political candidate in the NDC party.[39] Another pioneer, "Abogo owned a lot of land and sold a lot of land." A third, Chief Driver Alhaji Yuseif Ibrahim was a one-time chairman of the NDC: "He called me once to have me bring in the students to mobilize youth. He is very rich. He owns a lot of cattle. The rich men were supporting the teachers. This is how rich people came into politics."

Leaders were expected to serve the community first, and then they entered formal politics. The early leaders established private schools, health clinics, and settled disputes. They also led communal labor exercises, especially during the regime of President Jerry Rawlings who made communal labor central to his agenda. "People who refused to participate in clean up exercises," Selassie recalls that the elders "would not let them open their shops ... Those who refused were forcibly given shovels to do some digging. After a while we would all benefit."

---

[38] This is similar to Olson's (1993) concept of stationary bandit, though I do not imply that these leaders are autocratic or monopolistic, though they can be.

[39] His son is Tony Afenyo, a parliamentary candidate in 2012.

These founding pioneers form the roots of political development in Ashaiman. They are still opinion leaders today. For example, Baba Alhassan, one of the early Dagomba migrants served as assemblyman for two terms in the 1990s. He was instrumental in clearing the roadways to make way for two-lane roads. His deputy Honorable C succeeded Alhassan as assemblyman and represented the Dangbe community. He also was close to the Tema Chief, which helped legitimate his rule at first but later undermined him because he was accused of colluding with the customary authorities to sell off the land. Residents relied on these leaders for security of tenure because they did not have a formal title. At the same time, these men grew powerful because of their commitment to the neighborhood. Baba Alhassan would take in guests from the North on a regular basis. He was recognized as a very kind man. Honorable C had a large compound where youth would gather to discuss community affairs.

The close links that the "old pioneers" had with the traditional authorities contributed to an implicit bargain: Indigenes and migrants would work together for the improvement of the community.[40] Traditional authorities would rely on migrant leaders as intermediaries in land sales, while migrant leaders relied on authorities for tenure security and legal recognition. These sales would become more lucrative as urbanization increased, and the Ghanaian state invested in infrastructure and public service provision.

Demographically, the ethnic makeup of Tulako is similar to Old Fadama. There is a significant number of Dagombas and Ewes. But one tribe does not dominate leadership, as community members explain, "Since growing up different tribes have had their members as assembly member. The first assemblyman was an Ewe, and then we had Dagbani, Ga and Dagbani assembly members."[41] The authority patterns in Ashaiman neighborhoods differ because landlords settled early and purchased structures, and then became opinion leaders in the community. One resident explains how this plays an important role in community affairs, "Here, you rent a room in a house where there is a landlord who advises you, and stops you from misbehaving, but over there [in Old Fadama] people own their kiosks, they are not living in

---

[40] These relationships are well documented in other contexts in Schildkrout (1978); Barnes (1986); Pellow (2002).

[41] June 14, 2012.

houses, so they do what they want good or bad."[42] One resident added, "Here, we have older people who talk to us. They calm us down."[43]

Residents also rely on the elders for jobs. Youth work for elders who own butcher shops, transport companies, restaurants, and auto repair garages. Therefore, youth are forced to respect and submit to authority for daily livelihood and survival. One young university student explains how these landlords serve as de facto parents: "The landlord of this house, his name is Father Abdullai. Father Abdullai can serve as my father. If you have problem, you just go to him. Even if he does not solve [it] he will guide you to solve it."[44]

"Leaders gain power and authority from the way they talk, from the angle they come from, from the way they behave with the people when they get to know you," an Ashaiman resident explains.[45] Leaders must serve the community, and engage with residents on a daily basis. While tribal and family affiliations are important, they are not sufficient for the accumulation of a large group of followers. Leaders are expected to represent the neighborhood as a whole and not just one interest group. They assist with daily survival and coordinate public goods projects in the community.[46]

Most local politicians and assemblymen are new to formal politics, but they have stepped into formal positions of power after serving their neighborhoods for many years. They have proven to their constituents that they are viable leaders and hope to upgrade their communities. This gives them legitimacy and the political capital to lead. "Most of us here, we grew up here and we want to see it grow," former mayor Ibrahim Baidoo explained his rationale for working on behalf of the community.[47] The Zongo Chief agrees, "We are all born and bred here. Upon growing to see that the system is not right, we took it upon ourselves to fix things."[48] The elders and leaders are respected and

---

[42] June 3, 2012. I constantly asked people to compare the neighborhoods in which they settled with other neighborhoods. This helped me uncover the perceptions that people had of different neighborhoods, as well how people made decisions about where to live.

[43] March 9, 2012.   [44] June 3, 2012.   [45] May 5, 2012.

[46] For a longer discussion of perceptions of good and bad leaders, see: Paller (2018a). In this paper, I explain how leaders are expected to engage in face-to-face discussions with residents, and treat their neighbors with respect.

[47] February 13, 2012.   [48] February 16, 2012.

have fostered an environment of innovation and progress. As assemblyman Thomas Adongo said, "Our early elite has really opened the
door of democracy."[49] The old pioneers still play a central role in
neighborhood politics, and enter into party politics as the formal institutions gain strength.

Making Politicians from Opinion Leaders

In the second introductory vignette of this book, a drunk driver drove
his supply truck into an electricity pole in the Tulako neighborhood
of Ashaiman. The story is notable for the active response of community members and leaders to take care of the problem and get the
electricity back on by the end of the day. All of this occurred despite
the fact that the owner of the vehicle was a known "big man" in town
and could influence formal authorities. Yet, the assemblyman faced
intense pressure from the community to get the power back as soon
as possible and he was able to pressure the Electricity Company of
Ghana to fix the pole, and even upgrade the electricity line in the
process.

This story demonstrates how the Tulako neighborhood had the
collective capacity to get things done. They fixed the problem and
made sure that electricity was restored. The story includes a leader
who is accessible, legitimate, and has the ability to lead; community
members of different generations with the desire to participate in
the community decision-making; and the utility company who had
the incentive to get the power back on as soon as they could. But the
sequence of events also reveals how politics and decision-making
occurs in the informal realm, outside of formal institutions and official
space. Community members refused to report to the police, compile a
formal report to ECG, or seek the assistance of the Ashaiman Municipal Assembly (ASHMA). Instead, residents took matters into their own
hands to fix the problem.

Conventional accounts attribute this success to social capital or
collective efficacy. Studies of collective action in political science have
been strongly influenced by Putnam (1993), who defines social capital
as "connections among individuals – social networks and the norms of

---

[49] February 13, 2012.

reciprocity and trustworthiness that arise from them." In urban sociology, Robert Sampson draws from this concept and adds a layer of political action in the concept of collective efficacy, the "social cohesion among neighbors combined with their willingness to intervene on behalf of the common good" (Sampson et al. 1997).

Yet both of these theories fail to explain why leaders feel the need to act on behalf of the public good – why they are incentivized to act in the public interest. In addition, it does not explain why and when leaders actually follow through. This shortcoming has been addressed in previous critiques of the societal approach to collective action. In their critique of Putnam's (1993) theory of social capital, Boix and Posner (1998) suggest that scholars do not have a good sense of why social capital varies across contexts, and what mechanisms explain when social capital contributes to good governance. They point to formal institutional characteristics like electoral competitiveness, institutional design, political polarization, bureaucratic capacity, and socioeconomic modernity to help fill the gap.

My evidence provides an alternative logic: Leaders must contribute to the public good to legitimate their authority as opinion leaders. But rather than facing formal institutional pressure or social sanctions from coethnics, they resort to pressure from other informal norms. In stranger settlements, opinion leaders gain respect and authority through their service to the community. Opinion leaders provide service to the neighborhood because of their long time horizon: They plan on living there indefinitely. In this way, community well-being underlies governance in the neighborhood: If leaders do not serve the community interest, they will be shamed into action.

Community leaders are expected to act as parents and guides, and this bolsters their legitimacy in the community. It also provides them with the political capital to get things done. This does not mean all leaders are good. But the difference is that they have the collective capacity to choose new leaders and hold them accountable. Community leaders can then step into formal positions of power and become politicians. The neighborhoods have the underlying conditions to make these formal institutions work. Leaders hold each other to account because they have the incentive to improve the neighborhood, not simply their own house. As leader and politician Ibrahim Baidoo explains, "The people who gained a voice in Ashaiman were already leaders on the ground. Then they entered into formal positions. The community has nurtured leaders and they are taking up leadership positions."[50]

This collective behavior in Ashaiman is possible in part because the assemblymen are respected opinion leaders who have established themselves as community leaders. For example, the current assemblyman of Tulako has lived in the neighborhood for more than ten years and runs a small shop. The previous representative lived in the area for almost twenty years and runs a school, as well as several small businesses. Youth gather at his compound to discuss timely political and social issues. Both leaders are seen walking through the community on a daily basis. Residents even joke that the current assemblyman greets people too much. "He is always walking around greeting people!" one resident laughs.

Leaders are expected to be accessible in everyday affairs. This accessibility helps build admiration of its leaders, and strengthen bonds of respect between leaders and followers. For example, residents appreciate these face-to-face interactions with the current assemblyman of Tulako, and applaud "how he visits the people in their homes, how humane he is."[51] Residents refer to him as the father of the community because he is approachable and takes care of issues that are of interest to the community well-being.[52] Across all neighborhoods in Ashaiman, residents are very close to their assemblymen. They live together, eat together, and hang out with them. "Here, you are close to the assemblyman, they don't feel isolated," assemblyman Thomas Adongo explains.[53] "They will come knock on your door at all times. In some areas, the assemblyman is a lion—you are afraid to get close. But not here. In the chop bar, I eat with them. Our sandals are the same, we live here. We do everything on rank and file. Patronage of the assemblyman is very high. Sometimes I cannot even sleep!"

Adongo explains the pressure he feels to legitimate his authority: Residents come to his door in the middle of the night to make sure that the community is safe and secure. He even buys replacement streetlights himself because he does not trust that the municipal assembly will do its job. "If I waited for the Assembly to get it done, it would never get done," he said. "So I had to do it myself. And it was my own money! If I don't do it, I won't sleep."

[50] February 13, 2012.   [51] June 3, 2012.   [52] June 14, 2012.
[53] February 13, 2012.

Adongo's claim is even more surprising because while he is a politician, he serves the NPP, which is not perceived to have a chance to win the parliamentary seat in Ashaiman. Contrary to conventional theories of political clientelism, he is not incentivized only by winning elections. Because he is an important ally for the NPP on the ground in an opposition stronghold, the NPP rely on figures like him to distribute resources and gain support to carry out development projects. A broad-based coalition of support assists in this endeavor. This is not mere brokerage either: Adongo attempts to support as many people as possible because it could assist him to be appointed to a position in the NPP government in the future, including the position of Municipal Chief Executive.

How Opinion Leaders Become Politicians

Ibrahim Baidoo, aka Bronx, lives in a stranger neighborhood in Ashaiman called Zongo. His specific area is nicknamed Valco Flat, after a Tema-based manufacturing company who built apartments in the 1970s and the building remains one of the few multiple story buildings in the community. The area is well demarcated, with 50 × 50 plots, planned streets, and a central sewer that runs through the neighborhood. It has substandard housing, overcrowding, and inadequate sanitation and infrastructure. But since residents began settling there in the 1970s, people have upgraded their homes, streets have been tarred, and the community continues to improve its collective well-being.

Bronx was first an assemblyman, and then served as Municipal Chief Executive (MCE) between 2012 and 2016. He ran for MP in 2012, and came in second in the NDC primaries. He lives in the middle of the neighborhood. His blue Toyota Camry sits in front of his house, indicating whether he is at home or not. In the morning, young men give it a car wash. There is a large banner across his front wall that says "Spartan Youth Club." Bronx formed the self-help group for Muslim youth to "pull themselves up." It provides scholarships to young people, includes income-generating opportunities, and serves as a forum for residents to talk about and solve their own problems. The youth club meets every Sunday evening to discuss their issues and problems. It also serves a very important political purpose for Bronx, allowing him to build a support network that is well organized, yet formally apolitical. However, he can secure state goods and political party patronage and distribute through this seemingly apolitical enterprise. By building a club, Bronx has created a pressure group that youth must join if they want to receive any state benefits. To reap the benefits, followers must join his club.

Politicians and assembly persons in Ashaiman are expected to sponsor clubs, and make personal investments. This helped get Bronx elected assemblyman, and then appointed as MCE. The current MP Ernest Henry Norgbey was largely an unknown figure until he started a successful savings club for women entrepreneurs, legitimating his authority in the neighborhood. Every opinion leader has his or her followers. They are disguised as youth groups, friends clubs, and keep-fit clubs. In 2011, several of these youth clubs demanded that the MCE resign. In 2012, a number of Muslim Youth began agitating for the mayor to step down again. Local residents knew that Bronx was behind this resistance. Bronx was next in line to be MCE and he tried to demonstrate his popular support. As one local leader explained, "Every leader has people working for them privately, and then they say all the right things publicly. This is African politics."[54]

While political science literature might portray Bronx's behavior as clientelistic, residents in Ashaiman yearn for leaders like Bronx. As a community member in Tulako explains, "We have weak leaders. They are not vocal. If we had Bronx here, he would have convinced the Assembly and this place would be developed. This community and Taabo [a nearby poor neighborhood] are not well demarcated. Our new Assemblyman is not that vocal."[55] Bronx, on the other hand, educates his people on the political and decision-making process, and he gets them state goods. In return, they offer their political support to him.

Bronx is a community leader and a politician. These roles are complementary and not mutually exclusive. Local legitimacy complements formal procedures. Lauth (2000) describes this as a complementary arrangement: "Complementary informal institutions shape behavior in ways that neither violate the overarching formal rules nor produce substantively different outcomes" (Helmke and Levitsky 2006: 13).

---

[54] April 4, 2012.   [55] February 29, 2012.

Despite having little formal education, people constantly mention Bronx as a good leader because he is a loud talker, he lobbies for his people, and he secures contracts from the government. It is not surprising that people like him. He is charismatic, good looking, charming, and visible. During the biometric registration exercise he visited the polling agents and laughed with the workers. He flirted with the women and joked with the men. He is easily accessible. For example, by ten o'clock each morning, groups of youth enter his compound and wait for his assistance and guidance. There is often a large group of youth sitting at his compound discussing politics, and this extends to the governance of services and resources.

These practices give him a network of supporters. For example, he helped Mama Angela get involved with Ashaiman Women in Progressive Development and he participates in NGO activities. NGOs rely on him to mobilize people when they need participants at their events. This helps him maintain loyal followings in many different types of groupings in the community. But he is also a businessman, and he uses his political connections to profit. For example, he secured the contract for a neighborhood bridge, even though he has no contracting expertise that deals with building bridges.[56] He immediately subcontracted the project and he is alleged to have kept a 10percent cut for himself. After the deal went through, he traveled to the United States.[57]

Former President Mahama appointed Bronx the MCE of Ashaiman after a grueling vetting process. While Bronx has broad-based support across Ashaiman, his post is notable for one major factor: He is not an indigene, or member of the Ga Dangbe ethnic group. Nor is he Ewe, the group of the most powerful early settlers. Instead, he built his support from his close links and service to the NDC party, as well as his broad support from youth groups across Ashaiman. While he is undoubtedly a patron to many followers, his "clients" form a broad-based coalition of groups from different ethnic groups. His grassroots organizing capacity enabled him to step into power, which led him to control the second-most powerful position in the city.[58]

On the surface, Bronx and Vanderpuye (the politician described in the previous section) are very similar figures. They both legitimated

[56] Multiple sources say he won the contract for the Lebanon Bridge.
[57] March 23, 2012.
[58] Most people think the Member of Parliament is the most powerful position in the city.

their authority as opinion leaders before they entered formal politics, and they are expected to distribute goods and resources to their followers. But upon closer examination, Bronx's legitimacy rests on emboldening a broad-based coalition of supporters, extending beyond Muslims, men, and Northerners, while Vanderpuye must empower his indigenous base. The informal norms of settlement and belonging created very different rationales of authority for otherwise similar candidates.

Shame and Honor

In everyday settings, leaders in Ashaiman are susceptible to account-ability mechanisms of shame and honor. Unlike leaders like Nii Owoo in Ga Mashie, described as a shameless opinion leader earlier in this chapter, Ashaiman representatives are motivated by honor and seek to avoid public shame. They do not want to be viewed as narrowly self-interested, and fear public ridicule and labels of selfishness. Residents and leaders seek honor and prestige in front of their community members, and hope to be rewarded for cooperation (Goode 1979; Tsai 2007). This helps people, particularly local leaders and politicians, amass followers. This is in line with theoretical predictions suggesting that people might contribute to the public good when they otherwise would not be expected to if they receive favorable attention from other group members for doing so (Hawkes 1993).

The following example illustrates the claim. In February 2012 there was an emerging problem in Ashaiman. At a meeting earlier in the week, a local leader named Mama Angela was in charge of collecting money from participants to carry out a beautification exercise in the neighborhood. A lady who could not attend the meeting gave her money to an assemblyman, to give to Mama Angela. The assemblyman did not give the money to her, saying that he had every intention to but then had to use the money to rush his child to the hospital. Mama Angela sought the help of a community activist named Innocent Adamadu, who wrote the following text message to the assemblyman:

My bro. I sympathise with ur child situation n wish speedy recovery. However, de fact remain that as u wished people to sympathased with ur situ-ation, u shd also endeavor to do same to others situation. I will choose to go hungry than to end up reducing my credibility n creating suspescious around my stature. U know we all struggle to build credibility n lets guard around it before all people. I must b honest wth u as a brother dat things like dis may tarnish image as a leader.

The next day the assemblyman returned the money to Mama Angela, and it restored community cohesion in the neighborhood. The threat of public shame and the desire to keep the credibility and honor of local leaders proved to be the most important factor in the leader's decision.

Unlike Old Fadama and Ga Mashie, Ashaiman has the appropriate conditions to make shame and honor mechanisms work for the public good. Leaders in Ashaiman reside and sleep in the neighborhood and face the prospect of public shame and honor on a daily basis. Leaders do not have an exit option and they gain social status by meeting their residents face-to-face. The informal rules and procedures that shape daily life are expressed through formal institutions, leading to the successful process of collective decision-making. These requirements of a good leader underlie how leaders constitute legitimacy.

The Accessibility of Leaders

Over the course of the ethnographic research, the accessibility of leaders emerged as a crucial way for leaders to legitimate their authority. Leaders in all communities are expected to engage in face-to-face conversations with their constituents. The following vignette describes this process.

In early January 2012, a rumor spread through Ashaiman that Mama Angela was supporting parliamentary candidate Tony for Member of Parliament (MP). The rumor was based on a false claim that she hosted a meeting between Tony, the former MP, and another local "big man" at her house. This unsubstantiated claim was significant because informal networks of support underlie political power. If the rumor were true – that Mama Angela was supporting Tony as opposed to the incumbent MP – this would mean that Mama Angela turned her back on the incumbent and was actively supporting another candidate. But more importantly, this would signal that Mama Angela was abandoning and betraying a member of her political family, a serious act of disrespect. The act would signal disloyalty because the incumbent supported Mama Angela's recent campaign for a local elected office, demonstrating his allegiance to her; this also signified her position as a follower to him. Mama Angela, as constituent, has important obligations to her representative that extend beyond the ballot box.

Mama Angela is an important local figure because she is perceived as both an ordinary resident but also an aspiring politician with strong support from two important interest groups: women and her ethnic group. While the rumor signified potentially important local political divisions, the implications on the ground were far greater: Mama Angela might be accused of disrespecting her leader and being ungrateful, a dangerous combination for her future aspirations to be a community leader. The situation might also harbor dishonesty, resentment, and divisions among community leaders and followers. Leaders and followers are at the same time representatives, clients, protégés, and constituents, suggesting that the relationship between a leader and follower is a complicated one, as is the case with Mama Angela and the representative. But more was at stake than Mama Angela's need to save her budding political career. If the representative was allowed to get away with undermining his constituents, he could get away with far more, like stealing government funds and misappropriating development projects. The event sparked more than rational fears about politics and development: Mama Angela felt hurt and disrespected, as though a long relationship had been potentially broken.

When I met Mama Angela the morning she heard this rumor she was livid – and hurt. First, she claimed that the rumor was false and that she never facilitated a meeting with the incumbent's rivals. She did not like that somebody would make up what she deemed a "nasty lie." Second, and more significantly, she heard that the incumbent believed the rumor and was accusing her of turning her back on him. This drew her direct ire against the incumbent – "I don't know if I can ever support him again. What he is doing is so wrong." Third, the incumbent is inaccessible; she tried calling him and "begged" him to talk but he is unavailable.

The bonds of respect between the incumbent (leader) and Mama Angela (his follower) were threatened, and it endangered not only their relationship but potentially cohesion in the community as well. These bonds of respect are based on collective responsibility and social exchange, developing prior to the now-established political relationship. For Mama Angela and the leader, these bonds developed from many years of mentorship, partnership in their hometown association, and collective struggle in neighborhood affairs. Mama Angela spent the day visiting her friends and neighbors complaining about the man, building up support against him. Mama Angela would use these discussions with supporters as a collective endeavor to publicly shame the representative if he did not apologize.

The next morning, Mama Angela woke up at 4 AM and went to the incumbent's house before sunrise. "In our tradition, if you have a problem with a leader, you go to his house before sunrise and discuss your issue." They spoke face-to-face and she expressed her grievances, emphasizing that the leader turned his back not only on her, but all of the constituents as well. She mentioned that she spent the previous day visiting and explaining herself to supporters, mobilizing support to make these allegations public. While this meeting took place in the private home of the representative, the space is used as a public sphere for him and his followers to come together to express themselves. In this space, he explained himself. Whatever misinformation and rumors had spread were settled. She left the house having told him a clear message about spreading and believing false rumors.

The reciprocal practice of Mama Angela expressing herself, combined with the leader taking her ideas into account, allowed for their bonds of respect to be restored. That afternoon, Mama Angela saw the incumbent driving his big black truck through the neighborhood. She went up to his window and they talked for several minutes. They laughed throughout the entire conversation, signaling that the emotional attachment between the two remained strong. The public performance indicated that the bonds of respect between leader and follower persisted.

This story is a typical example of the importance of accessibility in urban Ghana. While democratic elections serve as an important context for political jockeying and electoral competition – both important aspects of democratic governance – the practice of politics takes place outside of these formal channels. As one campaign strategist for the aforementioned incumbent explains, "Go to his house before sunrise and you will see a line out the door. It takes him several hours before he can even leave for work." This also signals that private spaces like personal homes might have a public utility, in this case serving as a sphere of democratic expression. This demand must also be a collective endeavor: Mama Angela amassed her own support before she expressed herself to the representative, signaling the threat of public sanctioning by slighting human dignity.

But constituents also have obligations to their representatives and must reciprocate with loyalty. This pledge of allegiance is more than an economic or political relationship, as a long literature on neopatrimonialism in Africa implies (Bratton and van de Walle 1997). Instead, it requires a deep admiration for the qualities associated with that person, which is gained through social bonds that develop over the course of interactions and deliberation. Politics is public, relational, and practiced in the context of daily life.

In this example, the leader was accessible in everyday situations. But across the city, there is considerable variation. For example, in Old Fadama, which I will discuss next, residents complain that their assemblyman has not been seen since winning the election. To make matters worse, his phone is always turned off. Yet despite this inaccessibility, the assemblyman became an MP in his home constituency in the Northern Region.

Brokers and Opinion Leaders in a Sprawling Metropolis

Most of the scholarship on political clientelism in Global South cities – especially in its squatter settlements – derives from Latin America and South Asia.[59] Strong political machines and bureaucratic capacities characterize these settings. There is also robust union organizing among workers in many cases. This contributes to the political machine serving as the "only game in town." For example, Mike Davis writes, "Without formal land titles or home ownership, slum-dwellers are forced into quasi-feudal dependencies upon local officials and party bigshots" (Davis 2004: 16).[60] This is also the concern of Hernando de Soto (2000, 2003), who suggests the need to formalize land tenure so these arrangements will not persist. While there are certainly elements of these coercive relationships in urban Ghana, the importance of trust and respect gets lost when local leaders are reduced to "brokers." The following example describes the political networks that form, suggesting how more than coercion forms the bases of these relationships.

[59] Exceptions include Nelson (1979); Resnick (2013); Paller (2014).
[60] There is evidence of this in Mexico (Cornelius 1973); India (Boo 2012; Auerbach 2016); Argentina (Auyero 2001); Colombia, Chile, and Peru (Holland 2017).

Abdallah is a university student who came to Accra to attend the best university in the country. Boss is a powerful NDC party broker, alleged criminal, and scrap dealer. One fall morning, Abdallah woke up early to write a letter on Boss' behalf to secure a contract for cleaning sewers.[61] One of Boss's friends, a minister in government, was hiring for jobs at the fishing ports and Boss was trying to get jobs for some of the youth from his hometown, who were now living in Old Fadama. Boss has gained a reputation as a strong and honorable leader by providing jobs to youth, and working hard to get them enrolled in government youth programs for which programming had expanded.[62] Boss relied on his close connections to higher-ups in the NDC to build his following, capturing private goods to legitimate his authority and become a respected opinion leader.

While Boss is a powerful local leader, he cannot read or write and relies on youth like Abdallah to pen the official letters.[63] Abdallah wrote the letter at the NDC branch office, where there is a computer that was donated by the area's Minister of Parliament. This is one of the few concrete structures in his part of the neighborhood and it serves as a hangout for youth and space for local branch meetings. On the surface, the short-term exchange could be reduced to material needs. But the admiration that these men had for each other extends much deeper. Abdallah likes Boss because he thinks he is fair and honest. "He is a straight shooter," as one resident explains.[64] He buys food for Abdallah and they eat together; he purchases phone credit when Abdallah has no money; and they pray together at the same mosque on Friday afternoons.

These bonds of respect extend to Boss' larger social and political network. Abdallah's best friend is Boss' "Deputy Secretary." He has a whole organization of youth who follow him. Youth in the neighborhood are impressed by Boss' ideology. "People should have what is due to them," one resident explains, "and his main aim is to get the people who suffered to get government into power to get them what they want. He is very disappointed with government for not doing this."[65] These bonds of respect extend to another important opinion leader

---

[61] November 4, 2011.   [62] December 8, 2011.

[63] Abdallah is often asked by the local strongmen to write letters on their behalf. It is a very valuable resource to be literate and educated in Old Fadama (November 21, 2011).

[64] December 7, 2011.   [65] November 21, 2011.

named Chief, who explains that other leaders, like OFADA Chairman and PD Executive Director Farouk Braimah do not always pay people on time for the jobs they do. In contrast, he says, "This does not happen with Boss. He makes sure these things are fair." Boss speaks and listens to their ideas, which strengthens the respect people have toward him.[66]

But this particular social network is limited to mostly members of Boss' hometown.[67] Boss controls the territory under which these young men live, and they are protected by being closely aligned to him. Sometimes Boss even pays for their visits home to the North. His presence is simply felt. "Sometimes his name alone will stop things," one resident explained.[68] In a squatter settlement that does not provide basic public security, residents rely on figures like Boss for personal protection. Young people also rely on him for potential job opportunities and to link them up with his friends in powerful positions. While Boss and his followers engaged in numerous social gatherings, the bonds of respect that were outcomes of these social practices did not extend far beyond ethnic affiliation.

Despite the respect that Boss garnered among youth in his neighborhood, he is a controversial figure. In the early 2000s after the NPP government took over power (after twenty years of P/NDC government), Boss fled to Libya because he was suspected of criminal activity in the 2000 elections. The NPP had a warrant for his arrest – he is closely aligned with the NDC and is suspected of aiding them illegally in political mobilization.[69] He is labeled a "Rawlings boy" – a term given to supporters of former President Jerry John Rawlings. He returned in the mid-2000s and sought refuge in Old Fadama where he would be hard to find. His status in the community increased after the 2008 elections when the NDC regained power. NPP brokers from the community were forced out of the neighborhood, losing their businesses and properties. In 2009, four NPP supporters were killed after trying to return to the community. Boss' name always comes up in the news reports in relation to the killings. Many residents denounce

---

[66] In related research (Paller 2018a), I theorize how engaging in interactive modes of communication provide a basis for a logic of accountability.

[67] There were a few non-Dagombas who supported him politically. But the ties with the Dagombas were more persistent.

[68] November 21, 2011.   [69] April 19, 2012.

these allegations as false and maintain that he is innocent. Nonetheless, for this, "his name is tainted."[70]

Boss was one of the first squatters in Old Fadama. When he settled in the early 1990s, there were only 50–100 people living there.[71] In squatter settlements, early arrival greatly enhances a leaders' ability to amass power by extending his territorial authority. Boss has always been an ardent supporter of the NDC. His family was NDC and he credits President Rawlings with bringing development to the Northern Region, which has always been marginalized in Ghanaian politics (Abdulai 2017).[72] But he became an active political force when one of the MPs from the North, Alhaji Hudu Yahaya, became a patronage presence in the community.

Yahaya was Regional Secretary during the PNDC regime and became General Secretary of the NDC from 1992–2000. He was also from Tamale, and he wanted to bolster his hometown ties in the capital city. The MP opened an NGO, paid for some basic services, and handed out cash and contracts to mobilize and organize the youth. Yahaya provided Boss an important and formal link to NDC politics. Yahaya is credited as the main influence behind Northern migrants in Accra who entered into multiparty politics.[73] Yahaya in many ways politicized the residents of Old Fadama, solidifying the community as an NDC stronghold and potential NDC vote bank for politicians from the North. Boss found refuge in Yahaya's patronage network because it provided financial and employment opportunities, but it also provided a platform to bolster status and prestige.

Community leaders like Boss rely on politicians like Yahaya for security. For example, he "shielded" NDC insiders who would work for the party. But even ordinary residents need protection because they are stigmatized and considered criminals by the broader city population. Sometimes residents are thrown in jail without due process. They recount "join the line," when the police used to send buses in the middle of the night, round up residents, and throw them in jail. Politicians are expected to bail residents out of jail, especially party activists and insiders.

---

[70] October 31, 2011.   [71] April 19, 2012.

[72] This is a common narrative that Northerners often say about why they support Rawlings and the P/NDC.

[73] June 30, 2012.

How Opinion Leaders Become Political Brokers

Most residents in squatter settlements are citizens of Ghana and active voters, even though their neighborhoods lack legal recognition. Old Fadama residents are no exception. The NDC further consolidated its numerical strength in the community after the Dagbon King was killed in 2002, sparking a chieftaincy crisis and creating entrenched political divisions that remain today (Albert 2008; Issifu 2015). The majority Andani "gate" of the Dagombas (whose king was killed) aligned with the NDC, and the minority Abudu "gate" (who were accused of killing the king) aligned with the NPP. These divisions were reflected in Old Fadama politics, where Abudu political leaders lost considerable power and followers (due to lack of numbers), but maintained criminal gangs that they could maintain with the backing of the NPP government. These gangs were particularly strong between 2000 and 2004, when the NPP ruled the National Government and held the MP seat for the constituency.

NPP Branch leaders – with names like Yaw, Zachi, Gbrum, and "Old Man" – controlled territory, businesses, and property in the neighborhood. Some of them even allocated land to those from their own party.[74] According to one resident, "[Yaw] was so powerful in this community. He caused so many problems. He was a landlord and would just seize houses. He had a gang and was armed—he had a pistol. And he was a big drinker. There were lots of problems when he drank. When we tried to report his abuses, he would always be let off the hook because he was so close to the people in power."[75] Another explained how "Yaw would occasionally go around with the police and arrest NDC supporters. He would beat people and get away with it."[76] After the 2008 elections, these NPP-aligned community leaders, like Yaw, were forced out of the community. NDC aligned leaders and "thugs" seized their property and now run their businesses. Residents worried that if the NPP won the 2012 election they would seek revenge. In 2016 after the NPP won the election, the NPP leaders who had fled returned to control the bases, private services, and parks in the neighborhood. Those affiliated with the NDC were kicked out of the neighborhood.

---

[74] February 3, 2012.   [75] October 25, 2011.   [76] February 3, 2012.

People in squatter settlements are particularly reliant on informal security arrangements because public security services are under-provisioned. There is only one police station on the outskirt of the neighborhood and it has very little authority inside the settlement. Inside, community leaders have a powerful incentive to win elections: If their party loses the election, they might lose their business and property and have to relocate somewhere else. It is for these reasons that elections and campaigns are particularly tense and heated.[77]

Building the Political Machine

Power struggles are especially contentious within the governing political party networks. Internal rivalries within opposition parties have less of an impact on governance because they have fewer opportunities to distribute state resources, and hence have a smaller presence on the ground. During the NDC governing period (2008–2016), Old Fadama political struggles occurred within the NDC party. For example, the personal rivalry between Boss and the OFADA Chairman – nicknamed simply "Chairman" – represents an important cleavage that underscores how politics works in the neighborhood. But it also signals a shift in government–community linkages, with Boss representing the old guard and Chairman the new guard, as Ghanaian politics becomes more decentralized and democratic.

The climax of the rivalry between Boss and Chairman came in 2009 when they ran against one another for NDC Special Ward Chairman. The position is extremely powerful because they control the distribution of party goods to the community. Now that the NDC government is in power, and the NPP party activists have been forced out, the NDC executives control the flow of resources from the government to local structures. As a hierarchical organization, the NDC relies on its grassroots formal structures to distribute goods, including jobs, contracts, and government assistance like loans, vehicles, and labor contracts. The Chairman of the Old Fadama Special Ward is the first point of contact between the NDC government and the community. Therefore, he is able to control the sharing of resources with his own polity. This allows him to consolidate the party structures with

---

[77] There is evidence of this in other informal neighborhoods in Kenya (De Smedt 2009); South Africa (Fourchard 2012); Nigeria (Fourchard 2009).

his own supporters. Alternatively, residents who seek government or party assistance must go through him. While the race for Constituency Chairman was heated, Chairman won in a landslide, greatly bolstering his power and wealth in the community.

The roots of these political party battles extend deep into its history, and can be traced back to the early settlement of the neighborhood. Boss and Chairman are both early settlers in the community and even lived in the same house. "We were together," Boss explained. Since then, Boss and the Chairman have built their own followings and rival polities. Boss is perceived as rough and violent, yet principled, with political connections to the Ghanaian old guard and the top of the NDC party structure. These connections bring him private benefits, like plane tickets to his hometown and early notifications of recycled government vehicles and goods on which his scrap business depends.

Boss sometimes uses coercive strategies and threats of violence to secure goods from the state and from the NDC. As one resident explained, "If Boss is not getting support from people he would be causing lots of problems."[78] Taking former President Rawlings as his model, he is a populist who can rapidly mobilize people. He can create chaos and mobilize crowds. These qualities sometimes backfire. Many Old Fadama residents lost trust in him in 2009 when he secured goods from the government after a fire outbreak. But instead of sharing them with the affected residents, he brought them to his hometown and sold them. Residents in the neighborhood could not accuse him of wrong-doing because he still provided them with security and job opportun-ities. Dagomba youth found it particularly difficult to voice their concerns because he brought the goods home. They still went to "their own people" – coethnic Dagombas.

Some aspiring politicians rise through the party ranks by climbing the grassroots structures. But they still have the incentive to share party goods with their own ethnic group in order to hold onto power, increase their chances of future electoral success in their hometown, and ensure that they receive a greater share of the resources. For example, Chairman, in contrast to Boss, is a gentle leader who built his following by advancing through the grassroots structures in the local constituency, first as Vice Chairman and now as Chairman. He cooperates with the NGOs and aligns himself with the powerful

[78] February 3, 2012.

politicians of Odododiodioo Constituency, for which Old Fadama is a part. He grew wealthy and expanded his territorial authority by taking advantage of the informal land market and selling property.

He established power by owning a store in the neighborhood that served as a hangout for men to sit around and discuss politics. Sometimes his wife even made food and fed the group. And he is an impressive public speaker. "Some say he has special powers," a resident says of his speaking ability.[79] These meeting places served an important accountability function: They provided an avenue for a leader to hear the grievances and interests of his constituents, while providing him the platform to owe account for his actions (Paller 2018a). In the process, bonds of respect developed between him and his followers, as they discussed politics and community affairs on a daily basis.

But over time as Chairman gained more power through his alliances with the state and the NDC party, he was available to his constituents less and less. He is now criticized as being extremely corrupt and serving only his narrow self-interest. Residents who are not part of his inner core are disillusioned by his leadership and are unable to hold him to account. By 2016 he had too much power: He was Chairman of the NDC for the community, Chairman of OFADA, and is a core member of MP Nii Lantey Vanderpuye's mobilization team.

"You know, Boss and Chairman are very different types of people," one resident explains. "Chairman is soft and gentle; Boss is rough."[80] Despite these differences, both derive their authority from attracting coethnic followers and providing private goods to their networks. These bonds of respect took time to develop, nourished by countless hours talking and arguing about sports and politics, but were also bolstered by sharing food and Friday afternoon prayers.

Conclusion

This chapter complicates the notion that "brokers" and politicians serve a purely instrumental purpose. Instead, political actors constitute their authority by becoming opinion leaders in their communities. They need to control space and territory, as well as bolster their reputation by gaining admiration and respect among followers. But

---

[79] November 20, 2011.   [80] December 8, 2011.

these patterns of legitimacy vary across settlements, depending on the informal norms of settlement and belonging.

In indigenous settlements, leaders must subscribe to customary norms, as well as be from traditional families that control land. They are typically chiefs, family elders, religious leaders, and landowners. They can then step into formal positions of power. Leaders in stranger settlements must help people from different groups and ages, demonstrating a commitment to the neighborhood that expands beyond their family or clan. These opinion leaders include teachers, religious leaders, landlords, and other civic leaders. Finally, in squatter settlements, leaders can rely on fear and coercion to maintain authority, especially because residents rely on "big men" to secure their tenure. Leaders seek alliances with political parties, but capture goods and services to distribute to a narrow following from their hometown, using their newfound power to potentially enter formal positions of power back home. Opinion leaders are slumlords, scrap dealers, political party branch representatives, NGO workers, and youth club executives.

These insights support an institutional explanation based on informal norms of settlement and belonging to demonstrate why political clientelism in urban Ghana persists. The next chapter suggests that these clientelistic practices are embedded in a certain type of distributive politics in a neighborhood.

5 | *Distributive Politics for an Urbanizing Continent*

The study of distributive politics encompasses some of the most exciting research on Ghanaian politics in recent years. Political scientists focusing on elections have enhanced our understanding of accountability, voting behavior, and clientelism. Lessons from Ghana demonstrate that elections do matter, by enhancing democratic learning, promoting government responsiveness and effectiveness, and selecting better politicians.[1] An alternative literature derived from anthropology, development studies, and geography embeds distribution and service provision within a broader conception of governing the commons. For these sets of scholars, distributive politics is a process of collective decision-making that rests on norms of reciprocity.

Yet both of these approaches overlook the historical evolution of urban neighborhoods, as well as how certain residents and groups make meaning of specific goods and resources. This is particularly important in cities where land is scarce while property values rise, enabling politicians and leaders to politicize the commons. This chapter provides an alternative to conventional accounts of distributive politics by considering how informal norms of settlement and belonging shape certain types of distributive politics across neighborhoods.

As a scholar of politics, I focus on the local political economy of urban neighborhoods. I suggest that distributive politics is embedded in a broader struggle over control and authority in the city. Local leaders and politicians politicize urban neighborhoods – which can be conceived as a commons – by distributing goods and resources along club, public, or private lines. These distributive patterns coincide with indigenous, stranger, and squatter settlements, respectively.

---

[1] Studies include Lindberg (2006); Ichino and Nathan (2013); Harding (2015); Abdulai and Hickey (2016); Bob-Milliar and Paller (2018).

The chapter combines ethnographic observations with survey data. First, I explain how Ga residents in indigenous neighborhoods feel entitled to resources, state services, and government jobs. These goods are best conceptualized as club goods, whereby residents must subscribe to the norms of the Ga ethnic group to benefit from goods and services. This contributes to a distributive politics that is dominated by claims to indigeneity and first-comer status in the city. I then document how the conception of the commons extends to multiethnic populations in stranger communities like many neighborhoods in Ashaiman. This contributes to a distributive politics that serves the broader public interest. Finally, I discuss how the commons become privatized in squatter settlements, as local leaders empower themselves and their followers through the capture of state services and resources.

Customary Entitlement in the Indigenous Core of a City

Every Ghanaian city has an indigenous core, where the first comers to the land arrived before other migrants, and the evolution of leadership dates back to the earliest settlers. The historical evolution of these neighborhoods shapes the type of distributive politics that emerge. Residents and leaders feel entitled to important resources like water, land, housing, and government jobs. But these resources provide far more than material value; they also provide symbolic attachments to particular communities. These symbolic attachments are apparent in the everyday politics of indigenous neighborhoods like Ga Mashie, where the following event illustrates that the way goods and resources are distributed must be considered in a broader context of control over space, territory, and governing the city.

One block from the National Post Office in Central Accra, two Ga men walked past a group of young girls who were sleeping on the pavement. The girls were *kayayei,* or head porters from the northern regions of Ghana who migrated to Accra to find work. Most *kayayei* are under sixteen years of age, do not attend schools, and are extremely poor (Opare 2003; Agyei et al. 2016). One of the men sneered and displayed his disgust at the girls. The other man then complained, "Ahhh, these girls. And on Accra property!"[2]

---

[2] December 15, 2011.

This is a common view that Accra residents, especially the indigenous Ga, have against particular migrants in the city. Many Ga residents do not see the challenges facing the *kayayei* as a socioeconomic problem that confronts all Ghanaians, or portions of the urban poor. Instead, they portray the women as trespassers who are stains on the city. This belief also underlies policymaking, as the Ga dominate the Accra Metropolitan Assembly (AMA) and they form a strong interest group when it comes to development policy and urban development.

Many studies of migration in Africa focus on whether new residents encompass an economic, cultural, or political threat.[3] The comments from these men suggest an alternative logic: Incomers from certain regions – in this case the north – do not deserve a rightful place in the city. This is because they change the nature and form of the city, as well as threaten the authority over territory. Thinking about certain migrant populations as trespassers shifts the understanding of distributive justice. The definition of trespasser is "a person entering someone's land or property without permission" (*Oxford English Dictionary*). In this way, Ga residents living in the indigenous core believe that stranger groups need to seek permission from them to inhabit the city. The right to the city is not universal, but rather one that depends on seeking alliances with those already there first.

Indigenous ownership and control directly translates into municipal governance. As owners and custodians of Accra, the Ga leadership makes demands on the government by evoking the language of entitlement to the land. For example, AMA has identified more than eighty neighborhoods in need of investments in Accra, and Ga Mashie was chosen as a sight for slum upgrading, supported by UN-Habitat and other organizations. As Nii Tackie Tagoe, the Executive Director of the Ga Mashie Development Association, explained, "[Ga Mashie] is an indigenous area and it needs upliftment."[4] He explained that the next communities in line for upgrading are Korle Gonno and Chorkor, two indigenous neighborhoods. He explained that other communities include squatters, and they do not deserve state resources when "there are people here who 'need development.'" The ethnic nationalist organization Ga-Dangme Council makes a similar claim: "the Ga Dangme are falling behind as Ghana moves forward."[5]

---

[3] See: Adida (2014); Landau (2014); Honig (2016).   [4] June 21, 2012.
[5] Quoted in Grant (2009: 125).

It would be easy to dismiss this behavior as mere tribalism or nativism. While it certainly contains elements of ethnic chauvinism, it is rooted in historical and cultural understandings of power and authority across the country. As I explained in Chapter 3, the exchange of land for development projects – what I call a customary entitlement – has been a staple of urban policy throughout colonial and postcolonial governments. Customary ownership of land perpetuates these patterns. In the context of multiparty democracy and human rights, the informal norm of indigeneity shapes how Ga community leaders make claims to land and property in Accra – and how the logic of distribution works at the city level. Leaders evoke their indigenous ownership and make social justice assertions to reclaim land that their family members sold off several years before. This strategy can be particularly lucrative because land values in Accra are increasing rapidly.[6]

These nativist and legal claims have historical precedent, which can be observed by tracing the everyday politics of these neighborhoods. These claims date back to the early years of Independence. Ghana's first president Kwame Nkrumah was also the MP for Odododiodioo Constituency (in which Ga Mashie is a part) and he successfully consolidated Ga Mashie as a stronghold for the Nkrumah tradition. The strong indigenous narrative that developed in Ga Mashie due to its first-settler status developed in the precolonial era, and was incorporated into multiparty politics after Independence.[7] The first political crisis that independent Ghana faced was a riot instigated by the Ga Shifimo Kpee, a Ga nationalist political party that splintered off from

---

[6] Ato Kwamena Onoma (2009) provides an institutional explanation, suggesting that Ga family elders have no other productive use of their land, thus investing in speculative investments and selling multiple plot allocations for the same piece of land. Sackeyfio-Lenoch (2014) highlights how many land struggles today have their roots in colonial struggles of space and authority in the city. There is also a legal rationale, as Morrison (2017: 7) explains, "Since 1972, under Ghanaian law, if the land is not used for intended purpose, then the original land owners would be allowed a renewed claim to the land, or receive compensation after twelve years of occupation" (Grant 2006). Ghana's 1992 Constitution stipulates that 80 percent of land in Ghana is under the jurisdiction of traditional or customary authorities (Stacey 2018: 68).

[7] This narrative is propagated by Ga intellectuals and elites. For example, Josiah-Aryeh (1997) writes: "If the trend in the study of Ghanaian history persists, the Ga-Dangme stand in danger of becoming a people without a history; and even court the greater danger of denying their progeny the pride that arises from the knowledge of the heroic acts of one's forebears."

the CPP whose name translates to "The Ga Standfirm Society."[8] The Ga Shifimo Kpee organized in opposition to Nkrumah at the early years of Independence. They resisted government based on a combination of tribalism and economic grievances: They felt that President Nkrumah was favoring stranger groups for better jobs and housing, and they charged that cabinet ministers, who are not Ga, are "feathering their own nests by buying the better land and taking over homes upon which taxes have not been paid" (Houser 1957: 4).

The motto of the group was "gboi ngbe wo," or "the foreigners are killing us" (Osei-Tutu 2000: 78). The rise of the Ga nationalist group took the CPP by surprise because it took place in the capital and included former supporters of Nkrumah (Austin 1970: 44). But from the grassroots, the formation of the organization represented politics as usual. This fear of the outsider fueled rumors, resistance, and opposition to state policy throughout the postcolonial period. For example, in 1972 there was a proposal to put sewers in the entire city. But the people of Ga Mashie resisted because a rumor spread that the sewers were used to steal the sea and bring it to the hinterlands, especially Kumasi.[9] Ga Mashie residents were afraid that they were going to lose their sea. These fears of losing their sea and city fueled recent resistance to plans to modernize Bukom Park put forth by the former Minister for the Modernization of the Capital City (Afenah 2012).

President Jerry John Rawlings further consolidated the ethno-nationalist Ga Mashie voting base during his military rule (1979–1992) and his terms under democracy (1992–2000). Yet grassroots mobilization was intense throughout the decades. Nowhere was this more passionate than in the central markets, where the opposition organized under the guise of the Ghana Union of Trader's Association (GUTA). GUTA represented the interests of the traders, the majority of whom were Akan. This became the local stronghold for the NPP. Ghanaians were unable to publicly criticize the government under military rule, but instead used GUTA as a mouthpiece to express opposition and dissent to the military government's economic policies.

---

[8] Hodge writes: "Operating from the slum quarter of Accra gangs paraded the streets in distinctive dress, red armbands, sashes and headgear, shouting slogans and campaigning for the Ga cause, demanding that jobs and houses in Accra should be given to Gas, the local people, before strangers and migrants" (1964: 114–115).

[9] July 3, 2012.

The marketplace became a further source of political contention when the central market, called Makola Market, burned down in 1979 (Robertson 1983). This event had serious consequences. On the one hand, Ga women who had controlled the marketplace lost their powerful positions in the market. This is because the Revolutionary government did not discriminate with stalls when the new December 31 market was built. This emboldened the Akan traders to use the marketplace as an organizational space independent of the state. An opposition force grew, while leading to a reactionary narrative among Ga market women: "We are losing our markets." This further inflamed the indigenous narrative: *They* are taking over our market-places, and our city. Today, these historical roots continue to shape party politics, as the constituency is spatially divided between the central market (NPP territory) and indigenous Ga Mashie (NDC territory) (Klaus and Paller 2017).

In this way, development and infrastructure projects extend far beyond a narrow logic of electoral survival. In addition, while the development of the city certainly draws attention to neighborhoods as a commons, these examples highlight the different ways that space and territory are symbolic resources, as Erica Simmons (2016) suggests. Land and sea hold a special importance for the livelihoods of Ga residents. In her insightful study of linguistic development in Accra, Mary Esther Kropp Dakubu (1997) explains how the language of the Ga people, and the attachments given to land and sea, are embedded in broader political struggles over settlement and belonging. For example, the opposition between the Korle Lagoon (a waterway that extends through the city) and the sea signifies a distinction between "them and us," whereby "Korle" refers to that which is foreign while the sea belongs to the Ga people (Dakubu 1997: 12). She continues, "In Ga metaphor the Ga people are frequently linked with the sea, in opposition to inland people" (ibid).

As the city grew over time, the space surrounding the sea – inherently tied to the Ga people – extended inland. Meanwhile, "foreigners" settled along different waterways, which have deities that are seen as protectors of Accra – in extension the Ga people. Dakubu explains, "Water in Ga imagery includes a strong element of danger, often expressed as storm or flood" (Dakubu 1997: 13). The indigenous core of the city came into conflict with inland migrants, setting the context for contentious struggles over assimilation into Ga society, authority, and control over the city. Today, these struggles persist, as Ga residents fear the influx of outsiders as a threat to their livelihoods, language, culture, and city.

Distributive politics, therefore, is as much a struggle over identity and control of territory, as it is about material rewards and elections. But when resources and infrastructure do enter the equation, the logic of distribution manifests in a sense of entitlement to state resources and public services. This entitlement extends to other services, including markets and even public toilets. Not surprisingly, the struggle for contracts for public service projects becomes politicized.[10]

In line with my general theory, indigenous residents and leaders understand development projects as club goods – as customary entitlements. For example, jobs with public-private partnerships like Zoomlion are distributed as political favors to Ga youth groups. A local Ga nationalist youth gang has captured the public toilet in James Town, asserting its local dominance over the common space. Alternatively, the owner of the "public toilet" in Otubluhom takes pride in his business, and explains that he secured the contract as a customary entitlement for his role as custodian of the land. He takes great pride in his territorial authority over the people of Otubluhom – it brings him great pride and social approval. This logic extends beyond clientelism. Rather, the distribution enables him to be a good opinion leader – a legitimate authority among his family and neighborhood residents, as I outlined in the previous chapter. Therefore, the governance of public services has symbolic power, enabling leaders to serve the Ga community for which they are considered legitimate authorities.

Building a Political Family

The organizing power of indigeneity and entitlement extends to the way that political parties mobilize followers, and how residents vote for their candidates (Klaus and Paller 2017). The following example illustrates how political candidates are expected to build a political family, privileging the Ga ethnic group above all else.

---

[10] For example, in 2008 the rehabilitation project for Salaga Market was planned, but the contract was reprovisioned to a different family beneficiary after the NDC came to office. The rehabilitation project became a public debate and there was no work done on the project until 2012.

"He is my cousin!" a Ga Mashie resident happily proclaimed, explaining why she would vote for Nii Lantey Vanderpuye for MP.[11] Family lineage influences voters in traditional ways, especially among the elders.[12] Vanderpuye used the metaphor of family to create a "new political family." The creation of a new family is especially influential among the youth. In a focus group of Ga Mashie youth, two participants explained that they view Vanderpuye as the father of the community. This is because he is a vocal leader who provides jobs and opportunities to the youth.[13] Creating a "new political family" was strategic for Vanderpuye: He needed to be seen as a benevolent leader who can feed and provide for the community. He also needed to defeat the incumbent Tackie Komme who draws significant support from his traditional family ties. Politicians present themselves as father figures to legitimate their power in the community. He was serving his role as opinion leader, as I described in the previous chapter.

Vanderpuye built this new political family in various ways. He pays the school fees for children in the community.[14] He used his personal and professional connections to the President to submit letters of support for constituents for jobs or educational opportunities where the President might have some influence. He linked up a group of women with loans to support their businesses.[15] He hands out rice, clothes, and other gifts to constituents at various rallies and events.[16] He paved the alleyway in front of his family home, and claims that he will do the same for the entire community if he is voted in as MP. At a campaign rally in Old Fadama, he reached out to the women by saying, "You are all my wives. You are all part of my family."[17] Similarly, when he picked up his nomination form he called up "my brothers from Old Fadama" to join him on stage.[18] He wanted to make sure

---

[11] January 14, 2012. During my research, I closely followed the 2012 primary campaign of Odododiodioo Constituency. I had especially close ties to the Vanderpuye campaign. They allowed me entrance to their private office, as well as offering many interviews throughout the process.

[12] This section is adapted from Paller 2014.   [13] June 20, 2012.

[14] For example, Vanderpuye's administrative secretary claimed, "I brought over 300 cedis last week to pay for the school fees of one resident" (January 9, 2012).

[15] January 24, 2012.

[16] For example, on January 2, 2012 he supplied food for the New Year's celebration.

[17] March 4, 2012.   [18] December 16, 2011.

that the residents, many of whom are migrants from the North, felt part of his political family.

Vanderpuye attended and financially supported funerals and birth-day parties of influential members and politically connected residents. A member of Vanderpuye's campaign team explained, "This is how it works here. You have to pay for these personal things so that people see what you do."[19] Residents consider these opportunities when they support a candidate. There is also an instrumental dimension, as one resident said, "If Vanderpuye wins, I get the chance to make more money before the elections. If [the other candidate] Tackie Komme wins, I get nothing."[20]

The week before the primary election, especially the last night, is particularly expensive for the candidates.[21] NDC constituency admin-istrative secretary explained, "From what I hear, they [all three candi-dates] are saving their money for this week. For Friday. People change their minds so quickly that you have to be the last one to convince them."[22] Vanderpuye sponsored a big dinner at the local pool hall the night before the primary elections. The need for politicians to feed their constituents and keep them believing that they will personally benefit from the election contributes to the persistence of political clientelism, in spite of free and fair elections.

Vanderpuye was particularly effective at reaching out to the youth. The youth are most concerned about jobs, and they felt as though the incumbent did not provide employment opportunities to them. Van-derpuye's chief strategist explained that in the early 1990s, young boys would watch from their homes the police academy training, which was located in the community: "They would see people from their com-munity, young men they grew up next to. But now, they do not see anybody they know. These people want positions, but they are not getting them."[23] The belief is that in the 1990s, the MP was also a minister. Vanderpuye's campaign emphasized that if he is elected, he will not just be a "backbencher" like the incumbent, but rather a

---

[19] December 7, 2011.   [20] December 19, 2011.

[21] A report suggests that the cost of being a parliamentary candidate in Ghana increased 59 percent between 2012 and 2016: "On average candidates needed to raise GH₵389,803 (approximately US$85,000) to secure the party primary nomination and compete in the parliamentary election in their constituency" (Westminster Foundation for Democracy 2018).

[22] January 24, 2012.   [23] January 11, 2012.

minister who has the ability to link the youth up with jobs. Politicians in Ghana are expected to link up their own constituents, especially the youth, with state jobs.

One leader of the NDC Concerned Youth of Odododiodioo Constituency explained, "We need somebody to lobby for us, not someone who sits in Parliament and does nothing." Another young man explained, "The youth do not want money. We do not even want jobs directly from the MP. We want the MP to lobby for us. To make a call for us. To connect us with those who matter."[24] And another, "It is not that he is rich, but he has a link. We need people like that. He has links with people. He's all around. When you go to Brong Ahafo, he has friends. Go to Western, he has friends. Go to the North, he is known there."[25] Vanderpuye established youth groups, "keep-fit" clubs (athletic training teams), and friend's clubs to formally organize disparate clusters of youth throughout Odododiodioo Constituency. He placed banners throughout all parts of the constituency with emblems that read things like "Striker's Fan Club Votes Nii Lantey Vanderpuye for MP of Odododiodioo Constituency." The youth clubs are modeled after the popular fan clubs for Premier League football teams.

On the surface, Vanderpuye seems to be signaling that he is a credible candidate, one that voters can depend on once he is in office (Kramon 2016). This is certainly true. But Vanderpuye's tactics demonstrate more than just distributing the goods to win elections, but also include increasing his "political family" so that he can satisfy his role as an opinion leader in the neighborhood. This is important because while Vanderpuye clearly has electoral ambitions (that include his desire to be President one day), he also controls a valuable and historical part of the city. Even if the distribution of goods dries up, the goodwill he has gained from his political family can be transferred to business decisions he makes and involvement in chieftaincy affairs, both of which extend beyond electoral concerns. In these ways, leaders attempt to extend their political families as much as possible, allowing them to amass social approval and prestige. These assets help leaders extend control and authority in their neighborhoods. Vanderpuye is subscribing to what Michael Schatzberg calls the moral matrix of legitimacy, in which he must care for his family by providing to them,

[24] January 18, 2012.   [25] June 27, 2012.

but also enabling them to enter the decision-making sphere so that his family can carry on the legacy of his lineage (Schatzberg 1993: 452).

The concept political family broadens our understanding of distributive politics because it suggests that politicians in indigenous settlements are not attempting to provide resources to the broader public, nor to a private set of friends and colleagues. Politicians are serving a family – a club. Being a member of the club provides access to the division of spoils and a personal connection to not only the opinion leader, but the broader family network as well.

Indigeneity and the Politics of Resentment

Elinor Ostrom's insights into collective decision-making are applicable across Ghanaian cities, as residents are often forced to govern their own resources: managing sewers, public toilets, and property markets. But the simplified understanding of governing the commons overlooks the distinct political divisions that emerge from contentious historical events and episodes. This is most apparent in the way that the Ga indigenes fear the Ashanti ethnic group, and how politicians and leaders politicize this division with respect to distribution and service provision. This type of distributive politics extends far beyond the desire to win elections and manage the commons, but to the control and authority over urban space. Historical cleavages complicate the neat divisions between economic, cultural, and linguistic differences that are popular ways to conceptualize group difference and threat in the African politics literature (Adida 2011; Honig 2016). Baldwin and Huber's (2010) analysis, on the other hand, emphasizes the "substantive differences between groups," highlighting the importance of "between-group inequality." Their analysis finds robust evidence that "countries with higher levels of inequality between groups have lower levels of public goods" (645).[26] Despite this valuable finding, the mechanism, which requires local-level analysis, remains underspecified.

Katherine Cramer's (2016) concept of politics of resentment helps to specify the mechanism. In her conceptualization, citizens take out their frustration with distributive decisions – who gets what, when, and

---

[26] The argument relies on cross-national data. For African countries, it relies on the Afrobarometer.

how – on their fellow citizens. Rather than placing the responsibility on elite decision-makers or the state, they draw real boundaries between "us" versus "them" that "coincide with real geographic boundaries" (5). In Accra, many indigenes resent the Ashanti ethnic group – the core support base of the NPP – due to its historical accumulation of money and power through alliances made with whites during the slave trade and the colonial era (Wilks 1975; McCaskie 1983).[27] This contributes to a politics of resentment, where indigenes feel as though outsiders – and Ashantis in particular – are getting what is deservedly theirs. The following evidence demonstrates how political, economic, and cultural factors are embedded in broader struggles over authority in the city.

"We share, just not with the Ashantis," Vanderpuye's campaign strategist explains.[28] The sharing of state goods and resources is prevalent in Ga Mashie, but a core group of indigenous nationalists who hold considerable economic and political power will not form multi-ethnic coalitions with people of the Ashanti ethnic group. This is because these residents fear that the Ashantis will dominate – economically, politically, and culturally.[29]

This deep distrust is historically rooted. "In the history books, Ghanaian history is Ashanti history," the strategist explains.[30] "This is because Ashantis have dominated Academia, and most historians are Ashanti. They wrote the history of Ghana with their group at the center. This is something that belies politics in Ghana. It gives them the feeling of megalomania." There is a Ga folk belief that Ashantis tried to reach Accra decades ago, but were stopped, and were chased into nearby Dodowa Forest. A Ga saying developed: You don't know what is in Dodowa Forest. This serves as a warning: Be careful, you don't know what the Ashantis are up to. This distrust plays out in modern-day politics. "The Ashantis infiltrate all chieftaincy problems." "They have this higher-than-thou attitude toward all tribes. We are *here*. They have *come*."

This indigenous narrative is used to keep the Ashantis from moving in, organizing, and investing in Central Accra. Fear of a dominant ethnic group is common across Africa, and in poor indigenous settlements, leaders often use a language of indigeneity to score political

---

[27] Ga leaders also benefited from their role as middlemen (as described in Chapter 3), but many of these elites align with the NPP today.

[28] December 17, 2011.   [29] This portion is adapted from Klaus and Paller (2017).

[30] December 17, 2011.

points. The indigenous narrative has proven incredibly strong in relation to recent developmental plans for the community. During the NPP
government (2000–2008), there were several plans to modernize the
capital city. These plans included upgrading Bukom Park, a gathering
spot in the center of Ga Mashie. But local residents vehemently resisted
the NPP's plans to develop the park, and politicians like Vanderpuye
mobilized youth against the project (Obeng-Odoom 2013).

"Bukom is a place of free access," the strategist explains. "We go
there and we do whatever we like. It is ours. But we were afraid that if
the NPP came and developed the land they would sell the land like they
have done elsewhere across the city, to private businesses and individuals.[31] They have done this all over the city. We were worried that they
will take it from us."[32] Area youth verify these sentiments by claiming
that the NPP's plans were to benefit the wealthy and the government,
not the residents in the community. But they also realize that politicians easily manipulate them. This is a clear example of how the
commons gets politicized by local leaders, unemployed youth, and
other residents.

This example demonstrates why the provision of infrastructure must
be understood within a historical context. As Larkin (2008) suggests in
the context of Nigeria, providing infrastructure was a tool that colonial
regimes used in exchange for political subjection. It also contributed to
divide and conquer strategies that colonists used to prevent unity
among indigenous groups and families. In this case, the development
of a park has connotations that extend far beyond the mere development of a park. Rather, the control of the city was also under threat
because a section of the Ga community felt as though they were losing
their city.

The problem is intensified because of a lack of unified, strong
community leadership. During a focus group with Ga Mashie youth,
respondents admit that they contribute to the underdevelopment. One
man explained, "Our leaders are also not bold, they can't organize
a task force to let people stop selling in the street ... When there
was an attempt to provide WC toilets in every household, people
resisted saying "Do you want to use our sleeping place for WCs!"[33]
Yet this leadership must be understood in the indigenous context,

[31] Klopp (2000) discusses this problem in contemporary Kenya.
[32] December 17, 2011.   [33] June 20, 2012.

where residents organize along ethnic lines because the indigenous status provides a powerful mechanism to demand club goods and services from their leaders. The inclusion of outsiders, as well as outside development, is perceived as a disruption of the status quo, and maybe even a threat to their existence. In other words, the type of distributive politics undermines the development of a public sphere, where a collective identity can emerge, and instead privileges the state capture of services for club gain.

Therefore, political entrepreneurs respond to the norm of indigeneity, and create mobilization strategies that align with these interests. In the early 2000s, Ga Mashie witnessed a demographic change, whereby many new Akans were registering in the constituency. The in-migration of Akans worried the NDC because they typically vote NPP. This was a significant threat to the electoral dominance of the party, but also to the dominance of the Ga ethnic group.

Then, the NDC lost the 2000 election. Many in the NDC worried about the growing number of traders coming into the city from other parts of the country. Vanderpuye's campaign strategist explains the situation: "What happened was that *those people* came and outnumbered our votes. *They* outnumbered us. This is the commercial center of the country and people were creeping in all the time. Almost three million people each day are milling about. The groups that came in were actually parasitic groups. The NDC knew that their waterloo was there, and they tried to accommodate them. You can't trust those people."[34] He continues, "As the Akans were coming in, it changes the political action on the ground. And I was taking notice. The temperature was changing. The trend is changing. People are coming in with a different mindset and you always have to analyze that threat level."

The language that the campaign strategist uses is shaped by the indigenous nature of the neighborhood. He explains how Akan traders are "creeping in." He refers to them as "those people," in contrast to "us" – who are from here. His strongest claim is that they are "actually parasitic groups," claiming that they are a disease that is infiltrating their homeland and spreading rapidly: They need to be controlled and extinguished.[35] But he is adamant that the constituency is for the Ga,

---

[34] December 17, 2011.
[35] For a discussion about the difficulty of separating identity and homeland, and how struggles over territory can contribute to ethnic conflict, see: Shelef (2016).

and for the NDC. The party and identity group cannot be easily separated. Politicians benefit from the indigenous status of the settlement by using it to their own advantage during election time. The norm of indigeneity enables the NDC to play the ethnic card and use tribalism as a political tool to gain votes and win elections.

In this way, political entrepreneurs creatively devise rules of the game that favor their interests (Berk and Galvan 2009). The rules and procedures of multiparty democracy are fused with the underlying cultural and historical patterns of politics, creating syncretic institutions that incentivize politicians and followers to create distinct boundaries between the Ga and Ashantis. Of course, this extreme distrust is inherently political. In fact, the campaign strategist is not a Ga, and instead uses the language of indigeneity as a political tool. The strategist's story is framed by a very real threat of losing an election, and shaped even more by the recent loss in 2000. This fear translates directly to the campaign strategies that the NDC uses. One such tactic was to prevent Akans from registering to vote. "I am limiting their numbers," he admits. "In the voter's register. If they come I will challenge them. We know who are NPP and NDC."[36] The voter's register in the NDC office even has Akan names circled. They targeted these people to try to prevent them from registering and voting.

On the surface, this sounds like the classic racial threat that political scientists have documented in the context of African Americans in the southern United States, as well as with immigration to American cities (Key 1949; Putnam 2007). But this purely electoral perspective fails to account for the underlying norms of settlement and belonging that shape the practice of politics – in this case, the type of distributive politics.

Instead, norms of indigeneity shape how the NDC organizers interpret the electoral laws. During the registration process, the constituency experienced sporadic acts of violence between parties (Bob-Milliar 2014). The NPP claimed that the NDC prevented their voters from registering. The NDC claimed that they did not live in the constituency and therefore did not have the right to vote there. In the

---

[36] The strategist explains how they know who resides in the area: "People are neighbors. I know my neighbor and he also knows me. My other neighbor also knows me. So these are the houses. If you want to see the layout of all these areas, you have to see these places on Sunday. When there is no commercial traffic. So you can go there all the way and see who resides here." December 17, 2011.

areas of the constituency with large amounts of Akan migrants, the NDC challenged all residents who spoke Twi. But the NDC only had problems with the commercial migrants, typically Akan and NPP, who did not sleep in Odododiodioo, but not indigenous Ga who sleep elsewhere. The NDC interprets that those whose family are from the constituency can register, and these can only be indigenes of Ga Mashie.

From a purely electoral perspective, the decision to modernize parks, upgrade markets, and install sewers would be viewed as democratic accountability or government responsiveness. But what this section shows is that the process of distribution, as well as who is involved in the decision-making process, factors into the successful governance of resources in the indigenous core of the city. The politics of resentment helps explain how inequalities between groups can manifest in anti-outsider narratives, entitlement to space and territory, and potential ethnic conflict. Resource distribution, including the building of infrastructure, is embedded in much larger struggles for control and authority in the city.

Serving the Public Interest in a Diversifying City

A common misconception in much of the distributive politics literature, especially in the context of Africa, is that it assumes all state goods distributed by the government are "public." Even the overarching term "public goods distribution" is a misnomer because it fails to account for the ways in which local populations understand resources and services.[37] Instead, creating a public sphere – where populations deliberate, make decisions, and govern resources and services in the public interest – requires a long and contentious political process. This could be achieved at the national level, where top-down nationalization campaigns can create a sense of public goods at the local level, as opposed to ethnic entitlements (Miguel 2004).

But the construction of a public sphere can also be achieved locally, through the civic activism and collective action of diverse leaders and groups in neighborhoods. The growth of cities in Ghana has changed

---

[37] In a seminal article, Peter Ekeh (1975) goes so far as to say that there are two publics in Africa, a civic public that is an outcome of colonial rule and has no moral basis, and a primordial public that politicians have an affinity toward and to which they are held accountable.

the dynamics of its society by bringing together people from different ethnic groups into a limited physical space. These unsettled neighborhoods become arenas of politics where early settlers establish themselves as leaders, creating new authority structures distinct from existing indigenous chiefs and elders. These structures create a new type of distributive politics, where state goods and resources are governed publicly, in contrast to the pattern of club goods distribution in indigenous settlements.

As a city grows, new neighborhoods form, and the process of goods and resource distribution are politicized. One of the surprising realities of urbanization is that some neighborhoods evolve in a way where indigenous residents and migrant populations coexist and work together to demand change. The formation of a true public sphere is an active, practiced, and political process that I document in the following pages.

The Construction of a Public Sphere

From the very early years of settlement in the 1960s, Ashaiman had a robust organizational structure.[38] Residents formed rotating credit associations, landlord and occupational organizations, and hometown associations. Most of these organizations were ethnic by nature, mostly due to language barriers. The formation of the Ashaiman Traditional Council evolved, as elders from the different ethnic groups aligned with the indigenous traditional authorities to govern matters of land and territory. A public sphere that served the common interest did not exist in the early years of Ashaiman.

Nonetheless, these strong organizational ties made Ashaiman attractive to outside organizations, including political parties and foreign NGOs. As a leader explained, NGOs began coming here because "the community was already organized in groups."[39] Another leader added, "We have owned the community. We have owned the processes. Sometimes people just go and buy the lights and go to the Assembly to put them in. This gives us the advantage to go and get more funding because of our maintenance culture."[40] In 1989 the

---

[38] Studies of Ashaiman document this organizational structure (Peil 1974; Sandbrook and Arn 1977; Owunsu 1991).

[39] February 13, 2012.　　　[40] February 13, 2012.

NDC used Ashaiman as a pilot site for its new decentralization program. In the early 2000s, UN-Habitat worked on a pilot housing project. The dense networks of social engagement directly contributed to the growing presence of NGOs in Ashaiman. This is because NGOs need community partners on the ground, and preexisting local structures facilitate the success of the proposed project. Therefore, over time, Ashaiman was marked as an NGO-friendly community, and organizations based in Accra and internationally came to invest in the community. While NGOs have their own agenda, one of the important effects they have is that they bring people together publicly to discuss political issues.

With dense networks in place, NGOs and local government have better chances of success. Jennifer Brass (2016) explains how NGOs and the state can work in tandem to improve service delivery, as long as they work as partners. Further, residents and leaders on the ground benefit from what the NGOs teach them. As one party member said with respect to political parties, "They do not groom people. There is no training. It's the NGOs who have come here to show us the truth. We even have the talent but we did not know that we had it."[41]

The formation of a public sphere emerges out of these strong organizational ties. Until 2007, Ashaiman was part of Tema Municipal Assembly. Despite the growth of the settlement to nearly 200,000 people, it did not have its own form of political or administrative representation. This led to a broad-based political movement in Ashaiman, where residents and leaders from all groups came together to demand change. Residents of Ashaiman developed a common source of resentment – toward the formal government. In contrast to the politics of resentment in Ga Mashie that pit insiders versus outsiders, the lack of a strong indigenous group that claims entitlement to the city contributed to the formation of a broad-based coalition of actors to come together against a common enemy.

This was a long, slow, drawn out process, similar to what Asef Bayat calls the "quiet encroachment of the ordinary." Bayat describes this as "the discreet and prolonged ways in which the poor struggle to survive and to better their lives by quietly impinging on the propertied and powerful, and on society at large" (Bayat 2013: 15). Residents explain that Ashaiman had a very participatory culture. In the late 1990s and

---

[41] February 27, 2012.

early 2000s, residents recount a vibrant grassroots politics where every afternoon, neighbors would gather at the houses of their local leader and discuss community affairs. "It was a special time," one resident of Tulako said. These hang out spots became "sites for the performance of citizenship," as Wedeen (2008) calls them. These neighborhood spots of deliberation became critical to the development of a public sphere, where citizens discussed ways to set the agenda for what they wanted legislated, ensuring that they became part of the process of local decision-making, not just public opinion formation (Fraser 1990).

The quiet encroachment entered the public transcript in the 2000s after decades of feeling marginalized by the central government and the local government administrative unit. Residents and leaders began agitating for municipality status from the national government. They had one simple goal: They wanted to govern themselves. Up until this point they were part of Tema Metropolitan Assembly but as Ashaiman grew, they believed they were not getting their fair share of resources. More than everyday forms of resistance (Scott 1990), this struggle for urban citizenship becomes formalized "when the gains are formally recognized in the state law book" (Bayat 2013: 26). The process was notable for the incorporation of diverse factions into the movement.

"There was one enemy—the Castle," community activist Jonathan Avisah explained, referring to the resistance to national government policy. "It was a movement, a struggle. Let us organize and demonstrate."[42] The struggle for municipality status had its roots in the associational life and authority structures dating back to the initial settlement of the neighborhood. But the social movement gained traction in the early 2000s when political parties, traditional authorities, and assemblymen joined together in a broad-based coalition. This broad coalition was particularly unique because it included members from different ethnic groups, as well as both major political parties.

Several key members of Ashaiman civil society trace this collective action to the Ashaiman Youth Governance Forum that began in 2003. The forum was an attempt "to engage the duty bearers" and produce real change in the community. Local leaders wanted to shed the community's image as a "den of criminals." Avisah explains, "You could not identify yourself as being from Ashaiman because of the negative stigma associated with the community."[43] Instead, the community was

[42] February 8, 2012.   [43] February 8, 2012.

used as a political resource: "Political leaders would come here and bus people out to create mayhem."

The idea of the forum began when Professor Martin Adjei, a United States-based professor with ties to the University of Ghana, met an old friend wanting to promote good governance in Africa. Adjei was part of the NGO Nimba Community Support Services, or NIMCOSS, which was based in Legon. They partnered with Danish-based EBIS to fund the Ashaiman Youth Governance Forum in 2003. Ashaiman was selected as a test case for the forum because of its preexisting associational life, closeness to Accra, and extreme poverty.

In 2003, the leaders started holding monthly forums on good governance. A task force was assembled to find out how local leaders and assembly members were performing. The face-to-face forum grew out of this task force and was held publicly to hold leaders to account. At these forums, leaders and residents alike began expressing their grievances and demanding more local authority over the governance process. As one local leader explained, "You can be called upon to give account of your actions," he said. "The governance forum will expose you. You are watching and somebody is also watching."[44]

Of course, the forums had their challenges, as one resident made clear: "Some people are of the perception that those behind the Governance Forum are doing it for their own personal gain. But we try to mingle personal relationships into socio-economic development issues."[45] Another resident complained, "At the end of the day they push it under the floor. For example, there is a five-year action plan at the Assembly. We go to participate. But they do nothing. And they do it to get a big carpe diem for themselves, and give participants minerals and small chop . . . [But] They are good. They enlighten us. They create awareness in the community."[46] This quote illustrates Ghanaians' complicated relationships with NGOs and their leaders. On the one hand, most Ashaiman residents could point out the challenges of the forum, while at the same time appreciating the opportunity to come face-to-face with their leaders and discuss community issues. Like Ghanaian politics in general, personalities and personal rivalries

---

[44] February 13, 2012. See: Fujiwara and Wantchekon (2013) and Gottlieb (2016) on the role that information and deliberation can have on politics and governance in Africa.

[45] February 20, 2012.   [46] February 29, 2012.

matter. But the forum places these rivalries at the forefront, and brings various rivals face-to-face.

At the time, development was very difficult because Tema Municipal Assembly would not distribute sufficient funding to the decentralized zonal councils. The struggle grew particularly intense in 2007 when nearby town Adenta was selected as a new municipality, while the bigger Ashaiman was not. The selection of Adenta was seen as a political move because Adenta is a stronghold of the then governing NPP government, while Ashaiman is an NDC stronghold. This selection further emboldened the grassroots movement against the government.

The struggle for political representation included members from all different levels of society and political leanings. The MP lobbied at the National Level; the community agitated at the local level; the traditional authorities petitioned in their communities; and even NPP residents lobbied in party circles. A key moment of dissent occurred when Thomas Adongo, an influential NPP assemblyman, left his party's stance publicly and joined the youth in advocating for municipality status. This signaled an important political rupture because it is very rare for a partisan leader to break with his party and oppose its public stance. The market women's association soon joined. The assembly members then formed a caucus.

The struggle took on many forms of protest. For example, a group of Ashaiman women even threatened to march to the doorstep of the Deputy Minister of Local Government and Rural Development naked, and jump into his bed to sleep with him.[47] This kind of demonstration finds its roots in colonialism when women used diverse tactics to fight white rule. The women proposed this plan at a meeting that included traditional authorities, opinion leaders, assembly members, and leaders of the various community-based associations. The struggle culminated in a large demonstration. Three community leaders were all over the national radio stations.[48] Central to these grievances were the desire to "own the process," language that extended far beyond simply

---

[47] The threat of nakedness, especially from mature women, can be quite powerful in many African cultures.

[48] Ibrahim Baidoo (or Bronx) was leader of the Assemblyman Caucus, and later became the mayor; Prince Muhammed, President of the Ashaiman Youth Coalition (became leading assemblyman), and Avisah, representing the Ashaiman Youth Governance Forum and Civil Society.

demanding goods and services. Residents and leaders demanded self-governance over their own urban space.

They were able to get the attention of the media and over the next few days made "lots of noise." A few days later the announcement was reversed: Ashaiman got its own municipality.[49] Gaining formal political representation was a crucial moment in the development prospects of Ashaiman. But what it further shows is that political representation is not a given in urban Ghana. Neighborhoods and communities have to fight for it.[50] It is an outcome of vibrant collective action.

This story is similar to what Adam Auerbach (2016) describes in India as "demanding development." In this conceptualization, development is a demand-side proposition: Communities must organize themselves to either self-provision services; make claims on the state for resources, or; engage in collective protest. He finds that group claim-making, or "getting the attention of politicians and officials to improve the community," (Auerbach 2016: 118) was the most common strategy used by neighborhood residents in Indian squatter settlements.[51] In the case of Ashaiman, residents began with group claim-making, but were forced to engage in collective protests to demand a new administrative unit. Interestingly, their success stands in contrast to the argument advanced by Grossman and Lewis (2014) who find that administrative unit proliferation in Uganda occurs where there is a confluence of interests between the national executive and local citizens and elites. This suggests that in growing urban areas like Ashaiman, the demands of neighborhood residents might play a much larger role in decentralization.

Yet there is an additional factor that must be considered. Political economy explanations are limited in their explanatory power because they restrict development – and the distributive politics in which they are embedded – to an electoral game, underemphasizing the importance of the formation of a collective identity among the urban poor, as well as a space of politics where deliberation and face-to-face contact with representatives can occur. Instead, the case of Ashaiman represents something more: the construction of a public sphere among otherwise ethnic and parochial interests. The movement has important

[49] Adenta maintained its own as well.
[50] There is a similar effort in Nima, Accra. However, local political divisions undermine the effort.
[51] Eighty percent of his sample engaged in this type of activity.

lessons for other poor urban settlements: Collective decision-making and self-governance is the outcome of a long and contentious struggle. The outcome is a commons in which a broad coalition of actors can deliberate, engage, and shape their own image.

In other words, these dense associational forms are more than a demand for development. Rather, they are central to how democracy works in the neighborhoods of urban Ghana. Kwame Anthony Appiah (1993) characterizes these demands theoretically in the following way: "These organizations and their experiences with autonomous and relatively democratic organization are, I believe, of tremendous significance for the development of public life in Africa, and for the simplest of reasons: they give people a chance to practice participatory modes of organizing communal life; they offer the experience of autonomy" (Appiah 1993: 171). But these spheres of democratic expression must be able to demand formal change, by gaining administrative units where local self-governance of goods and services fall under the jurisdiction of neighborhoods.

Beyond Elite Capture

Decentralization is not a silver bullet for development. Decentralization can replace central government corruption with elite capture of local governments (Bardhan and Mookherjee 2006). Elite capture is quite durable, and has been a problem that local administrative units struggle with across diverse contexts (Sheely 2015). The challenge of elite capture has certainly plagued the municipal assembly in Ashaiman, but has not stalled its governmental prospects.

Since 2007, Ashaiman has struggled to incorporate its structures that existed prior to political recognition into formal administration. One of the biggest problems with the provision of services is that political parties co-opt the process. The following example involving public toilets illustrates this. In 2000, the NPP took over the management of public toilets after they won the election. Local branch leaders seized the toilets by force. In 2002 after many arguments and complaints, the Assembly reclaimed management of the toilets. However, the Assembly simply awarded the contracts back to the NPP foot soldiers and leaders. In 2008, after the NDC won the election, NDC youth seized the toilets and regained control. The Assembly reclaimed control after people made numerous complaints. But political influence dictated the process: The Assembly abrogated the contracts to the NPP and re-awarded them to the NDC. NDC branch leaders and other party insiders now run the operations, and profit from them.

Not all public toilets operate in the same way.[52] Some operators only share with their friends. This creates problems because people do not feel as though they are getting a fair share. People fight and argue about the sharing. The toilet in the neighborhood called Zongo operates differently. The toilet is managed by an organization of representatives from various groups, including clubs, opinion leaders, churches, and mosques. The coordinator explains that the most important thing is to make sure that the Christians get some of the proceeds. If they do not do this they will claim that the Muslims are dominating and this will create problems. "Everybody knows how much it costs," he said. "You cannot cheat them."

The public toilets serve a political agenda. The proceeds are often used for NDC functions and campaigns. During voter registration, the proceeds went to feeding the NDC polling agents. The party leaders make these decisions. For example, the Chief Executive asked the operators to donate the money for the exercise. The operators complied. "This is how you distribute goods," the organizer said, emphasizing the groupings. Without the organized groups, people do not know how things are shared. This creates confusion and mistrust. But with the organized groups, goods are shared through the outlets and they cannot be accused of empowering their own pockets. By creating organized groupings, Zongo has established a network that serves the interests of a diverse group of residents.

Though the governance of public services in this way certainly serves club interests – as it does in Ga Mashie – the structures enable a minimum level of transparency and accountability. This pattern of behavior is similar to evidence from urban Uganda where the few examples of successful collective action occurred among a small subset of homogenous groups, rather than broad-based multiethnic activity (Habyarimina et al. 2009: 146). The case of Ashaiman demonstrates that organized "capture" of public services still maintain a level of accountability, because more elites are pulled into the governance structure. While certain public services are "captured" by local elites, the informal rules and norms provide the possibility for a diverse set of

---

[52] August 14, 2012.

leaders to benefit from the governance of services. In addition, organizations learn from the neighboring and better functioning governance structures, creating a knowledge spillover through institutional learning. Distributive politics thus emerges out of a vibrant public sphere, which allows for different organized groups to be incorporated into the process of governance.

This is not to say that the commons is not politicized in Ashaiman. But the space of distributive politics extends far beyond political parties, and there are spheres of deliberation that underlie the rules of the game. In other words, there is space outside of formal politics for residents and leaders to seek civic advancement.[53] But perhaps more importantly, there is a growing space for residents to secure personal advancement without engaging in multiparty politics. This sets Ashaiman on an alternative path that is optimal for development. The case of the opinion leader Innocent illustrates this fact.

Members of political parties are the first people to receive state benefits when resources are limited. Innocent explains that if he joined the NDC, "I would be the first person that they help. They help out people who follow them, who work for them."[54] The assistant secretary for Ashaiman constituency of the NDC confirmed, "Party work is sacrificial work. It's for love of the party. But when something flows, we extend it to them. If there is a job opening, especially if it's governmental, we help them get the job."[55] Joining political party ranks can bring immediate opportunities, like jobs, educational opportunities, and contracts (Bob-Milliar 2012).[56] Citizens and residents, therefore, make rational calculations about whether they join "politics."

But Innocent also understood the problems it brings: It immediately "outs" you as partisan. This can be used against people in all matters of daily life. Partisans are accused of furthering their party's agenda at the expense of the common good. In all neighborhoods across urban Ghana, joining a political party is one important pathway for social

---

[53] In the context of Uganda, Aili Tripp (1997) refers to this as state autonomy. Fox (1994) suggests that this is a crucial aspect of being a citizen, in contrast to client.

[54] February 20, 2012.   [55] August 8, 2012.

[56] The NDC even has a "Hero's Fund" that rewards "political victims," supporters of the party who sacrificed time and energy for the party during a prior campaign. It provides scholarships and other employment opportunities for dedicated members of the NDC. The fund is modeled after a previous initiative of the NPP.

mobility. While he admits that he would get assistance from the political parties if he joined, he knows that it comes with consequences. "It would completely compromise my work as a social worker."[57] In this way, gaining legitimacy as an opinion leader extends beyond the ability to win elections, to gaining the support and trust and respect of residents on the ground.

These alternative pathways of empowerment only work under two conditions. First, if being a social worker who advocates on behalf of a broad population of residents is respected and admired in the neighborhood. Second, if there are other avenues of social mobility outside of politics. Both of these conditions hold in Ashaiman. I've noted how the development of a public sphere contributes to a spirit of civic engagement in the neighborhood. But residents also have other opportunities outside of formal politics, including serving as teachers, health workers, restaurant operators, butchers, and shop owners. Perhaps most importantly, leaders have the space to serve outside of multiparty channels, including working with NGOs, churches, mosques, and other social organizations. In Ashaiman, leaders like Innocent have choices to work outside the realm of political parties because there are economic and social opportunities that are tied to politics, but not consumed by the parties themselves. This does not exist in communities like Old Fadama, as I will explain next. It is this interaction between political parties and the underlying distributive logic that is often left out of conventional studies of public goods provision.

This is not to say that leaders like Innocent are not engaged in politics at all. Innocent always mentions that he is "working at the grassroots" and is "close to the people." He uses NGO buzzwords like, "We need to build capacity at the grassroots." As a member of the Ewe ethnic group, residents perceive Innocent to be affiliated with the NDC. But this is not a problem in Ashaiman, an NDC stronghold. Nonetheless, he makes sure to stay out of formal politics publicly. Instead, he supports candidates underground, by providing information at the grassroots to political candidates.[58] For example, he often meets with the MP of Ashaiman. He is able to get meetings with him because the MP likes to know what is going on at the grassroots. Other politicians rely on insights from him because they need to make sure that the men who are assisting on political campaigns are real followers, and

[57] February 20, 2012.   [58] March 26, 2012.

not informants of a political opponent.[59] Politicians consulted him "usually at midnight, late into the process they call us."[60]

The concepts associated with elite capture and clientelism do not capture the real incentives that residents and leaders face in the context of daily life. Nor do they accurately represent the motivations that drive people like Innocent. Leaders and residents are motivated by far more than a desire for political survival or economic empowerment. But the underlying rules and procedures of a neighborhood condition the opportunities available to them.

The Production of Democracy

In some ways, multiparty democracy in Ghana has become a production or performance.[61] It creates new spaces for economic empowerment, everyday enjoyment, and daily struggles. Nowhere was the performance of multiparty democracy on greater display than during the voter registration exercise that consumed one month of people's lives. The exercise provided a good opportunity for people like Innocent because he is affiliated with a local NGO called SYPPA, who received a contract to observe the elections. He was tasked with visiting polling stations over the course of the month, and assigning volunteers to potential hotspots.

The registration exercise symbolizes the logistical challenges of democratization in African societies. For example, at one polling station, there was a long delay because one old man did not know what his surname was because he never identified himself as such.[62] At another polling station, an eighty-four-year-old woman could not find a ride home because she did not bring two cedis with her. This caused a fight in line when one of the young men paid for her taxi and then asked her for money.[63]

---

[59] April 16, 2012.   [60] April 4, 2012.
[61] Kertzer's (1988) book is the classic account of the role that rituals play in politics. Englund (2002) discusses the role of culture and performance in Malawi. Nugent (1996) examines the political culture of Ghana. Fraser (2017) uses the concept of political theatre to analyze the role of post-populist politics in Zambia. Jourde (2005) assesses the role of drama and performance in presidential campaign visits in Mauritania.
[62] March 26, 2012.   [63] April 2, 2012.

During the second week, a fight broke out at one of the polling stations when a man skipped ahead in line. A woman then smacked the man.[64] The next day at Starlight Elementary School, dozens of people waited in the hot sun for hours to register. There were no trees under which people could wait.[65] That same day, two of the registration stations started more than two hours late because the EC worker with the computers did not show up on time. At another, the biometric machine would not work. This same day, one of the EC agents was accused of extorting money from people to allow them to jump the line.

The production of democracy illustrated by the voter registration exercise provided a stage for local "big men" to assert their authority at the polling stations. The mayor used the chance to drive around in his state-provisioned truck.[66] An MP aspirant used the chance to promote his community service, as one of the polling stations was his school. He also sought to attract new voters by handing out t-shirts in his office.[67] Assemblymen used the chance to inform residents about the meeting the previous Wednesday where new roads in town were discussed.[68]

One politician used the chance to organize youth supporters to pressure higher-ups in the NDC party to make a change at Chief Executive, threatening to cause disturbances if nothing was done.[69] The Constituency Chairman used the chance to assert his power and barked orders at his party faithful. He brought snacks to the workers in a public display of generosity.[70] Another man was formally employed by the Electoral Commission to register voters and the process gave him the chance to make some extra money and greet his neighbors. But more importantly, as an older man inherently interested in learning and strengthening his social networks, he hoped that it would help him establish links to maybe start his own NGO one day.[71]

Similarly, students used the exercise as a way to make some money and put a line on their resume. One young woman explained how she was in the middle of a gap year and the exercise provided something to do outside of her daily chores.[72] Innocent used the chance to be close to the grassroots and establish his authority as a social worker.

---

[64] April 4, 2012.   [65] April 5, 2012.   [66] March 26, 2012.
[67] April 2, 2012.   [68] March 26, 2012.   [69] April 4, 2012.
[70] April 16, 2012.   [71] April 10, 2012.   [72] April 16, 2012.

His personality shined through, and he glowed in the prestige it gave him. Residents and politicians alike seek advice from people like Innocent from a governance and local government standpoint. While he is not a central player in the intense negotiations, his voice is heard and they seek his advice. In this way, he is an important stakeholder in the political game.

Clearly, the state offered different resources to different people, and residents and leaders navigated the arena of politics in a way to secure their own advantage. This process of creative syncretism adds an additional layer to understandings of distributive politics, giving people and groups agency to the process, rather than simply conceiving distribution as an instrumental patronage exchange.

Political parties took the registration exercise particularly seriously. The NDC placed two polling agents at each station to make sure there were no problems. The parties trusted neither the Electoral Commission nor the NPP, so they had to send their own watchdogs. The NPP also had agents, but not as many due to their lower levels of support in Ashaiman. This also provided opportunities for young, unemployed youth to volunteer for the party and show their political commitment. Women were employed as caterers to feed the polling agents and they provided takeaway food for all workers. During this process, incumbency advantage proved strong.[73] The NDC was able to fund the catering and extra money necessary to serve as watchdogs with revenue from the public toilets. The interplay between political party struggles, working for the party, and public services underlie the production of democracy during the registration exercise.

There is a growing research agenda about how political parties manipulate the electoral process. For example, Asunka et al. 2017 find that Ghanaian political parties relocate fraud to polling stations that do not have an election observer. This is similar to Ichino and Schündeln's (2012) finding that electoral observers reduce the number of registration irregularities in the country. The management of elections can impact the trust that citizens have in state institutions, greatly affecting the democratization process (Erlich and Kerr 2016). Most of these studies focus on the formal electoral process, neglecting the important contextual factors that shape trust in electoral institutions.

---

[73] Klaus and Paller (2017) discuss the role that incumbency plays in choosing campaign strategies.

Most importantly, they are unable to account for the production of elections – how the democratic process is actually embedded in the daily lives of citizens. This is important because it contributes new understandings to Ghana's democratic development.

The misallocation of funds was on the front of people's minds during the month of the biometric registration exercise, and was a constant topic of conversation while residents waited in the long lines.[74] Rumors spread when people gathered at the registration centers. Ghanaians needed the registration exercise for more than just the right to vote. It also signaled an important action of exercising citizenship.[75] They need the picture ID as a form of identification because without state ID cards residents rely on the voter's ID cards to help secure bank loans and other potential assistance from the state. Further, they are proud of the card as it symbolizes their Ghanaian identity. Many residents carry it with them everywhere they go.

While the registration exercise was certainly important for the elections in December 2012, it was also important for the production and performance of democracy in people's daily lives. It offered the chance for leaders to establish their authority. It allowed economic opportunities for unemployed but educated youth. It legitimized the work of social workers and NGOs. It allowed the chance for ordinary residents to exercise their citizenship. It highlighted important aspects of the democratic process that are crucial for its success, and embodied in the daily practices of Ashaiman residents. The centers opened up important spaces for residents and their leaders to engage in governance and decision-making. Residents were not just voting, but claiming a space in Ghana's democratic, and also distributive, politics.

The registration exercise was important in all communities across the country, but it took different forms depending on the underlying informal institutional context and the nature of local political competition. For example, in Ga Mashie fights broke out over registration as members of the NDC tried to prevent outsiders from registering. They couched the debate both in ethnic terms, but also exploited the lack of legal property rights in some areas by suggesting that many of the opponents work in the constituency, but do not sleep there. This presented a preview to the forms of political mobilization that

---

[74] April 18, 2012.
[75] For more about citizen engagements with the state, see: Lauren M. MacLean (2011) on the exercise of citizenship.

would be used during the subsequent campaign. Despite similar ethnic demographics and comparable settlement patterns in some neighborhoods, Ashaiman did not have the same problems. As one resident explained a polling station , "Nothing like that happens here in Ashaiman. It is very calm."[76]

This ethnographic analysis of the voter registration exercise provides insights into why formal democratic procedures and practices take different forms and produce different results in various contexts. The daily practices of residents, leaders, and political parties shed light on the production of democracy in Ashaiman. While the exercise is a formal procedure and is guided by official rules and regulations, the underlying informal norms tell us as much, if not more, about the success of the exercise in Ashaiman as opposed to the difficulties in places like Ga Mashie and Old Fadama.

In Ashaiman, leaders are able to assert their informal authority through formal means. In other words, they are able to act as parents, caretakers, and personal rulers to their followers as assembly persons, constituency executives, and politicians. Similarly, young people have alternatives to political parties for social mobility. They can work as EC agents and for NGOs. This is in contrast to youth in other neighborhoods like Ga Mashie, where one youth resident explains that he works for the NDC because they give him jobs and a motorbike: "They feed me and make me happy," he said.[77] In other words, youth do not rely solely on political parties for their daily livelihoods. Members from different ethnic groups have opportunities to come together and engage in daily activities. The long waiting lines at the polling stations provided a vibrant public space for cross-ethnic dialogue and discussion. In the end, formal processes like voter registration perform better in settlements like Ashaiman, but only because the underlying institutional context forges strong leaders and cross-ethnic social engagement. This type of distributive politics incentivizes the governance of resources for the public interest.

Privatizing the Commons in Rapidly Growing Cities

The growth of squatter settlements in the past twenty years has coincided with significant tension over claims to urban space. As

[76] April 10, 2012. There is a history of low-intensity electoral violence (Bob-Milliar 2014) in Ashaiman.
[77] May 13, 2012.

opposed to the growth of stranger settlements during the colonial era when migrant leaders negotiated plots of land directly with indigenous landowners, these new neighborhoods formed illegitimately and extralegally. This distinction contributed to a very different type of distributive politics, where populations privatized the commons to empower their narrow population of settlers. These inhabitations were different from squatter invasions in many Latin American countries, where massive collective action and protest eventually contributed to the political recognition of these neighborhoods (Gilbert 1981; De Soto 2000; Holston 2008). In urban Ghana, populations lay a claim to the urban economy and a democratic dividend from the government, but the distribution of goods does not take the form of brick and mortar improvements, but rather private goods like jobs and contracts to a narrow, politically connected segment of the population. Local strongmen are able to politicize the commons for their personal empowerment.

Property developers, internationally backed NGOs, and indigenous landowners are making new claims to the land on which squatter settlements rest, contributing to a very contentious politics in these areas (Paller 2017). These neighborhoods are some of the most contentious political spaces in cities today, and questions over who gets what and how are highly combative and often play out in the courts and public media. For example, the struggle over Old Fadama is constantly stuck in a public battle between those who see residents as deserving of basic goods of survival, to those who demand they move to other neighborhoods or head back home. Less understood is the process by which this unfolds in the context of daily life. Political entrepreneurs and opinion leaders expertly navigate this terrain to seek their own advantage, capturing state goods for their own narrow segment of the population. I document the privatization of the commons in the rest of this chapter.

Private Services, Public Power

Despite the insecure political situation, squatter settlements provide a vibrant commercial market for residents (Gulyani and Talukdar 2008; Fox 2014). The following examples describe the different commercial opportunities available to its residents.

Every day, Kwame walks through the community carrying a large bag of cash.[78] He collects cash profits from several different shower operators in Old Fadama and brings it to the bank. Each month, one person gets a loan from the group, interest free. Kwame donates to local CBOs, youth groups, NDC branches, and other festivities, bolstering his status and prestige. His role as shower owner provides him significant clout in the community: His neighbors visit his compound every day, and unlike formal jobs, he receives an influx of cash.

Squatter settlements provide plentiful business opportunities, but also platforms for personal empowerment. Entrepreneurs take advantage of the insecure and informal property rights institutions to enhance their wealth, power, and prestige through private operations of "public" services like shower and toilet businesses, scrap recycling, and exploiting the informal land market. There are approximately 400 shower operators and their association forms an important interest group in the neighborhood. They are invited to all community functions and even have representatives when the community meets with AMA.[79] Showers cost more than those in other poor Ghanaian neighborhoods.[80] This is because when Kwame needed money, he called the association together and told them to raise the price ten peswas, and they all agreed.[81]

Running a shower business – a commercial enterprise that provides showers to residents because homes do not have running water – is extremely profitable. For example, an influential opinion leader named Frederick Opoku inherited a shower business from his father, who was a very early settler in the community. He also inherited a hotel business where people rent rooms mostly on an hourly rate. He controls a large compound that is used for outdoorings – funerals, weddings, or baby-naming ceremonies. He explains that his shower business is one of the smaller ones in Old Fadama and he makes approximately 1,050 Ghana cedis ($525) each month.

Many of the operators own multiple shower businesses. Opoku also owns a toilet facility. There are approximately 300 toilet businesses in the community, and they are equally as lucrative. Shower and toilet operators are some of the wealthiest people in the community, along

---

[78] October 31, 2011.   [79] November 29, 2011.

[80] In 2013, the shower price in Old Fadama was forty peswas (twenty cents), more than the average in the city.

[81] April 1, 2012. In other words, the shower association runs like a cartel.

with scrap dealers and transport operators. They do not pay taxes, although they sometimes pay municipal rates and rents, and earn consistent, daily income. Opoku's businesses have been so successful that he has purchased land and built a house outside of the community, where he often sleeps. Many of the business owners no longer sleep in the community.

Squatter settlements are not entirely off the grid in the way that they are often portrayed. People in government positions own businesses in the neighborhood, and residents are often tipped off early when there is an eviction rumor. Similarly, residents accuse cinema owners of colluding with the Electricity Company of Ghana and turning off the electricity during popular football matches. For example, a rumor spread during the Champion's League Final when electricity was shut down, and people with generators profited (Paller 2014).

With a population of more than 80,000 the business opportunities in Old Fadama are plentiful. One of the most lucrative businesses is the informal land market. Dagombas dominate the land market, having taken it over from the early Ga settlers. They have ruled with force since. But because the sales are unofficial and extralegal, leaders seek protection from political patrons. For example, when local strongman Yaw was forced out of the community after the NDC won the 2008 election, Hanaan and his small gang immediately stepped in to control his territory. If somebody wants to purchase a plot of land, they go to one of the seven landlords in the community.[82] This includes several Dagomba Youth Chiefs and even Chairman. As an NDC foot soldier, Hanaan maintains control.

The landlords all have various ways that they accumulated power, including wealth, early settlement, chieftaincy status, coercion, and even spiritual power. One Chief, the Daboli Lana is "based in the North. On and off he comes and goes. He's a magician. He does amazing things."[83] These landlords call in "the Thugs," like Hanaan and his boys, to come in and "create the necessary order for the deal to go through." They make sure that the person moving in will be safe on the ground, and they take their cut of the financial deal. Community leaders in squatter settlements craft creative strategies to

[82] For a good discussion of the land market in Old Fadama, see: Morrison (2017). For an ethnographic account of four property transactions, see: Stacey (2018).
[83] November 21, 2011.

take advantage of their informal living environment. In the absence of formal institutions, leaders find informal means to consolidate power through the amassing of wealth, extension of territorial authority, accumulation of followers, and connections to politicians. Powerful opinion leaders use the commons as a way to enrich themselves.

Beyond Vote Buying

Political parties understand the importance of squatter settlements, and they consolidate support through the distribution of private goods. In 2004, the NDC decided to extend their grassroots party structures into Old Fadama.[84] They designated the community a "Special Ward" and inaugurated four new branches. This was done for electoral reasons: Eight new delegates were created, and the people behind the creation of these new branches hoped that the eight delegates would support their primary candidate. Establishing branches makes it easier to distribute patronage and strengthen the organizational machinery of the party. A party insider explains how the growth of Old Fadama "handed us [the NDC] a victory on a silver platter."[85] In 2012, there were thirteen party branches in the community, with new groups constantly being officially inaugurated. But the branches are organized along ethnic lines: Eleven are Dagomba, one is Kokomba, and one is "other ethnic groups." By 2016, there were twenty-seven branches in the neighborhood. While electoral concerns and multiparty politics are central to power relations, the political practices of parties and individuals are embedded in an institutional environment where leaders capture state resources for their own, private agenda.

Old Fadama is a big vote bank. Over 80,000 residents live there, and they have connections to their extended families back in their hometown. Politicians find different ways to win votes, through distributing private goods, giving tickets to Hajj, linking them up with jobs, and providing personal security. But it would be a mistake to attribute this type of distributive politics to mere vote buying. While the residents might vote for their leader come election time, most people are motivated by everyday challenges. Residents rely on leaders for their daily problem-solving skills, as Javier Auyero calls them (Auyero 2001). But they are also motivated by historical grievances that they bring with

---

[84] January 11, 2012.   [85] January 11, 2012.

them to the city. For example, the battle between the Andani and the Abudu gate in the Dagomba chieftaincy crisis plays out in the squatter settlements of Accra and Ashaiman.[86] Leaders of these residents politicize the commons in order to bolster their side in the fight.

For example, in 2009, a large group of Old Fadama youth staged a press conference and burned NDC paraphernalia, setting off a small riot in the community. The youth were furious about a recent statement made by the NDC government. The statement said that there was not enough evidence to charge the suspects in the 2002 death of the Dagbon King. These youth, who were members of the Andani gate – a clan whose chief representative was king of the Dagomba nation in 2002 – were angry, and felt betrayed by "their" government. They expected the NDC government, who they helped put in government and with whom they allied largely because of this issue, to bring the perpetrators to justice.

While this was a local conflict that resonated in the Northern Region, migrants from this area now lived in Old Fadama. Youth posted messages on social media, and anger quickly spread throughout the neighborhood. Many of these residents had close political connections to both parties. In fact, the Dagbon Chieftaincy dispute is sometimes fought in Old Fadama, where formal security is weak, populations are dense, and young men are abundant. For these reasons, policymakers and politicians view Old Fadama as a "ticking time bomb" that could explode at any time.[87] Squatter settlements are often sources of instability, and politicians have the incentive to maintain peace. The eruption of violence, especially in the capital city, can affect the national economy. It could also spark violence or riots in other parts of the country.

But without formal institutions of security, politicians devise creative strategies to keep the peace. One strategy is to pay off leaders and residents in order to keep quiet and stay calm. Leaders can even use the potential for chaos as a threat against government, increasing their bargaining power in the process. Community leaders sometimes use this potential for conflict and instability to their advantage by

---

[86] For a good history of political history in Northern Ghana, see: Staniland (1975). For contemporary accounts of the Dagbon Chieftaincy dispute, see: Tonah (2012); Issifu (2015).

[87] The community is designated a "National Security Zone" and is under special government surveillance.

threatening government. Politicians are forced to deal with these threats informally, without solving the underlying political deadlock.

Therefore, when youth in Old Fadama staged a protest in 2009, those in government were worried. In response, NDC constituency executives called together thirty-six opinion leaders from Old Fadama and urged them to excise patience.[88] Residents explain that at this meeting, David Lamptey, a former minister, NDC donor, Chief Executive of Sidalco, and close friend of Nii Lantey Vanderpuye, paid off these leaders with $30,000 cash.[89] The money was supposed to be shared with residents so that they would keep calm. But most opinion leaders kept the money.

Word got out to residents that money was distributed but it was not shared fairly. In protest a group of youth stole the soda machine from the local NDC chairman's store, which they accused of stealing most of the money. The Dagomba Youth Chief Zachi was also rumored to have taken $7,000, and other chiefs took $2,000. Others began agitating and making noise. This worried Lamptey and the NDC constituency executives. The next day, they called all residents from the community to a meeting and distributed $100 to anybody who showed up. Approximately 300 people attended the meeting. Most residents did not even know who the man was, and he was simply referred to as a "very rich man." Today, residents constantly worry that if they do not show up for meetings they will be left out when politicians or other "big men" are sharing any money. Alternatively, residents and community leaders try to keep meetings where goods or money will be distributed secret so they can share with as few people as possible. The norms and politics of sharing are central to community governance in the neighborhood.

The relationship between politicians and residents of squatter settlements is in constant flux, with politicians reaching out for votes and residents attempting to secure as many private favors as possible. But the relationship is also akin to employer-employee, with residents working for the party as valuable political muscle and the politician distributing payment for the necessary work. But politicians do this in a larger network of personal problem-solving, whereby

---

[88] October 18, 2011.

[89] I could not independently verify this story, but many residents told me the same thing.

they help residents secure housing, employment opportunities, and daily entertainment.

Politicization of Evictions

Residents lived in the space that is now Old Fadama in the 1950s and 1960s, but they were relocated to a neighborhood called New Fadama by President Nkrumah in the early years of Independence.[90] In the 1980s, new settlers arrived and began squatting along the Korle Lagoon, eventually building up the swampland into a human settlement with thousands of residents. From the very early years, the neighborhood emerged as a private and commercial space. The most powerful and salient threat to squatter settlements like Old Fadama is forced eviction and demolition. Yet these threats are embedded in a context of distributive politics, and the politicization of urban space.[91] This reality is typically overlooked in studies of African squatter settlements. The following story documents how evictions become politicized, and empowers a small network of powerbrokers in the process.

"We were literally outgunned," explained former Accra Mayor Nat Nunoo Amarteifio. "On paper we held all the marbles, but in reality there were too many people who wanted the status quo."[92] Governing a city is never easy, even when the law is on one's side. In this case, the squatters of Old Fadama illegally inhabited the settlement. By 2002, the courts issued an eviction notice to all inhabitants. But the political underpinnings of the settlement were well entrenched, with numerous constituencies benefitting from the arrangements of the status quo.

As is the case with all modernization campaigns, development is political and there are always winners and losers. In this case, the future of Old Fadama is a very public subject, filled with intense political jockeying and debate. Politicians accuse each other of preventing a lasting solution to the Old Fadama crisis because of pandering for votes. For example, during the August 14, 2008 parliamentary debates when parliamentarians discussed a potential loan for sanitation improvements, MP I. K. Asiamah stated, "Most often, when

[90] I document the building of Old Fadama in Paller (2018b).
[91] Politicization of urban space refers to the struggle for control over land and territory, as well as the social institutions that have authority over the rules and procedures of everyday life.
[92] March 22, 2012.

such national projects are to be carried out and people will have to be moved … you will hear interested parties, more so, people who will benefit politically, politicizing the whole exercise."

In the same session, MP C. S. Hodogbey responded, "Why are we now trying to impress upon the Sodom and Gomorrah people, that we are very nice to them, when for so many years this has not been done? Now that it is an election year, they have brought this kind of a loan so that the thirty thousand people will vote for them." MP Lee Ocran added, "Initially, they tried to induce settlers with cash for them to move voluntarily. It did not work because some of the issues … were raised by certain politicians in the year 2000, trying to let the people not to move."

Numo Blafo, the Public Relations Officer from AMA describes similar frustrations as to why the Mayor is unable to act, "The Chief Executive is a political appointee, so sometimes he has to bow to pressure."[93] Governments often use the threat of forced eviction against the community when the country experiences a natural disaster, like a flood. The community becomes a scapegoat for larger structural or institutional problems that the government is unable to solve. Politicians are particularly active during eviction threats to the community.[94]

"Behind the scenes, the NPP had our side," one community activist explained. "When we are tasked with anything, they provide us with information."[95] In Ghana, the opposition [regardless of party] often politicizes issues in order to make it as difficult as possible to move forward with policies and development. But national politicians also have their own incentives, which often differ from those of the municipal authorities. For example, then President Mills addressed the Ghanaian community in New York in 2011 at a fundraiser. He made it clear that "forced eviction in Sodom and Gomorrah is not an option, and

---

[93] June 15, 2012. Public perception on the ground is that the former NPP Vice President, Aliu Mahama, is the person who was tasked with "solving" the crisis, but when the NDC came to power the plans stalled.

[94] For example, on July 16, 2009 the Regional Minister issued an eviction threat to Old Fadama. The Mayor of Accra supported the threat. Alternatively, in September, the Deputy Minister of Information contradicted the threat by saying the national government was examining relocation packages. Public opinion leaders like Kwesi Pratt, Nana Oye Lithur, and the leader of CHRAJ all made statements in the media in support of Old Fadama.

[95] July 30, 2012.

that any relocation must happen with a human face."[96] While municipal administrators are tasked with the day-to-day governance of a
city's neighborhoods, the incorporation of squatter settlements become
a national concern, and is politicized by the host city population and
political parties alike.

The political deadlock is further intensified because squatters are not
just prospective voters, but also valuable "political muscle."[97] In new
democracies where formal institutions are weak, political parties rely
on party activists, "foot soldiers," and "macho-men" to patrol polling
stations during voting and registration periods, attend rallies, and
mobilize voters (Bob-Milliar 2012; Klaus and Paller 2017). Old
Fadama is comprised mostly of youth working in the informal sector,
and they are willing to work for the party on a short-term basis.
Political parties view squatter settlements like Old Fadama as a valuable source of labor.

For example, during the 2008 elections, the NDC shipped four buses
of Old Fadama residents to Tain Constituency during the final round
of voting to "show force and numbers."[98] The busloads of people also
were "to put NDC people on the ground to make sure that the NPP did
not use extra-legal means for their advantage—such as stuffing ballot
boxes or busing in NPP voters from elsewhere."[99] They provided a de
facto electoral vigilante group.[100] Opinion leaders in the neighborhood
explain that NDC higher-ups like Constituency Executives, National
Security personnel, and politicians often call them to organize youth
from the community.

This "political muscle" is also utilized to come together and fight
eviction when the government threatens demolition. For example, on
September 9, 2009 more than 20,000 Old Fadama residents stayed
home from work and attended a large demonstration against the
earlier forced eviction notice. Community leaders woke up at 4 AM
and prevented people from going to their businesses. By 10 AM,
thousands of people covered the main street, with people sitting and
hanging from walls, trees, cars, and rooftops. Leaders addressed the

---

[96] *Daily Graphic*, September 27, 2011.
[97] Former Mayor Nat Nunoo Amarteifio explained, "Political parties find muscle
there. We also had our own connections with them" (March 22, 2012).
[98] April 19, 2012.   [99] April 19, 2012.
[100] January 28, 2012. In personal communications, George Bob-Milliar explains
that electoral vigilantism is built into the political system in Ghana.

crowd, radio and TV stations, and challenged the government to fulfill their responsibilities to the Old Fadama people and not demolish their structures. Two days later, the Deputy Minister of Information stated that the government was pursuing relocation options, not forced eviction.

Squatters also can threaten chaos. The Ghanaian government worries that instability in Old Fadama is a national security concern. But squatter settlements can also provide residents new opportunities to demand inclusion into the national polity, legitimate property ownership, and participate as equal citizens in social life (Holston 2008). The squatter status of the neighborhood creates differing incentives for diverse actors and institutions. Leaders, politicians, NGOs, and squatters themselves find ways to benefit from their insecure environments and profit from extra-legality and informality. The power in numbers that voters have does not translate to public goods. Instead, distributive politics in these communities takes a very specific logic: the provision of private goods to individuals who do not serve the public interest.

In June 2015 municipal authorities demolished thousands of structures along the outside of the neighborhood, evicting more than 25,000 people from their homes without due process. The situation closely resembled the scene at the beginning of the book: poor residents with nowhere to go; sold out by the very leaders they helped put into power. But at the grassroots, the demolition signaled a change in state-society relationships. On the one hand, the demolition asserted the control of the city and national government, demonstrating that an NDC government might make the hard decision to demolish the settlement. Some of the most influential leaders directly lost power: Local leader Hanaan's territory was demolished, limiting his power in the neighborhood. The chief Dagbola-Na also lost his home and territory in the demolition. NDC partisan Boss moved north after losing the NDC chairmanship, limiting the power of a broad-based coalition of the opposition to the community leaders. Chief Zachi, the youth chief of the Dagomba people in Accra, no longer lives in the community.

In December 2016, the governing party NDC lost the presidential elections. The party lost nearly 8,000 votes in Odododiodioo Constituency, mostly from Old Fadama, as NDC supporters decided to sit out the election. As resident Alhassan Ibn Abdallah explains:

As a voter in the constituency, I think the reason is one: Mr. Mahama's insensitive directive for nationwide demolition to be carried out without due process in June 2015 caused us the over 8000 votes in Odododiodioo. The authority he gave to [mayor] Oko Vanderpuije to evict people in the rainy season and later deport them back to "where they came from" made the difference in Odododiodioo and beyond. I hope we learn this time. If we so wish, we can continue to deny its impact as we have done always. But I am sure those who were at the polling stations in and around #Agbogbloshie will understand.

The government might not recognize squatters in Old Fadama. But they still have their votes, and eviction notices and legal insecurity continue to provide opportunities to various decision-makers on the ground. But it does so privately, with no public sphere available to all residents.

A Quantitative Illustration: State Services and Public Spheres

Extending the logic of distribution beyond electoral politics has important implications for how social scientists measure public goods provision. In their important article "Who Benefits from Distributive Politics? How the Outcome One Studies Affects the Answer One Gets," Eric Kramon and Daniel Posner make a poignant point about the burgeoning distributive politics literature: "The pattern of favoritism that has been identified with respect to the outcome in question may be counterbalanced by a quite different, even opposite, pattern of favoritism with respect to other outcomes that are not being measured" (2013: 462). They emphasize that studies primarily focus on one particular distributed good. But in doing so, they demonstrate that there are very different logics depending on what type of good is in question.

My analysis suggests a further challenge to the academic literature on public goods provision. In cities, where elections are often embedded in broader struggles over urban space, informal norms of settlement and belonging can shape whether neighborhoods are eligible for certain goods in the first place. Settlement recognition – both legal and political – is not a given across urban space.[101] Informal norms of

---

[101] Rains et al. 2017 provide a similar finding in slums across India.

settlement shape the entire process of distribution, from the demands by the community, to the provision by the government, to the maintenance by neighborhood residents.

This reality calls for the need to disaggregate public goods distribution into categories of *government provision* and *community management*. Government provision entails access to basic goods, services, and infrastructure. Community management, on the other hand, is the ability of a neighborhood to govern infrastructure and development projects effectively (Sheely 2013). These are two distinct concepts: Government provision provides a possible measure of electoral logics of distribution, while community management refers to collective efficacy and level of collective action in a neighborhood (Sampson 2012).

By examining both types of public goods provision, and embedding them in the context of informal norms of settlement and belonging, we gain a more complete picture of distributive politics in urban neighborhoods. With this in mind, I collected data on 150 distinct enumeration areas across sixteen poor urban neighborhoods. I documented the quality of the following services: roads, sewers, garbage collection, streetlights, and toilets. I then constructed a *Provision Index* and a *Management Index* (Figure 5.1). By devising indices, I overcome some of the concerns of examining only one good. The *Provision Index* includes the quality of the road, construction of sewers, collection of garbage, existence of streetlights, and location of toilets. The *Management Index* includes the openness of the road, cleanliness of the sewers, amount of litter, maintenance of streetlights, and neatness of toilets.

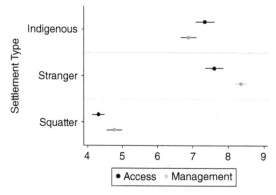

Figure 5.1 Access and management of basic services

The difference between indigenous and stranger settlements is telling. Indigenous settlements score highest on the *Provision Index*, suggesting that they are able to secure the most government resources. This is likely because residents in indigenous settlements feel entitled to state goods, and the close connections with municipal authorities strengthen the bargaining position. In other words, they are able to demand and secure access to public goods and services. Indigenes are able to capture state services for their own populations. There is very little variation between stranger and indigenous settlements when it comes to the provision of public services, suggesting that both types of neighborhoods have equal ability in demanding development from the state (Auerbach 2016).

On the other hand, stranger settlements score the highest on the *Management Index*. They do better at maintaining infrastructure when it is under the community's jurisdiction. The substantive difference is strong: Stranger settlements score more than one full point better, suggesting that their public services are better maintained due to neighborhood supervision. This is even more surprising because these communities tend to have higher levels of ethnic diversity. Unsurprisingly, and in line with my general theory, squatter settlements score poorly on both measures. Squatter settlements are not eligible at all for most infrastructure projects and brick and mortar development projects. Instead, residents in these neighborhoods demand private goods like employment contracts. The next section reports evidence for why stranger settlements are able to manage their services effectively once they are under the neighborhood's jurisdiction.

Operationalizing Public Spheres

The changing nature of urban neighborhoods requires new ways of operationalizing public spheres. For the most part, the concept of an African urban public sphere has been restricted to studies of critical urban theory or anthropology.[102] But insights from scholars like Lisa Wedeen (2007) suggest that detailed observations of deliberation in everyday life can inform theories of democracy. In places where formal institutions are weak, citizens need an alternative to elections to influence their leaders. Governance often requires physical spaces where people come together to engage in collective decision-making, or

---

[102] See: Larkin (2008); Chalfin (2014); Roitman (2013); Hoffman (2017).

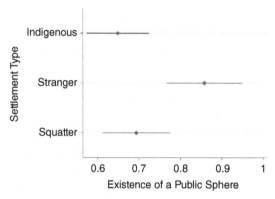

Figure 5.2 The emergence of public spheres

spheres of democratic expression (Wedeen 2008). In this context, decision-making becomes a give-and-take process whereby residents publicly express their concerns and leaders actively listen to the claims made. Then they come to an agreement together.

In my survey, I ask respondents, "Within a five minute walk of your house, is there a spot where neighbors come together to discuss community affairs and development?" By operationalizing public spheres in this way, I am able to show variation in spheres of democratic expression at a very local level. Importantly, these hangout spaces are more than just places to watch sports or discuss party politics. Instead, residents and leaders come face-to-face to discuss issues that affect the entire neighborhood.

Notably, stranger settlements are far more likely to have these spaces than the other neighborhoods. Perhaps more interestingly, residents in squatter settlements respond that these spaces exist in their neighborhoods more so than residents in indigenous settlements. These data help confirm my qualitative evidence that public spheres are more likely to emerge in stranger settlements. Figure 5.2 provides a very simple visual illustration of the differences in public spheres across the three settlement types.

Conclusion

This chapter complicates the notion that the distribution of goods and services is the same across neighborhoods, and can be explained by formal institutional features like political competition and electoral demography. Instead, distributive politics is embedded in a broader struggle over control and authority in the city. Local leaders and politicians politicize urban neighborhoods by distributing goods and resources along club, public, or private lines. Residents in these neighborhoods have different understandings of power and authority, and this shapes the entire distribution process – from the demands, to the distribution, to the management of goods once under the neighborhood's jurisdiction.

In indigenous settlements, leaders distribute state goods and services along club lines. They are restricted to indigenous members of the neighborhood. In stranger settlements, goods and services are distributed in a public or common fashion; they are accessible to all. In addition, public spheres of democratic expression develop so that residents and leaders from different walks of life can enter the decision-making process. Finally, in squatter settlements, the commons is privatized, and leaders co-opt goods and services to empower themselves and their narrow base.

These insights support an institutional explanation based on informal norms of settlement and belonging to demonstrate why distributive politics take different forms across local contexts. The next chapter suggests that these forms of distribution contribute to ethnic politics in some neighborhoods, and multiethnic power structures in others.

6 | *The Organization of Civic Life*

Ethnic politics – the distribution of power along shared cultural attributes, consciousness, and boundaries (Young 2014) – has not deteriorated with the urbanization of Ghanaian society. Noah Nathan's insightful research demonstrates how ethnic voting still occurs at high rates in Ghana's cities (Nathan 2016a, 2016b). But these patterns cannot only be explained by differences in the salience of ethnic identities, or by the individual-level characteristics of voters. Nathan finds that these patterns are attributed to the diversity and wealth of particular neighborhoods. These neighborhood-level characteristics signal a certain type of distributive politics, which "determine voters' expectations of the benefits of electing ethnically aligned politicians" (Nathan 2016b: 1897). Ethnic politics still characterize elections in urban Ghana, but only in certain neighborhoods.

There is an emerging political science literature that pays close attention to local ethnic geography in African politics (Ichino and Nathan 2013; Kasara 2013; Nathan 2016a, 2016b; Hassan 2017). Yet missing in these studies is the control over space and authority, especially in the city.[1] In particular, by focusing primarily on ethnic demography and formal institutions like elections and the rule of law, they miss the differences in everyday politics across neighborhoods. This is important because neighborhoods contain enduring patterns of political behaviors that persist throughout history, extending from the precolonial era, through colonial times, to Ghana's multiparty democracy today.

A focus on everyday politics provides a lens into the organization of civic life in urban neighborhoods. By the organization of civic life, I refer to the patterns of authority and structure of associational life – how daily affairs are constructed and institutionalized in a

---

[1] Exceptions include the recent special issue on urban land conflicts in *Urban Studies* edited by Lombard and Rakodi (2016), as well as Klaus and Paller (2017).

neighborhood. This approach magnifies the persistence and social resilience of underlying institutions, especially traditional authorities and the chieftaincy (Swidler 2013). In some neighborhoods, ethnicity continues to be the defining feature of the organization of civic life, while in others it dissipates into the background. A focus on the informal norms of settlement and belonging help explain these divergent outcomes.

The chapter combines ethnographic observations with survey data. First, I explain how the organization of civic life in indigenous neighborhoods is restricted along ethnic lines – to members of the Ga ethnic group. I then document how a multiethnic civic life emerges in stranger communities like those in Ashaiman. This contributes to a civic life that is open to the public. Finally, I discuss the persistence of ethnic politics in squatter settlements, as local leaders empower coethnics through the capture of state services and resources. I document the role that nonstate actors and politicians play in the persistence of ethnic politics, and how governing by the largest ethnic group can become a "tyranny of the majority." In line with Varshney's claim, "Structures of civic life constrain political strategies and their outcomes" (2001: 13).

An Ethnic Civic Life in the Indigenous Core of the City

The indigenous core of a city privileges an ethnic politics because local society is organized along indigenous lines. This organizing principle shapes daily interactions between residents, political party strategies and behaviors, and the provision of collective goods. The following examples demonstrate how norms of indigeneity structure an everyday politics based on ethnic ties, which quickly can turn political as nativist chauvinism.

"We say *ablekuma aba kuma wo*—meaning we want to welcome strangers so as to make progress together," Professor Oquaye, a well-known NPP politician and prominent Ga leader told the crowded press conference.[2] "I say so as a proud Ga," he said, basking in his position as a representative of the Ga people. But he also said so as a leader in the NPP political party, using the ethnic proverb to try and make the case that his party is not only an Akan-based party, but is open to

[2] April 12, 2012.

members from all groups. In the process, he borrows from a narrative derived from their rich history: that the Ga people welcome outsiders or strangers into their society and city, and they take great pride in this sentiment.[3]

But this narrative is also contentious, as the relationship between migrants and settlers in Accra, the center of the Ga homeland, has been violent, politicized, and a main staple of multiparty politics in the city. Moreover, many Accra residents did not agree with Oquaye's sentiment. Instead, they worried that ethnic outsiders, especially Akan from the Ashanti region, were settling in Accra in great numbers, threatening to take over their city. During the electoral campaign, the NDC campaigned on this fear of outsiders, and strategically limited the registration of non-Ga residents in their constituencies. Both narratives used in the electoral campaigns represent institutional syncretism, in this case the blending together of multiparty democracy and ethnic authority. Ga leaders actively and purposefully recombined rules and norms from multiple sociocultural origins into syncretic political institutions (Galvan 2004).

For the Ga people, the answer to the question "who settled first, and how" is unequivocal: the indigenous Ga people. This simple answer shapes the overarching view that their ethnic group owns the city because Accra is their ancestral homeland. Owning the city extends to its economic system, military presence, and municipal affairs. But this organizing principle only resonates in certain spaces within the city – neighborhoods where indigenous authorities structure the civic life, and where patterns of ethnic life become institutionalized over time. In these indigenous settlements, these patterns of everyday politics are shaped by ethnic networks of engagement, where residents primarily associate and engage with members of their own group. These spaces are still dominant in the indigenous core of a city.

This structure of civic life privileges nativist control over the city, and extends to anti-outsider attitudes. These sentiments are expressed in the numerous examples of everyday politics observed in these areas. For example, on a hot day, a fight broke out among young men outside

---

[3] Numerous Ga informants articulated this public narrative to me, despite underlying beliefs that might run counter to what is said in public.

of Salaga Market, Ga Mashie's largest food market.[4] A group of men were cleaning the sewers as a form of communal labor, a practice that was repopularized during the presidential tenure of Jerry John Rawlings (Adedeji 2001). The fight started because a Ga opinion leader came by the market and was pleased at the work they were doing. He gave two of the men 100 Ghana cedis in appreciation. The men who received the cash thought they should split the money between the two of them, allowing them to keep fifty cedis each. The other workers were angry and demanded that the money be shared among all the workers. They began fighting for the money. An onlooker remarked, "We just let people fight it out here." The young men fought for ten minutes until a group of local opinion leaders divided them, split up the money, and the two original men left the scene angry.[5] The rest of the men and onlookers laughed and continued cleaning out the gutters.

The young men who cleaned the gutters were members of the Ussher Town football team. They had won an important match the past Sunday, which happened to be a holiday that coincided with festivities. In good spirits, local opinion leaders organized a community cleanup exercise and the football team provided the labor. Youth groups in Ga Mashie are deeply established and active, with football clubs, boxing groups, fan clubs, keep-fit clubs, and church organizations. On the surface, Ga Mashie has an active civil society – it contains high levels of social capital, or dense networks of trust and reciprocity. But without accountability mechanisms to internally govern these associations, and without external institutions to make sure that these energies are productively utilized, clubs and associations are easily used by power holders and by individuals for personal gain and group (or club) patronage.[6]

In indigenous neighborhoods like Ga Mashie, civic life is governed along ethnic lines. Community members play the ethnic card, organizing effectively around the fact that they are the rightful owners of the land. They use this as a rallying cry to control the city (Klaus and Paller 2017). Residents resort to a narrative of keeping strangers or outsiders out, especially during elections when political parties attach ethnicity

---

[4] November 10, 2011.

[5] For an account of the role of boxing in Ga culture and society, see: Akyeampong (2002).

[6] This finding is consistent with those of Habyarimana et al. 2009.

to political affiliation (Nathan 2016a). In this way, the norm of indigeneity undermines trust between different ethnic groups, making it very difficult for members of diverse groups to come together for development projects. In other words, bonds of trust and respect develop along ethnic lines, creating dense networks of social engagement and association based on ethnic ties. These ethnic bonds provide the basis for politicians and elites to use divide and rule strategies along ethnic lines to divide the community, hampering productive collective action among all residents.

These social ties are strengthened by the daily interactions between residents, what Erica Simmons calls quotidian communities, or those "built on face-to-face, routine interactions where members know each other personally" (Simmons 2014). Rather than solidifying national communities, the governance of the city – and the associational life that underlies it in the indigenous core of the city – promotes an ethnic politics over national belonging.[7]

Ga Nationalists as Foot Soldiers

Many scholars have written about how political parties use unemployed youth to win elections (Anderson 2002; Bob-Milliar 2012; LeBas 2013; Brierley and Kramon 2018). But there is far less attention paid to who these young (usually) men are, and how parties tap into underlying organizational structures to mobilize support. The political clientelism literature accurately characterizes political parties as an avenue for social mobility for unemployed youth. But young people also have agency in the process, using political parties to broaden their own authority and power. In indigenous settlements, the residents' love for the party can overlap with ethnic chauvinism. The strength of the indigenous narrative and its impact on political behavior is especially apparent. In the case of Ga Mashie, support for the NDC political party is indistinguishable from Ga nationalism. The following case of Nii Addo, a local political activist – termed foot soldier in Ghana – illustrates how the structure of civic life shapes political imaginaries and identities. It demonstrates how Nii Addo

---

[7] This is not to say that these residents are not proud Ghanaians. Instead, they think urban and national citizenship are distinct entities, with different claims.

interacts with residents and outsiders, and how this conditions his connection to the city, as well as his vote choice.

"Phobia! Phobia!" Nii Addo yelled to a man across the busy street, "Phobia!" The man looked up and waved. Nii Addo and the man were both fans of the Accra Hearts of Oak, the local football club that gained its support from the Ga faithful (Fridy and Brobbey 2009). Nii Addo seems to know everybody in Ga Mashie. At the chop bar, he argues about why the NDC is the best party for Ghana. At Blue Gate, the hang out spot for local NPP members, he argues about the latest newspaper headline about an embattled MP. Across from Bukom Park, he argues with a group of youth why Islam "holds the truth." He constantly runs into mates from school and family members he calls "boss." He will only speak his local Ga language. When somebody addresses him in Twi, he goes on a long outburst about how when people are in Accra, they need to speak the indigenous Ga language.

Nii Addo gains his livelihood from the different ethnic associations in which he participates. He is a leader in the Concerned Youth of Odododiodioo Constituency, a forum that has been supported by Nii Lantey Vanderpuye to support the local youth, but also bolster the aspiring politician's electoral chances. He is involved in the Ga Dangbe Youth Association, a Ga nationalist organization that seeks to advance the interests of the Ga community. He provides some promotional assistance for the boxer Joseph Agbeko, who is from Ga Mashie but is currently boxing internationally and is allegedly promoted by Don King. He occasionally runs errands for various family members; a "big man" in the family will need a few letters dropped off to various government buildings, and he will ask Nii Addo to deliver the envelope. He will give Nii Addo "something small."[8] He relies on some support from the family head of the moment, a man who works in the Sports Ministry.[9]

Nii Addo's entire political narrative is one of "standing ground." He constantly talks about how "we cannot let them [the NPP] in." He mentions how NDC has never lost a polling station in Ussher Town, a portion of Ga Mashie. He talks about how they must stand firm and

---

[8] In the Ga language, this is translated to *nokofio*. This is also the term used for money distributed to voters during campaign events.

[9] The term "errand boy" is used to describe youth who do these tasks.

not allow the NPP, and specifically the Ashantis, to come in. His whole narrative is very territorial. When he walks by the post office, he says, "This is ours. We oversee this land." He does not talk about winning people over. Rather, it is about standing ground and "keeping them out." He is in charge of hanging banners of his politicians at every main intersection, and he explains that they must mark their territory. They need to make it clear that people know it is NDC territory, and that outsiders do not "trespass."[10] For him, and many youth in Ga Mashie, the "real" Ga people support NDC. The NPP, on the other hand, is an Ashanti party.[11]

On one summer day, Nii Addo discussed his future.[12] He explained his desire to get a job so he could pay for his education. He also needed some money so he could propose to his girlfriend. To do so, he has to give gifts to the woman's family, and he estimated that the gifts would cost 3,000 Ghana cedis. He explained the bind he was in, unable to pay for the engagement. "Tackie Komme really let us down," he said. Tackie Komme was the current Member of Parliament, and had promised to get a number of the youth in the area jobs at Immigration. Immigration is one of the few government departments where jobs do not require a college education. People are also known to seek Immigration jobs because of the many lucrative opportunities to take bribes.

Nii Addo expected that due to his many years of work for the party, he would be rewarded with a job at Immigration. Nii Addo really expected this to happen and he views this failure as a large contributor to his challenges today. "We had a list and everything and he never submitted the list," Nii Addo continued, "He did not do what he was supposed to do." Nii Addo's emotions should not be discounted. His feelings of disillusionment stem from a sense of political betrayal, which in other research I call political sting: feelings of betrayal, insult, and disrespect among ordinary citizens stemming from a government's failure to protect and provide for its population (Paller 2013).

After a long back and forth about dependence on politicians, Nii Addo explained how he has a job lined up "as soon as the new districts are created." He has a politically connected friend who has promised

---

[10] April 3, 2012.

[11] Many people I spoke with fear the Ashanti ethnic group's history of accumulation. This included people from different classes and social groups. For academic research on this topic, see: McCaskie (1983).

[12] June 16, 2012.

him a job in one of the new district offices. Soon, forty-five new
districts would be created for the election.[13] However, this will take
several months and there is no guarantee that this job will go to him.
Many youth in Ga Mashie rely on politicians and leaders for job
opportunities and daily sustenance. In many cases, youth hang around
when they expect a "big man" to come through the community. They
hope for *nokofio*, or something small.[14] Nii Lantey Vanderpuye has
been accused of winning over the youth by handing out *nokofio* at
campaign rallies and other events. But youth like Nii Addo rely on this
money and expect it to improve their lives.

It would be easy to discount this behavior as pure vote buying or
turnout buying, but the motivation for this behavior extends much
deeper and is better understood as part of a daily problem-solving
network (Auyero 2001). It has been a social norm and source of
political authority since precolonial times that family heads in Ga
Mashie provide welfare to their followers. In indigenous settlements,
these personal networks form along ethnic lines. Youth treat their role
in these personal networks as employees: They run errands for "big
men," and they get compensated in return. In places where jobs are
scarce, this reciprocal exchange enforces clientelistic politics, but is also
an ordinary part of daily life. Reducing these problem-solving networks to instrumental mechanisms to garner votes obscures the historical and sociological dimension that this norm of reciprocity takes.

The "big men" who Nii Addo relies on do not live in Ga Mashie. His
most important patron lives in the nearby suburb of North Kaneshie.
The MP, Tackie Komme bought a house in a far suburb and rarely
walks through the community. Former MP Nii Ayi Bonte does not live
in Ga Mashie because "There's no accommodation space. I cannot live
there with my wife and children. How many people have their own
private toilets?"[15] Rather than improving the community and upgrading the poor neighborhood, leaders tend to move out and only return
during election time. They are accused of using youth like Nii Addo for
their own political gain.

---

[13] For a discussion of the political roots of administrative unit proliferation, see:
   Grossman and Lewis (2014); Hassan (2016); Hassan and Sheely (2017).
[14] For a discussion of the culture of corruption in daily African politics, see: Smith
   (2010).
[15] June 8, 2012.

Former Mayor Nat Nunoo Amarteifio explains that Ga Mashie suffers from a lack of good leaders. "When Gas become successful they move out of the community," he says. "They rarely come back to the community. There is a dislocation between Ga Bourgeoisie and relatives in Bukom."[16] The youth admit that this undermines accountability, as one man asked rhetorically, "Like you are a parent, and you sleep in Dansoman and your children sleep at Kinka, how can you control him?"[17] Nii Addo said that the one person who can mentor him and offer advice is Vanderpuye, the current MP. "But he is too busy for me right now."[18]

Nii Addo's story fits into the broader pattern of community organization in Ga Mashie. One resident tells the story of a police forum that the NDC organized to recruit community members into the police service. However, one family who was supposed to organize the event took the money for themselves, and police recruits were never chosen from the community. But this behavior is so embedded in daily life that residents do not see it as stealing. As one man explained, "It is not exactly stealing. Their family just took the money."[19] Because family lineage is so important to the structure of civic life, transparency of public funds is less important than allegiance to the Ga social organization.

Amarteifio described his frustration with dealing with Ga Mashie, "I used to go there for party outreach programs. They always complained about lack of jobs. Unfortunately most of them don't have skills. We tried to give them employment but it was inevitably menial work. If we hired them to start at 9, by eleven seven would disappear. By four, two more would leave. The rest would take our tools. But they are quite vocal about their entitlements."[20] There is an institutional explanation for this behavior: Norms of indigeneity privilege a situation where residents feel entitled to state resources, including public services and jobs.

Indigenous neighborhoods like Ga Mashie are structured by families, or institutionalized clubs that organize the community. Claiming to be part of these clubs provides an important source of power and an answer to the important question "who settled first, and how." Residents like Nii Addo internalize these narratives and act on them.

---

[16] March 22, 2012.   [17] June 20, 2012.   [18] June 16, 2012.
[19] November 22, 2011.   [20] March 22, 2012.

Norms of indigeneity provide a particularly powerful impetus to secure state resources, thereby undermining other potentially powerful alliances like class, business, or cosmopolitan demands. These norms are hard to break, and have become a guiding principle in Ghanaian politics.

The Emergence of Cross-Ethnic Social Engagement

The growth of Ghanaian cities has contributed to new interactions between people of different ethnic groups. While this creates new experiences for individuals, hybrid social structures also develop and replace traditional institutions. Urban neighborhoods become far more than "villages in the city." Instead, they are spaces for the emergence of a new type of social organization and multiethnic civic life. In the following pages, I document how a multiethnic civic life emerges in Ashaiman, providing evidence that Tocqueville's ideal of a vibrant associational life can emerge in the unlikeliest of places.

Tocqueville's Ideal

In his treatise *Democracy in America,* Alexis de Tocqueville admires the density of associational life that settlers developed in the United States. For him, the strong civil associations contributed directly to a flourishing democracy. Tocqueville writes:

> The more the number of these minor communal matters increases, the more men acquire, even unknowingly, the capacity to pursue major ones in common. Civil associations, therefore, pave the way for political associations; on the other hand, political associations develop and improve in some strange way civil associations ... So when a nation has a public life, the idea of associations and the desire to form them are daily in the forefront of all citizens' minds; whatever natural distaste men may have for working in partnership, they will always be ready to do so in the interests of the party. (Tocqueville 2003: 604)

Tocqueville's insights have been felt far and wide across the social sciences, as the study of associational life and social capital has proliferated across the world. The case of Ashaiman demonstrates how this associational life must also incorporate all residents of society, a challenge for ethnically diverse neighborhoods with weak formal institutions.

Yet spaces of cross-ethnic social engagement are apparent in the everyday politics of stranger settlements, especially in *zongo* communities where residents from many different ethnic groups are forced to govern their neighborhoods together, and coexist peacefully. The following examples from Ashaiman demonstrate how the organization of multiethnic civic life emerges from the very early years of settlement. I argue that the structure of a multiethnic civic life can be traced to the pattern of settlement and belonging.

On a Sunday in May 2012, there were forty people sitting in plastic chairs waiting for the Friend's Club to begin its meeting. Three-quarters of the audience were men, but all wore matching green wax print fabrics with the Friend's Club insignia on it. The club started in 2006 to serve as a self-help group for its members. When people are in need, they can go to the club and ask for financial assistance or other support. For example, at this meeting the leadership discussed the money that was given to a member to travel to a funeral that was several hours away in the Volta Region. At the beginning of each meeting, participants pay one cedi. If they are late to the meeting, they pay a small penalty. If their phone rings, they also owe a penalty. At this particular meeting, some of the members had not paid their dues so the leader was naming aloud those who still needed to pay. He publicly shamed the people to pay their balance.

Sundays in Ashaiman are Tocqueville's dream: days when the democratic spirit is flourishing and the collective capacity of its citizens is visibly evident. At four o'clock in the afternoon, chairs throughout the city are set up, youth club and friend's groups banners hang, and residents have changed their church clothes to association t-shirts and outfits. Some of the clubs are ethnically based, like the Frafra Youth Group. Others are self-help groups made up of friends, like the Friend's Club and the Executive Youths. The Ashaiman Women in Progressive Development is based along gender lines, while the Spartan Youth Club comprises mostly Muslim youth.

Nearby the meeting of the Friend's Club, the Executive Club held its meeting. This was a smaller group, with only ten people gathered. A few former members of the Friend's Club split off in 2009 to begin their own club: There was an internal power struggle and the new leaders wanted more control. The club focused on married couples. Individuals came with their spouse and the mission was to help couples live moral lives together. Two women sat at the front table and signed people in. They wore matching orange collared shirts. Several hundred meters from the meeting, two youth groups were busy playing football at Starlight School. Community members sat along the sidelines watching their friends.

Groups in Ashaiman also organize along occupational lines. For example, the Minister's Association of Ashaiman meets the first Monday of every month to discuss the challenges facing Ashaiman and the church. They also discuss personal problems facing the ministers. The most recent concern is that pastors felt they had been sidelined from the political decision-making process. The group was particularly disappointed because they played an important part in advocacy for municipal status, which was explained in Chapter 5. One youth pastor explains, "The ministers were sidelined. Our local government does not include the ministers in the decision-making process. We are still figuring out what our role is."[21]

The organization also serves an accountability function: It is used to hold each other to account. One pastor explains, "Because of our network, we caution each other. We are our brother's keeper. We talk to each other. We are not far from each other." They also serve to help each other out and reward one another for their good work. At the meetings, church leaders discuss dues and fees, reward amounts for graduations and certificates, and upcoming events to preach peace for the 2012 election. Political parties, NGOs, and religious organizations are all active in Ashaiman, and they continue to fund projects and invest in the community because they have been relatively successful. Much of this success can be attributed to the fact that Ashaiman is well organized and has been for many years. In other words, they are only successful because of the collective capacity of the community that already exists on the ground.

The development of cross-ethnic networks of social engagement underlies political party behavior, as the discussion about toilet revenue in Chapter 5 suggests. The social expectation of sharing goods and resources with non coethnic members contributes to broader political cooperation among residents from different ethnic groups. Without formal transparency mechanisms in place, the social norm provides the incentive for leaders and residents to share goods with members from different groups, particularly with respect to state resources.

---

[21] February 16, 2012.

In a focus group of Dagomba youth, for example, participants were asked what they would do if their leader provided jobs to only members of his own family and ethnic group, when the contract was intended to employ members from all tribes. "We will call him and tell him that by doing that it tarnishes the image of Dagombas, so he should stop," a respondent explains.[22] "We can also call for [an] executive meeting to sit him down and talk to him because that can also affect the party's popularity, the tribe, so we will call him." Residents take their group identity seriously, and the accusation of ethnic chauvinism or tribalism tarnishes group identity in Ashaiman. In other words, the residents in Ashaiman have pioneered a new form of ethnic mobilization: They mobilize to *prevent* the ethnicization of identity in the form of excessive in-group patronage. The structure of civic life privileges a public articulation of politics, one that extends beyond private or group interest.

The design of urban space can also go a long way toward facilitating cooperation and cross-ethnic social engagement.[23] For example, Ashaiman homes are constructed as compound houses, facilitating the need to share a common space, water, and maybe even a bathhouse. In this situation, people from different ethnic groups even live in the same compound. One resident explains that this fosters interethnic engagement that promotes unity, "In these compound houses there are people from different tribes, so there is harmony among the people. We are all born here, and grew up with people from different tribe[s] so we have learnt to speak each other's language and eat their food."[24]

The importance of eating together and sharing one's food displays the intimacy of daily life. In West Africa, a household is defined as those eating from the same pot. The sharing of food brings people from diverse backgrounds together, even allowing them to join the same household. The interethnic households even extend to leadership, as the NPP MP aspirant, who is a member of the Ewe ethnic group explains, "You will hardly find an intertribal conflict in Ashaiman. We are closely bonded. In one house you will find all different types of people. Even me, I married an Ashanti."[25]

---

[22] June 3, 2012.
[23] For a fascinating account of the role that architecture plays in enabling collective action, see: Hoffman (2017).
[24] June 14, 2012.   [25] February 15, 2012.

The rise of dense networks of associational life preceded formal civil society and NGO activity. The political organization on the ground, with different tribes being represented by their leaders, enabled further cooperation between groups. The dense networks of social engagement contribute to the growing presence of NGOs in Ashaiman. This is because NGOs need community partners on the ground, and preexisting local structures facilitate the success of the proposed project. Therefore, Ashaiman has become marked as an NGO-friendly community, and NGOs based in Accra and international NGOs continue to invest in the community. While NGOs have their own agenda, one of the important effects that they have is they bring people together publicly to discuss political issues.

Blurring Boundaries between NGOs and the State

On a quiet morning in January, a group of Ashaiman women from different ethnic groups met at a USAID-funded health clinic.[26] But the women were not meeting to discuss health concerns, nor did they come to talk about the NGO's agenda. Instead, they came to discuss problems in the community, as they did every Tuesday morning. They used the space paid for by USAID to gather and talk. Immediately, the women started complaining about the public toilet. It was not cared for, was very dirty, and they had to pay ten peswas for their young children to use it. They felt that this was not fair. They did not like that the proceeds go to the NDC party, and most of the money goes directly to the assemblyman.[27] The women are so displeased with the toilet that they walk ten minutes farther to another public toilet that is cleaner, and run by another assemblyman. The farther toilet is much cleaner because the assemblyman's family uses it. Therefore, he takes care of it. The assemblyman who operates the closer toilet has a private one in his own house, and does not feel the need to clean it properly.

While the women discussed the issues, the assemblyman walked by on the street. The leader of the women's group walked outside and called him in. He entered the room to speak to the group. He said that he would discuss the issue later and told them to write a formal

---

[26] January 23, 2012.
[27] The assemblyman received the contract because of his close connections to the NDC, as well as his strong bargaining position with the Municipal Assembly.

letter to him and the Assembly. He tried to leave, but the women continued complaining to him and would not let him go. The back-and-forth lasted several minutes, until they all started laughing and smiling. The assemblyman left and the women immediately started drafting a letter. They had a formal letter by the end of the session. The leader of the group then used the USAID-provided computer to type the letter formally. The rest of the meeting was spent complaining about the "Dagomba boys" who speed through the streets on their motorbikes.

This event illustrates what Jennifer Brass (2016) calls "blurring boundaries" between NGOs and the state, where the government and nonprofit organizations share collaborative working environments and form public-private partnerships. In contrast to theories that suggest NGOs undermine the state or replace it, in Ashaiman they often work as partners or collaborators. But perhaps more importantly, the women's group creatively recombined their role as health workers – and the materials and office for which USAID expected health work – for general improvements in the community, providing a case of creative syncretism (Berk and Galvan 2009). While foreign aid is often co-opted and captured for personal use, as Swidler and Watkins (2017) demonstrate in Malawi, this group of Ashaiman women leveraged their resources to improve wellbeing in other sectors.

Women have a long history of governing urban space in Africa's informal neighborhoods (Robertson 1984; Tripp 1997). They play a vibrant role in market associations, hometown clubs, and religious organizations. But two things make Ashaiman women's role in associational life different. First, women from many different ethnic groups participate in civic life, extending beyond indigenous lines as they do in Ga Mashie. Second, these groups pressure formal authorities directly, playing a central role in "demanding development," as Adam Auerbach (2016) describes claims to the state for public services in the context of India.

This story of women entering the decision-making process to fix the problems in the community is part of a broader form of institutional learning that is taking place in Ashaiman. As Assemblyman Thomas Adongo explained to me: "Anything you can think of here we have it here in Ashaiman. Crime combatting. You name it. We have what it takes to educate ourselves. Even if you are an ignorant man in an area, you will learn from the other social groupings. We have these networks."[28] In other words, local pressure groups form, compete, and learn from one another to advance their interests and strengthen their agenda. In the process, broad-based democratic learning takes place. And women are at the center of many of these networks.

With dense networks in place, NGOs and local government have better chances of success. Further, residents and leaders on the ground benefit from what the NGOs teach them. The NGOs leverage a vibrant multiethnic associational life into real institutional performance, similar to the ways Putnam (1993) suggests.

Complementary Institutions and Hybrid Governance

The multiethnic civic life in Ashaiman has contributed to a vibrant participatory culture that extends to municipal governance. Every day, residents, technocrats, and politicians fill the halls of the Ashaiman Municipal Assembly. Assemblymen park their motorbikes outside and walk through the staircases. Youth groups gather to try and get hired for communal labor exercises. NGO representatives meet with assembly workers to try to find ways to collaborate with the city government. It is unclear how much this form of coproduction, as Ostrom (1996) calls it, strengthens the institutional performance of the municipal assembly. Residents are still expected to self-provide public services, as the introductory anecdote regarding the electricity pole suggests. But what is clear is that the Assembly building provides residents – and leaders especially – a stake in the governing of the city. Moreover, it enables them to imagine their "city yet to come," as Simone (2004) calls it, providing a claim to urban citizenship and the potential to govern themselves.

Assembly persons and opinion leaders want to be the first to hear when projects are announced and the bidding process opens; they want a leg up on the contract bid.[29] All assembly persons in town have private businesses that are registered as companies so they can secure these contracts. The Municipal Assembly provides them the physical space to be close to power. But perhaps more importantly, the Assembly is a gathering place for outsiders and visitors to the community. Researchers begin their studies there; NGOs seek permission from the

[28] February 13, 2012.   [29] February 27, 2012.

authorities; and utility companies sign contracts there. Ashaiman residents and leaders hope to spark a relationship that might bolster future power or employment opportunities.

On the one hand, the Assembly symbolizes the importance of formal politics. Leaders gain formal recognition by becoming assemblymen. The Chief Executive and Minister of Parliament hold budget meetings to discuss the distribution of funds. A staff of professional bureaucrats controls the funds for the provision and management of public services. But to limit the importance of the Municipal Assembly to the formal and official realm would be to undermine the real value that the Assembly has to the Ashaiman community. As importantly, it serves as a public meeting place for local-level decision-making and as a symbol of democratic self-governance. Ashaiman leaders and residents take pride in their struggle for political recognition and self-governance, and the physical building where the Assembly is housed maintains a central presence in the city.

In his book *Monrovia Modern,* Danny Hoffman (2017) draws attention to the importance of architecture in the public life of a city. In Liberia's capital city, "Physically, socially, and politically, there are few spaces in the city in which collectivities gather and form" (Hoffman 2017: 164). Therefore, there are no public spaces in which citizens can challenge those in power (Mbembe and Roitman 1995). But the Municipal Assembly in Ashaiman serves this purpose, bringing together residents from all walks of life to demand answers from government. The physical building provides the space for Ashaiman residents to "imagine a democratic future," as Hoffman suggests. The building serves a far greater purpose than simply an administrative apparatus that efficiently governs the city.

Local representatives like Gifty Avorgbedor, an NDC party activist and local leader, visit the Assembly often. She tries to secure contracts and to visit with other leaders to scheme potential projects. But she also visits the Assembly to let off steam and air her grievances. Sitting directly underneath the open window of the MCE's office, she complains about a slew of governance problems in the community. "There is also a problem with the Coordinating Director," she says. "The man is too old. Most of our things go wrong here. All of the staff do what they like. There is no order of authority from the head. Lack of leadership. There is no respect ... People at the revenue site go for bribes. There is no authority." Avorgbedor recounts the previous

leader who had respect and governed with discipline. "He had initia-
tive and vision." And she immediately went back to the current leader.
"I do not [care that] he's my party man. If anybody steps on me now,
I will eat the person."[30]

The study of the performance of bureaucrats has recently gained
traction in the political science literature. Sarah Brierley (2017) finds
that giving politicians tools to punish bureaucrats can increase administrative malfeasance, contrary to conventional expectations. Drawing
on evidence from Ghana, politicians actually use these tools to control
bureaucrats and extract rents from the state – in contexts of low
accountability. While these studies go a long way toward advancing
our understanding of the incentives of bureaucrats and politicians, they
fail to account for the numerous ways that bureaucrats interact with
the constituents they serve. Embedding oversight mechanisms in the
broader context of associational life provides a more complete picture
of the practices of accountability that bureaucrats and politicians face
with respect to governance and urban development.

Avorgbedor has many complaints about the leaders, and she is not
afraid to go straight to the Assembly and tell the people off. Creating
noise also places pressure on authorities and can act as a symbol of
power: She recently received a contract to cater lunches for public
schools in town. One resident provided the following rationale for
how she secured the contract: "Let's give it to her to shut her up."[31]
This is not uncommon in Ashaiman. When individuals or pressure
groups begin to make lots of noise, they are often given a contract or
other good to keep them quiet. This leads to a situation where residents
on the ground want their leaders to be loud and strong because this is
one mechanism to secure development projects in the community.

As Avorgbedor's statements suggest, the relationship between the
Assembly and the community members is a tense one. Most of the
technocrats are outsiders brought in to govern the city, and this contributes to problems. Residents and community leaders on the ground want
more power in the decision-making process. Technocrats in the Assembly
want more assistance from community leaders and less political partisanship. Neither the Assembly workers nor the community members trust
one another. The President appoints the mayor. Therefore, the mayor is
not directly accountable to the community members.

[30] February 24, 2012.   [31] February 24, 2012.

This example demonstrates some of the major challenges of decentralization in Ghana. Contrary to expectations of clientelism or corruption, Martin J. Williams (2017) finds that assemblies struggle to deliver – in his case completed development projects – because of collective choice commitment problems. After a project is started, it's difficult to finance the completion of the project because another neighborhood or village demands their own projects, and these pressures take priority in the funding cycle. This theory provides a powerful explanation as to why so many development projects remain unfinished across the country. While there is evidence of these commitment problems in Ashaiman, the underlying associational structure mitigates the problem because there is a centralized space for residents and their leaders to participate in the deliberations. The Assembly building is open to all.

Of course, urban governance remains a challenge. Perfect, the Administrator in the Coordinating Office has worked in Ashaiman since the Assembly opened in 2007. She expressed serious concerns: "The major issue in Ashaiman is the youth. They don't want to learn. They don't understand this is a government establishment. People come here and beat the workers. People are afraid to work here. It was not easy at first. We had to start running. But now there is a change."[32] She explained that community members do not understand the decentralization process. While this is part of the problem, a larger problem is that community residents and leaders want more power in the decision-making process and do not trust Assembly technocrats to do what is in the best interests of Ashaiman. Municipal technocrats are not from the community, and there is a long history of misallocation of funds and government ineffectiveness.

The mistrust extends to daily activities, as well as allocations for development projects. For example, one morning a group of tomato sellers was very angry because a new market that was being built did not include stalls for them. They staged a demonstration against the development exercise and marched directly to the Municipal Assembly chanting, singing, and they barged into the meeting hall and demanded an answer.[33] They were worried that the market would only benefit those connected to the politicians, and not the women selling there now. Their concerns were legitimate because there was historical

---

[32] March 1, 2012.   [33] May 14, 2012.

precedent for this in the community. Further, there is a history of "white elephants" when it comes to markets in Ashaiman.[34] The situation illustrates that there is very little trust between the ordinary residents and ASHMA. Moreover, these issues become politicized. Politicians can easily take advantage of the situation to score cheap political points. Community leaders quickly connected themselves to the grievances by the market women and added their resistance to the Municipal Assembly.

Despite the ongoing challenges of decentralization and local government, Ashaiman residents and leaders still take pride in the Municipal Assembly building because it symbolizes all that they have accomplished over the past forty years: the struggle from a squatter settlement to a functioning city. Governing through the Municipal Assembly is the prize for all local leaders in Ashaiman. It provides them the economic opportunities to socially advance, the political recognition to act as representatives of their constituents, and the prestige to uplift their leadership status. But more than anything, the Municipal Assembly is suspended above preexisting authority structures and associational bodies, and the constant process of governance depends on creatively combining these structures together. State building is the constant recombination of institutional rules and procedures with local norms and cultural practices.[35]

Everyday State Building

The process of everyday state building is especially evident with respect to police-resident relations. The relationship between police, residents, workers, and soldiers in Ashaiman is a tense one, but also a very personal one. On the one hand, soldiers have been settling in Ashaiman since the 1960s and established their authority from the time they purchased their plot. In fact many of the neighborhoods are named after countries or regions of the world where the soldiers did their foreign service, like Lebanon and Middle East.

In the center of town at the lone traffic lights, police officers squawk orders at *tro tro* drivers, harass hawkers, and try to direct

---

[34] May 15, 2012.
[35] This is similar to what Ostrom (1996) calls coproduction, as well as Berk and Galvan's (2009) concept of creative syncretism.

traffic. Police are often getting into heated arguments with residents, demanding authority and getting very little. Residents know the names of the officers, and talk about them behind their back in personal terms. They know whom they should be afraid of and whom they can ignore. But the relationship between police, ordinary residents, and local leaders has a long history, and is part of the process of state building and developing Ashaiman from a squatter settlement to a functioning city.

The process of rapid urbanization in Africa coincides with a potentially massive state-building project. The state must invest in infrastructure, services, and institutions, or risk large areas governed informally by non-state providers of services (Cammett and MacLean 2013). While these areas of limited statehood persist in urban Africa (Krasner and Risse 2014), local governments attempt to develop and modernize their towns and cities by investing in their police stations and legal institutions. But the success of these state building enterprises often depend on daily negotiations between multiple authorities, civic organizations, and local leaders (Chalfin 2010). More importantly, they depend on the underlying civic life and networks of engagement that are apparent in the everyday politics of a neighborhood. The following example of police reform in Ashaiman demonstrates this process.

"The way bullets were flying I had to run away," a witness to the shooting recounts. "The military came in to calm the tension. Otherwise this would have degenerated into something else."[36] In 2009, a dispute erupted between drivers and the police. The drivers accused the police of extorting money from them. A fight broke out and stray police bullets killed two innocent people, including one small boy who was selling pure water. The military was already in the community and had to rush to the scene. A committee was set up to investigate the issue. Compensation was given to the victim's family. The Governance Forum was one avenue used to mend the relationship between citizens and the police. In the end, the entire police leadership was transferred to another municipality.

Residents tell stories of police cooperating with criminals and drug dealers by "handing rifles to armed robbers" and collecting money from them. For example, "There is a 'drug addict spot' just behind the

[36] February 24, 2012.

school, and there are often cops walking in and out of there," one resident explains.[37] He suggests that things used to be so bad that mothers even tried to get their own kids arrested but could not. "We started noticing that the police were wearing flashy clothes and driving fancy cars," he explained. "There was no way they could make that much money on police salaries." They began to notice that the CID was "in bed with the drug peddlers."[38] Prominent leaders in the community came together and pushed for reform. The issue was taken up by the Governance Forum, and after several meetings, the government institutionalized a reform that no CID could work in Ashaiman for more than three years. Once the CID started getting "comfortable" with the terrain, they must transfer.

While Ashaiman has long been considered a "den of criminals," it has always been a point of concern for community members and leaders. From the earliest years of settlement, leaders have tried to find ways to rid the municipality of crime: "In Ashaiman, security issues are really important. The community can rally together to solve the problem," as one leader explains.[39] This does not always mean relying on the police. For example, long-time residents remember the infamous criminal named Alimenu, who was the most notorious criminal in town. His father was also a criminal, and residents recount how he even gave birth to a criminal. Several years ago, a group of community residents went to the police complaining about his activity, and the police gave them the go ahead to "do what you need to do to take care of it." They were a watchdog, or vigilante, group. So they killed the man.[40] While vigilante groups exist in many neighborhoods, this example is notable because they consulted the police first.

Security concerns and dispute resolution often fall on informal institutions in contexts of weak state institutions (Blattman et al. 2014; Sowatey and Atuguba 2014). In Ashaiman, the police worked closely with leaders on the ground to secure the peace. This process of coproduction was essential for building trust between residents and the state.

---

[37] January 26, 2012.   [38] February 8, 2012.   [39] February 8, 2012.
[40] February 16, 2012. For excellent research on the role of vigilantism in South African urban settlements, see: Smith (2015).

Developing Trust and Networks of Social Engagement

In August 2012, the Governance Forum began a series of decentralized forums based on building bridges between the police and the community. With the financial support of IBIS and the partnership of SYPPA, the forums brought residents, community leaders, and the police together with an attempt to collectively problem solve issues that are of concern to the community. The police would report on the data they gathered about the concerns of residents, as well as personally introduce themselves to leaders in the community.

For police officers, this provided them the chance to go into neighborhoods they had never entered previously. As one officer explained, "I did not even know this street existed. I am learning so much."[41] The exercise was part of a broader "community policing" initiative meant to "change the face of policing in Ashaiman," explained the new Divisional Commander of Ashaiman, David Eklu.[42]

At one forum, the police commander explained the role of the service and how they can work with the community to improve security.[43] The commander then took questions from the residents. The forum provided an interesting account of honesty and frankness. One resident aired a grievance, "It is ridiculous that the police view everyone they don't know as a suspect. If I am arrested, you must tell me why." The commander empathized with the resident and even admitted that the police service has had its problems, and reiterated that the service is learning. He continued, "If you have a problem, come and see the Commander directly." He went on to emphasize that residents do not need to pay bribes, "You do not need to pay this," he explained, admitting that this had been a problem.

One week later in a nearby neighborhood, Commander Eklu introduced the concept of community policing to a different crowd of residents and leaders. "Policing has changed all over the world," he said. He described how it is much more personal and the challenges are different. He explained that he wanted a relationship built on trust and

---

[41] June 13, 2012.

[42] August 1, 2012. Community policing has mixed results across Africa. In Kenya it has democratized security but there are also instances of decentralizing repression (Ruteere and Pommerolle 2003). There have been similar challenges in South Africa (Pelser 1999).

[43] August 1, 2012.

"face-to-face—you can know our names. We can learn from each other."[44] He kept emphasizing how the police could not do their jobs without a good working relationship with the communities. Eklu explained that crime had decreased since January, but that fear was still a problem. He called on residents to work with the police. "Once in a while, come by and you can know us," he urged. "We can exchange numbers. You are the ones who know the criminals. This is a partnership." The dialogue continued, with residents asking police what was being done with the problems at notorious ghettos called P-Squared and Soweto Lane, as well as the smokers around market square. "They smoke their gonja and their cocaine and snatch the mobile phones," a resident complained.

Eklu had a direct answer: Come work with us. "Members of the police force will be going to your study area. If the community wants to support us with a tent, then we will work with you," he responded. He explained the concept of Tent City Policing, where there could be a tent in each neighborhood that was used as a space to report and solve crimes. This is crucial in areas where there is no office space and budgets are low. But he also emphasized that this would only happen in places where the community put up the tent: "If the community can mobilize themselves and help us, by all means we will come." But the community must make the initiative. Pressure and capacity for security improvements must come from below.

Eklu made a final plea: "I plead. If you know of a Big Man, then ask for us." He was attempting to fund raise for the police force. "If the community speaks, people listen. I need your support. Add your voice. I am trying but I need your help!" Eklu needed the help of the community to help him lobby, reduce crime, and raise resources. It clearly was not going to come from the top, or through tax revenue. For him to do a good job, he needed the support of the residents and leaders at the grassroots.

The Ashaiman police force has one truck to serve a population of more than 230,000 people. It has a few motorbikes but those are often used to make trips from Ashaiman to Tema. It suffers from a history of mistrust and ineffectiveness. But this does not mean that the process of state building is not occurring in Ashaiman. Rather, it is an everyday process that involves constant interactions and negotiations between

---

[44] August 7, 2012.

local communities, leaders, politicians, and state technocrats. Further, as this section demonstrates, the success of state building depends on the underlying dynamics in the community: the strength of community leadership, the underlying networks of social engagement, and the effectiveness of its pressure groups. State capacity does not rest solely on state coercion, nor does it fuel unmitigated community resistance. Instead, it is mitigated by personal relationships, public discussion, and hard work in daily life.[45]

The Endurance of Ethnicity in Squatter Settlements

Old Fadama is Ghana's largest squatter settlement, and has been under the threat of forced eviction since 2002. The Ghanaian government has recommended numerous proposals for the area, ranging from the Korle Lagoon Restoration Project meant to clean up and turn into a tourist hub, to private development that would most likely benefit the elite (Grant 2009). Like other squatter settlements across the continent, Old Fadama is valuable for its affordable housing and proximity to employment – Makola Market #2 and the largest scrap recycling market border the neighborhood, providing numerous jobs to residents.

Though informal and unrecognized by city authorities, the settlement has a vibrant social organization. Ties to migrants' hometowns bond rows and clusters of homes together, establishing dense ethnic networks. As I describe in Chapters 3 and 4, early in the settlement process, settlers established themselves as local leaders by controlling territory and accumulating wealth. They seized property and acted as de facto landlords. These early settlers established themselves as opinion leaders by providing a sense of security of tenure, and by linking followers up to jobs. As electoral competition intensified, many of these leaders made inroads to the two major political parties and incorporated residents into the broader party organizational machinery (Bob-Milliar 2012).

Many Old Fadama leaders attained political value from this institutional ambiguity. In some cases, indigenous landowners and migrant squatters benefited from the insecure property rights regime because

---

[45] This is consistent with an anthropological approach to state building advanced by scholars like Gupta (1995).

they could extract rents and allocate land plots (Onoma 2009). Without tenure security, residents relied on these de facto landlords for property safekeeping. But more importantly, leaders bolstered their status by acting as spokespeople for marginalized groups, establishing working ties to international actors like NGOs, in this case the Shack/Slum Dwellers International (SDI) affiliate called People's Dialogue on Human Settlements (PD) and Amnesty International (Elyachar 2003). For example, many leaders allied with these organizations because they provided job opportunities, logistical expertise, and connections to new financial and political networks. As "slum rights" have become an international human rights concern, community leaders sought political advancement through opportunities funded by international organizations.[46]

Over time, the neighborhood has gained various levels of recognition. The yam market has been formalized and now collects taxes, giving significant power to the Konkomba Chief who controls the surroundings. Waste bins have been set up on the main road. But the neighborhood continues to be fraught with local political battles. After the 2016 election, foot soldiers from the New Patriotic Party (NPP) reestablished control in much of the settlement, seizing land and services and barring the opposition from entering the settlement.

The most significant outcome of this institutional insecurity and ambiguity is the persistence of ethnic social organization, and residents' ties to their rural homeland. Without tenure security or political recognition, residents rely on their ethnic headmen for protection, similar to the ways in which ethnic politics took on new meanings in towns and cities in the early years of independence, as described in Chapters 2 and 3. A notable difference is that ethnic leaders have competing incentives in today's environment, seeking to gain close connections to the state in order to accumulate political power, while also seeking alliances with internationally backed NGOs, enabling them to achieve empowerment that translates to political power in their rural districts. Without opportunities for formal positions of power in the city, they satisfy the demands of their coethnics, institutionalizing the ethnic associational life in these spaces.

---

[46] An expanded version of this argument is included in Paller (2018b).

Eviction as Opportunity

In the third introductory vignette at the beginning of this book, I told the story of Old Fadama's own community leaders collaborating with municipal authorities to demolish residents' structures, leaving them with nowhere to go. Community leaders saw the exercise as an opportunity to lead the demolition, providing an employment contract and a way to show strength and bolster their power in the community. Even more surprising was the leaders' close partnership with internationally backed NGOs advocating for human rights. Why would community leaders collaborate with state authorities to undermine the interests of residents in their neighborhood? Why would community leaders comply with an otherwise weak state – at least with respect to governance of the informal settlement – and extract resources from and demolish the homes of their neighbors? And why would they do so in partnership with an internationally recognized NGO that espoused that "slum rights" are human rights?

Demolitions do not necessarily serve the interests of the broader public (Moncada 2013; Lombard and Rakodi 2016). They tend to enrich a business and political class that benefits from the formal development process (Davis 2006; Harvey 2008; Roy 2009). The urban poor are often left out of the process (Satterthwaite and Mitlin 2013). Yet very little academic scholarship has interrogated the local leaders who help facilitate the process, and who emerge from the structures of associational life.

Pierre Englebert provides one possible answer. In his book *Africa: Unity, Sovereignty, Sorrow*, Englebert suggests that "nonstate actors of different hues have often ended up contributing one way or another to the reproduction of weak African states" (2010: 2).[47] Englebert suggests:

Even though people may live in regions or belong to minorities that are neglected or repressed by their government, many of them have a vested interest in maintaining the state so as to preserve their own sovereign

---

[47] The dominant explanation is that state elites benefit from weak states (Bayart et al. 1999; Reno 1999). There is evidence of this in informal settlements in Kenya (Gulyani and Talukdar 2008), and the continent as a whole (Fox 2014). But this does not explain why leaders in these neighborhoods would comply with state bureaucrats.

connection, and the resources and power they derive from it. They exchange national submission for local sovereign domination or exploitation. (2010: 6)

Compliance with the state enables community leaders local command, or the ability to order people around and extract rents from their neighbors. An added benefit in this case, is that local leaders derive additional power from their connections with international NGOs who provide legitimacy to their actions without closely monitoring the situation.

These actions are only possible given certain conditions of associational life. As I have demonstrated earlier in this chapter, the underlying civic life of a neighborhood provides the opportunities for residents to gain a voice in the process of urban development. This is least likely in squatter settlements, where leaders can comply with state authorities and sell their neighbors out. This is because social life is splintered along ethnic lines, and leaders pit their own groups against others, while maintaining close ties to their rural hometown. Without understanding how social life is organized, municipal bureaucrats and NGOs contribute to the persistence of ethnic politics in these neighborhoods at the expense of the most marginalized populations. The following example tells a more complete story of the demolition introduced earlier, which demonstrates how leaders in squatter settlements view evictions as opportunities to empower themselves, at the expense of the poorest residents. Without a vibrant and multiethnic civic life, the poorest residents are left without due representation and compensation.

On an otherwise ordinary morning, a bulldozer crashed into buildings, demolishing all structures on the outer edge of the settlement.[48] Hundreds of people gathered on the road, trying to stay out of the path of the bulldozer. Members of the task force for OFADA wore bright green t-shirts and led the exercise. Since 2006, they have assisted with moving kiosks off an access road so that cars could pass by, building a community center funded by Shack/Slum Dwellers International (SDI), and organizing the community for various programs called for by PD. OFADA task force leaders directed the bulldozer and signaled which structures should be demolished.

---

[48] December 21, 2011.

Residents panicked as homes were bulldozed. Men tried to salvage any usable materials like electricity wires and copper. Some residents complained that if they waited only a few hours, then people could have saved their kiosks. Families worked hard to move their belongings from their house. Men carried TVs while women carried their cookware. A group of men carried a wooden kiosk while another group used hammers to salvage any wood that they could. When the bulldozer entered Hanaan's territory, a community leader known to be extremely violent and feared by residents, he jumped up on the bulldozer and controlled the exercise. He was smiling and clearly liked leading the exercise. He started smoking a cigarette. A group of young men were on the ground laughing. He started throwing them cigarettes as if they were party favors.

While the actual demolition of houses occurred on this Wednesday morning, municipal authorities in partnership with international human rights organizations and community leaders planned the exercise. The exercise was implemented to respond to the floods of the previous month that killed fourteen people, in which the mayor responded, "We're going all the way to the beginning to where it ends. We just lost 14 lives, we can't sit down to lose more in this country. So the next thing to do is to go to Sodom and Gomorrah and move the structures along the lands closest to the lagoon so we can desilt the place. We are taking this very seriously" (Citi FM 2011a). AMA commissioned $85 million to dredge the lagoon (Accra Metropolitan Assembly). This was part of the mayor's larger plan to make Accra a "Millennium City" (Ghana News Agency 2010). As a representative of the Ghanaian state, the mayor emphasized state power through coercion: its ability to "go to Sodom and Gomorrah," evict people, and destroy structures that he claims are the root of floods in Accra (Ghana News Agency 2012).

Confronted by the threat of forced eviction and potential demolition by the city, community leaders creatively and strategically found ways to benefit personally from the uncertainty. When the threat of forced eviction persists for long periods of time, it can become institutionalized in ways that enable rent-seeking behavior and privilege leaders to act in deceitful ways. In this case, local leaders actually used the eviction exercise to bolster their own political power and consolidate their base of support, seeking reputational benefits by acting as spokespeople for the community.

For example, a month before the demolition, Opoku, the former secretary of OFADA, was angry. He was unhappy with the leadership of OFADA because he thinks that the leaders are corrupt and that they serve the interests of the Dagomba ethnic group, the majority group in Old Fadama. On this day as he walked through the neighborhood, he said, "Us Akans [another ethnic group], we must stick together." He started talking about how he supports the government's plan to evict squatters and demolish structures along the lagoon.[49] He claimed that he had made enough money in the last seventeen years as a de facto landlord and shower operator that he would not lose much if the neighborhood were demolished. His feelings complicate the conventional wisdom that community leaders are united, and resisted the demolition.[50] There were further fissures in the dominant narrative: Some felt that AMA was trying to fix the problem with the floods, while others believed that local chiefs support the beautification exercise as a power grab. Many people thought traditional authorities simply wanted to profit off the land. "They will simply go off and sell the land to developers. This is prime real estate," one leader said.

Publicly, Opoku acted differently. Two days after expressing his opinions privately, Opoku was one of the loudest leaders speaking against the proposed eviction. Due to his connection with a Citi FM journalist, the station published an online article with a headline "8,000 squatters to be rendered homeless" and quoted Opoku extensively. He made up this number because it would sway public opinion to their side. It would also spark fear in the government and force National Security to get involved, thereby limiting the power of AMA. The station published another article that further pit the state versus the community called, "AMA declares war on Sodom & Gomorrah residents." While Opoku was instrumental in the framing of the public narrative, when he called a meeting at the OFADA office, only three people showed up. Opoku had very few followers on the ground and admitted that he used the strategy to build support for his political party [the CPP], which had very little support from residents, and his women's rights NGO [WISEEP], which was constantly struggling for funding.

[49] Opoku now claims to be the Secretary-General of the National Tenants Association of Ghana.

[50] The community is portrayed as united by Du Plessis (2005); Grant (2006, 2009); Braimah (2010); Afenah (2012).

Somewhat surprisingly, community leaders did not resist the state's desire to evict squatters along the Korle Lagoon. Instead, they cooperated with authorities with the hope of securing an employment contract and serving as political representatives of their people. In line with Englebert's theory, it provided them legal command to order their neighbors around, as well as make money in the process. Further, if there was any opportunity for relocation, they wanted to be the first leaders to gain a plot of land, or secure the contract to assist with the relocation of people, allowing them to distribute these opportunities to their own personal following.

A few weeks before the demolition, AMA invited "community leaders" to the Assembly to discuss the dredging exercise. AMA sent out a paper invitation and the letter was distributed around the community so that leaders would come together for the discussion. AMA explained that they needed to dredge the lagoon so that there is free flow of water from the city to the sea. In order to complete the exercise, AMA explained that they needed to demolish all structures within fifty meters of the lagoon. The forum offered community members the opportunity to jockey for leadership positions and position themselves as spokespeople of their community. While the meeting was a performance of democratic deliberation, not all residents or leaders received the invitation and the forum was a closed-door affair.

A week before the exercise, Braimah invited approximately thirty-five Old Fadama leaders to the PD office to discuss the demolition. Each participant was given twenty cedis, refreshments were served, and the group was hired to conduct the demolition exercise themselves, without AMA and the police. The OFADA leadership was pleased because the exercise was a job for them, and they believed it would strengthen their status and prestige in the community. One leader who refused to be part of the exercise expressed his disappointment, a feeling that many community members felt: "The executive committee is doing it for their own self-interest." The organized structure of OFADA masked the real divisions in civic life, encompassing very little collaboration or trust between members from different ethnic groups.

A Battle for a Voice

The demolition exercise provided a platform of resistance for some leaders in the community. It allowed a small batch of leaders to take the moral high ground and express their displeasure with the authorities and the OFADA leadership. For example, Boss expressed his sentiment, "I support moving the people for the betterment of the community, but I do not support the exercise when it is for their own self-interest [the leadership of OFADA]. And they have not educated the people." Boss would not support the exercise because proper education was not carried out, relocation options were not finalized, and he did not trust OFADA leadership. But the exercise provided him the opportunity to gain popular support at the expense of his political rival, the Chairman of OFADA. He could paint the Chairman as colluding with authorities to make money while he made populist appeals to protect his people and "do what is right." He could take the moral high ground to increase his status in the community.[51]

Two days before the proposed exercise, Boss prevented the demolition from continuing because he resisted it. It could not move forward without his support because he had the power to mobilize hundreds of people and instigate violence. Boss walked outside to calm tempers and discuss things with residents whose houses were to be affected. People express their frustrations publicly, and Boss's spontaneous actions in the community are important because they shed light on how decision-making works among community members. He walked with an assured presence. People flooded to him. They all wanted to know what he knew and what he would do. He met people face-to-face, listened to them, and gave the final word. Boss replied with an answer that sought to calm tensions.

Boss wanted the lagoon dredged, and he understood why the shacks along the lagoon had to be cleared. But he did not want the OFADA leadership to take advantage of the situation without due process. Boss and Chairman met for twenty minutes and then walked around the community to educate the people. After they did this, Boss was still not convinced. He explained, "See how I do this. I had to negotiate the number down. I had to take care of my people. I will go back and not agree at all." By "my people," he was referring to a

---

[51] It is possible that Boss was simply sabotaging the exercise to make his political opponent look bad. More likely, however, is that by aligning himself with the popular masses and those affected by the demolition exercise, he would be able to portray himself as the "just leader" who wanted "the right thing" to be done to the vulnerable citizens.

group of people from the Dagomba ethnic group who viewed him as their opinion leader.

Boss's "deputy secretary" verified these actions via text message the next morning: "Boss informed OFADA yersternight [last night] that he will not agree for the exercise to take off until he is fully convinced. He said that to even Farouk and he got panicked and rushed to Boss immediately to listen to him and he called off the bulldozers and promised to be here early this morning." For the first time during this process, Braimah came to the community to try and convince Boss and the other leaders to agree to the exercise. He lobbied Boss to support the exercise. He tried to explain to him that AMA demanded certain measures and that it was in the best interests of the community to move the structures. Braimah, Chairman, and Boss walked around the community and made decisions about what structures would be affected. Braimah was finally able to convince Boss to support the exercise.

The payment for the exercise was not transparent and fueled rumors. Leaders said that the OFADA Chairman gave Braimah a list of sixty-two people who would manage the exercise, knowing that only half of those people would participate. Braimah apparently gave 800 cedis to Chairman to distribute: He allegedly distributed 300 cedis and kept the remaining 500 for himself. Rumors began spreading that the same leaders who demolished the structures would turn around and sell the land before the AMA comes to dredge the lagoon.

Residents were extremely angry about the exercise and placed most of the blame on their own leaders. One man who lives in the back of the settlement explained how the leader who controls the area where he lives was previously told that his structure was safe. He even moved the structure inside to avoid demolition. The local Chief came by three days before to collect ten cedis from each person whose structure might be affected. But their structures were demolished anyway. Another resident expressed the perception that the leaders colluded with the authorities: "The authorities selected leaders to turn them against the community so that we would fight. Then they could portray us as criminals and could demolish the place."

The distrust that residents have of their leaders in Old Fadama is immense and was only worsened after the demolition exercise. Many think that their leaders are only concerned with their self-interest. In many cases, residents were not angry about the exercise itself, but rather the way that it was done by their so-called community leaders.

As one resident explained, "The exercise is not a bad idea but the people doing it are lazy—they are turning it into a money thing." Many of the grievances that residents have of their leaders are the result of years of mismanagement of community funds, and the non-transparent provision of private goods.

After the exercise, hundreds of women and children sat along the edge of the lagoon on top of their belongings. One couple said they would sleep outside with mosquito nets. Others said they would stay with family members. Young men cleaned up debris. Many of them seemed fine with the exercise because they heard that the government was coming in to make a road. They said they moved inside and cooperated. They now expect the government to deliver what they promised. The demolition exercise had severe repercussions for the relationship between community leaders and its residents. Rather than viewing the leaders as representing their best interests, they lost even more trust in them. One resident expressed the common sentiment: "The community leaders have sold us out."

Several months after the demolition, the lagoon was still not dredged. Authorities did not patrol the area and structures cropped up on the land where structures were demolished. Leaders continue to take rents for the use of the land. The AMA Public Relations Officer provided the following statement as to why the lagoon had not been dredged. He replied, "Actually we need funds to do that job. We have a whole lot of procedures we have to complete before it can be completed. We are still in the process."[52] In June 2015, AMA demolished hundreds more structures in Old Fadama, reacting to flooding in the city.[53]

Tyranny of the Majority

Old Fadama's status as a squatter settlement can explain the underlying logic of these leadership patterns. The majority ethnic group dominates leadership positions because there are no formal institutions to provide representative bodies of checks and balances. This can sever bonds of respect between people from different ethnic groups. The

---

[52] June 15, 2012. The Mayor of Accra announced in February 2014 that the dredging exercise would continue soon, more than two years after this demolition (Dredging Today 2014). By 2015, the funds were still not secured.

[53] Reuters (2015).

potential for a tyranny of the majority is greater than in other settlements. Leaders build their political support with future payoffs in
mind, and the future requires running for political office in their hometown region. Boss and Chairman are both Dagombas, and they draw
their support from their Dagomba followers. Dagombas are the majority ethnic group in Old Fadama, and because there are no formal
structures of representation they do not need to reach out to other
tribes for inclusive governance.[54] They also do not need to provide any
public services in return for support.

Dagomba aspiring politicians like Boss and Chairman still consider
the settlement temporary and are building their support in order to run
for political office in the Northern Region. They act like ethnic chau-
vinists because they have the incentive to empower their own people
and share with other Dagombas because this is whom they consider
their future prospective voters. As one opinion leader named Alhaji
explains, "I want to be a politician. To be a DC or constituency
chairman back in the North, back home. I have been here 13 years,
but I was not bred here so I don't want to be MP or anything here."[55]
According to residents, previous Assemblyman Otie Bless severely
underperformed and people even laugh when asked if he is seen in
the community. "Once he won the election, his phone immediately
stopped working," one resident said, but he ran for MP in his home
region, with support from the NDC, and he won.

Residents are forced to form local political alliances, even with
members from different ethnic groups, to improve their daily living
situation and increase their personal power. But trust and respect
remains low, and squatter status incentivizes sharing of goods with
coethnics. For example, sometimes when goods are shared across
ethnic groups, those who did the sharing are often punished or accused
of selling out. In Old Fadama, this arrangement fuels great distrust
among residents, with minority groups often complaining that Dagombas dominate and do not share resources and goods with other groups.
Even leaders who form alliances with people from different groups find
it difficult to trust others; one prominent leader explained how he
cannot shed his distrust of a Dagomba he works closely with, "I like

---

[54] OFADA includes members from different ethnicities, but the general belief on
the ground is that Dagombas dominate positions of power.
[55] June 30, 2012.

Abdallah, but still, his tribal affiliation. He still has a soft spot for his people. This is the problem. The blood relation."

The distrust does not stem from primordial hatreds, but rather institutionalized norms of sharing that have developed over time. Opinion leaders who are not Dagombas complain that they only share among themselves. Due to having the largest ethnic group in the settlement, Dagombas now control most positions of power in the community, especially the coveted NDC special ward executives and OFADA leadership positions. One way that the minority groups are trying to counter "Dagomba dominance" and ensure that they will be included in sharing of party goods is by starting NDC branches. For example, one leader launched the NDC Sankofa Branch, made up of entirely non-Dagombas, but had trouble officially registering it. To do so, he needed approval from Chairman, a Dagomba who is not forthcoming with linking non-Dagomba residents with the constituency executives who will make branch designations official.

NGOs and the Organization of Civic Life

NGOs like PD and Amnesty International (AI) are known entities in Old Fadama. But they are not perceived as democratic organizations fighting on behalf of the poor, rather as contractors for community leaders fighting to secure contracts from government technocrats and politicians, as well as donor funding from international agencies. PD, for example, has a long history of acting as a broker between the AMA and Old Fadama (Braimah 2010). Executive Director Farouk Braimah is an expert on urban issues in Ghana and across the world and has helped the community fight eviction threats, first as a member of CEPIL when the community took the government to court in 2002 and lost, and then as an advocate trying to open up space for dialogue and engagement. But now he uses this leverage to serve as a de facto spokesperson of the community. Other NGOs like AI started working on behalf of Old Fadama residents in 2009 after urban development issues became an international human rights concern. AI launched a campaign claiming that forced evictions violate international human rights law.[56]

---

[56] In 1993 the UN Commission on Human Rights indicated, "forced eviction constitutes a gross violation of human rights." And in 1998, the UN Sub-

Braimah takes credit for establishing OFADA; he paid the initial registration fee.[57] This leads to the perception in the community that PD controls OFADA by providing its leadership with money and jobs, painting a perception that OFADA is simply PD's puppet. Another allegation is that PD establishes committees on the ground with Old Fadama residents, but controls them with the power of funding and information. For example, Braimah helped start a health committee in partnership with the government, but the representatives of the committee are the same residents who have leadership roles in OFADA, local NDC branches, and GHAFUP [the CBO affiliated with PD].[58] In the face of eviction threats, the community organizes to fight against the government. But in daily governance, the community is far from united, and NGOs contribute to personal rivalries, lack of accountability, and power struggles.

Governments often seek the help from NGOs working in squatter settlements if they want to carry out any projects in the community. Without any formal representative, governments rely on these private organizations as an entry point into the community. But the view from within the settlement in daily life uncovers the complexities of these relationships. Residents take advantage of international NGOs for their own personal empowerment, while NGOs espouse a public narrative of social welfare and human rights without confronting the informal norms that help keep the status quo in place. More damaging, NGOs fuel distrust within squatter settlements and heighten existing personal rivalries.

A major problem is that NGOs and municipal workers are not accountable to the residents. Therefore, the interests and concerns of ordinary residents are not integrated into political decision-making. Instead, the interests and motivations of a few leaders trump the public good, funneling state resources to individuals in the form of private goods.

Commission on the Protection and Promotion of Human Rights reaffirmed that "the practice of forced eviction constitutes a gross violation of a broad range of human rights; in particular the right to adequate housing, the right to remain, the right to freedom of movement, the right to privacy, the right to property, the right to an adequate standard of living, the right to security of the home, the right to security of the person, the right to security of tenure and the right to equality of treatment." (COHRE Global Survey 11).

[57] April 27, 2012.   [58] November 21, 2011.

For example, many Old Fadama residents think that when Braimah receives funding from organizations like SDI, he will funnel the money to his personal account, invest it, and only use a portion of the funding for programs.[59] Braimah has positioned himself so that PD will be commissioned to carry out resettlement and other development projects whenever there is a proposal for the neighborhood. As one person hypothesized with regards to the demolition exercise, "It is a stepping stone for him to demand more: [t]o secure contracts, enumerations, and other exercises."[60] Another resident explains, "Farouk [Braimah] is an opportunist who always uses the community to his benefit."[61] A local leader in Ashaiman views the NGO as a business, and explained how this undermines PD's projects. He said, "Farouk's approach is all business—'I want to get funding.'" This even affects the success of its projects: "It was too much for his own personal business. He should have come to work with existing groups in the community."[62]

Without spheres of public expression where NGO leaders and politicians can deliberate with citizens and residents and must owe account of their actions, democratic accountability is not achieved. This contributes to the spread of numerous allegations against those in power, and weakens the bonds of respect between leaders and followers. NGOs are not immune to these charges. Due to the underlying lack of legitimacy of the settlement, NGOs have little incentive to care for the public interest (that of all community residents), but rather support a small group of people who they can rely on to assist them with securing funding in the future. Residents complain that NGOs like PD and AI empower community leadership and themselves, but not the vulnerable residents for whom they claim to be advocating. For example, one resident feels used by Braimah. "I am getting old, and I do not want to be thrown to the road anymore," he said.[63] Residents are especially aggravated that they are not paid fairly when they do a project for PD. One resident explains that he and a group had to go to the PD offices and "make noise" to demand their payment after their work in an enumeration exercise.[64]

International NGOs have the incentive to support resettlement of squatters because it means they might be contracted to support the

---

[59] October 13, 2011.   [60] December 29, 2011.   [61] November 20, 2011.
[62] February 13, 2012.   [63] October 28, 2011.   [64] October 21, 2011.

resettlement. Part of the problem between PD and Old Fadama dwellers is that residents have to live there and deal with immediate issues like poor sanitation, disease outbreaks, and bad drainage. PD, on the other hand, views the status quo as a good thing: It means that the authorities do not have any immediate plans to demolish the structures. A PD associate explains why they are not currently advocating for the community: "We want to show the authorities that things are quiet and calm there so we do not need to make noise. GHAFUP and OFADA are still there. When we need to mobilize people we call them."[65] In other words, PD still treats the community as a space that needs to be protected, not upgraded. PD advocates resettlement, and hopes to be a stakeholder in the resettlement process if it ever progresses.

But this angers some residents who do not see any progress being made in their community. Instead they simply see Braimah acquiring contracts, securing more funding from international donors, and buying more cars. The rumor is that he has four of them.[66] As one angry resident complains, "Ask Farouk: Has he ever slept here before? We were here before PD came. The destiny of Old Fadama is in the hands of us, not PD."[67]

Working on "slum issues" has brought Braimah close to politicians, and interested in joining politics himself. One resident explained, "When the NPP was in power he was close to them. Now he is close to the NDC. He is very politically connected."[68] Braimah has told some people that he has ambitions to be a minister from the North, but if the NDC loses the elections he will be left with nothing. He has already used his political connections to secure government contracts, as he did for his "brother" who he helped link up and secure the construction of a gutter in Ashaiman.[69] But he has also learned that to get anything done with development, you have to "go political." "If you are not at the table," he said, "you will not get a thing."[70]

But community leaders also view NGOs as an opportunity to empower themselves and raise their status in the community. One leader tells a story about how PD asked him and the Chairman to

---

[65] October 24, 2011.

[66] These are rumors; I cannot verify them as facts. But the perception is important to how residents view NGOs in the neighborhood.

[67] September 21, 2011.   [68] October 13, 2011.   [69] May 11, 2012.

[70] May 11, 2012.

search for land in the community for a special economically friendly toilet facility for a partnership for which PD was a part.[71] He and Chairman purchased a plot of land for 3,500 Ghana cedis ($1,750). They then told PD that it cost 5,000 Ghana cedis ($2,500) and they pocketed the remainder of the money. In another example, the current spokesperson for OFADA does not even live in the community.[72] When asked if his structure was demolished after the recent fire outbreak, he angrily sneered, "Oh no no. I don't live in this place." Contrary to common understandings that NGOs serve a nonprofit and social welfare function, many Ghanaians view NGOs as profit-generating enterprises with valuable political payoffs.[73] As more global public attention is placed on urbanization and the growth of informal settlements, private donor-funded projects for issues regarding urban development have escalated as well. Residents and community leaders see this as an opportunity to expand their personal power.

NGOS are often embedded in local community divisions and politics, meaning they are not apolitical. For example, Women in Slums Economic Empowerment (WISEEP) formed in 2010 when four disgruntled leaders split from OFADA. They claimed that OFADA was corrupt, citing the time when the leadership taxed people in the community to improve basic infrastructure, but they kept the money for themselves. They were frustrated that Dagombas dominated these organizations and shared the money only with coethnic members.

These leaders from non-Dagomba ethnic groups hoped that WISEEP would serve as an avenue to bring other groups into leadership positions, raise money from new funding sources, and bolster their own power. They also had their personal reasons. One leader explained, "I just needed to make some money for my family because I was not doing well in the shop. We opened the NGO because we needed to improve our lives. We need to benefit and feed our families too."[74] WISEEP faced fierce resistance from OFADA, PD, and other community leaders when they announced the new organization. The personal and organizational rivalries continue to be felt in daily governance.

Local NGOs in squatter settlements are often reliant on larger international organizations for funding, and therefore lose a lot of their autonomy. WISEEP receives most of its funding through small

[71] December 15, 2011.   [72] May 24, 2012.   [73] October 31, 2011.
[74] December 13, 2011.

AI projects. Several times a year AI will have stakeholder forums and program meetings at upscale hotels. They partner with WISEEP to invite residents from the community. Leaders use these opportunities to build their own coalition of followers and loyalists. AI has provided international travel opportunities for several members of WISEEP. These trips provide international networking opportunities and educate participants on the "rights of slum dwellers." But they also impact the community when the participants return, contributing to extreme internal jealousy and raised expectations. For example, one leader came back from the Netherlands with a new laptop computer and digital camera. After securing a contract to show educational movies about the "rights of slum dwellers," he talks about how he wants to use the purchased projector to show regular movies each night as a business.

These travel opportunities are highly sought after. There are rumors that one leader tried to sell off these opportunities for personal profit. On one trip to the Netherlands, the participant fled the conference hotel and never returned. While this is an extreme case, some people view international NGOs as a path out of poverty. Most see them at least as a short-term employment option or opportunity for material rewards. Most participants do enjoy the events and learn a lot about informality and human rights.

AI and other international NGOs attempt to construct a narrative of human rights and fairness that does not confront the informal norms of settlement and belonging. In fact, applying the dominant international narrative of human rights to domestic urban issues sometimes has a backlash domestically.[75] In some cases, this sparks a backlash against human rights organizations by policymakers who view these NGOs as supporting illegality and instilling a culture of indiscipline.[76] One policymaker explains how international human rights have meddled in Ghanaian affairs: "They are always talking about people's rights when people are doing the wrong thing. This leads to resistance instead of leading to rules and enforcement and common sense."[77] Another man similarly states, "I do not understand human rights. These days you have people urinating everywhere, throwing their trash

[75] Autesserre (2012) documents this in the case of the Congo.
[76] This is similar to Smith's (2015) concept of "rejecting rights" in South Africa.
[77] June 21, 2012.

all over the place. Young men will speak to elders with no respect. All because they can claim human rights. Human rights is indiscipline."[78]

NGOs are limited in their transformative potential. They might help individuals, but only to a certain point. For example, one participant feels as though he is used: "I like the training but nothing comes of it. These organizations use us. They say they do this, that, and this, they get funding and we get nothing."[79] While residents are educated at AI and PD conferences and trainings, they still must follow orders and are not given the space to act independently or empower themselves. This leads to a situation where residents do not have the incentive to organize the community by themselves. Rather, they must wait and take orders from the international organizations if they want any of the material benefits that come along with the partnership. Meanwhile, organizations are fighting against one another for limited resources, and they create strategies depending on what will secure them international funding. They are upwardly accountable to foreign donors, but not downwardly accountable to residents.

While NGOs work in squatter settlements and attempt to speak on behalf of its residents, they do not engage with residents on a daily basis. They are embedded in broader structures of civic life. Further, NGOs attempt to speak on behalf of the residents without putting in place the interests of the public and those they claim to serve. Finally, they construct narratives that do not confront the informal institutions that frame domestic politics; in this case the extralegal norms that shape the relations between host city populations and new migrants.

A Quantitative Illustration: Associational Life and Quotidian Interactions

The qualitative evidence offers very different organizations of civic life across settlement types. Each settlement pattern privileges certain social practices. In indigenous settlements, residents cling to their indigenous identity in all forms of daily life. Yet in stranger settlements, residents extend their social networks to include people from different ethnic groups, coalescing in daily practices of eating with, talking to, and visiting people from other ethnic groups. Multiethnic spheres of

---

[78] November 2, 2011.   [79] October 13, 2011.

decision-making emerge in these spaces. In squatter settlements, people maintain strong ethnic ties, as residents are often new to the city and cluster themselves ethnically in specific neighborhoods.

My survey data confirm these patterns across a larger sample of neighborhoods. My survey captured novel ways to measure quotidian interactions and associational life. Descriptive evidence indicates that urban residents interact with members of different ethnic groups on a daily basis, but in ways we would not expect. I operationalize cross-ethnic social engagement by asking residents how often they visit the houses of people from different ethnic groups, eat with people from other ethnic groups, and attend outdoorings of people from other ethnic groups. These variables capture everyday forms of social engagement in urban Ghana.[80]

Ethnic visits are common, and while they bring people together in the context of daily life, they do not require long conversation or deep integration. Attending outdoorings of people from other ethnic groups is more intimate, and often requires making financial contributions to families from other ethnic groups. These outdoorings are festive events, and the process of celebrating with others strengthens social ties between neighbors. Ethnic eating is the most intimate activity, and not surprisingly least common. Food, like language, has deep cultural roots and ties to ethnic homelands. But eating also brings people together, as people often share the same bowl and chat and discuss politics – when they are done eating, of course. Seventy-four percent of respondents indicate that they visit the houses of people from other groups, 67 percent of respondents indicate that they do go to out-doorings of people from other ethnic groups, while only 48 percent of respondents eat with non-oethnics.

These ethnic engagements vary statistically across settlement types (Figure 6.1). I combine these behaviors in an index that captures these quotidian interactions. In line with my theoretical predictions, individuals in stranger settlements score on average more than one point higher than those in indigenous settlements, and nearly one point higher than those in squatter settlements. In other words, they report engaging with people from different ethnic groups significantly more. I also show how these behaviors vary across the sixteen different neighborhoods that are included in the study (Figure 6.2). This behavior appears to carry over

---

[80] This is similar to the approach taken by Varshney (2001).

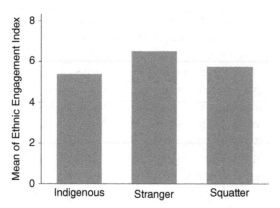

Figure 6.1 Ethnic interactions across settlements

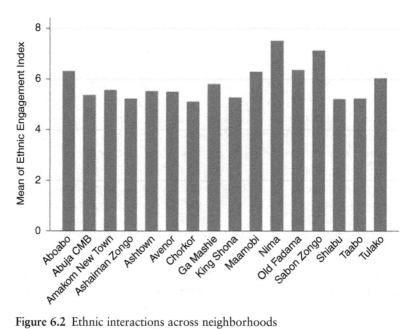

Figure 6.2 Ethnic interactions across neighborhoods

into community decision-making as well, as respondents report that the public spheres discussed in the previous chapter extend to members of different ethnic groups. More patterns of social engagement are included in the Appendix in Table A.1.

Conclusion

In this chapter, I trace how the development of cross-ethnic social engagement is most closely associated with the institution of indigeneity and belonging. In indigenous settlements, the organization of civic life is restricted along ethnic lines – to members of the Ga ethnic group. Yet in stranger neighborhoods, a multiethnic civic life develops. This contributes to a civic life that is open to the public. On the other hand, ethnic politics persists in squatter settlements, as local leaders empower coethnics through the capture of state services and resources. Nonstate actors – including international human rights organizations – and politicians play an important, yet under-examined role in the persistence of ethnic politics. In sum, ethnic politics still shape politics in urban Ghana, but only in certain neighborhoods. The informal norms of settlement and belonging explain these divergent outcomes.

7 | *Everyday Politics in Urban Africa*

Ethnically diverse urban neighborhoods with high poverty, weak state capacity, and troubling colonial histories are unexpected places to find a functioning democracy. Scholars and pundits portray these neighborhoods as "dens of criminals," "brown areas," and breeding grounds for the new urban guerilla and urban proletariat (O'Donnell 1993; Davis 2004; Kilcullen 2013). Yet this book demonstrates how clientelism can sometimes lead to better governance, distributive politics can serve the public good, and ethnic politics can be overcome in African cities. By paying close attention to the everyday politics of African urban neighborhoods, we gain a better understanding of the mechanisms and processes that contribute to Ghana's democracy.

In recent years, anthropologists, sociologists, and political scientists have studied democracy in unexpected places, including health groups in Chile (Paley 2004), gas stations in Wisconsin (Walsh 2012), *qaˉt* chews in Yemen (Wedeen 2007), soccer clubs in Uganda (Schatzberg 2006), dance clubs in the Congo (White 2008), and street preaching in Ghana (Shipley 2009). All of these studies focus on public spheres and seek to expand upon conventional and procedural conceptions of the political. In other words, they locate the site of politics beyond formal institutions like elections and legislatures to the site of daily life where political decision-making takes root. These studies also involve understanding political culture in an inductive manner, by examining societies through categories and analytical frames that mean something to local populations. This requires examining political behavior for what it actually is and does – not what intellectuals, foreign policymakers, and technocrats would like it to do (Scott 1998; Easterly 2014).

Local people build institutions and apply local knowledge to their own political realities, and they do this in very different ways depending on certain social, economic, and political circumstances. They also draw on a number of available cultural and institutional resources to create novel combinations (Berk and Galvan 2009). These "syncretic institutions" become the guiding rules and procedures of the political game in daily life. This book applies these insights to urban Ghana, and shows how ordinary people follow institutional norms in the attempt to serve their interests and bolster their status and prestige.

The focus on everyday politics in urban Africa contributes to an emerging research agenda that brings new meanings, fosters innovative concepts, and highlights new directions in the study of politics, particularly the study of democracy. It does so by uncovering the motivations, incentives, interests, and emotions that guide people's daily behaviors, and in turn, shapes their political choices and patterns of political participation. I was able to uncover the logics of collective action, and found that the basis of this collective effort was a desire for social recognition and respect. This is not entirely surprising: Behavioral economists and law scholars have shown that in small groups people are likely to cooperate when they face the threat of social sanction (Gächter and Fehr 1999; Kahan 2003). But how these behaviors scale up, and contribute to multiparty politics, are less understood by social scientists.

The connections between local communities and the state is far less understood, and an exciting avenue of future research. What is especially missing in current analyses of urban politics is the site of daily life where politicians and community leaders actually interact with their supporters and followers. This site of inquiry exposes the "personal problem solving networks" that leaders and followers form to deal with the difficulties of urban life and to enhance daily survival (Auyero 2001).

This book demonstrates the need for innovative and unconventional ways to study insecure and rapidly changing environments. Perhaps most importantly, it requires that social science not be done "behind people's backs," as James Scott says (West and Plender 2015). Social science must consider the very people who are the actors in the story; they must be consulted with, spoken to, and placed front and center in the study of democracy. Of course, this is not a new endeavor, as researchers have been conducting field research in Africa for many years; the *Afrobarometer's* public attitude survey has expanded across the continent; and scholars are using innovative experimental methods to study interpersonal relations among residents and leaders (Wantchekon and Vicente 2009). But the mechanics of how democracy works takes place in the hidden transcript in daily life (Scott 1990).

Observational and experimental survey research can assist with the study of politics in daily life, but only if the questions are relevant to people's lives. My survey was designed to probe and understand political decision-making in urban Ghana. To make sure I asked context-appropriate questions about political participation and democratic accountability, I supplemented the ethnographic research with in-depth focus group discussions with community leaders and residents. Focus group discussions are useful because they ask open-ended questions and give participants the ability to deliberate and discuss issues that might be sensitive or difficult to ask in close-ended survey formats or one-on-one interviews.

I used the insights from the focus groups to construct questions that made sense to people's daily experiences and to how they think about politics. My survey includes questions that document how individuals participate in politics and hold their leaders accountable in daily life. This includes expanding notions of the political to unofficial spaces like community hang out spots, outdoorings, and politicians' houses. It demands asking questions that have cultural relevance, like asking about whether leaders are parents to their communities and whether they eat with them and sleep in the neighborhood.

While I developed the questions to understand the urban Ghanaian context, the next step is to ask similar questions in other cities across Africa to uncover patterns of everyday politics across the continent. Comparing and contrasting the site of daily life across neighborhoods in Africa and across the world would help us understand the challenges that the urban poor face in today's world. The use of in-depth focus groups and context-specific household surveys could assist with this endeavor, and should be used more often in social science research.

Informal Institutions and Everyday Politics

Informal institutions might be doing more of the work in shaping democratic politics than most studies give them credit for. While scholars are beginning to consider informal institutions in the study of democracy, they still are largely described as secondary to, complementary to, or outcomes of formal institutional arrangements. They are typically studied as separate from state power, divorcing them from the ways in which historical legacies of state formation impact informal institutions.[1] Most importantly, informal institutions are largely understood as an outcome or reaction to weak state institutions. For these reasons, they are rarely studied in their own right, but rather as factors in a larger official political game.

This book suggests that informal institutions play a more important role than previously understood. Rather than serving a subsidiary role to official activity, they are a primary element of politics, and can shape the way formal institutions work, particularly with respect to the distribution of power and resources. Ghana, and all African countries, has undergone significant change over the past 300 years, from Western interventions during the slave trade and colonialism, to foreign influence via structural adjustment and promotion of human rights. But throughout these significant changes in the official transcript, the struggle for political space and the rules and procedures that guide power dynamics in daily life have remained incredibly resilient. A focused study of the hidden transcript over time uncovers these enduring trends in the struggle for political power (Scott 1990). A major conclusion of this study is that the informal institutions in daily life, particularly the norms of settlement and belonging, continue to shape relationships of clientelism, the type of distributive politics, and the persistence of ethnic politics. In other words, they shape the practice of democracy in urban Africa.

But why do some informal institutions matter more than others? Informal institutions include traditional and customary institutions (Englebert 2000; Williams 2004), solidary groups (Tsai 2007), Pentecostalism (McCauley 2013), friendship (Hart 1973, 2000), parenthood (Schatzberg 2001), entrepreneurialism (Shipley 2009), witchcraft (Ashforth 2005), vigilante groups (Smith 2015), and personal rule (Price 1974; Nugent 1996). All of the informal norms associated with these institutions play an important role in shaping the motivations and desires of ordinary urban residents. They play a particularly important role in how leaders legitimate power and gain status and prestige (Paller 2014). But during my fieldwork I found that they were secondary to concepts of first-comer status and settlement. The question "who settled first, and how" was of utmost importance, and shaped daily discourse, struggles for leadership, and multiparty politics. All other informal institutions were secondary.

---

[1] An important exception is MacLean (2010).

While the importance of indigeneity and belonging are ubiquitous in contemporary politics, I show in Chapter 3 that these claims are part of a historical struggle for political space and the extension of territorial authority that dates back to early settlement of a city. The sometimes controversial question "who settled first, and how" has shaped local control, political legitimacy, and access to resources in precolonial and colonial eras. I document how indigeneity is a political resource that leaders use to control followers and establish control (Bailey 1969). In other words, mobilizing followers around narratives of belonging and exclusion, as well as exploiting extralegality in squatter settlements, are options in leaders' cultural "tool kits" (Swidler 1986), making a certain kind of politics "thinkable" (Schatzberg 2001). They serve as the guiding rules and procedures that govern daily life. These norms include powerful sanctioning mechanisms if leaders and residents do not follow these rules. It is for these reasons that I advocate using the concept of informal institutions, and show how they continue to shape contemporary politics.

Chapters 4–6 demonstrate how these informal norms and procedures continue to structure everyday politics in Ghana's multiparty democracy. Most importantly, I show how they relate to formal institutions to complement, accommodate, substitute, or compete with formal institutions (Helmke and Levitsky 2006). I find that a stranger settlement is the optimal institutional environment, serving a substitutive role of the state in the complete absence of state power, or serving a complementary role with the state to provide public goods. Squatter and indigenous settlements are suboptimal. Indigenous settlements privilege the distribution of club goods and compete with the rules of the state, while squatter settlements substitute for state activity but privilege the distribution of private goods. The extent to which these settlement patterns explain political behavior in the rest of the world remains an empirical question, but has been largely ignored in social science research.

While significant attention has been paid to the importance of property rights, land tenure security, and public goods provision, more research is needed on the informal underpinnings of land security and public goods provision. While strengthening formal institutions like property rights and tenure security might be a desired outcome (De Soto 2000; World Bank 2013), this is not possible without reforming the informal institutional environment as well. This further necessitates the study of nonstate providers of public goods, as well as further interrogating the relationship between informal and formal institutions (Cammett and MacLean 2013; Kushner and MacLean 2015).

The next challenge is for scholars to place informal institutions in a comparative perspective to examine whether these different contexts have similar institutional environments that shape democratic practices. In other words, there is a need for more empirical research on the informal institutions that underlie democratic governance, especially relating to the different ways that leaders in new democracies amass funds of power and accumulate followers at the local level. Without this, the study of politics remains incomplete, and the real sources of political struggle in African societies might continue to fuel suboptimal outcomes, like the persistence of political clientelism and elite capture, despite the continuing success of formal institutional development.

Implications for the Study of Democracy

Empirically, the book provides an optimistic view of the prospects of democratization in Africa. While scholars and pundits warn of a "democratic rollback" or "democratic recession" across the world (Diamond 2008), including much of Africa, this study shows how the urban poor engage in democratic behavior in their daily lives. They actively participate in party politics, cooperate in community decision-making, and sanction their leaders. As the continent rapidly urbanizes, the conventional wisdom that African countries are experiencing urban crises is only part of the story. Instead, as the book shows, the rise of poor urban neighborhoods provides new political opportunities for previously marginalized communities, local leaders, and the urban poor to engage the state and participate in the construction of their democratic governments. Yet more research is needed to probe the impact of the dual transition of rapid urbanization and political liberalization on African societies.

While the vast majority of African politics scholarship explains why African nations and states fail,[2] this book shows how African societies can overcome these structural and institutional obstacles to reach democratic self-government. This study does not just explain why African politicians and leaders make economically irrational decisions

---

[2] These volumes include Van de Walle (2001); Bates (2008); Englebert (2010).

or use disorder as a political instrument (Bates 1981; Chabal and Daloz 1999), but rather why and when leaders will make decisions that benefit the public interest. This provides an empirically grounded explanation for how leaders and communities can overcome under-development and ethnic diversity – factors that have puzzled social scientists for many years.

But the study does not simply confirm the popular "Africa rising" narrative (Mahajan 2008). It provides many instances and examples where democratization strengthens personal or club interests. Rather, it uncovers the conditions and incentives that contribute to democratic practices. This means that I also show when and where multiparty competition contributes to nondemocratic outcomes, an unfortunate yet enduring reality across African societies. Nonetheless, my evidence shows that factors like informal institutions, social engagement, and accessible leadership need to be at the center of studies of democracy. This requires a further examination of the everyday politics as a site of social and political inquiry.

This shift in the space of politics has significant theoretical implica-tions as well. It suggests that we rethink underlying assumptions and key concepts about democracy and political decision-making. Since Robert Putnam's groundbreaking work on the importance of social capital to active citizenship and democratization (Putnam 1993, 2001), the study of social capital and associational life has been front and center in studies of democracy (Kamrava and OMora 1998; Chambers and Kymlicka 2002; Howard 2002). Yet, at the same time, the simple existence of social capital has been shown to serve exclu-sionary purposes as well, as in the case of 1930s Germany and the power of the Chieftaincy in Sierra Leone (Berman 1997; Acemoglu, Reed and Robinson 2014; Voth, Voigtländer, and Satyanath 2017). The response to this has been that without strong formal institutions, "destructive" social capital cannot be reined in (Levi 1996; Woolcock and Narayan 2000).

This book offers an alternative possibility. Instead of focusing on the strength of formal institutions to rein in "unsocial capital," more attention should be paid to the informal institutions that shape the type of social engagement and accountability of leadership. This is because different informal institutional environments have different logics of collective action. In other words, certain types of norms serve the public interest. Likewise, strong leaders are required to mobilize followers and instigate collective action. In the case of urban Ghana, cross-ethnic social engagement and accessible leaders are shaped by the settlement pattern of the neighborhood. Whether this is the case in the rest of the world is an empirical question, but one that requires further analysis. More research needs to be done on how cross-ethnic social engagement develops in ethnically diverse settings, and why public spheres evolve in some contexts while in others they do not.

The Study of Urban Africa

This book provides an innovative framework for studying urban Africa. My empirical evidence suggests that the best way to compare African neighborhoods is via norms of settlement and belonging, or whether they are settled as stranger communities, squatter settlements, or indigenous to the territory. Future questions include: Do these categories extend beyond Ghana? How useful is the model presented in this book for the study of African cities across the continent? Preliminary evidence suggests that these categories do stand up to empirical scrutiny, and are useful for the comparative study of African cities.

The model is best generalizable to other West African countries, particularly countries like Nigeria, Cote d'Ivoire, and Senegal, where customary law structures land access and the historical experience of indigeneity, and settler dynamics are similar. In addition, cities with precolonial histories are most likely to have similar development patterns. The case of democracy in indigenous settlements is especially relevant to Nigeria where conflicts over ethnic identity, religion, and resources can often be understood through the lens of indigene-settler dynamics.[3]

Consider the city of Jos, situated geographically in the center of Nigeria, and considered one of the most cosmopolitan cities in Nigeria due to its historical importance as a mining town. According to the 2006 census, it has approximately 900,000 people and has most likely grown each year since. But it has also been beset by communal and

---

[3] Nigeria is further notable because the indigene/settler dichotomy is institutionalized in the 1999 Constitution. While this distinction plays an informal role in Ghana, in Nigeria it is part of the official rules and procedures of government.

religious violence throughout the early 2000s. Like Ga Mashie in
Accra, the tensions between indigenes and settlers in poor urban
neighborhoods in Jos have gained increased importance during multiparty elections, particularly as the Christian minority has "voted out"
all Muslim representatives from government. Danfulani explains that
"In 1999, no Hausa-Fulani Muslim was voted to either the Senate or
the National House of Assembly and only one was voted to the Plateau
State of Assembly," leading to a strong feeling by the Muslim minority
that they are losing political control (Danfulani 2004).

But at the core of these political divides is a struggle over ownership
of the city of Jos, with Muslim Hausa-Fulanis on one side, and
Christian Yoruba, Urhobo, and Igbo on the other. For example, the
struggles over political and economic space were at the forefront of the
September 2001 conflicts (Gora 2001). The struggle to retain or claim
ownership of the city is the most important political struggle there is in
indigenous settlements, and multiparty politics only intensifies these
conflicts.

In the case of Jos, the most immediate parallels to Ga Mashie are the
neighborhoods where the Afisare (Izere or Jarawa), Anaguta (Nara-
guta), and Berom people live. This is because these groups have been
determined as the "true indigenes" of Jos dating back to precolonial
times. Yet, not surprisingly, "The Plateau Peace Conference [of 2004]
noted that certain individuals and groups distort history concerning
land ownership for selfish purpose and in order to cause confusion"
(Danfulani 2004). A Human Rights Watch report indicates a similar
phenomenon, and quotes a prominent Hausa civil society figure: "Indigene and non-indigene is a distinction used to manipulate the minds of
the people and drag them into crisis, just like religion and ethnicity.
[The elites] use this to drag innocent people into war with their neighbors." Additionally, former Nigerian President Obasanjo similarly
stated that the issue of indigeneity is used to manipulate people into
serving as "foot-soldiers to the designs and machinations of power-
seekers" (Human Rights Watch 2006).

The Berom are a particularly interesting parallel to the Ga of Accra.
While only numbering 300,000 nationwide (as opposed to more than
30 million Hausas), their indigenous status in local government offers
them the only opportunity for political control. As Human Rights
Watch explains, "Because of the political realities all of this implies
and in order to protect their cultural heritage, the argument goes, these

groups have no choice but to jealously guard their status as the only "true indigenes" of the state" (ibid: 38).

Muslim Hausa and Jarawa communities of Jos also claim indigeneity to the city, but are not officially recognized. This is particularly difficult for these communities because they do not have official indigenous status in any parts of the country. This leaves neighborhoods of these groups, like Anguwan Rogo, Gangare, and Rikkos under-resourced and with poor provision of public services, much like *zongo* communities in Ghana. The tensions over indigeneity and settler status are more severe than in Ghana due to the official importance indigenous status provides: access to scholarships, jobs in the civil service, and access to resources. Nonetheless, the politics of indigeneity guides multiparty politics and the process of democratization, and undermines democratic accountability in Jos, Nigeria. Similar dynamics arise in other cities of Nigeria as well, including Kano, Kaduna, and Warri. In Lagos, the rise of squatter settlements is a growing problem, as governance and authority structures in Makoko and Agogo appear similar to that of Old Fadama in Ghana (Adelekan 2010; Olaniyan 2018). The next step is to compare indigenous, stranger, and squatter settlements in these cities to determine how these informal institutional contexts shape distributive politics, political clientelism, and cross-ethnic social engagement.

This framework of African cities is not limited to former British colonies, but applies to Francophone Africa as well. For example, more than 50 percent of Cote d'Ivoire's population lives in urban areas.[4] Like the Ga in Accra, the indigenous ethnic group "Ebries" has seen their total percentage of the Abidjan population decrease from 37 percent of the total population of the city in the 1936 census, 6.8 percent in 1955, 5.5 percent in 1963, and 3.3 percent in 1975.[5] The initial settlement of neighborhoods in Abidjan is documented in similar fashion to those of Ghana and Nigeria. For example, the settlement Zoé

----

[4] 51.3 percent as of 2011.

[5] Antoine et al. (1987) quoted in Appessika (2003). Yet, like the Ga, the Ebries have maintained control over significant land and have stepped into positions as landlords. Freund (2001) argues that this is one reason that strict racial control and discrimination did not occur in Cote d'Ivoire like it did in South Africa. Freund writes: "The thriving development of Adjame and Treichville, and the real and growing importance of Ebrie claims and power, worked against any possibility of a clinically segregated city in Abidjan, not merely by race but also by class or by function" (540).

Bruno, in the commune of Koumassi, dates from the early 1960s and is named after the founder of the settlement, a leader who settled in 1964 to extend his territorial authority (Appessika 2003). Residents of Abidjan poor neighborhoods include migrants from all over the country, as well as numerous non-Ivorians mostly from Burkina Faso.

Officially, the Abidjan Urban Development Agency – the agency that governs Abidjan – distinguishes between "precarious" and "slum/spontaneous neighborhoods." The distinction is based on legality: Precarious neighborhoods are poorly resourced and have poor infrastructure, but are legal and therefore eligible for upgrading. Slum/spontaneous neighborhoods are illegal and not eligible for government services. These distinctions are critical in Abidjan, as the local authorities have been extremely aggressive in demolishing slum areas since Independence (Freund 2001). Between 1969 and 1973, for example, one-fifth of the urban population was forced to move as the authorities demolished unauthorized structures (Joshi et al. 1976: 66). These distinctions were at the forefront of urban divisions in post-Independence Abidjan, and remain that way in contemporary politics. For example, Freund describes the development of Treichville, a commune that can be compared to Ga Mashie:

Treichville, in particular, became a zone of freedom and sociability for the emerging African elite of the Ivory Coast. The ruling party was founded in there and this is where its leaders met in the course of their long struggle for power and independence (Rapley 1993: 45). Treichville, after independence, became the site of the *Maison du parti*. And even if the elite increasingly repaired to grand villas near the lagoon in Cocody, they continued to look back over the water to Treichville with considerable affection. They were certainly never inclined to plan its destruction. As Dembele mentions, the state was always tolerant of what were called "habitatse volutifs," typical of Treichville (Dembele 1987: 488). Such housing was characterized by its licit or near-licit status and its construction in solid, difficult-to-destroy materials. Such toleration was seen as part of the battle against the spread of *bidonvilles*. (Haeringer 1985)[6]

These areas stand in direct contrast to squatter settlements like Abobo, which Freund describes as developing "outside the law" (Freund 2001: 541). Today, Abobo includes some of the poorest and under-serviced neighborhoods in Abidjan, and were the site of some of the worst

---

[6] This description of Treichville is included in Freund (2001: 27).

violence following the 2010 election (Smith 2011). Residents do not have land tenure security, and often distrust the process of land titling – they view it as a distribution of state patronage. Many of these residents are not Ivorian citizens, making it even more difficult for them to gain formal rights. Nonetheless, the removal of these settlements through demolition has subsided since the 1980s, leading to authority structures that are consistent with the pattern of politics that I document in squatter settlements like Old Fadama. But electoral politics play an increasingly important role in residents' ability to gain access to the state and secure their tenure. Not surprisingly, this is where conflict is most likely. The underlying tensions between host societies and settlers continue to structure politics in these communities.

While the number of people living in squatter settlements is growing rapidly in West Africa today, the historical development of squatter settlements has not been as ubiquitous. This has been attributed to the customary land tenure systems, as well as traditional norms of ownership and other spiritual beliefs (Peil 1976; Konadu-Agyemang 1991). The dynamics I describe in this book are providing new opportunities across West Africa for political entrepreneurs to extend their political power. Yet opportunities in squatter settlements are nothing new to East and Southern Africa, where squatter settlements have developed since the colonial period as a space for "native" Africans to provide an important cheap labor supply. During the Independence period, these settlements persisted and provided an important source of political muscle for aspiring politicians.

Consider the Kibera neighborhood in Nairobi, Kenya. According to Brian Ekdale's excellent history of Kibera, the relationship between state and society in the neighborhood is fraught with political struggle, patron-client relationships, and constant maneuvering between leaders, residents, developers, landlords, and politicians (Ekdale 2011). The neighborhood was founded in 1899 as a site of reserve labor for Britain's growing colonial presence. The early settlers were Sudanese "Nubians" who served in the British East African army. As the neighborhood developed, the area grew haphazardly and was beset by crime, neglect, and underdevelopment. The colonial government attempted to demolish the neighborhood to no avail in the late years of colonial rule, turning their attention to more important matters like the Mau Mau insurgency and decolonization (Parsons 1997). The early

Nubian settlers were unable to gain formal, secure land rights and lost their special privilege with the British colonial authorities in the early years of Independence.

In 1969 the Kenyan government declared all Kibera land state property (Clark 1972). The government and residents could not come to a conclusion about relocation packages, and the neighborhood continued to develop and grow rapidly. In the 1970s, the government offered permits to build in Kibera, but these permits were a source of political patronage, "paying back favours, consolidating political clients, rewarding friends or fellow tribesmen by informally giving out free land for urban development" (Amis 1984: 90). While the state provides very few services to Kibera, the local leaders and landlords exploit extralegal opportunities to make a hefty profit. Fox sums this up succinctly: "Urban underdevelopment can be very profitable for some" (Fox 2014: 198). The lack of government services provides significant business opportunities for de facto landlords and private service operators. For example, in 2004 an estimated $31 million in rents were paid to landlords (Gulyani and Talukdar 2008). Like Old Fadama, this leads to a situation where community leaders have the incentive to maintain informality due to the huge profits they enjoy from its extralegal status.

Extralegality in Kibera creates incentives for politicians to extend private goods to political supporters, often members of their own ethnic group. Residents, in turn, rely on these politicians for access to state resources and security of tenure, particularly protection from eviction by landlords (Amis 1984). In the same way that I demonstrate in Old Fadama, residents need their politician in power to protect their security of tenure (Klopp 2008). This is one reason why Raila Odinga has become so popular in Kibera, particularly to Luo migrants who view him as critical to protecting their interests (De Smedt 2009). This is even more important as many of the landlords in the neighborhood are Kikuyus or Nubians. It is for these reasons that cross-ethnic social engagement does not develop in squatter settlements like Kibera. In the absence of strong property rights, residents perceive elections and multiparty politics to be a very important source of daily security.

The study of cities is an emerging field in comparative politics research. These studies include uncovering logics of political party network expansion in Indian slums (Auerbach 2016), geography of governance and informal leadership in India (Jha, Rao and Woolcock 2007; Huntington and Wibbels 2014), the politics of forbearance in Latin America (Holland 2015, 2016, 2017), order in informal markets in Lagos (Grossman 2018), and the political economy of slums in Africa (Fox 2014). My study has attempted to incorporate insights from these diverse studies, and demonstrate how conditions that underlie urban governance in India, Latin America, and even the United States exist and shape prospects for democratization in Africa.

More research is required to build a generalizable theory of democratic practices and everyday politics in urban Africa. In particular, studies of local leadership and informal institutions would benefit from examining them in a comparative perspective. Why do some communities develop strong leaders while others do not? How does cross-ethnic social engagement develop? Do norms of settlement differ between societies? A starting point is to examine the informal institutions that shape political behavior. Further, there is a need to uncover the reputational incentives that enable leaders and residents to place the public interest above narrow club or private interests. As the world urbanizes at a rapid rate, these questions are crucial for a prosperous and healthy urban future.

Overcoming Urban Poverty

The type of everyday politics that I outline is not relevant to all contexts, due to the scale of operations and cultural differences. Yet elite capture, political clientelism, and ethnic politics persist in many societies across the African continent, even in cities. Governments, international organizations, and NGOs are using social media to combat corruption, fund civic education campaigns to bolster political education, and to track World Bank projects using digital technology. But while these innovations should not be discredited, they do not replace the everyday interactions between citizens and representatives. This is not just the case in Africa and the developing world, but in the developed and industrialized world as well.

Studies and policies to support African development have mostly focused on rural challenges. Poverty alleviation strategies focus on the rural poor. Technological innovations focus on electrification of the hinterland and connectivity across villages. Yet an emerging problem of African development is urban poverty. As the continent becomes increasingly urban, these problems will only be intensified. As this study shows, the urban poor face different obstacles and challenges than the rural poor. Dealing with these challenges requires new and innovative solutions, including policies that confront politics and local authority structures.

One of the most important challenges that the urban poor face is difficulty in accessing basic public goods like toilets, sanitation, security, and housing. These challenges are distinct from the rural poor, who have a harder time accessing healthcare, education, and food security but do not face housing and sanitation challenges. By and large, the urban poor have access to food and water (especially in Ghana), but might not have security of tenure or live in safe neighborhoods. My study argues that this type of challenge requires confronting local collective action problems, rather than focusing solely on economic growth and technocratic "good governance" (Booth and Cammack 2014). To do so requires policy prescriptions that include a dynamic decision-making process that brings together local communities and state administrators and politicians. This book suggests three potential strategies to address urban poverty and achieve sustainable urban development: strengthening mechanisms of political accountability; providing state legal recognition; and designing creative solutions for urban upgrading.

Throughout Ghana's urban development, change comes from pressure from below. For example, I document how residents and leaders in Ashaiman overcame high poverty and insecurity to fight for political representation and effect developmental change. They were able to develop accountability mechanisms at the community level that fostered strong, accessible, and accountable leadership. To apply these lessons to other communities requires strengthening the shaming, sharing, and claims-making mechanisms that already exist. This involves "going with the grain" of African cultures and societies (Kelsall 2010). This can be done in a few ways. One way is to make sure community leaders live in the community. Residents find it much easier to confront their leaders when they can go to their house and speak to them. Leaders are able to respond faster and more efficiently. This also helps build trust between a leader and his or her followers. Leaders will also have the incentive to improve services because he or she personally benefits from the improvements.[7]

Another policy is to implement participatory governance forums in all communities (Fujiwara and Wantchekon 2013). These forums give residents the opportunity to air their grievances. But they also allow the leaders the chance to educate and explain how local governance works. Information is shared to members of all political leanings, allowing a space for diverse interests to come together to effect community change. A third strategy is to strengthen transparency in sharing of goods, foods, and jobs by leaders. They need to be clear how they share their resources. This will prevent rumors from spreading and undermine clientelist behavior. This is especially important at the level of the political party. All three of these prescriptions will strengthen the bonds of respect between leaders and their followers, a crucial aspect of governance and decision-making.

The non-recognition of squatter settlements is perhaps the biggest barrier to socioeconomic development of these neighborhoods. Without legal recognition, communities cannot receive public services and residents live in constant fear of forced eviction, making it difficult for them to invest in their neighborhoods. Lack of land security also creates incentives for opportunistic leaders to exploit informality, leading to the persistence of the status quo. All communities need to be incorporated into city planning or presented with relocation options that satisfy international human rights standards. But as this book shows, this process is not as simple as formalizing or regularizing the informal sector, as analysts like Hernando De Soto (2000, 2003) advocate. This is because informal norms of settlement and belonging provide an alternative logic to tenure security than a liberal model suggests.

Therefore, bolstering tenure security requires a political settlement where underlying land tensions and disputes must be settled. Otherwise these problems will be postponed to a later date. This requires political negotiations between communities, city authorities, politicians, and traditional authorities. It might also include incorporating alternative dispute resolution mechanisms into community life to change behavior (Blattman, Hartman, and Blair 2014). But difficult decisions must be made: There will be winners and losers.

---

[7] Olson 1993 calls these types of leaders "stationary bandits."

"Slum clearance" has been the major strategy to deal with poor neighborhoods since colonial times. This strategy has failed. Therefore, a new strategy is in order. Many residents in Old Fadama and other poor neighborhoods have the financial capital to upgrade their community if they are given the green light by city authorities. A recent fire in Old Fadama demonstrates this point: After hundreds of structures burned down, dozens of new structures were immediately built (Paller 2018b). These structures were a huge upgrade over the wooden structures that burned down. Residents used cement block, iron sheets, and bright paint. These creative solutions should be part of a broader strategy of strengthening decentralization by building the capacity of district assemblies and sub-metro units so they can better negotiate the challenges facing poor urban neighborhoods. These three policy prescriptions have one thing in common: For transformative change to occur in urban Africa, it must come from below.

Toward a Sustainable Urban Future

This book set out to explain why democracy works in some local contexts but not others. Accessible and accountable leadership, public deliberation, and cross-ethnic social engagement contributes to democratic practices in Ghanaian neighborhoods. Whether these factors explain democratic decision-making in other developing societies remains an empirical question, but preliminary evidence suggests that it does. The development of these factors can be attributed to the informal institutions that underlie official political activity. This finding suggests the need for more research on informal institutions in the study of democracy, how they foster political participation in local decision-making, and cooperation in community affairs. A theory of everyday politics in urban Africa provides a preliminary attempt at explaining democratic decision-making across the urbanizing continent. The politics of urban development will be central to a sustainable future across Africa for years to come.

Methodological Appendix

Table A.1 *Survey of sixteen urban neighborhoods: Summary statistics*

Question	Indigenous	Stranger	Squatter	Mean
Demographics				
Gender (Female = 1)	0.54	0.56	0.54	0.55
Age	36.65	38.73	33.10	36.16
Level of education	1.18	0.97	1.01	1.05 (0/2)
Literate	0.78	0.69	0.64	0.70
Employment	1.35	1.37	1.57	1.43 (0/2)
Employed in formal sector	0.90	0.87	0.92	0.90 (0/2)
Household income (*GH*)	23.57	21.80	20.48	21.93
Languages spoken	2.78	3.77	3.18	3.25
Lived poverty (gone without medicine)	2.08	1.95	2.01	2.01 (0/5)
National health insurance coverage	0.65	0.76	0.54	0.65
Settlement Status				
Ownership status (rent/own)	0.77	0.66	0.67	0.70
Years in neighborhood	20.43	21.35	12.46	18.05
Title deed (no/yes)	0.58	0.55	0.35	0.49
Pays property rate	0.54	0.52	0.32	0.46
Ethnic diversity: # of non coethnic neighbors (perceived)	2.72	2.89	3.04	2.89 (1/4)
Tenure security (perceived)	1.50	1.61	1.01	1.38 (0/2)
Local Leadership				
Leader acts as "father" to community	2.22	2.31	2.45	2.33 (1/4)
Leaders listens to concerns about public services	2.53	2.72	2.42	2.56 (1/4)

Table A.1 (*cont.*)

Question	Indigenous	Stranger	Squatter	Mean
Leaders respond to needs of residents	3.23	3.78	3.32	3.44 (1/6)
Leaders respond to public service problems	3.42	3.77	3.36	3.52 (1/6)
Leaders responds to problems	3.41	3.97	3.45	3.62 (1/6)
Leaders care about well-being of residents	3.23	3.61	3.24	3.36 (1/6)
Level of unity among leaders in neighborhood	3.70	4.47	3.85	4.01 (1/6)
Strong leader index	15.70	18.62	16.18	16.86 (1/32)
Ethnic dominance: perception that one ethnic group dominates politics	0.55	0.51	0.62	0.56 (0/1)

Everyday forms of accountability: How often does the respondent do the following?

Goes to leader's house to tell he has done something wrong	1.73	1.72	1.50	1.65 (1/4)
Stops leader on road to tell him he has done something wrong	1.69	1.53	1.57	1.59 (1/4)
Calls leader on phone to tell him he has done something wrong	1.55	1.42	1.32	1.43 (1/4)
Accountability index	2.97	2.67	2.39	2.68 (1/10)

Associational Activity

Attends political party branch meeting	0.72	0.79	0.75	0.75 (0/3)
Attends friends meeting or youth club	0.72	0.67	0.68	0.69 (0/3)
Attends hometown association	0.63	0.66	0.70	0.66 (0/3)
Attends community meeting	0.49	0.42	0.56	0.49 (0/3)
Attends prayer group or religious meeting	1.70	0.72	1.14	1.18 (0/3)
Attends trade/professional association	0.57	0.22	0.61	0.46 (0/3)
Attends other local meeting	0.42	0.24	0.30	0.32 (0/3)

Table A.1 (*cont.*)

Question	Indigenous	Stranger	Squatter	Mean
Trust and reciprocity				
Lends neighbors money	2.12	1.98	1.99	2.03 (1/4)
Contribute to community group	0.28	0.28	0.13	0.23 (0/1)
Trust in the community	2.72	2.78	2.48	2.66 (1/4)
Clientelistic Activity: Respondent's experience with the following:				
Parties target w/ gifts/money	0.53	0.52	0.46	0.50 (0/2)
Parties target w/ promises of social welfare benefits	0.46	0.52	0.50	0.50 (0/2)
Parties target w/ promises of employment	0.48	0.51	0.53	0.51 (0/2)
Parties target with promises of government contracts	0.38	0.30	0.32	0.33 (0/2)

Note: Complete codebook available on author's professional webpage

Interviews, informal conversations, and events (referenced)

Ga Mashie Interviews, Conversations, and Observations

November 10, 2011: Ussher Town, Ga Mashie

November 18, 2011: Community leader, Old Fadama

November 22, 2011: NDC foot soldier, Odododiodioo Constituency

November 22, 2011: Ga Mashie resident

December 7, 2011: Assemblyman, Asiedu Keteke District

December 17, 2011: Campaign Manager, Vanderpuye campaign, Odododiodioo Constituency

December 19, 2011: Old Fadama resident

December 7, 2011: Administrative secretary, Vanderpuye campaign, Odododiodioo Constituency

December 15, 2011: Ga Mashie, outside Vanderpuye campaign office

December 15, 2011: James Town resident

December 16, 2011: Vanderpuye campaign event, Odododiodioo Constituency

December 17, 2011: Nii Lantey Vanderpuye political campaign, Odododiodioo Constituency

January 2, 2012: Vanderpuye campaign event, Odododiodioo Constituency

January 9, 2012: Administrative secretary, Vanderpuye campaign, Odododiodioo Constituency

January 11, 2012: Campaign Manager, Vanderpuye campaign, Odododiodioo Constituency

January 14, 2012: James Town resident

January 18, 2012: NDC foot soldier, Odododiodioo Constituency

January 24, 2012: Administrative secretary, Vanderpuye campaign, Odododiodioo Constituency

January 24, 2012: NDC administrative secretary, Odododiodioo Constituency

March 4, 2012: Vanderpuye campaign event, Odododiodioo Constituency

March 22, 2012: Former Accra Mayor Nat Nunoo Amarteifio

April 3, 2012: NDC foot soldier and Ga Mashie resident, Odododiodioo Constituency

April 5, 2012: Ga Mashie fetish priest Samuel Ashalley Addey-Ashley

April 9, 2012: Vehicle spotting, James Town, Ga Mashie

April 12, 2012: NPP press conference, Ussher Town

June 7, 2012: Gbese Homowo Festival, Ussher Town

June 8, 2012: Nii Ayi Bonte, former MP Odododiodioo Constituency

June 16, 2012: NDC foot soldier and Ga Mashie resident, Odododiodioo Constituency

June 20, 2012: Ga Mashie youth focus group

June 21, 2012: Nii Tackie Tagoe, Executive Director of Ga Mashie Development Association

June 27, 2012: Robert Esmon Otorjor, Ga Mashie

July 3, 2012: NPP youth organizer, Nii Lankai, Odododiodioo Constituency

July 5, 2012: Nii Kwatelei Owoo, James Town

July 5, 2012: Nii Amarkai III, Asere Dzazetse

Old Fadama Interviews, Conversations, and Observations

September 21, 2011: Old Fadama leader and resident

September 26, 2011: Old Fadama leader

October 13, 2011: Old Fadama resident

October 13, 2011: Old Fadama leader and resident

October 18, 2011: Old Fadama resident

October 20, 2011: Nii Tackie Tagoe, Amnesty International Stakeholder's Meeting

October 24, 2011: Old Fadama leader and resident

October 25, 2011: Old Fadama resident

October 28, 2011: Ashaiman leader and resident

October 31, 2011: Old Fadama resident

October 31, 2011: Old Fadama leader and resident

November 2, 2011: Accra resident

November 4, 2011: Old Fadama

November 20, 2011: Old Fadama resident

November 20, 2011: Old Fadama leader and resident

November 21, 2011: Old Fadama resident

November 29, 2011: AMA public meeting

December 8, 2011: Old Fadama resident

December 7, 2011: Old Fadama resident

December 7, 2011: Old Fadama elder and resident

December 13, 2011: Old Fadama leader

December 15, 2011: Old Fadama leader

December 21, 2011: Old Fadama

December 29, 2011: Old Fadama leader and resident

January 11, 2012: Campaign Manager, Vanderpuye campaign, Odododiodioo Constituency

January 28, 2012: Old Fadama leader and resident

February 3, 2012: Old Fadama resident

February 9, 2012: Old Fadama Mallam, elder, and resident

February 9, 2012: Chairman, OFADA, leader and resident

February 13, 2012: Ibrahim Baidoo, Ashaiman mayor

March 22, 2012: Former Accra mayor Nat Nunoo Amarteifio

April 1, 2012: Old Fadama resident and leader

April 27, 2012: Slum Union of Ghana organizational meeting

April 19, 2012: Old Fadama resident

April 19, 2012: Old Fadama leader and resident

April 27, 2012: Farouk Braimah, Executive Director, PD

May 11, 2012: Farouk Braimah, Executive Director, PD

May 24, 2012: Old Fadama resident

May 24, 2012: OFADA spokesperson

June 4, 2012: Old Fadama elder and resident

June 15, 2012: Numo Blafo, Public relations representative, AMA

June 20, 2012: Ga Mashie youth focus group

June 21, 2012: Nii Tackie Tagoe, Executive Director of Ga Mashie Development Association

June 28, 2012: Nima elders focus group

June 30, 2012: Old Fadama leader, NDC branch organizer, and resident

July 30, 2012: Old Fadama leader

Ashaiman Interviews, Conversations, and Observations

January 23, 2012: Zongo Laka, Ashaiman

January 26, 2012: Innocent Adamadu Onyx, social worker, Ashaiman

January 26, 2012: Emmanuel Zonyira, teacher and leader

February 8, 2012: Jonathan Avisah, Executive Director, SYPPA

February 13, 2012: Thomas Adongo, Ashaiman Assemblyman

February 13, 2012: Ibrahim Baidoo, mayor of Ashaiman

February 15, 2012: Seji Amedonu, NPP MP aspirant

February 16, 2012: Ashaiman youth pastor

February 16, 2012: Chief of Ashaiman Zongo

February 16, 2012: Chief Yero, Ashaiman

February 20, 2012: NGO worker and activist, Ashaiman

February 20, 2012: Agbena Ahetu, Chairman, Amuidjor Zonal Council

February 24, 2012: Innocent Adamadu Onyx, social worker, Ashaiman

February 24, 2012: Gifty Avorgbedor, Assemblywoman, Ashaiman

February 27, 2012: Gifty Avorgbedor, Assemblywoman, Ashaiman

February 27, 2012: Selassie, teacher and leader, Ashaiman

February 29, 2012: Tulako-Ashaiman resident

February 29, 2012: Emmanuel Zonyira, teacher and leader

March 1, 2012: Administrator, Coordinating Director Office

March 9, 2012: Tulako-Ashaiman resident

March 23, 2012: Ashaiman resident

March 26, 2012: NGO worker and activist, Ashaiman

March 26, 2012: Ashaiman

April 2, 2012: Ashaiman

April 4, 2012: Ashaiman

April 4, 2012: Jonathan Avisah, Executive Director, SYPPA

April 4, 2012: NGO worker and activist, Ashaiman

April 5, 2012: Ashaiman

April 10, 2012: Emmanuel Zonyira, teacher and leader

April 10, 2012: Ashaiman

April 16, 2012: NGO worker and activist, Ashaiman

April 16, 2012: Ashaiman-Tulako

April 18, 2012: Ashaiman

May 5, 2012: Ashaiman leader

May 5, 2012: Emmanuel Zonyira, teacher and leader, Tulako-Ashaiman

May 5, 2012: Tulako-Ashaiman Slum profile focus group

May 13, 2012: Ga Mashie resident

May 14, 2012: Taabo, Ashaiman

May 15, 2012: Emmanuel Zonyira, teacher and leader

June 3, 2012: Tulako-Ashaiman focus group

June 13, 2012: Police officer, Ashaiman

June 14, 2012: Tulako-Ashaiman focus group

August 1, 2012: David Eklu, Divisional Commander of Ashaiman

August 7, 2012: David Eklu, Divisional Commander of Ashaiman

August 8, 2012: Assistant secretary, Ashaiman NDC

August 14, 2012: Ibrahim Baidoo, mayor of Ashaiman

Focus Group Information

To conduct the focus groups, I used a "snowball" sampling strategy to recruit participants because representative lists were not available, and I required respondents who had a basic understanding of associational and political life. Recruiters targeted community leaders in one series of groups (ten total) to ask about the political history of the neighborhood, while targeting ordinary residents (sixteen total) to uncover the different ways that individuals participate in politics. Recruiters selected participants who varied along gender, age, ethnicity, and political party lines. Recruiters targeted working class men and women including petty traders, students, fishermen, drivers, healthcare workers, and the unemployed (Table A.2). The ages of the participants ranged from eighteen to seventy-two, with the mean age of thirty-nine.

The first series of focus groups were conducted in ten communities and asked local leaders how residents hold them to account, the

Table A.2 *Jobs of focus group participants*

Student	15%
Trader/Businessperson	30%
Independent/Informal worker	24%
Community worker/Volunteer	11%
Fishermen	9%
Other	10%

developmental and political challenges facing the community, and how the community grew over time. Focus groups were conducted in Ashaiman-Taabo, Ashaiman-Tulako, Agbogbloshie, Chorkor, Ga Mashie, King Shona, Avenor, Abuja, ECOMOC, and Old Fadama. The interviews were conducted in Twi and Ga and translated into English. They lasted approximately two hours each.

The second series of focus groups consisted of sixteen groups in ten different neighborhoods. Focus groups were conducted in Old Fadama (three), Agbogbloshie, Ga Mashie (two), Nima (two), Abuja, Chorkor, Ashaiman-Valco Flat, Ashaiman-Taabo, Ashaiman-Tulako (three), and King Shona. Each group consisted of six to seven residents of each community; 102 residents participated in total. In Old Fadama and Ashaiman-Tulako, I varied ethnic composition of the groups because I inducted from ethnographic immersion that ethnic divisions play an important role in community affairs. Therefore, I conducted one focus group with all members of the Dagomba ethnic group, one with entirely non-Dagombas, and one with three Dagombas and three non-Dagombas. Similarly, in Nima and Ga Mashie I varied the composition along the lines of age: I conducted one group with youth and another group with elders. Each group lasted approximately three hours and participants were compensated 10 cedis ($7) for their participation. The group interviews were conducted in Twi, Ga, Hausa, and Dagomba.

Household Survey

I administered the survey "Public Service Provision in Urban Ghana" in tandem with the Ghana Center for Democratic Development (CDD). CDD is the preeminent organization in Ghana that has experience conducting social science research surveys. The enumerator training took place on April 10–11, 2013 at CDD in Accra, and the enumeration team administered the survey April 15–20, 2013. Twenty-five Ghanaian enumerators participated in the survey. Enumerators had experience working with CDD on other survey projects. Many of them served as enumerators for the *Afrobarometer* survey project. They were from Accra, Ashaiman, and Kumasi.

The survey used an "as if" stratified two-stage sampling procedure. I purposively selected three cities in Ghana to conduct the survey. Accra is the largest city with an estimated 4.3 million people.[1] As a primate city, it also has the largest number of poor neighborhoods and a growing migrant population. It is the economic and political center of the country. Ashaiman is a city on the outskirts of Tema in the Greater Accra Region. Ashaiman provides an interesting comparison to Accra because they are both in the Greater Accra Region and the Ga Dangbe customary authorities control land. Further, because the cities are only thirty minutes apart from one another, migrant patterns are very similar, with large populations of Northerners and Ewe migrants settling in the two cities.

Kumasi is the third city selected. It is widely considered the second-most politically and economically important city (behind Accra) and the capital of the Ashanti Region. Kumasi adds important variation along several important variables of interest. Unlike Accra and Kumasi, it is a stronghold of the opposition NPP political party. Some scholars have suggested that political dynamics and party activity differ in opposition strongholds (Resnick 2012). Further, the Ashanti ethnic group controls land. The Ashanti are notable for their proud history, centralized governance apparatus, and large population (they are the largest ethnic group in Ghana making up 47 percent of the population). By including Kumasi in the survey, I am able to broaden the scope of the survey from a Greater Accra project (where most recent studies of informal settlements have taken place) to a more national sample. Further, I am able to test whether political dynamics can be attributed to certain patterns of ethnic arrangements or specific ethnic group dynamics, or underlying institutional factors as my analysis suggests.

I then selected sixteen neighborhoods across the three cities: ten in Accra, three in Ashaiman, and three in Kumasi. I created a list of poor

[1] Ghana Statistical Service 2012.

urban neighborhoods in Accra, Kumasi, and Ashaiman. I started with AMA's "slum inventory," and added a list of neighborhoods from Ashaiman and Kumasi (Table A.3). I did not include neighborhoods that have an estimated population of less than 2,000 people. With lack of census data on these communities, the estimate was a crude approximation based on local knowledge. I then classified these neighborhoods into three categories: indigenous, stranger, and squatter. In total, twenty-

Table A.3 *List of poor Ghanaian neighborhoods*

Neighborhood name	City	Institutional type
Aboabo *+	Kumasi	Stranger
Abuja CMB *+	Accra	Squatter
Agbogbloshie +	Accra	Squatter (part indigenous)
Alajo	Accra	Indigenous
Amakom New Town *	Kumasi	Squatter
Asawase	Kumasi	Stranger
Ashaiman Zongo *+	Ashaiman	Stranger
Ashtown (Ashanti New Town) *	Kumasi	Indigenous
Avenor *+	Accra	Squatter (part indigenous)
Chorkor *+	Accra	Indigenous
Darkuman	Accra	Stranger
ECOMOC +	Accra	Squatter
Ga Mashie *+^	Accra	Indigenous
Gbegbeyise	Accra	Indigenous
King Shona (James Town Beach) *+	Accra	Squatter
Kotobabi	Accra	Strenger
Maamobi *	Accra	Stranger
Nima *+	Accra	Stranger
New Fadama	Accra	Stranger
New Town	Accra	Stranger
Nii Boi Town	Accra	Indigenous
Old Fadama *+^	Accra	Squatter
Sabon Zongo *	Accra	Stranger
Shiabu *	Accra	Indigenous
Sukura	Accra	Stranger
Taabo *+	Ashaiman	Indigenous
Tulako *+^	Ashaiman	Squatter
Zongo Laka +	Ashaiman	Squatter

*Included in household survey; +Included in focus groups; ^Included in ethnography

nine neighborhoods made my list. I selected five indigenous and five stranger, and six squatter settlements. This was necessary because Abuja and King Shona are small, but have similar institutional characteristics.

Squatter settlements are the least ubiquitous neighborhoods. Nonetheless, they are crucial for three important reasons. First, many of the settlements with a population under 2,000 people are squatter settlements, and have the potential to develop into bigger neighborhoods. With increasing migration, new migrants might settle in these young communities. Second, settlements like Tulako and Old Fadama have huge populations and are growing every day. Many experts estimate Old Fadama to have more than 100,000 residents. Third, squatter settlements are increasing rapidly across the developing world, from India and Brazil to South Africa and Egypt.

I used a spatial sampling technique. Having selected sixteen neighborhoods to conduct the survey, I then created boundaries of neighborhoods using Google Earth. I combined information from "AMA's Slum Inventory" with my local knowledge of neighborhood borders. Local knowledge included residents' own perceptions of where the neighborhood begins and ends. I corroborated this information during focus group interviews with leaders in twelve of the sixteen neighborhoods.

The point of the spatial sampling approach is to make sure that all spaces within the neighborhood are equally represented in the sample. This is particularly important in Ghana because ethnic groups live in spatial clusters (Agyei-Mensah and Owusu 2010). The spatial sampling technique, therefore, allows me to include different ethnic clusters within my sample with equal probability. The key outcome of my sampling procedure allows me to make generalizations and inferences at this level of analysis: There is a random chance that all "neighborhoods" might be included in the sample.

The enumeration area is a subset of the "neighborhood" and is meant to represent the population in the broader neighborhood. I include 150 point markers representing 150 clusters. I led a research team to each GPS point to find an easily identifiable starting point as close to the GPS point as possible. At each starting point, I recalculated the GPS point. The small research team collected data on local public goods provision around each starting point, serving as indicators of public goods provision for each clusters. Data was collected on road quality, sanitation, streetlight provision and maintenance, electricity, water, public toilet availability and cleanliness, and shower access. The team recorded directions for enumerators that they would use to carry out the survey. Enumerators used a random walk protocol at each starting point. They interviewed six to eight residents at each starting point. Gender parity was imposed.

Interviewers spoke with respondents face-to-face at their homes. There were twenty-five interviewers; most had experience carrying out household surveys. Only one respondent per household took part in the survey. A total of 1,432 visits were made to households; 82 percent of those resulted in successful interviews. I substituted all nonresponse households with an interview with the household next door. Therefore, all spatially sampled units were represented and interviewed. I substituted respondents for 249 households. Of those households that were not interviewed: 47 percent refused; 20 percent were empty; 16 percent did not have a respondent home who could satisfy requirement; 9 percent had no adults; and 8 percent could not communicate with the interviewer.

References

Abdulai, Abdul-Gafaru, and Sam Hickey. 2016. "The Politics of Development under Competitive Clientelism: Insights from Ghana's Development Sector." *African Affairs* 115 (458): 44–72.

Abdulai, Abdul-Gafaru. 2017. "Rethinking Spatial Inequality in Development: The Primacy of Power Relations." *Journal of International Development* 29 (3): 386–403.

Acemoglu, Daron, Tristan Reed, and James A. Robinson. 2014. "Chiefs: Economic Development and Elite Control of Civil Society in Sierra Leone." *Journal of Political Economy* 122 (2): 319–368.

Acemoglu, Daron, and Matthew O. Jackson. 2015. "History, Expectations, and Leadership in the Evolution of Social Norms." *The Review of Economic Studies* 82 (2): 423–456.

Acquah, Ione. 1958. *Accra Survey*. London: London University Press.

Adedeji, John L. 2001. "The Legacy of J. J. Rawlings in Ghanaian Politics: 1979–2000." *African Studies Quarterly* 5 (2): 1–27.

Adejumobi, Said. 2001. "Citizenship, Rights and the Problem of Conflicts and Civil Wars in Africa." *Human Rights Quarterly* 23 (1): 148–170.

Adelekan, Ibidun O. 2010. "Vulnerability of Poor Urban Coastal Communities to Flooding in Lagos, Nigeria." *Environment and Urbanization* 22 (2): 433–450.

Adida, Claire L. 2011. "Too Close for Comfort? Immigrant Exclusion in Africa." *Comparative Political Studies* 44 (10): 1370–1396.

2014. *Immigrant Exclusion and Insecurity in Africa*. New York: Cambridge University Press.

Adsera, Alicia, Carles Boix, and Mark Payne. 2003. "Are You Being Served? Political Accountability and Quality of Government." *The Journal of Law, Economics & Organization* 19 (2): 445–490.

Afenah, Afia. 2012. "Engineering a Millennium City in Accra, Ghana: The Old Fadama Intractable Issue." *Urban Forum* 23 (4): 527–540.

African Development Bank Group. 2012. "Urbanization in Africa." Available: www.afdb.org/en/blogs/afdb-championing-inclusive-growth-across-africa/post/urbanization-in-africa-10143/.

Agyei, Yaa Ankomaa, Emmanuel Kumi, and Thomas Yeboah. 2016. "Is Better to Be *Kayayei* than to Be Unemployed: Reflecting on the Role of Head Portering in Ghana's Informal Economy." *GeoJournal* 81 (2): 293–318.

Agyei-Mensah, Samuel, and George Owusu. 2010. "Segregated by Neighbourhoods? A Portrait of Ethnic Diversity in the Neighbourhoods of the Accra Metropolitan Area, Ghana." *Population, Space, and Place* 16 (6): 499–516.
  2012. "Ethnic Residential Clusters in Nima, Ghana." *Urban Forum* 23 (1): 133–149.

Akinyele, Rufus T. 2009. "Contesting for Space in an Urban Centre: The Omo Onile Syndrome in Lagos." In Francesca Locatelli, and Paul Nugent, eds. *African Cities: Competing Claims on Urban Spaces*. Leiden: Brill: 109–134.

Akyeampong, Emmanuel. 2002. "Bukom and the Social History of Boxing in Accra: Warfare and Citizenship in Precolonial Ga Society." *The International Journal of African Historical Studies* 35 (1): 39–60.

Albert, Isaac Olawale. 2008. "From 'Owo Crisis' to 'Dagbon Dispute': Lessons in the Politicization of Chieftaincy Disputes in Modern Nigeria and Ghana." *The Round Table* 97 (394): 47–60.

Allman, Jean Marie. 1991. "'Hewers of Wood, Carriers of Water': Islam, Class, and Politics on the Eve of Ghana's Independence." *African Studies Review* 34 (2): 1–26.

Allport, Gordon W. 1954. *The Nature of Prejudice*. Cambridge, MA: Addison-Wesley.

Almeida, Teresa. 2012. "Neoliberal Policy and the Growth of Slums." *The Prospect Journal of International Affairs at UCSD* 4 (5).

Amis, P. 1984. "Squatters or Tenants: The Commercialization of Unauthorized Housing in Nairobi." *World Development* 12 (1): 87–96.

Anderson, David M. 2002. "Vigilantes, Violence and the Politics of Public Order in Kenya." *African Affairs* 101 (405): 531–555.

Appadurai, Arjun. 1996. *Modernity at Large, Cultural Dimension of Globalization*. Minneapolis: University of Minnesota Press.
  2001. "Deep Democracy: Urban Governmentality and the Horizon of Politics." *Environment and Urbanization* 13 (23): 23–43.

Appessika, Kouamé. 2003. "The Case of Abidjan." *Ivory Coast, Case Study for the Global Report*.

Appiah, Kwame Anthony. 1993. *In My Father's House: Africa in the Philosophy of Culture*. New York: Oxford University Press.

Apter, David E. 1955. *The Gold Coast in Transition*. Princeton, NJ: Princeton University Press.

Arendt, Hannah. 1958. *The Human Condition*. Chicago: University of Chicago Press.

Arguello, Jose E. M., Richard Grant, Martin Oteng-Ababio, and Bethlehem M. Ayele. 2013. "Downgrading – An Overlooked Reality in African Cities: Reflections from an Indigenous Neighborhood of Accra, Ghana." *Applied Geography* 36: 23–30.

Arhin, Kwame. 1971. "Strangers and Hosts: A Study in the Political Organisation and History of Atebubu Town." *Transactions of the Historical Study of Ghana* 12: 63–82.

Arimah, Ben C. 2010. "The Face of Urban Poverty: Explaining the Prevalence of Slums in Developing Countries." *UNU-WIDER Working Paper* 2010–2030.

Arku, Godwin. 2009. "Housing Policy Changes in Ghana in the 1990s: Policy Review." *Housing Studies* 24 (2): 261–272.

Arn, Jack. 1996. "Third World Urbanization and the Creation of a Relative Surplus Population: A History of Accra, Ghana to 1980." *Review* 19 (4): 413–444.

Arthur, Peter. 2010. "Democratic Consolidation in Ghana: The Role and Contribution of the Media, Civil Society and State Institutions." *Journal of Commonwealth and Comparative Politics* 48 (2): 203–226.

Ashforth, Adam. 2005. *Witchcraft, Violence, and Democracy in South Africa*. Chicago: University of Chicago Press.

Asunka, Joseph. 2016. "Partisanship and Political Accountability in New Democracies: Explaining Compliance with Formal Rules and Procedures in Ghana." *Research & Politics* 3 (1): 1–7.

2017. "Non-Discretionary Resource Allocation as Political Investment: Evidence from Ghana." *Journal of Modern African Studies* 55 (1): 29–53.

Asunka, Joseph, Sarah Brierley, Miriam Golden, Eric Kramon, and George Ofosu. 2017. "Electoral Fraud or Violence: The Effect of Observers on Party Manipulation Strategies." *British Journal of Political Science*: https://doi.org/10.1017/S0007123416000491.

Auerbach, Adam Michael. 2016. "Clients and Communities: The Political Economy of Party Network Organization and Development in India's Urban Slums." *World Politics* 68 (1): 111–148.

Auerbach, Adam Michael and Tariq Thachil. 2016. "Capability, Connectivity, Co-Ethnicity: The Origins of Political Brokerage in India's Urban Slums." Working paper.

Austin, Dennis. 1970. *Politics in Ghana, 1946–1960*. London: University of Oxford Press.

Austin, Gareth. 2005. *Labour, Land and Capital in Ghana: From Slavery to Free Labour in Asante, 1807–1956*. Rochester, NY: University of Rochester Press.

Autesserre, Severine. 2010. *The Trouble with the Congo: Local Violence and the Failure of International Peacekeeping*. New York: Cambridge University Press.

2012. "Dangerous Tales-Dominant Narratives on the Congo and their Unintended Consequences." *African Affairs* 111 (443): 202–222.

Auyero, Javier. 2001. *Poor People's Politics: Peronist Survival Networks and the Legacy of Evita*. Durham, NC: Duke University Press.

Awuvafoge, Samson Abapale. 2013. "Affordable Housing in Urban Areas of Ghana: Issues and Recommendations." Master's Thesis, Ball State University.

Ayee, Joseph, and Richard Crook. 2003. "'Toilet Wars': Urban Sanitation Services and the Politics of Public-Private Partnerships in Ghana." *IDS Bulletin* No. 123.

Azarya, Victor, and Naomi Chazan. 1987. "Disengagement from the State in Africa: Reflections on the Experience of Ghana and Guinea." *Comparative Studies in Society and History* 29 (1): 106–131.

Bailey, F. G. 1969. *Stratagems And Spoils: A Social Anthropology Of Politics*. New York: Westview Press.

Baldwin, Kate, and John D. Huber. 2010. "Economic versus Cultural Differences: Forms of Ethnic Diversity and Public Goods Provision." *American Political Science Review* 104 (4): 644–662.

Baldwin, Kate. 2016. *The Paradox of Traditional Chiefs in Democratic Africa*. New York: Cambridge University Press.

Banégas, R., and R. Marshall-Fratani. 2003. "La Côte d'Ivoire en guerre. Dynamiques du dedans, dynamiques du dehors." *Politique Africaine* 89: 5–11.

Banerjee, Abhijit, Lakshmi Iyer, and Rohini Somanathan. 2005. "History, Social Divisions, and Public Goods in Rural India." *Journal of the European Economic Association* 3 (2/3): 639–647.

Bank of Ghana. 2007. *The Housing Market in Ghana*.

Bardhan, Pranab, and Dilip Mookherjee. 2006. "Decentralisation and Accountability in Infrastructure Delivery in Developing Countries." *The Economic Journal* 116 (508): 101–127.

Barnes, Sandra T. 1974. *Becoming a Lagosian*. University of Wisconsin–Madison. Unpublished PhD manuscript.

1986. *Patrons and Power: Creating a Political Community in Metropolitan Lagos*. Bloomington: Indiana University Press.

Bates, Robert H. 1981. *Markets and States in Tropical Africa: The Political Basis of Agricultural Policies*. Berkeley: University of California Press.

1983. *Essays on the Political Economy of Rural Africa*. Cambridge: Cambridge University Press.

2008. *When Things Fell Apart: State Failure in Late-Century Africa*. New York: Cambridge University Press.

Bayart, Jean-François. 2005. *The Illusion of Cultural Identity*. Chicago: University of Chicago Press.

Bayart, Jean-François, Stephen Ellis, and Béatrice Hibou. 1999. *The Criminalization of the State in Africa*. Oxford: Currey.

Bayat, Asef. 2013. *Life as Politics: How Ordinary People Change the Middle East*. Palo Alto, CA: Stanford University Press.

Berk, Gerald, and Dennis Galvan. 2009. "How People Experience and Change Institutions: A Field Guide to Creative Syncretism." *Theory & Society* 38 (6): 543–580.

Berman, Sheri. 1997. "Civil Society and the Collapse of the Weimar Republic." *World Politics* 49 (3): 401–429.

Berry, Sara. 1993. *No Condition Is Permanent: The Social Dynamics of Agrarian Change in Sub-Saharan Africa*. Madison: University of Wisconsin Press.

2009. "Property, Authority and Citizenship: Land Claims, Politics and the Dynamics of Social Division in West Africa." *Development and Change* 40 (1): 23–45.

Besley, Timothy. 1995. "Property Rights and Investment Incentives: Theory and Evidence from Ghana." *Journal of Political Economy* 103: 903.

Besley, Timothy, and Robin Burgess. 2002. "The Political Economy of Government Responsiveness: Theory and Evidence from India." *The Quarterly Journal of Economics* 117 (4): 1415–1451.

Blattman, Christopher, Alexandra Hartman, and Robert Blair. 2014. "How to Promote Order and Property Rights under Weak Rule of Law? An Experiment in Changing Dispute Resolution Behavior through Community Education." *American Political Science Review* 108 (1): 100–120.

Blocher, Joseph. 2006. "Building on Custom: Land Tenure Policy and Economic Development in Ghana." *Yale Human Rights and Development Law Journal* 9: 166–202.

Blumer, Herbert. 1958. "Race Prejudice as a Sense of Group Position." *Pacific Sociological Review* 1 (1): 3–7.

Boas, Morten. 2009. "'New' Nationalism and Autochthony – Tales of Origin as Political Cleavage. *Africa Spectrum* 44 (1): 19–38.

Bob-Milliar, George M. 2011. "'Te NyɔgeyƐng Gbengbenoe!' ('We Are Holding the Umbrella Very Tight!'): Explaining the Popularity of the NDC in the Upper West Region of Ghana." *Africa: Journal of the International African Institute* 81 (3): 455–473.

2012. "Political Party Activism in Ghana: Factors Influencing the Decision of the Politically Active to Join a Political Party." *Democratization* 19 (4): 668–689.

2014. "Party Youth Activists and Low-Intensity Electoral Violence in Ghana: A Qualitative Study of Party Foot Soldiers' Activism." *African Studies Quarterly* 15 (1): 125.

Bob-Milliar, George M., and Jeffrey W. Paller. 2018. "Democratic Ruptures and Electoral Outcomes in Africa: The Ghana 2016 Election." *Africa Spectrum* 53 (1): 5-35

Bobo, Lawrence, and Vincent Hutchings. 1996. "Perceptions of Racial Group Competition: Extending Blumer's Theory of Group Position to a Multiracial Social Context." *American Sociological Review* 61 (6): 951–972.

Boix, Carles, and Daniel N. Posner. 1998. "Social Capital: Explaining Its Origins and Effects on Government Performance." *British Journal of Political Science* 28 (4): 686–693.

Boo, Katherine. 2012. *Behind the Beautiful Forevers: Life, Death, and Hope in a Mumbai Undercity*. New York: Random House.

Boone, Catherine. 2014. *Property and Political Order in Africa: Land Rights and the Structure of Politics*. New York: Cambridge University Press.

Booth, David, and Diana Cammack. 2014. *Governance for Development in Africa: Solving Collective Action Problems*. London: Zed Books.

Borocz, Joszef. 2000. "Informality Rules." *East European Politics and Societies* 14 (2): 348–380.

Bowles, Samuel. 1998. "Endogenous Preferences: The Cultural Consequences of Markets and Other Economic Institutions." *Journal of Economic Literature* 36 (1): 75–111.

Brady, Henry E., and David Collier. 2004. *Rethinking Social Inquiry: Diverse Tools, Shared Standards*. New York: Rowman & Littlefield Publishers, Inc.

Braimah, Farouk. 2010. "A Decade of Struggles and Lessons at Old Fadama." *SDI.net Blog*. Available: www.sdinet.org/blog/2011/11/8/old-fadama-decade-struggles-and-lessons/.

Braimah Farouk, R., and Mensah Owusu. 2012. "'If in Doubt, Count': The Role of Community-Driven Enumerations in Blocking Eviction in Old Fadama, Accra." *Environment and Urbanization* 24 (1): 47–57.

Brand, Richard R. "The Spatial Organization of Residential Organizations in Accra, Ghana, with Particular Reference to Aspects of Modernization." *Economic Geography* 48 (3): 284–298.

Brass, Jennifer. 2016. *Allies or Adversaries: NGOs and the State in Africa*. New York: Cambridge University Press.

Bratton, Michael, and Nicolas Van de Walle. 1994. "Neopatrimonial Regimes and Political Transitions in Africa." *World Politics* 46 (4): 453–489.

1997. *Democratic Experiments in Africa: Regime Transitions in Comparative Perspective*. New York: Cambridge University Press.

Brierley, Sarah. 2017. "Unprincipled Principals: Co-Opted Bureaucrats and Corruption in Local Governments in Ghana." Working paper.

Brierley, Sarah, and Eric Kramon. 2018. "Party Campaign Strategies: Rallies, Canvassing and Handouts in a New Democracy." Working paper.

Bruce-Myers, J. M. 1927. "The Origin of the Gãs: Part I." *Journal of the Royal African Society* 27 (105): 69–76.

Cammett, Melani, and Lauren M. MacLean. 2013. *The Politics of Non-State Social Welfare*. Ithaca, NY: Cornell University Press.

Casely-Hayford, J. E. 1903. *Gold Coast Native Institutions: With Thoughts Upon a Healthy Imperial Policy for the Gold Coast and Ashanti*. London: Cass.

Ceuppens, Bambi, and Peter Geschiere. 2005. "Autochthony: Local or Global? New Modes in the Struggle over Citizenship and Belonging in Africa and Europe." *Annual Review of Anthropology* 34: 385–407.

Chabal, Patrick, and Jean-Francois Daloz. 1999. *Africa Works: Disorder as Political Instrument*. Bloomington: Indiana University Press.

Chabal, Patrick. 2008. *Africa: The Politics of Suffering and Smiling*. London: Zed Books.

Chalfin, Brenda. 2008. "Sovereigns and Citizens in Close Encounter: Airport Anthropology and Customs Regimes in Neoliberal Ghana." *American Ethnologist* 35 (4): 519–538.

2010. *Neoliberal Frontiers: An Ethnography of Sovereignty in West Africa*. Chicago: University of Chicago Press.

2014. "Public Things, Excremental Politics, and the Infrastructure of Bare Life in Ghana's City of Tema." *American Ethnologist* 41 (1): 92–109.

Chambas, Mohammed Ibn. 1979. "Leadership and Policies in Nima, a Slum Community in Accra." M. A. Thesis, University of Ghana.

Chambers, Simone, and Will Kymlicka, eds. 2002. *Alternative Conceptions of Civil Society*. Princeton, NJ: Princeton University Press.

Charnysh, Volha, Christopher Lucas, and Prerna Singh. 2015. "The Ties That Bind National Identity Salience and Pro-Social Behavior toward the Ethnic Other." *Comparative Political Studies* 48 (3): 267–300.

Chauveau, Jean-Pierre. 2001. "How Does an Institution Evolve? Land, Politics, Intergenerational Relations and the Institution of the *Tutorat* amongst Autochthons and Immigrants (Gban region, Côte d'Ivoire)." In R. Kuba and C. Lentz, eds. *Land and the Politics of Belonging in West Africa*. Leiden: Brill.

Chazan, Naomi, and Donald Rothschild. 1988. *The Precarious Balance: State and Society in Africa*. Boulder, CO: Westfield Press.

Citi MF. 2011a. "Odor Dredging to Cost GHc2 Million." Available: www.ghanaweb.com/GhanaHomePage/NewsArchive/artikel.php?ID=223865.

Claassen, Christopher. 2014. "Group Entitlement, Anger and Participation in Intergroup Violence." *British Journal of Political Science* 46 (1): 127–148.

Clark, D. 1972. *Social Dynamics of a Low Income Neighborhood in Nairobi.* Kampala: Makerere University.

Cohen, Abner. 1969. *Custom & Politics in Urban Africa: A Study of Hausa Migrants in Yoruba Towns.* London: Routledge.

Cooke, Edgar, Sarah Hague, and Andy McKay. 2016. "The Ghana Poverty and Inequality Report." Available: www.unicef.org/ghana/Ghana_Poverty_and_Inequality_Analysis_FINAL_Match_2016(1).pdf.

Cooper, Frederick. 1983. *Struggle for the City: Migrant Labor Capital and the State in Urban Africa.* London: Sage Publications.

Cornelius, Wayne A. 1973. *Political Learning among the Migrant Poor: The Impact of Residential Context.* Vol. 4. London: Sage Publications.

Cramer, Katherine. 2016. *The Politics of Resentment: Rural Consciousness in Wisconsin and the Rise of Scott Walker.* Chicago: University of Chicago Press.

Crawford, Sue E. S., and Elinor Ostrom. 1995. "A Grammar of Institutions." *American Political Science Review* 89 (3): 582–600.

Croese, Sylvia, and M. Anne Pitcher. 2017. "Ordering Power? The Politics of State-Led Housing Delivery under Authoritarianism–The Case of Luanda, Angola." *Urban Studies.* Available: doi: 10.1177/0042098017732522.

Daaku, KY. 1970. "Pre-Ashanti States." *Ghana Notes and Queries* 9: 1600–1720.

Daes, Erica. 1996. Working paper on the Concept of "Indigenous Peoples." UN Doc. E/CN.4/Sub.2/AC.4/1996/2.

Dakubu, Mary Esther Kropp. 1997. *Korle Meets the Sea: A Sociolinguistic History of Accra.* New York: Oxford University Press.

Danfulani, Habila Dadem. 2004. "The Jos Peace Conference and the Indigene/Settler Question in Nigerian Politics." Working paper.

Daniell, William F. 1856. "On the Ethnography of Akkrah and Adampe, Gold Coast, Western Africa." *Journal of the Ethnological Society of London* 4: 1–32.

Datta, Ansu K., and R. Porter. 1971. "The Asafo System in Historical Perspective." *The Journal of African History* 12 (2): 279–297.

Davis, Mike. 2004. "Planet of Slums: Urban Involution and the Informal Proletariat." *New Left Review* 26: 5–26.

   2006. *Planet of Slums.* London: Verso.

Dembele, Ousmane. 1987. "Le modèle d'urbanisme ivoirien face à la crise économique: Observations à propos de l'habitat métropolitain." In Bernard Contamin, and Harris Memel-Fotê, eds. *Le modèle ivoirien en questions: crises, adjustments, recompositions.* Paris: Karthala Editions.

De Smedt, Johan. 2009. "'No Raila, No Peace!' Big Man Politics and Election Violence at the Kibera Grassroots." *African Affairs* 108 (433): 581–598.

De Soto, Hernando. 2000. *The Other Path.* New York: Basic Books.

2003. *The Mystery of Capital: Why Capitalism Triumphs in the West and Fails Everywhere Else.* New York: Basic Books.

De Tocqueville, Alexis. 2003. *Democracy in America.* Vol. 10. Washington, DC. Regnery Publishing.

Diamond, Larry. 2008. "The Democratic Rollback: The Resurgence of the Predatory State." *Foreign Affairs* 19 (2): 138–149.

Dionne, Kim Y. 2015. "Social Networks, Ethnic Diversity, and Cooperative Behavior in Rural Malawi." *Journal of Theoretical Politics* 27 (4): 522–543.

Djankov, Simeon, Rafael La Porta, Florencio Lopez-de-Silanes, and Andrei Shleifer. 2010. "Disclosure by Politicians." *American Economic Journal: Applied Economics* 2 (2): 179–209.

Dredging Today. 2014. "Ghana: Korle Lagoon Dredging Begins in February." Available: www.dredgingtoday.com/2014/01/27/ghana-korle-lagoon-dredging-begins-in-february/.

Dunning, Thad, and Lauren Harrison. 2010. "Cross-Cutting Cleavages and Ethnic Voting: An Experimental Study of Cousinage in Mali." *American Political Science Review* 104 (01): 21–39.

Du Plessis, Jean. 2005. "The Growing Problem of Forced Evictions and the Crucial Importance of Community-Based, Locally Appropriate Alternatives." *Environment and Urbanization* 17 (1): 123–134.

Durand-Lasserve, Alain. 2006. "Informal Settlements and the Millennium Development Goals: Global Policy Debates on Property Ownership and Security of Tenure." *Global Urban Development* 2 (1): 1–15.

Easterly, William. 2014. *The Tyranny of Experts: Economists, Dictators, and the Forgotten Rights of the Poor.* New York: Basic Books.

Ejdemyr, Simon, Eric Kramon, and Amanda Lea Robinson. 2017. "Segregation, Ethnic Favoritism, and the Strategic Targeting of Local Public Goods." *Comparative Political Studies.* Available: doi: 10.1177/0010414017730079.

Ejobowah, John Boye. 2012. "Ethnic Conflict and Cooperation: Assessing Citizenship in Nigerian Federalism." *Publius: The Journal of Federalism* 43 (4): 728–747.

Ekdale, Brian. 2011. "A History of Kibera." Available: www.brianekdale.com/the-history-of-kibera/.

Ekeh, Peter. 1975. "Colonialism and the Two Publics: A Theoretical Statement." *Comparative Studies in Society and History* 17 (1): 91–112.

Elischer, Sebastian. 2013. *Political Parties in Africa: Ethnicity and Party Formation*. New York: Cambridge University Press.

Elleh, Nnamdi. 2002. *Architecture and Power in Africa*. Westport, CT: Praeger.

Elyachar, Julia. 2003. "Mappings of Power: The State, NGOs, and International Organizations in the Informal Economy of Cairo." *Comparative Studies in Society and History* 45 (3): 571–605.

Emerson, Robert M., Rachel I. Fretz, and Linda L. Shaw. 2011. *Writing Ethnographic Fieldnotes*. Chicago: University of Chicago Press.

Englebert, Pierre. 2000. "Pre-Colonial Institutions, Post-Colonial States, and Economic Development in Tropical Africa." *Political Research Quarterly* 53 (1): 7–36.

2002. *State, Legitimacy and Development in Africa*. Boulder, CO: Lynne Rienner.

2010. *Africa: Unity, Sovereignty, and Sorrow*. Boulder, Co: Lynne Rienner.

Englund, Harri, ed. 2002. *A Democracy of Chameleons: Politics and Culture in the New Malawi*. Uppsala: No. 14. Nordic Africa Institute.

Enos, Ryan D. 2015. "What the Demolition of Public Housing Teaches Us about the Impact of Racial Threat on Political Behavior." *American Journal of Political Science* 60 (1): 123–142.

Erlich, Aaron, and Nicholas Kerr. 2016. "'The Local Mwananchi Has Lost Trust': Design, Transition and Legitimacy in Kenyan Election Management." *The Journal of Modern African Studies* 54 (4): 671–702.

Ermakoff, Ivan. 2011. "Patrimony and Collective Capacity: An Analytical Outline." *The ANNALS of the American Academy of Political and Social Science* 636 (1): 182–203.

Epstein, Arnold Leonard. 1958. *Politics in an Urban African Community*. Manchester: Manchester University Press.

Eyoh, Dickson, and Richard Stren, eds. 2003. *Decentralization and the Politics of Urban Development in West Africa*. Washington, DC: Woodrow Wilson International Center for Scholars.

Fay, Marianne and Charlotte Opal. 2000. "Urbanization-without-Growth: A Not-So-Uncommon Phenomenon." *The World Bank*. Policy research working paper 2412.

Fearon, James D. 1999. "Electoral Accountability and the Control of Politicians: Selecting Good Types versus Sanctioning Poor Performance." In Adam Przeworksi, Susan C. Stokes, and Bernard Manin, eds. *Democracy, Accountability, and Representation*. New York: Cambridge University Press.

Fearon, James D., and David Laitin. 1996. "Explaining Interethnic Cooperation." *American Political Science Review* 90 (4): 715–735.

Ferguson, James. 1992. "The Country and the City on the Copperbelt." *Cultural Anthropology* 7 (1): 80–92.

1999. *Expectations of Modernity: Myths and Meanings of Urban Life on the Zambian Copperbelt*. Berkeley: University of California Press.

Ferraz, Claudio, and Frederico Finan. 2008. "Exposing Corrupt Politicians: The Effects of Brazil's Publicly Released Audits on Electoral Outcomes." *Quarterly Journal of Economics* 123 (2): 703–745.

Field, Margaret J. 1937. *Religion and Medicine of the Ga People*. London: Oxford University Press.

1940. *The Social Organization of the Ga People*. London: Crown Agents.

Finan, Frederico, and Laura Schechter. 2012. "Vote-Buying and Reciprocity." *Econometrica* 80 (2): 863–881.

Fortes, Meyer. 1975. *African Political Systems*. Oxford: Oxford University Press.

Fortescue, Dominic. 1990. "The Accra Crowd, the Asafo, and the Opposition to the Municipal Corporations Ordinance, 1924–25." *Canadian Journal of African Studies* 24 (3): 348–375.

Fourchard, Laurent. 2009. "Dealing with 'Strangers': Allocating Urban Space to Migrants in Nigeria and French West Africa, End of the Nineteenth Century to 1960." In Francesa Locatelli, and Paul Nugent, eds. *African Cities: Making Claims on Urban Spaces*. Leiden: Brill. 187–218.

2012. "Security and Party Politics in Cape Town." *Geoforum* 43 (2): 199–206.

Fox, Jonathan. 1994. "The Difficult Transition from Clientelism to Citizenship: Lessons from Mexico." *World Politics* 46 (2): 151–184.

Fox, Sean. 2014. "The Political Economy of Slums: Theory and Evidence from Sub-Saharan Africa." *World Development* 54 (2): 191–203.

Fraser, Alastair. 2017. "Post-Populism in Zambia: Michael Sata's Rise, Demise and Legacy." *International Political Science Review* 38 (4): 456–472.

Fraser, Nancy. 1990. "Rethinking the Public Sphere: A Critique of Actually Existing Democracy." *Social Text* 25(26): 56–80.

French, Howard. 2013. "How Africa's New Urban Centers Are Shifting Old Colonial Boundaries." *The Atlantic*. Available: www .theatlantic.com/international/archive/2013/07/how-africas-new-urban-centers-are-shifting-its-old-colonial-boundaries/277425/.

Freund, Bill. 2001. "Contrasts in Urban Segregation: A Tale of Two African Cities, Durban (South Africa) and Abidjan (Côte d'Ivoire)." *Journal of Southern African Studies* 27 (3): 527–546.

Fridy, Kevin S. 2007. "The Elephant, Umbrella, and Quarrelling Cocks: Disaggregating Partisanship in Ghana's Fourth Republic." *African Affairs* 106 (423): 281–305.

Fridy, Kevin S., and Victor Brobbey. 2009. "Win the Match and Vote for Me: The Politicisation of Ghana's Accra Hearts of Oak and Kumasi Asante Kotoko Football Clubs." *The Journal of Modern African Studies* 47 (1): 19–39.

Frohlich, Norman, Joe A. Oppenheimer, and Oran Young. 1971. *Political Leadership and Collective Goods.* Princeton, NJ: Princeton University Press.

Fujiwara, Thomas, and Leonard Wantchekon. 2013. "Can Informed Public Deliberation Overcome Clientelism? Experimental Evidence from Benin." *American Economic Journal: Applied Economics* 5 (4): 241–55.

Gächter, Simon, and Ernst Fehr. 1999. "Collective Action as a Social Exchange." *Journal of Economic Behavior & Organization* 39 (4): 341–369.

Gadjanova, Elena. 2017. "Electoral Clientelism as Status Affirmation: Evidence from Ghana." *Journal of Modern African Studies* 55 (4): 593–621.

Gale, Thomas S. 1995. "The Struggle against Disease in the Gold Coast: Early Attempts at Urban Sanitary Reform." *Transactions of the Historical Society of Ghana* 16 (2): 185–203.

Galvan, Dennis. 2004. *The State Must Be Our Master of Fire: How Peasants Craft Culturally Sustainable Development in Senegal.* Berkeley: University of California Press.

Gay, Robert. 1998. "Rethinking Clientelism: Demands, Discourses and Practices in Contemporary Brazil." *European Review of Latin American and Caribbean Studies* 65: 7–24.

Geertz, Clifford. 1973. *The Interpretation of Cultures.* New York: Basic Books.

George, Alexander L., and Andrew Bennett. 2005. *Case Studies and Theory Development in the Social Sciences.* Boston: MIT Press.

Geschiere, Peter, and Josef Gugler. 1998. "Introduction: The Urban-Rural Connection: Changing Issues of Belonging and Identification." *Africa* 68 (3): 309–319.

Geschiere, Peter, and Francis Nyamnjoh. 2000. "Capitalism and Autochthony: The Seesaw of Mobility and Belonging." *Public Culture* 12 (2): 423–452.

Geschiere, Peter, and Stephen Jackson. 2006. "Autochthony and the Crisis of Citizenship: Democratization, Decentralization, and the Politics of Belonging." *African Studies Review* 49 (2): 1–14.

Ghana News Agency. 2010. "Accra Declared Millennium City." *Ghana News Agency.* January 15, 2010. Available: http://news.peacefmonline.com/news/201001/36628.php.

  2012. "Courage Needed to Deal with Pollution of Korle Lagoon–Accra Mayor." *Ghana News Agency.* March 22, 2012. Available: http://

vibeghana.com/2012/03/22/courage-needed-to-deal-with-pollution-of-korle-lagoon-accra-mayor/.

Ghana Statistical Service. 2012. "2010 Population & Housing Census: Summary of Final Results."

Gilbert, Alan. 1981. "Pirates and Invaders: Land Acquisition in Urban Colombia and Venezuela." *World Development* 9 (7): 657–678.

Gluckman, Max. 1960. "Tribalism in Modern British Central Africa." *Cahiers d'études africaines* 1 (1): 55–70.

Gocking, Roger. 1999. *Facing Two Ways: Ghana's Coastal Communities under Colonial Rule*. Lanham, MD: University Press of America.

2005. *The History of Ghana*. Westport, CT: Greenwood Press.

Golden, Miriam, and Brian Min. 2013. "Distributive Politics Around the World." *Annual Review of Political Science* 16: 73–99.

Goldstein, Markus, and Christopher Udry. 2008. "The Profits of Power: Land Rights and Agricultural Investment in Ghana." *Journal of Political Economy* 116 (6): 981–1022.

Goode, William J. 1979. *The Celebration of Heroes: Prestige as a Control System*. Berkeley: University of California Press.

Gora, Daniel. 2001. "Remote Causes/Suggestions on September 7, 2001 Crisis." Memorandum submitted to the Nikki Tobi Judicial Commission of Inquiry into the Jos and Environs Communal/Religious Crisis, Azi Nyako Youth Centre, Dadin Kowa, Jos.

Gottlieb, Jessica. 2016. "Greater Expectations: A Field Experiment to Improve Accountability in Mali." *American Journal of Political Science* 60 (1): 143–157.

Gouldner, Alvin W. 1960. "The Norm of Reciprocity: A Preliminary Statement." *American Sociological Review* 25 (2): 161–178.

Grant, Richard. 2006. "Out of Place? Global Citizens in Local Spaces: A Study of the Informal Settlements in the Korle Lagoon Environs of Accra, Ghana." *Urban Forum* 17 (1): 1–24.

2009. *Globalizing City: The Urban and Economic Transformation of Accra, Ghana*. Syracuse, NY: Syracuse University Press.

Grant, Richard, and Martin Oteng-Ababio. 2012. "Mapping the Invisible and Real 'African' Economy: Urban E-Waste Circuitry." *Urban Geography* 33 (1): 1–21.

Granovetter, Mark S. 1973. "The Strength of Weak Ties." *American Journal of Sociology* 78 (6): 1360–1380.

Green, Elliott D. 2014. "The Political Economy of Urbanization in Modern Botswana." Available at SSRN 2251935.

Grossman, Guy. 2014. "Do Selection Rules Affect Leader Responsiveness? Evidence From Rural Uganda." *Quarterly Journal of Political Science* 9 (1): 1–44.

Grossman, Guy, and Delia Baldassarri. 2012. "The Impact of Elections on Cooperation: Evidence from a Lab-in-the-Field Experiment in Uganda." *American Journal of Political Science* 56 (4): 964–985.

Grossman, Guy, and Janet Lewis. 2014. "Administrative Unit Proliferation." *American Political Science Review* 108 (1): 196–217.

Grossman, Guy, and Kristin Michelitch. 2018. "Information Dissemination, Competitive Pressure, and Politician Performance between Elections: A Field Experiment in Uganda. *American Political Science Review* 112 (2): 280–301.

Grossman, Shelby. 2018. "The Politics of Order in Informal Markets: Evidence from Lagos." Working paper.

Gruffyd Jones, Branwen. 2009. "'Cities without Slums'? Global Architectures of Power and the African City." *African Perspectives 2009: The African Inner City: [Re]sourced*. Conference proceedings, 57–68.

Gulyani, Sumila, and Debabrata Talukdar. 2007. "Retrieving the Baby from the Bathwater: Slum-Upgrading in Sub-Saharan Africa." *Environment and Planning C: Politics and Space* 25 (4): 486–515.

2008. "Slum Real Estate: The Low-Quality High-Price Puzzle in Nairobi's Slum Rental Market and its Implications for Theory and Practice." *World Development* 36 (10): 1916–1937.

Gupta, Akhil. 1995. "Blurred Boundaries: The Discourse of Corruption, the Culture of Politics, and the Imagined State." *American Ethnologist* 22 (2): 375–402.

Gyimah-Boadi, Emmanuel. 2009. "Another Step Forward for Ghana." *Journal of Democracy* 20 (2): 138–152.

Habermas, Jurgen. 1991. *The Structural Transformation of the Public Sphere: An Inquiry into a Category of Bourgeois Society.* Cambridge, MA: MIT Press.

Habyarimana, James, Macartan Humphreys, Daniel N. Posner, and Jeremy M. Weinstein. 2009. *Coethnicity: Diversity and the Dilemmas of Collective Action: Diversity and the Dilemmas of Collective Action.* New York: Russell Sage Foundation.

Haeringer, Philippe. 1985. "Vingt-cinq ans de politique urbaine à Abidjan ou la tentation de l'urbanisme intégral." *Politique africaine* 17: 20–40.

Hanagan, Michael P., and Charles Tilly, eds. 1999. *Extending Citizenship, Reconfiguring States.* Lanham, MD: Rowman and Littlefield Publishers, Inc.

Hardin, Garrett. 1968. "The Tragedy of the Commons." *Science* 162 (3859): 1243–1248.

Harding, Robin. 2015. "Attribution and Accountability: Voting for Roads in Ghana." *World Politics* 67 (4): 656–689.

Hart, Jennifer. 2016. *Ghana on the Go: African Mobility in the Age of Motor Transportation*. Bloomington: Indiana University Press.

Hart, Keith. 1973. "Informal Income Opportunities and Urban Employment in Ghana." *The Journal of Modern African Studies* 11 (1): 61–89.

2000. "Kinship, Contract, and Trust: The Economic Organization of Migrants in an African City Slum." In Diego Gambetta, ed. *Trust: Making and Breaking Cooperative Relations*. Oxford: Oxford University Press.

Harvey, David. 2008. "The Right to the City." *The City Reader* 6: 23–40.

Hassan, Mai. 2016. "A State of Change: District Creation in Kenya after the Beginning of Multi-Party Elections." *Political Research Quarterly* 69 (3): 510–521.

2017. "The Strategic Shuffle: Ethnic Geography, the Internal Security Apparatus, and Elections in Kenya." *American Journal of Political Science* 61 (2): 382–395.

Hassan, Mai, and Ryan Sheely. 2017. "Executive–Legislative Relations, Party Defections, and Lower Level Administrative Unit Proliferation: Evidence From Kenya." *Comparative Political Studies* 50 (12): 1595–1631.

Hawkes, Kristen. 1993. "Why Hunter-Gatherers Work: An Ancient Version of the Problem of Public Goods." *Current Anthropology* 34 (4): 341–361.

Helmke, Gretchen, and Steven Levitsky. 2004. "Informal Institutions and Comparative Politics: A Research Agenda." *Perspectives on Politics* 2 (4): 725–740.

eds. 2006. *Informal Institutions and Democracy: Lessons from Latin America*. Baltimore, MD: Johns Hopkins University Press.

Herbst, Jeffrey. 2000. *States and Power in Africa: Comparative Lessons in Authority and Control*. Princeton, NJ: Princeton University Press.

Hicken, Allen. 2011. "Clientelism." *Annual Review of Political Science* 14: 289–310.

Hilgers, Mathieu. 2011. "Autochthony as Capital in a Global Age." *Theory, Culture & Society* 28 (1): 34–54.

Hilgers, Tina. 2011. "Clientelism and Conceptual Stretching: Differentiating among Concepts and among Analytical Levels." *Theory & Society* 40 (5): 567–588.

Hodge, Peter. 1964. "The Ghana Workers Brigade: A Project for Unemployed Youth." *The British Journal of Sociology* 15 (2): 113–128.

Hodgson, Dorothy. 2002. "Introduction: Comparative Perspectives on the Indigenous Rights Movement in Africa and the Americas." *American Anthropologist* 104 (4): 1037–1049.

Hoffman, Danny. 2017. *Monrovia Modern: Urban Form and Political Imagination in Liberia*. Durham, NC: Duke University Press.

Holland, Alisha C. 2015. "The Distributive Politics of Enforcement." *American Journal of Political Science* 59 (2): 357–371.

2016. "Forbearance." *American Political Science Review* 110 (2): 232–246.

2017. *Forbearance as Redistribution: The Politics of Informal Welfare in Latin America*. New York: Cambridge University Press.

Holston, James. 2008. *Insurgent Citizenship: Disjunctions of Democracy and Modernity in Brazil*. Princeton, NJ: Princeton University Press.

Honig, Lauren. 2016. "Immigrant Political Economies and Exclusionary Policy in Africa." *Comparative Politics* 48 (4): 517–537.

Houser, George M. 1957. "Africa Revisited." *Africa Today* 4 (5): 3–7.

Howard, Marc Morje. 2002. "The Weakness of Postcommunist Civil Society." *Journal of Democracy* 13 (1): 157–169.

Huchzermeyer, Marie. 2011. *Cities with Slums: From Informal Settlement Eradication to a Right to the City in Africa*. Cape Town: Juta Academic.

Human Rights Watch. 2006. "'They Do Not Own This Place:' Government Discrimination against "Non-Indigenes" in Nigeria." 18 (3a): 1–68.

Huntington, Heather, and Erik Wibbels. 2014. "The Geography of Governance in Africa: New Tools from Satellites, Surveys and Mapping Initiatives." *Regional & Federal Studies* 24 (5): 625–645.

Hyden, Goran. 1983. *Beyond Ujamaa in Tanzania: Underdevelopment and an Uncaptured Peasantry*. Berkeley: University of California Press.

Ichino, Nahomi, and Matthias Schündeln. 2012. "Deterring or Displacing Electoral Irregularities? Spillover Effects of Observers in a Randomized Field Experiment in Ghana." *The Journal of Politics* 74 (1): 292–307.

Ichino, Nahomi, and Noah L. Nathan. 2013. "Crossing the Line: Local Ethnic Geography and Voting in Ghana." *American Political Science Review* 107 (2): 344–361.

2016. "Democratizing the Party: The Effects of Primary Election Reforms in Ghana." Working paper.

Inglehart, Ronald, and Christian Welzel. 2009. *Modernization, Cultural Change, and Democracy: The Human Development Sequence*. New York: Cambridge University Press.

Issifu, Abdul Karim. 2015. "An Analysis of Conflicts in Ghana: The Case of Dagbon Chieftaincy." *The Journal of Pan African Studies* 8 (6): 28–44.

Jackson, Stephen. 2006. "Sons of Which Soil? The Language and Politics of Autochthony in Eastern D. R. Congo." *African Studies Review* 49 (2): 95–123.

Jha, Saumitra, Vijayendra Rao, and Michael Woolcock. 2007. "Governance in the Gullies: Democratic Responsiveness and Leadership in Delhi's Slums." *World Development* 35 (2): 230–246.

Jockers, Heinz, Kohnert Dirk, and Paul Nugent. 2010. "The Successful Ghana Election of 2008: A Convenient Myth?" *Journal of Modern African Studies* 48 (1): 95–116.

Joshi, Heather, Harold Lubell, and Jean Mouly. 1976. "Abidjan: Urban Development and Employment in the Ivory Coast."

Josiah-Aryeh, Nii Armah. 1997. "The GaDangme People – A Historical Sketch." The King Tackie Memorial Lectures delivered in the UK and in Ghana.

Jourde, Cédric. 2005. "'The President Is Coming to Visit!': Dramas and the Hijack of Democratization in the Islamic Republic of Mauritania." *Comparative Politics* 37 (4): 421–440.

Kahan, Dan M. 2003. "The Logic of Reciprocity: Trust, Collective Action, and Law." *Michigan Law Review* 102 (1): 71–103.

Kamrava, Mehran, and Frank O. Mora. 1998. "Civil Society and Democratisation in Comparative Perspective." *Third World Quarterly* 19 (5): 893–916.

Kasara, Kimuli. 2013. "Separate and Suspicious: Local Social and Political Context and Ethnic Tolerance in Kenya." *Journal of Politics* 75 (4): 921–936.

Keefer, Philip. 2007. "Clientelism, Credibility and the Policy Choices of Young Democracies." *American Journal of Political Science* 51 (4): 804–821.

Keller, Edmund J. 2014. *Identity, Citizenship, and Political Conflict in Africa*. Bloomington: Indiana University Press.

Kelsall, Tim. 2010. "Going with the Grain in African Development? *Development Policy Review* 26 (6): 627–655.

Kendhammer, Brandon. 2013. "The *Sharia* Controversy in Northern Nigeria and the Politics of Islamic Law in New and Uncertain Democracies." *Comparative Politics* 45 (3): 291–311.

Kertzer, David I. 1988. *Ritual, Politics, and Power*. New Haven, CT: Yale University Press.

Key Jr., V .O. 1949. *Southern Politics in State and Nation*. Knoxville: University of Tennessee Press.

Kilcullen, David. 2013. *Out of the Mountains: The Coming Age of the Urban Guerrilla*. Oxford: Oxford University Press.

Kirchherr, E. C. 1968. "Tema 1951–1962: The Evolution of a Planned City in West Africa." *Urban Studies* 5 (2): 207–217.

Kitschelt, Herbert, and Steven Wilkinson, eds. 2007. *Patrons, Clients, and Policies: Patterns of Democratic Accountability and Representation*. New York: Cambridge University Press.

Klaus, Kathleen. 2015. "Claiming Land: Institutions, Narratives, and Political Violence in Kenya." PhD dissertation, University of Wisconsin-Madison.

Klaus, Kathleen, and Jeffrey W. Paller. 2017. "Defending the City, Defending Votes: Campaign Strategies in Urban Ghana." *Journal of Modern African Studies* 55 (4): 681–708.

Klaus, Kathleen, and Matthew I. Mitchell. 2015. "Land Grievances and the Mobilization of Electoral Violence Evidence from Côte d'Ivoire and Kenya." *Journal of Peace Research* 52 (5): 622–635.

Klopp, Jacqueline M. 2000. "Pilfering the Public: The Problem of Land Grabbing in Contemporary Kenya." *Africa Today* 47 (1): 7–26.

2008. "Remembering the Destruction of Muoroto: Slum Demolitions, Land and Democratisation in Kenya." *African Studies* 67 (3): 295–314.

Kobo, Ousman. 2010. "'We Are Citizens Too': The Politics of Citizenship in Independent Ghana." *The Journal of Modern African Studies* 48 (1): 68–94.

Konadu-Agyemang, Kwadwo O. 1991. "Reflections on the Absence of Squatter Settlements in West African Cities: The Case of Kumasi, Ghana." *Urban Studies* 28 (1): 139–151.

Koter, Dominika. 2013. "King Makers: Local Leaders and Ethnic Politics in Africa." *World Politics* 65 (2): 187–232.

Kramon, Eric. 2016. "Electoral Handouts as Information: Explaining Unmonitored Vote Buying." *World Politics* 68 (3): 454–98.

Kramon, Eric, and Daniel N. Posner. 2013. "Who Benefits from Distributive Politics? How the Outcome One Studies Affects the Answer One gets." *Perspectives on Politics* 11 (2): 461–474.

Krasner, Stephen D., and Thomas Risse. 2014. "External Actors, State-Building, and Service Provision in Areas of Limited Statehood: Introduction." *Governance* 27 (4): 545–567.

Kruks-Wisner, Gabrielle. 2018. "The Pursuit of Social Welfare: Citizen Claim-Making in Rural India." *World Politics* 70 (1): 122–163.

Kuper, Adam. 2003. "The Return of the Native." *Current Anthropology* 44 (3): 389–401.

2005. *The Reinvention of Primitive Society: Transformations of a Myth*. London: Routledge.

Kushner, Danielle Carter, and Lauren M. MacLean. 2015. "Special Issue: The Politics of the Nonstate Provision of Public Goods in Africa." *Africa Today* 62 (1).

Laitin, David L. 1986. *Hegemony and Culture: Politics and Religious Change among the Yoruba*. Chicago: University of Chicago Press.

Landau, Loren B. 2014. "Conviviality, Rights, and Conflict in Africa's Urban Estuaries." *Politics & Society* 42 (3): 359–380.

Landry, Pierre F., and Mingming Shen. 2005. "Reaching Migrants in Survey Research: The Use of the Global Positioning System to Reduce Coverage Bias in China." *Political Analysis* 13 (1): 1–22.

Larkin, Brian. 2008. *Signal and Noise: Media, Infrastructure, and Urban Culture in Nigeria*. Durham, NC: Duke University Press.

Larreguy, Horacio, John Marshall, and Pablo Querubin. 2016. "Parties, Brokers, and Voter Mobilization: How Turnout Buying Depends upon the Party's Capacity to Monitor Brokers." *American Political Science Review* 110 (1): 160–179.

Lauth, Hans-Joachim. 2000. "Informal Institutions and Democracy." *Democratization* 7 (4): 21–50.

Lawson, Chappell, and Kenneth F. Greene. 2014. "Making Clientelism Work: How Norms of Reciprocity Increase Voter Compliance." *Journal of Comparative Politics* 47 (1): 61–85.

LeBas, Adrienne. 2011. *From Protest to Parties: Party-Building and Democratization in Africa*. Oxford: Oxford University Press.

2013. "Violence and Urban Order in Nairobi, Kenya and Lagos, Nigeria." *Studies in Comparative International Development* 48 (3): 240–262.

Lentz, Carola. 1995. "'Tribalism'and Ethnicity in Africa." *Cahiers des sciences humanes* 31 (2): 303–328.

1998. "The Chief, the Mine Captain and the Politician: Legitimating Power in Northern Ghana." *Africa* 68 (1): 46–67.

2003. "This Is Ghanaian Territory: Land Conflicts on a West African Border." *American Ethnologist* 30 (2): 273–89.

2013. *Land, Mobility, and Belonging in West Africa: Natives and Strangers*. Bloomington: Indiana University Press.

Levi, Margaret. 1996. "Social and Unsocial Capital: A Review Essay of Robert Putnam's *Making Democracy Work*." *Politics & Society* 24 (1): 45–55.

Li, Tanja Murray. 2000. "Articulating Indigenous Identity in Indonesia: Resource Politics and the Tribal Slot." *Comparative Studies in Society and History* 42 (1): 149–179.

Lieberman, Evan S., and Gwyneth H. McClendon. 2013. "The Ethnicity-Policy Preference Link in Sub-Saharan Africa." *Comparative Political Studies* 46 (5): 574–602.

Lindberg, Staffan. 2003. "It's Our Time to 'Chop': Do Elections in Africa Feed Neo-Patrimonialism rather than Counter-Act It?" *Democratization* 10 (2): 121–140.

2006. *Democracy and Elections in Africa*. Baltimore, MD: Johns Hopkins University Press.

Lindberg, Staffan I., and Minion K. C. Morrison. 2008. "Are African Voters Really Ethnic or Clientelistic? Survey Evidence from Ghana." *Political Science Quarterly* 123 (1): 95–122.

Lindberg, Staffan I. 2010. "What Accountability Pressures Do MPs in Africa Face and How Do They Respond? Evidence from Ghana." *The Journal of Modern African Studies* 48 (1): 117–142.

Locatelli, Francesca, and Paul Nugent, eds. 2009. *African Cities: Competing Claims on Urban Spaces*. Vol. 3. Leiden: Brill.

Logan, Carolyn. 2009. "Selected Chiefs, Elected Councillors and Hybrid Democrats: Popular Perspectives on the Co-Existence of Democracy and Traditional Authority." *The Journal of Modern African Studies* 47 (1): 101–128.

Lombard, Melanie, and Carole Rakodi. 2016. "Urban Land Conflict in the Global South: Towards an Analytical Framework." *Urban Studies* 53 (13): 2683–2699.

Loraux, Nicole. 1996. *Né de la terre–Mythe et Politique à Athènes*. Paris: Le Seuil.

Lukes, Steven. 1974. *Power: A Radical View*. New York: Palgrave MacMillan.

Lund, Christian. 2006. "Twilight Institutions: Public Authority and Local Politics in Africa." *Development and Change* 37 (4): 685–705.

MacLean, Lauren M. 2004. "Mediating Ethnic Conflict at the Grassroots: The Role of Local Associational Life in Shaping Political Values in Cote d'Ivoire and Ghana." *Journal of Modern African Studies* 42 (4): 589–617.

2010. *Informal Institutions and Citizenship in Rural Africa: Risk and Reciprocity in Ghana and Côte d'Ivoire*. New York: Cambridge University Press.

2011. "State Retrenchment and the Exercise of Citizenship in Africa." *Comparative Political Studies* 44 (9): 1238–1266.

Mahajan, Vijay. 2008. *Africa Rising: How 900 Million African Consumers Offer More Than You Think*. New York: Pearson Prentice Hall.

Mahmud, Tayyab. 2010. "'Surplus Humanity' and the Margins of Legality: Slums, Slumdogs, and Accumulation by Dispossession." *Chapman Law Review* 14 (1): 1–76.

Maier, Donna. 1980. "Competition for Power and Profits in Kete-Krachi, West Africa, 1875–1900." *The International Journal of African Historical Studies* 13 (1): 33–50.

Mamdani, Mahmood. 1996. *Citizen and Subject: Contemporary Africa and the Legacy of Late Colonialism*. Princeton, NJ: Princeton University Press.
2002. "Citizenship and African States." *International Affairs* 78 (2): 493–506.

Manby, Bronwen. 2009. *Struggles for Citizenship in Africa*. London: Zed Books.

Manin, Bernard, Adam Przeworkski, and Susan C. Stokes. 1999. "Elections and Representation." In Adam Przeworksi, Susan C. Stokes, and Bernard Manin, eds. *Democracy, Accountability, and Representation*. New York: Cambridge University Press.

Marcus, George E. 1995. "Ethnography in/of the World System: The Emergence of Multi-Sited Ethnography." *Annual Review of Anthropology* 24 (1): 95–117.

Marx, Colin. 2016. "Extending the Analysis of Urban Land Conflict: An Example from Johannesburg." *Urban Studies* 53 (13): 2779–2795.

Mayer, Philip. 1962. "Migrancy and the Study of Africans in Towns." *American Anthropologist* 64 (3): 576–592.

Maylam, Paul, and Iain Edwards. 1996. *The People's City: African Life in Twentieth Century Durban.* Pietermaritzburg: University of Natal Press.

Mazeau, Adrian, Rebecca Scott, and Benedict Tuffuor. 2012. "Sanitation – A Neglected Essential Service in the Unregulated Urban Expansion of Ashaiman, Ghana." Working paper, presented at *Sustainable Futures: Architecture and Urbanism in the Global South*, in Kampala, Uganda, June 27–30, 2012.

Mbembe, Achille, and Janet Roitman. 1995. "Figures of the Subject in Times of Crisis." *Public Culture* 7 (2): 323–352.

Mbembe, Achille. 2001a. *On the Postcolony.* Vol. 41. Berkeley: University of California Press.

2001b. "Ways of Seeing: Beyond the New Nativism–Introduction." *African Studies Review* 44 (2): 1–14.

2002. "Les nouveaux Africains: entre nativisme et cosmopolitanisme." *Esprit* 10: 1–10.

McAuslan P. 2003. "Land Policy: A Framework for Analysis and Action." In P. McAuslan, ed. *Bringing the Law Back in, Essays in Land, Law and Development.* Aldershot: Ashgate Press.

McCaskie, Tom C. 1983. "Accumulation, Wealth and Belief in Asante History: To the Close of the Nineteenth Century." *Africa* 53 (1): 23–43.

McCauley, John. 2013. "Africa's New Big Man Rule? Pentecostalism and Patronage in Ghana." *African Affairs* 112 (446): 1–21.

McMichael, Gabriella. 2016. "Land Conflict and Informal Settlements in Juba, South Sudan." *Urban Studies* 53 (13): 2721–2737.

McPhee, Allan. 1926. *The Economic Revolution in British West Africa.* Vol. 106. New York: Psychology Press.

Meagher, Kate. 2010. *Identity Economics: Social Networks & the Informal Economy in Nigeria.* Suffolk: Boydell & Brewer Ltd.

Miguel, Edward. 2004. "Tribe or Nation? Nation Building and Public Goods in Kenya versus Tanzania." *World Politics* 56 (3): 328–362.

Miguel, Edward, and Mary Kay Gugerty. 2005. "Ethnic Diversity, Social Sanctions, and Public Goods in Kenya." *Journal of Public Economics* 89 (11/12): 2325–2368.

Mitchell, James Clyde, ed. 1969. *Social Networks in Urban Situations: Analyses of Personal Relationships in Central African Towns.* Manchester: Manchester University Press.

Mitchell, Matthew I. 2012. "Migration, Citizenship and Autochthony: Strategies and Challenges for State-Building in Cote d'Ivoire." *Journal of Contemporary African Studies* 30 (2): 267–287.

Moncada, Eduardo. 2013. "The Politics of Urban Violence: Challenges for Development in the Global South." *Studies in Comparative International Development* 48 (3): 217–239.

Moore, Barrington. 1978. *Injustice: The Social Bases of Obedience and Revolt*. White Plains, NY: ME Sharpe.

Morgan, David L. 1997. *Focus Groups as Qualitative Research*. New York: Sage Publications.

Morrison, Nicky. 2017. "Playing by the Rules? New Institutionalism, Path Dependency and Informal Settlements in Sub-Saharan Africa." *Environment and Planning A: Economy and Space* 49 (11): 2558–2577.

Myers, Garth A. 2005. *Disposable Cities: Garbage, Governance, and Sustainable Development in Urban Africa*. Aldershot: Ashgate Press.

Nathan, Noah L. 2016a. "Does Participation Reinforce Patronage? Policy Preferences, Turnout, and Class in Urban Ghana." *British Journal of Political Science*. Available: https://doi.org/10.1017/S0007123416000351.

2016b. "Local Ethnic Geography, Expectations of Favoritism, and Voting in Urban Ghana." *Comparative Political Studies* 49 (14): 1896–1929.

Ndegwa, Stephen N. 1997. "Citizenship and Ethnicity: An Examination of Two Transition Moments in Kenyan Politics." *American Political Science Review* 91 (3): 599–616.

Nelson, Joan M. 1979. *Access to Power: Politics and the Urban Poor in Developing Nations*. Princeton, NJ: Princeton University Press.

Nichter, Simeon. 2008. "Vote Buying or Turnout Buying? Machine Politics and the Secret Ballot." *American Political Science Review* 102 (1): 19–31.

Ninsin, Kwame A. 2016. "Elections and Representation in Ghana's Democracy." In: Kwame A. Ninsin, ed. *Issues in Ghana's Electoral Politics*. Dakar: CODESRIA: 115–134.

Njoh, Ambe J. 2006. *Planning Power: Town Planning and Social Control in Colonial Africa*. London: University College of London Press.

2009. "Urban Planning as a Tool of Power and Social Control in Colonial Africa." *Planning Perspectives* 24 (3): 301–317.

North, Douglass C. 1990. *Institutions, Institutional Change and Economic Performance*. New York: Cambridge University Press.

Ntewusu, Samuel A. 2012. *"Settling in and Holding on," a Socio-Historical Study of Northerners in Accra's Tudu: 1908–2008*. Leiden: African Studies Centre.

Ntsebeza, Lungisile. 2005. *Democracy Compromised: Chiefs and the Politics of the Land in South Africa*. Leiden: Brill.

Nugent, Paul. 1996. *Big Men, Small Boys and Politics in Ghana: Power, Ideology and the Burden of History, 1982–1994*. London: Pinter Pub. Limited.

2001. "Ethnicity as an Explanatory Factor in Ghana's 2000 Elections." *African Issues* 29 (1/2): 2–7.

2007. "Banknotes and Symbolic Capital: Ghana's Elections under the Fourth Republic." In Matthias Basedau, Andreas Mehler, and Gero Erdmann, eds. *Votes, Money and Violence: Political Parties and Elections in Sub-Saharan Africa*. Durban: University of KwaZulu Natal Press.

Nworah, Kenneth D. 1971. "'The Aborigines' Protection Society, 1889–1909: A Pressure-Group in Colonial Policy." *Canadian Journal of African Studies/La Revue canadienne des études africaines* 5 (1): 79–92.

Nzongola-Ntalaja, Georges. 2011. "Citizenship and Exclusion in Africa: The Indigeneity Question." Keynote address at a national workshop on citizenship and indigeneity conflicts in Nigeria. Organized by the Centre for Democracy and Development (CDD). Abuja, Nigeria, February 8–9, 2011.

Obeng-Odoom, Franklin. 2010. "An Urban Twist to Politics in Ghana." *Habitat International* 34 (4): 392–299.

2012. "Neoliberalism and the Urban Economy in Ghana: Urban Employment, Inequality, and Poverty." *Growth and Change* 43 (1): 85–109.

2013. "Degeneration for Others." In Michael E. Leary, and John McCarthy, eds. *The Routledge Companion to Urban Regeneration*. London: Routledge.

Ocheje, Paul D. 2007. "'In the Public Interest': Forced Evictions, Land Rights and Human Development in Africa." *Journal of African Law* 51 (2): 173–214.

O'Connor, Anthony. 1993. *Poverty in Africa*. Manchester: Wiley.

Odoi-Larbi, Stephen. 2012. "Demolish Sodom & Gomorah Now." *The Chronicle*. Available: http://thechronicle.com.gh/demolish-sodom-gomorah-now-ga-chiefs/.

O'Donnell, Guillermo. 1993. "On the State, Democratization and Some Conceptual Problems: A Latin American View with Glances at Some Postcommunist Countries." *World Development* 21 (8): 1355–1369.

1996. "Illusions about Consolidation." *Journal of Democracy* 7 (2): 34–51.

Odotei, Irene. 1991. "External Influences on Ga Society and Culture." *Research Review* 7 (1–2): 61–71.

Olaniyan, Gideon Olaniyi. 2018. "Urbanization, Land Rights and Development: A Case Study of Waterfront Communities in Lagos, Nigeria." Master's thesis in international studies. University of San Francisco.

Ollenu, N. A. 1962. *Customary Land Law in Ghana*. London: Sweet and Maxwell.

Ollenu, N. A., and G. R. Woodman. 1985. *Ollenu's Principles of Customary Land Law*. Birmingham: CAL Press.

Olson, Mancur. 1965. *The Logic of Collective Action: Public Goods and the Theory of Groups*. Cambridge, MA: Harvard University Press.

——— 1993. "Dictatorship, Democracy, and Development." *American Political Science Review* 87 (3): 567–576.

Onoma, Ato Kwamena. 2009. *The Politics of Property Rights Institutions in Africa*. Cambridge: Cambridge University Press.

Opare, J. A. 2003. "Kayayei: The Women Head Porters of Southern Ghana." *Journal of Social Development in Africa* 18 (2): 6-20.

Osei-Tutu, John Kwadwo. 2000. "'Space', and the Marking of 'Space' in Ga History, Culture, and Politics." *Transactions of the Historical Society of Ghana* 4 (5): 55–81.

Ostrom, Elinor. 1990. *Governing the Commons: The Evolution of Institutions for Collective Action*. New York: Cambridge University Press.

——— 1996. "Crossing the Great Divide: Coproduction, Synergy, and Development." *World Development* 24 (6): 1073–1087.

——— 2000. "Collective Action and the Evolution of Social Norms." *Journal of Economic Perspectives* 14 (3): 137–158.

Owusu, Maxwell. 1970. "Culture and Democracy in West Africa: Some Persistent Problems." *Africa Today* 18 (1): 68–76.

Owunsu, Thomas Y. 1991. "Rural-Urban Migration and Squatter Settlement Formation in African Cities: A Case Study of a Ghanaian Squatter Settlement (Tema)." PhD dissertation, Wilfred Laurier University.

——— 1999. "The Growth of Ashaiman as a Squatter Settlement in the Tema District of Ghana, 1950–1990." *The Arab World Geographer* 2 (3): 234–249.

——— 2004. "Urban Migration and the Growth of Squatter Settlements in African Cities: Some Theoretical and Empirical Observations." *National Social Science Journal* 21 (2): 68–78.

Paley, Julia. 2004. "Accountable Democracy: Citizens' Impact on Public Decision Making in Postdictatorship Chile." *American Ethnologist* 31 (4): 497–513.

Paller, Jeffrey W. 2013. "Political Struggle to Political Sting: A Theory of Democratic Disillusionment." *Polity* 45 (4): 580–603.

——— 2014. "Informal Institutions and Personal Rule in Urban Ghana." *African Studies Review* 57 (3): 123–142.

——— 2015. "Informal Networks and Access to Power to Obtain Housing in Urban Slums in Ghana." *Africa Today* 62 (1): 30–55.

2017. "The Contentious Politics of African Urbanization." *Current History* 116 (790): 163.

2018a. "Dignified Public Expression: A New Logic of Political Accountability." Working paper.

2018b. "Building Permanence: Fire Outbreaks and Emergent Tenure Security in Urban Ghana." Working paper.

Parker, John. 2000a. *Making the Town: Ga State and Society in Early Colonial Accra.* Oxford: James Currey.

2000b. "The Cultural Politics of Death and Burial in Early Colonial Accra." In David Anderson, and Richard Rathbone, eds. *Africa's Urban Past.* Oxford: James Currey.

Parnell, Susan, and Edgar Pieterse, eds. 2014. *Africa's Urban Revolution.* London: Zed Books.

Parsons, Timothy. 1997. "'Kibra Is Our Blood': The Sudanese Military Legacy in Nairobi's Kibera Location, 1902–1968." *The International Journal of African Historical Studies* 30 (1): 87–122.

Payne Geoffrey. 2001. "Urban Land Tenure Policy Options: Titles or Rights?" *Habitat International* 25: 415–429.

Peil, Margaret. 1971. "The Expulsion of West African Aliens." *The Journal of Modern African Studies* 9 (2): 205–229.

1974. "Ghana's Aliens." *The International Migration Review* 8 (3): 367–381.

1976. "African Squatter Settlements: A Comparative Study." *Urban Studies* 13 (2): 155.

Pelican, Michaela. 2009. "Complexities of Indigeneity and Autochthony: An African Example." *American Ethnologist* 36 (1): 52–65.

Pellow, Deborah. 1985. "Muslim Segmentation: Cohesion and Divisiveness in Accra." *The Journal of Modern African Studies* 23 (3): 419–444.

2002. *Landlords and Lodgers: Socio-Spatial Organization in an Accra Community.* Chicago: University of Chicago Press.

Pelser, Eric. 1999. "The Challenges of Community Policing in South Africa." *Institute for Security Studies Papers* 42: 10.

Piattoni, Simona. 2001. *Clientelism, Interests, and Democratic Representation: The European Experience in Historical and Comparative Perspective.* New York: Cambridge University Press.

Pierson, Paul. 2004. *Politics in Time: History, Institutions, and Social Analysis.* Princeton, NJ: Princeton University Press.

Pitcher, Anne, Mary H. Moran, and Michael Johnston. 2009. "Rethinking Patrimonialism and Neopatrimonialism in Africa." *African Studies Review* 52 (1): 125–156.

Pogucki, R. J. H. 1954. *Report on Land Tenure in Customary Law of the Non-Akan Areas of the Gold Coast (Now Eastern Region of Ghana).* Volume II. Accra: Lands Department.

1955. "Land Tenure in Ghana." *Ghana Lands Department.*

Posner, Daniel. 2005. *Ethnic Politics and Political Institutions in Africa.* New York: Cambridge University Press.

Post, Alison E., Vivian Bronsoler, and Lana Salman. 2017. "Hybrid Regimes for Local Public Goods Provision." *Perspectives on Politics* 15 (4): 952–966.

Price, Richard. 1974. "Politics and Culture in Contemporary Ghana: The Big-Man Small-Boy Syndrome." *Journal of African Studies* 1 (2): 173–204.

Przeworksi, Adam, Susan C. Stokes, and Bernard Manin, eds. 1999. *Democracy, Accountability, and Representation.* New York: Cambridge University Press.

Putnam, Robert D. 1993. *Making Democracy Work: Civic Traditions in Modern Italy.* Princeton, NJ: Princeton University Press.

2001. *Bowling Alone: The Collapse and Revival of American Community.* New York: Simon and Schuster.

2007. "*E Pluribus Unum*: Diversity and Community in the Twenty-First Century." *Scandinavian Political Studies* 30 (2): 137–174.

Quarcoopome, Samuel S. 1987. "The Rejection of the Municipal Corporations Ordinance of 1924 at Accra: A Review of the Causes." *Research Review* 3 (1): 24–49.

1992. "Urbanisation, Land Alienation, and Politics in Accra." *Research Review* 8 (1/2): 40–54.

1993. "A History of the Urban Development of Accra: 1877–1857." *Research Review* 9 (1/2): 20–32.

Quartey-Papafio, A. Boi. 1914. "The Use of Names among the Gas or Accra People of the Gold Coast." *Journal of the Royal African Society* 13 (5): 167–182.

1920. "The Ga Homowo Festival." *Journal of the Royal African Society* 19 (74): 126–134.

Rains, Emily, Anirudh Krishna, and Erik Wibbels. 2017. "Slummier than Others: A Continuum of Slums and Assortative Residential Selection." *Policy.* Working paper.

Rakodi, Carole. 1997. *The Urban Challenge in Africa: Growth and Management of its Large Cities.* Tokyo: United Nations University Press.

2016. "Addressing Gendered Inequalities in Access to Land and Housing." In Caroline O. N. Moser, ed. *Gender, Asset Accumulation and Just Cities: Pathways to Transformation.* London: Routledge.

Rapley, John. 1993. *Ivoirian Capitalism: African Entrepreneurs in Côte d'Ivoire.* Boulder, CO: Lynne Rienner.

Rathbone, Richard. 2000. *Nkrumah & the Chiefs: The Politics of Chieftaincy in Ghana, 1951–60*. Columbus, OH: State University Press.

Ravallion, Martin, Shaohua Chen, and Prem Sangraula. 2007. "New Evidence on the Globalization of Urban Poverty." *Population and Development Review* 33 (4): 667–701.

Razzu, Giovanni. 2005. "Urban Redevelopment, Cultural Heritage, Poverty and Redistribution: The Case of Old Accra and Adawso House." *Habitat International* 29 (3): 399–419.

Reno, William. 1999. *Warlord Politics and African States*. Boulder, CO: Lynne Rienner Publishers.

Republic of Ghana. 1991. "Strategic Plan for the Greater Accra Metropolitan Area. Volume 1: Context Report."

2012. "Accra Metropolitan Assembly Medium-Term Development Plan (2010-2013)." National Development Planning Commission.

Resnick, Danielle. 2012. "Opposition Parties and the Urban Poor in African Democracies." *Comparative Political Studies* 45 (11): 1351–1377.

2013. *Urban Poverty and Party Populism in African Democracies*. New York: Cambridge University Press.

2015. "The Political Economy of Africa's Emergent Middle Class: Retrospect and Prospects." *Journal of International Development* 27 (5): 573–587.

Reuters. 2015. "Ghana Destroys Hundreds of Homes in Accra to Tackle Floods." *Reuters*. June 21, 2015. Available: www.hindustantimes.com/world-news/ghana-destroys-hundreds-of-homes-to-tackle-floods-in-accra/article1-1361147.aspx.

Riedl, Rachel Beatty. 2014. *Authoritarian Origins of Party Systems in Africa*. New York: Cambridge University Press.

Robertson, Claire C. 1983. "The Death of Makola and Other Tragedies." *Canadian Journal of African Studies/La Revue canadienne des études africaines* 17 (3): 469–495.

1984. *Sharing the Same Bowl?: A Socioeconomic History of Women and Class in Accra, Ghana*. Bloomington: Indiana University Press.

Robertson, Roland. 1992. *Globalization: Social Theory and Global Culture*. London: Sage.

Robinson, Amanda L. 2016. "Nationalism and Ethnic-Based Trust Evidence From an African Border Region." *Comparative Political Studies* 49 (14): 1819–1854.

Roitman, Janet. 2013. *Anti-Crisis*. Durham, NC: Duke University Press.

Roniger, Luis. 2004. "Review: Political Clientelism, Democracy, and Market Economy." *Journal of Comparative Politics* 36 (3): 353–375.

1994. "The Comparative Study of Clientelism and the Changing Nature of Civil Society in the Contemporary World." In Luis Roniger, and Ayşe

Güneş-Ayata, eds. *Democracy, Clientelism and Civil Society.* Boulder, CO: Lynne Rienner.

Roniger, Luis, and Ayşe Güneş-Ayata, eds. 1994. *Democracy, Clientelism and Civil Society.* Boulder, CO: Lynne Rienner.

Rouch, Jean. 1956. "Migrations au Ghana." *Journal de la Société des Africanistes* 26 (1): 33–196.

Roy, Ananya. 2009. "Why India Cannot Plan Its Cities: Informality, Insurgence and the Idiom of Urbanization." *Planning Theory* 8 (1): 76–87.

Ruteere, Mutuma, and Marie-Emmanuelle Pommerolle. 2003. "Democratizing Security or Decentralizing Repression? The Ambiguities of Community Policing in Kenya." *African Affairs* 102 (409): 587–604.

Sackeyfio, Naaborko. 2012. "The Politics of Land and Urban Space in Colonial Accra." *History in Africa* 39: 293–329.

Sackeyfio-Lenoch, Naaborko. 2014. *The Politics of Chieftaincy: Authority and Property in Colonial Ghana, 1920–1950.* Vol. 61. Suffolk: Boydell & Brewer.

Sampson, Robert J. 2012. *Great American City: Chicago and the Enduring Neighborhood Effect.* Chicago: University of Chicago Press.

Sampson, Robert J., Stephen W. Raudenbush, and Felton Earls. 1997. "Neighborhoods and Violent Crime: A Multilevel Study of Collective Efficacy." *Science* 277 (5328): 918–924.

Sandbrook, Richard, and Jack Arn. 1977. *The Labouring Poor and Urban Class Formation: The Case of Greater Accra.* Montreal: Centre for Developing-Area Studies, McGill University.

Sanjek, Roger. 1972. "Ghanaian Networks: An Analysis off Inter-Ethnic Relations in Urban Situation." Diss. PhD dissertation, Department of Anthropology, Columbia University.

Satterthwaite, David, and Diana Mitlin, eds. 2013. *Empowering Squatter Citizen: Local Government, Civil Society and Urban Poverty Reduction.* London: Routledge.

Satyanath, Shanker, Nico Voigtländer, and Hans-Joachim Voth. 2017. "Bowling for Fascism: Social Capital and the Rise of the Nazi Party." *Journal of Political Economy* 125 (2): 478–526.

Scacco, Alexandra, and Shana S. Warren. 2018. "Can Social Contact Reduce Prejudice and Discrimination? Evidence from a Field Experiment in Nigeria." *American Political Science Review.* 1–24. Available: doi:10.1017/S0003055418000151.

Schaffer, Frederic Charles. 1998. *Democracy in Translation: Understanding Politics in an Unfamiliar Culture.* Ithaca, NY: Cornell University Press.

Schaffer, Frederic C., and Andreas Schedler. 2007. "What Is Vote Buying? The Limits of the Market Model." In Frederic C. Schaffer, ed. *Elections for Sale: The Causes and Consequences of Vote Buying*. Boulder, CO: Lynne Rienner.

Schatz, Ed, ed. 2009. *Political Ethnography: What Immersion Contributes to the Study of Power*. Chicago: University Chicago Press.

Schatzberg, Michael G. 1993. "Power, Legitimacy, and 'Democratisation' in Africa." *Africa* 63 (4): 445–461.

2001. *Political Legitimacy in Middle Africa: Father, Family, Food*. Bloomington: Indiana University Press.

2006. "Soccer, Science, and Sorcery: Causation and African Football." *Afrika Spectrum* 41 (3): 351–369.

2014. "Transformation and Struggle." In Lucy Koechlin, and Till Forster, eds. *The Politics of Governance: Actors and Articulations in Africa and Beyond*. London: Routledge.

Schildkrout, Enid. 1970. "Strangers and Local Government in Kumasi." *The Journal of Modern African Studies* 8 (2): 251–269.

1978. *People of the Zongo: The Transformation of Ethnic Identities in Ghana*. New York: Cambridge University Press.

Schmidt, Steffen W., ed. 1977. *Friends, Followers, and Factions: A Reader in Political Clientelism*. Berkeley: University of California Press.

Scott, James C. 1972. "Patron-Client Politics and Political Change in Southeast Asia." *American Political Science Review* 66 (1): 91–113.

1990. *Domination and the Arts of Resistance: Hidden Transcripts*. New Haven, CT: Yale University Press.

1998. *Seeing Like a State: How Certain Schemes to Improve the Human Condition Have Failed*. New Haven, CT: Yale University Press.

Shaloff, Stanley. 1974. "The Cape Coast Asafo Company Riot of 1932." *The International Journal of African Historical Studies* 7 (4): 591–607.

Sheely, Ryan. 2013. "Maintaining Local Public Goods: Evidence from Rural Kenya." Working paper, Center for International Development at Harvard University.

2015. "Mobilization, Participatory Planning Institutions, and Elite Capture: Evidence from a Field Experiment in Rural Kenya." *World Development* 67 (3): 251–266.

Shelef, Nadav G. 2016. "Unequal Grounds: Homelands and Conflict." *International Organization* 70 (1): 33–63.

Shipley, Jesse Weaver. 2009. "Comedians, Pastors, and the Miraculous Agency of Charisma in Ghana. *Cultural Anthropology* 24 (3): 523–552.

Shipton, Parker. 1994. "Land and Culture in Tropical Africa: Soils, Symbols, and the Metaphysics of the Mundane." *Annual Review of Anthropology* 23 (1): 347–377.

Simensen, Jarle. 1974. "Rural Mass Action in the Context of Anti-Colonial Protest: The Asafo Movement of Akim Abuakwa, Ghana." *Canadian Journal of African Studies* 8 (1): 25–41.

1975. "Commoners, Chiefs and Colonial Government." *Akim Abuakwa, Ghana, under British Rule*. PhD Thesis, University of Notterdam.

Simmel, George. 1908. "The Stranger." In Donald N. Levine, ed. *On Individuality and Social Forms*. Chicago: University of Chicago Press.

Simmons, Erica. 2014. "Grievances Do Matter in Mobilization." *Theory & Society* 43 (5): 513–546.

2016. *Meaningful Resistance: Market Reforms and the Roots of Social Protest in Latin America*. New York: Cambridge University Press.

Simone AbdouMaliq. 2001. "On the Worlding of African Cities." *African Studies Review* 44(2): 15–43.

2004. *For the City Yet to Come: Changing African Life in Four Cities*. Durham, NC: Duke University Press.

Singh, Prerna. 2011. "We-Ness and Welfare: A Longitudinal Analysis of Social Development in Kerala, India." *World Development* 39 (2): 282–293.

Skinner, Elliot P. 1963. "Strangers in West African Societies." *Africa* 33 (4): 307–320.

1972. "Political Conflict and Revolution in an African Town." *American Anthropologist* 74 (5): 1208–1217.

Smith, Daniel Jordan. 2010. *A Culture of Corruption: Everyday Deception and Popular Discontent in Nigeria*. Princeton, NJ: Princeton University Press.

Smith, David. 2011. "Ivory Coast 'on the Brink of a Bloodbath.'" *The Guardian*. March 11, 2011. Available: www.theguardian.com/world/2011/mar/11/ivory-coast-abobo-abidjan-gbagbo.

Smith, Nicholas Rush. 2015. "Rejecting Rights: Vigilantism and Violence in Post-Apartheid South Africa." *African Affairs* 114 (456): 341–360.

Sowatey, Emmanuel Addo, and Raymond A. Atuguba. 2014. "Community Policing in Accra: The Complexities of Local Notions of (in) Security and (in) Justice." In Peter Albrecht, and Helene Maria Kyed, eds. *Policing and the Politics of Order-Making*. London: Routledge.

Stacey, Paul. 2015. "Political Structure and the Limits of Recognition and Representation in Ghana." *Development and Change* 46 (1): 25–47.

Stacey, Paul, and Christian Lund. 2016. "In a State of Slum: Governance in an Informal Urban Settlement in Ghana." *Journal of Modern African Studies* 54 (4): 591–615.

Stacey, Paul. 2018. "Urban Development and Emerging Relations of Informal Property and Land-Based Authority in Accra." *Africa* 88 (1): 63–80.

Staniland, Martin. 1975. *The Lions of Dagbon: Political Change in Northern Ghana*. New York: Cambridge University Press.

Stokes, Susan C. 2005. "Perverse Accountability: A Formal Model of Machine Politics with Evidence from Argentina." *American Political Science Review* 99 (3): 315–325.

Stokes, Susan C., Thad Dunning, Marcelo Nazareno, and Valeria Brusco. 2013. *Brokers, Voters, and Clientelism: The Puzzle of Distributive Politics*. New York: Cambridge University Press.

Swidler, Ann. 1986. "Culture in Action: Symbols and Strategies." *American Sociological Review* 51 (2): 273–286.

2013. "Lessons from Chieftaincy in Rural Malawi." In Peter A. Hall, and Michèle Lamont, eds. *Social Resilience in the Neoliberal Era*. New York: Cambridge University Press.

Swidler, Ann, and Susan Cotts Watkins. 2017. *A Fraught Embrace: The Romance and Reality of AIDS Altruism in Africa*. Princeton, NJ: Princeton University Press.

Tonah, Steve. 2012. "The Politicisation of a Chieftaincy Conflict: The Case of Dagbon, Northern Ghana." *Nordic Journal of African Studies* 21 (1): 1–20.

Tostensen, Arne, Inge Tvedten, and Mariken Vaa. 2001. *Associational Life in African Cities: Popular Responses to the Urban Crisis*. Oslo: Nordiska Afrikainstitutet.

Tripp, Aili Mari. 1997. *Changing the Rules: The Politics of Liberalization and the Urban Informal Economy in Tanzania*. Berkeley: University of California Press.

Tsai, Lily. 2007. *Accountability without Democracy: Solidary Groups and Public Goods Provision in Rural China*. New York: Cambridge University Press.

UN-Habitat. 2003. "Slums of the World: The Face of Urban Poverty in the New Millennium." Nairobi: United Nations Human Settlements Programme.

2012. "State of the World's Cities 2010/11: Cities for All: Bridging the Urban Divide." Available: www.unhabitat.org/content.asp?cid=8051& catid=7&typeid=46.

United Nations, Department of Economic and Social Affairs. 2014. "World Urbanization Prospects." Available: https://esa.un.org/unpd/wup/publications/files/wup2014-highlights.Pdf.

United Nations, Global Urban Observatory. 2003. *Slums of the World: The Face of Urban Poverty in the New Millennium?* New York.

Van de Walle, Nicolas. 2001. *African Economies and the Politics of Permanent Crisis, 1979–1999*. New York: Cambridge University Press.

Van der Ploeg, Frederick, and Steven Poehlhekke. 2008. "Globalization and the Rise of Mega-Cities in the Developing World." *Cambridge Journal of Regions, Economy and Society* 1 (3): 477–501.

Van Leeuwen, Mathijs, and Gemma Van Der Haar. 2016. "Theorizing the Land–Violent Conflict Nexus." *World Development* 78 (2): 94–104.

Varshney, Ashutosh. 2001. "Ethnic Conflict and Civil Society: India and Beyond." *World Politics* 53 (3): 362–398.

2002. *Ethnic Conflict and Civic Life.* New Haven, CT: Yale University Press.

Varughese, George. 1999. "Villagers, Bureaucrats, and Forests in Nepal: Designing Governance for a Complex Resource." PhD dissertation, Indiana University.

Vidal, John. 2010. "227 Million People Escape World's Slums, UN Report Finds." *The Guardian.* Available: www.guardian.co.uk/world/2010/mar/22/slums-un-report.

Vigneswaran, Darshan, and Joel Quirk. 2012. "Quantitative methodological dilemmas in urban refugee research: A case study of Johannesburg." *Journal of Refugee Studies* 26 (1): 110–116.

Waldron, Jeremy. 2003. "Indigeneity? First Peoples and Last Occupancy." *New Zealand Journal of Public Law* 1: 1–58.

Walsh, Katherine Cramer. 2012. "Putting Inequality In its Place: Rural Consciousness and the Power of Perspective." *American Political Science Review* 106 (3): 517–532.

Wantchekon, Leonard, and Pedro Vicente. 2009. "Clientelism and Vote Buying: Lessons from Field Experiments in African Elections." *Oxford Review of Economic Policy* 25 (2): 292–305.

Wedeen, Lisa. 2002. "Conceptualizing Culture: Possibilities for Political Science." *The American Political Science Review* 96 (4): 713–728.

2007. "The Politics of Deliberation: Qāt Chews as Public Spheres in Yemen." *Public Culture* 19 (1): 59–84.

2008. *Peripheral Visions: Publics, Power, and Performance in Yemen.* Chicago: University of Chicago Press.

2010. "Reflections on Ethnographic Work in Political Science." *Annual Review of Political Science* 13: 255–272.

Westminster Foundation for Democracy. 2018. "The Cost of Politics in Ghana." Available: www.wfd.org/wp-content/uploads/2018/03/Cost_Of_Politics_Ghana.pdf.

West, Harry G., and Celia Plender. 2015. "An Interview with James C. Scott." *Gastronomica: The Journal of Food and Culture* 15 (3): 1–8.

White, Bob W. 2008. *Rumba Rules: The Politics of Dance Music in Mobutu's Zaire.* Raleigh, NC: Duke University Press.

Whitehouse, Bruce. 2012. *Migrants and Strangers in an African City: Exile, Dignity, Belonging.* Bloomington: Indiana University Press.

Whitfield, Lindsay. 2011. "Competitive Clientelism, Easy Financing, and Weak Capitalists: The Contemporary Political Settlement in Ghana." DIIS Working paper.

Wilfahrt, Martha. 2018a. "The Politics of Local Government Performance: Elite Cohesion and Cross-Village Constraints in Decentralized Senegal." *World Development* 103 (3): 149–161.

2018b. "Precolonial Legacies and Institutional Congruence in Public Goods Delivery: Evidence from Decentralized West Africa." *World Politics* 70 (2): 239–274.

Wilks, Ivor. 1975. *Asante in the 19th Century: The Structure and Evolution of a Political Order*. New York: Cambridge University Press.

1989. Asante in the Nineteenth Century: The Structure and Evolution of a Political Order. New York: Cambridge University Press.

Williams, J. Michael. 2004. "Leading from Behind: Democratic Consolidation and the Chieftaincy in South Africa." *Journal of Modern African Studies* 42 (1): 113–136.

Williams, Martin J. 2017. "The Political Economy of Unfinished Development Projects: Corruption, Clientelism, or Collective Choice?" *American Political Science Review* 111 (4): 705–723.

Woolcock, Michael, and Deepa Narayan. 2000. "Social Capital: Implications for Development Theory, Research, and Policy." *World Bank Research Observer* 15 (2): 225–250.

World Bank. 2013. "Project Performance Assessment Report Ghana: Land Administration Project." Available: www-wds.worldbank.org/external/default/WDSContentServer/WDSP/IB/2013/06/19/000445729_20130619150703/Rendered/PDF/750840PPAR0p0711570Box377346B00OUO090.pdf.

Yakah, Theophilus A. 2016. "The Rise of 'Ethnic Parties' in Africa: The Case of Ghana." Working paper.

Yeboah, Ian E. A. 2000. "Structural Adjustment and Emerging Urban Form in Accra, Ghana." *Africa Today* 47 (2): 60–89.

Yeboah, Ian E. A., Samuel N. A. Codjoe, John K. Maingi. 2013. "Emerging Urban System Demographic Trends: Informing Ghana's National Urban Policy and Lessons for Sub-Saharan Africa." *Africa Today* 60 (1): 99–124.

Young, Crawford. 1994. *The African Colonial State in Comparative Perspective*. New Haven, CT: Yale University Press.

2012. *The Postcolonial State in Africa: Fifty Years of Independence, 1960–2010*. Madison: University of Wisconsin Press.

2014. "Ethnicity and Politics." In Paul Tiyambe Zeleza, ed. *Oxford Bibliographies in African Studies*. Oxford: Oxford University Press.

Index